THE OCEAN IN HUMAN AFFAIRS

THE OCEAN IN HUMAN AFFAIRS

Edited by

S. Fred Singer

An ICUS Book

PARAGON HOUSE
New York

Published in the United States by the
International Conference on the Unity of the Sciences
481 8th Avenue
New York, New York 10001

Distributed by Paragon House Publishers
90 Fifth Avenue
New York, New York 10011

An ICUS Book

The International Conference on the Unity of the Sciences (ICUS) convenes international, distinguished scientists and scholars from every field of study to pursue academic discussion of theoretical and practical concerns. ICUS seeks an integrated world-view based on absolute values generated through multi-disciplinary, academic dialogue.

Library of Congress Cataloging-in-Publication Data

The Ocean in human affairs / edited by S. Fred Singer.—1st ed.
p. cm.
"An ICUS book."
Bibliography: p.
Includes index.
ISBN : 0-89226-037-8
ISBN : 0-89226-070-X (pbk.)
1. Oceanography. 2. Man—Influence on environment. I. Singer, S. Fred (Siegfried Fred), 1924–
GC28.023 1990
551.46—dc19 87-30840
CIP

Other books in this series
Edited by S. Fred Singer

GLOBAL CLIMATE CHANGE:
HUMAN AND NATURAL INFLUENCES
ISBN 0-89226-033-5
ISBN 0-89226-071-8 (pbk.)

THE UNIVERSE AND ITS ORIGIN:
FROM ANCIENT MYTHS TO PRESENT REALITY
AND FUTURE FANTASY
ISBN 0-89226-049-1

TABLE OF CONTENTS

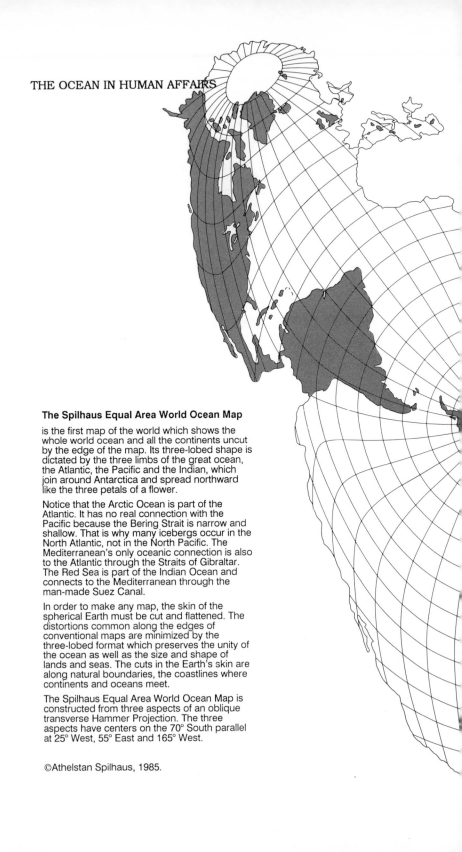

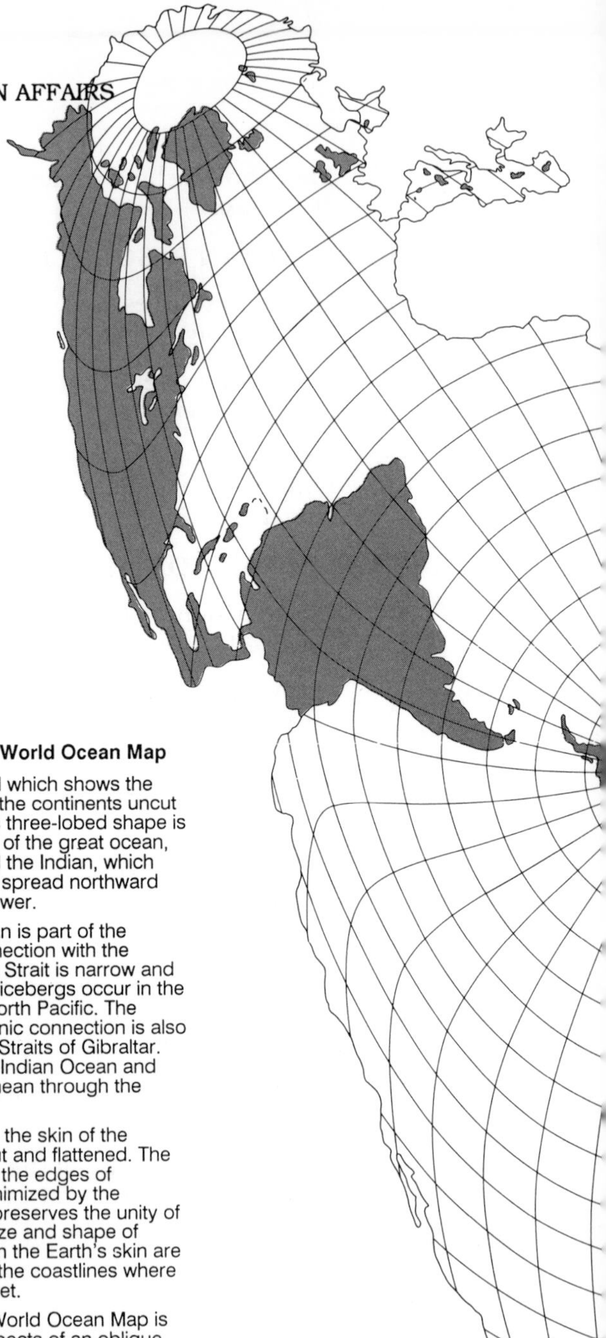

The Spilhaus Equal Area World Ocean Map

is the first map of the world which shows the whole world ocean and all the continents uncut by the edge of the map. Its three-lobed shape is dictated by the three limbs of the great ocean, the Atlantic, the Pacific and the Indian, which join around Antarctica and spread northward like the three petals of a flower.

Notice that the Arctic Ocean is part of the Atlantic. It has no real connection with the Pacific because the Bering Strait is narrow and shallow. That is why many icebergs occur in the North Atlantic, not in the North Pacific. The Mediterranean's only oceanic connection is also to the Atlantic through the Straits of Gibraltar. The Red Sea is part of the Indian Ocean and connects to the Mediterranean through the man-made Suez Canal.

In order to make any map, the skin of the spherical Earth must be cut and flattened. The distortions common along the edges of conventional maps are minimized by the three-lobed format which preserves the unity of the ocean as well as the size and shape of lands and seas. The cuts in the Earth's skin are along natural boundaries, the coastlines where continents and oceans meet.

The Spilhaus Equal Area World Ocean Map is constructed from three aspects of an oblique transverse Hammer Projection. The three aspects have centers on the 70° South parallel at 25° West, 55° East and 165° West.

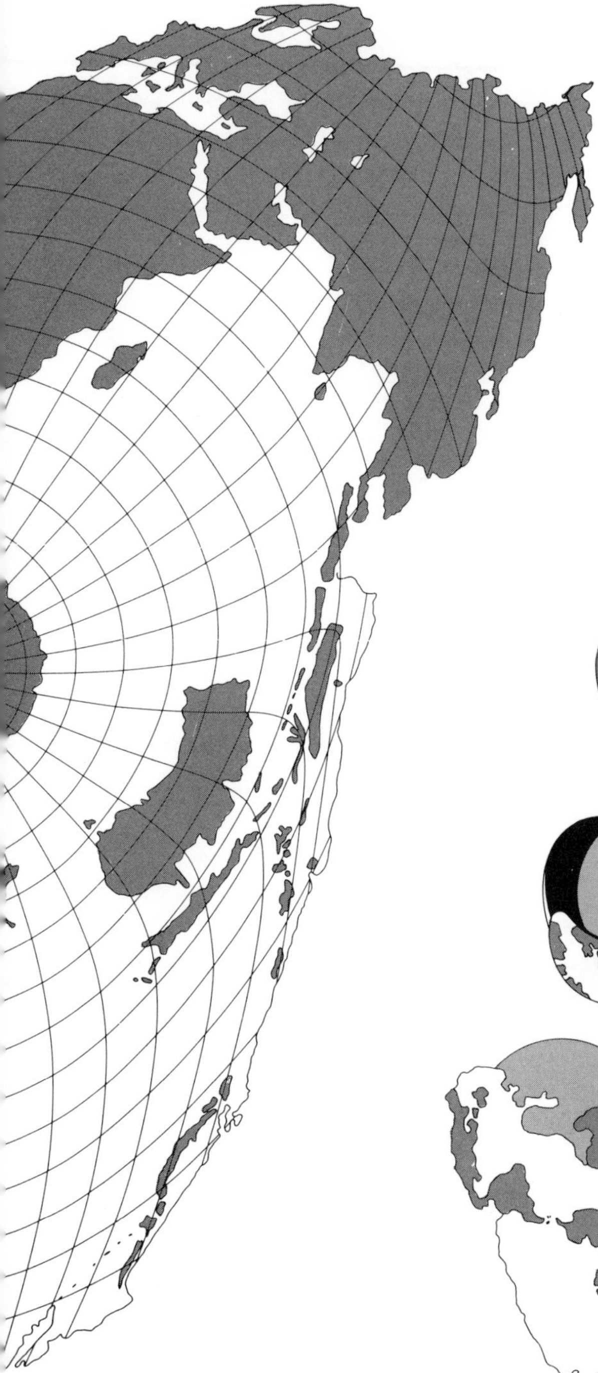

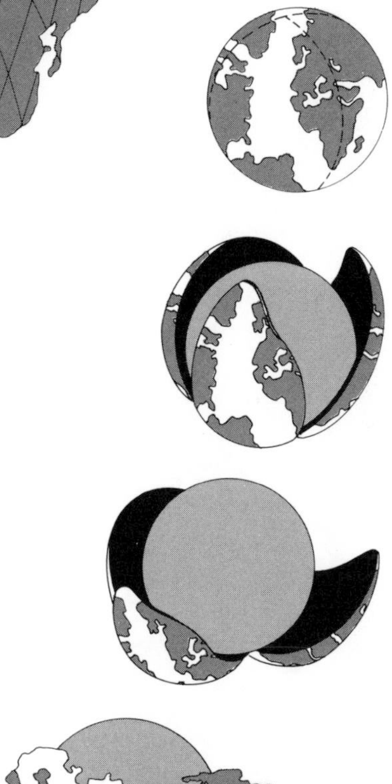

INTRODUCTION

S. Fred Singer

The planet Earth is alone in the solar system in possessing a water ocean and living things. The existence of this ocean may be responsible for the evolution of life and of mankind. Throughout the history of the planet, the ocean controlled the earth's climate, as it still does today. The ocean has assumed increasing economic importance as an avenue of commerce and as a source of fish, oil and minerals. It is used for recreation, as well as for the disposal of the wastes created by our increasingly affluent society. It is still a frontier of exploration on this planet—ocean research and ocean technology have increased to meet that challenge. New ways are being found to exploit the ocean for the benefit of mankind. Finally, and inevitably, the ocean's importance in human affairs throughout history has led to increased international attention to the management of its resources.

This volume starts with basic scientific issues of the history and evolution of the earth, of its ocean and of life itself. It then deals with the fundamental yet practical question of the interactions, research and technology, resources, and advanced technological projects. Finally, the discussion turns to the role to the ocean in human commerce, from the earliest times to the present.

Ocean Science

Why is it, that among the many planets and other large bodies of our solar system, most have an atmosphere, but only the earth has liquid-water oceans? Only the earth seems to have been the cradle of life.

It is generally agreed that the earth's atmosphere is of secondary origin—the result of outgassing the original planetesimals, chunks of primordial material that came together to form the earth. But did the earth form hot so that melting, volcanism and outgassing occurred quickly, or did the earth form cold and heat only subsequently? Opinions are divided. Yet we believe that the oceans are some four billion years old. And thus the outgassing (including that of water vapor) must have occurred soon after the earth's formation, about 4.6 billion years ago.

One widely held view is that the earth owes its special properties to the fact that it happens to be at just the right distance from the sun: not too close to prevent water vapor from condensing, not so far that liquid water would freeze. Perhaps so, but the earth's orbit has been at times quite eccentric, and the sun was some 30% weaker 4.6 billion years ago. If the ocean were ever to freeze over, it might never remelt again because the high reflecting power of sea ice reflects rather than absorbs solar energy.

Yet another view holds that the moon has been responsible for the special properties of our planet: namely, the early development of the world ocean and of life. Capture of the moon would indeed heat the earth to melting temperature through the friction of the tides within the solid earth, and would quickly produce an atmosphere and ocean through outgassing of the primeval rocks.

Be this as it may, a liquid ocean was essential for the development of life, in the form of self-replicating molecules. Much evidence, observational and experimental, exists to suggest that organic molecules would readily form on the earth in an initially reducing atmosphere and turn the ocean into an organic "soup." But once life formed, it evolved along a path which eventually changed the chemistry of atmosphere and ocean in a profound way; free oxygen gradually accumulated in the earth's atmosphere—another feature unique in the solar system.

While oxygen may be the most striking example of chemical change, other exchanges developed between atmosphere, ocean and rocks on land. Eventually, biogeochemical cycles were established for carbon, nitrogen, phosphorus and other, less abundant, elements. These cycles were punctuated by various natural events and catastrophes, for example, by continent building and erosion, continental drift, volcanism, and even impacts of extraterrestrial bodies. Many believe that the mass extinctions of biota that mark the different geologic periods (e.g., the sudden disappearance of the dinosaurs 65,000,000 years ago) are due to events that disturbed the climate so severely as to cause major ecological catastrophes.

More recently, human activities have started to make an important impact on biogeochemical cycles. For example, the increased use of energy since the beginning of the industrial revolution has been raising the level of atmospheric carbon dioxide. It is generally believed that the resultant "greenhouse" effect will lead to a noticeable warming of the global climate.*

Our understanding of past climatic changes and of the mechanisms responsible for them has been greatly aided by two developments: (i) access to new data through deep-sea sediment cores and ice cores from polar regions; and (ii) sensitive techniques for measuring isotopes, together with other significant improvements in instrumentation.

But the role of the ocean in climatic change is not always clear. For example, are observed changes in global sea levels the result of, or the cause of, sea ice that is correlated with glacial episodes? Complicating the issue are the effects of ocean circulation, involving various parts and depths of the oceans on different time scales and being affected by both temperature and salinity differences. Furthermore, changes in biota can be important enough to affect ocean properties and even ocean processes on the surface.

On a shorter time scale, i.e., days or months instead of millennia, the interactions between atmosphere and ocean are controlled by dynamic and thermal factors. The higher density of water leads to ocean cyclonic and anticyclonic systems small in size (about 20–100 km) and cyclones long in duration

* For a more detailed discussion see articles in *Global Climate Change: Human and Natural Influences* (S. Fred Singer, editor). Paragon House Publishers, New York, N.Y. 1989.

(20–200 days), as against about 2000 km and five days for atmospheric systems. At the same time, a thin top layer of the ocean, less than 3 meters thick, has a heat capacity equal to that of the whole atmosphere. The detailed analysis of the interactions, and especially the prediction of atmospheric events, is a challenging problem indeed, yet of immense commercial importance. A major El Niño event, such as occurred in 1982, can and did have major weather consequences and cause widespread ecologic and economic losses.

Tropical cyclones (generally called hurricanes or typhoons) may also be related to ocean temperature anomalies. While providing much-needed rainfall, tropical cyclones also take more human lives than other natural events, as many strike without sufficient advance warning.

Ocean Technology

Observations form the basis of all our understanding of ocean-atmosphere phenomena. And the major new tool promises to be the earth satellite. Starting with weather satellites and "Landsats," "Seasats" are needed to carry out specialized observations of the ocean surface. However, *in situ* measurements will always be needed to obtain "ground truth" and data below the ocean surface. Great strides have been made in instrumentation, yet such fundamentals as ocean current measurements are still less than satisfactory. Chemical and isotopic tracers, acoustic techniques, and specialized buoys are among promising new methods.

Human exploration of the ocean in submersibles has always presented an exciting frontier. Based on the experience gained over the last 50 years, bathyscaphes now being built in several countries will routinely explore down to 6,000 meters (having access thereby to 98% of the ocean floor). This advance opens up the prospects of fuller development of the mineral resources of the ocean floor.

From the mining of ocean minerals, off-shore oil development, and the exploration of fish stocks, it may be only a short step to the use of other ocean resources. One such resource is the heat content of the surface layer, which in some parts of the globe provides the energy for the evaporation that feeds rain clouds. Research in the eastern Mediterranean has established a strong correlation between the summer heat input and the winter rainfall. Beyond the predictive value of this discovery, it suggests active intervention to increase the heat stored in summer by artificial mixing (in order to increase the thickness of the warm surface layer), and thus enhance much-needed precipitation over the arid Levant.

Other projects to exploit the ocean would use the gravitational energy released when Mediterranean Ocean water is conducted by tunnel to natural depressions, such as the Dead Sea (400 meters below sea level) or the Qattara Depression in Egypt. The hydroelectric power and other benefits may be sufficient to make the high initial investments worthwhile.

In the meantime, tunnels are being built under the ocean floor for purposes of commerce. The 53 km-long Seikan Tunnel—the longest in the world, linking the Islands of Honshu and Hokkaido in Japan—has just been completed. Plans for a 235 km-long tunnel and highway between Korea and Japan are under study.

Of course, the use of the ocean for commerce is quite old. Voyaging may have started more than 40,000 years ago and continued throughout human history, driven by different motivations. Ocean crossings, perhaps accidental, are known to have occurred as far back as 5,000 years ago; suitable boats were available and people are known to have survived at sea for several months. Certainly, King Cheops' ship (of 2590 B.C.) was twice as long as that of Christopher Columbus' vessel over 4,000 years later.

Ocean commerce was conducted from ports which developed into cities, each with a different character. Perhaps the most unique is Venice, a paradigm of an ocean city with special environmental problems. The study of these problems may be of value to other ocean cities, especially if global climatic changes induced by human activities should result in a rise of sea level and the inundation of low-lying coastal areas.

The ocean is both ancient and new. It has played a role in human affairs for millennia. With science advances and resources accessible to modern technology, it promises to be the last frontier on this planet.

PART ONE:

OCEAN SCIENCE

ONE

OCEANS Of WATER On EARTH

A UNIQUE EVENT IN THE SOLAR SYSTEM

S. Ishtaque Rasool

The last two decades have witnessed very intensive and extensive exploration of the solar system both by space probes and with powerful ground-based telescopes. A new description of the planets and of their satellites is now emerging. For example, we now know that the atmospheres of Venus and Mars, our neighboring planets, are largely made up of carbon dioxide, that the surface of Venus is extremely hot, about 450°C, and that the clouds which enshroud the planet perpetually are composed of sulfuric acid; that the Martian surface is devoid of any organic matter and the polar caps on Mars may be both water ice and carbon dioxide ice. Small bodies like the moon and Mercury do not possess any atmosphere at all, while the giant planets, Jupiter and Saturn, are made up of hydrogen and helium with traces of methane and ammonia in their atmospheres. Far out in the solar system the temperatures get very low; and we see many of the satellites of Jupiter and Saturn covered with "frost" but with no atmosphere until we come to Titan where temperatures are so low, -200°C, that ethane flows as liquid on the surface.*

With such an exotic description of the other planets, Earth stands out as a unique object in the entire planetary system in that it has an atmosphere of nitrogen and free oxygen, has liquid water on the surface and has life. Obviously the three circumstances are related. Presence of water in liquid state facilitated the origin of life because the first organic molecules formed in the atmosphere or on the surface accumulated, grew, and were sustained in the liquid environments of an ocean; while subsequently, and as discussed later, the germination of life created free oxygen which in turn determined the path of evolution of life itself.

The principal question that needs to be answered, therefore, is what combination of circumstances produced oceans of water on Earth and not on Mars or Venus? The answer can perhaps be developed with the following account of the history of planetary formation.

The First Billion Years

About 5,000,000,000 years ago, earth accumulated into a solid body out of a swarm of rocks, dust, ice, and cosmic gas circling around the sun. Other planets, Mercury, Mars, and Venus, also formed in the neighboring regions of the earth at about the same time. The size of the planets differed, depending on the amount of material available in the solar "rings"; but the composition was probably about the same, mostly silicates and iron. However, calculations indicate that if the planets were formed in about 200,000,000 years, which in geological terms is fairly rapid, the bombardment of the surface during the last phases of planetary accumulation must have been extremely frequent and intense, so much so as to raise the temperature above the melting point of rocks. So it appears that, at least for

* For a more detailed discussion see, e.g. Lewis (1990).

the first billion years, the climate of the earth was extremely torrid: oceans of molten rocks, an atmosphere mostly of fumes of silicates and other toxic gases and temperatures in the lower atmosphere reaching about 1000°C. Support for such a scenario comes from the fact that the oldest rocks on earth are not older than 3.8 billion years, while on the moon they go back to 4.6 billion years. The intervening time of about 800,000,000 years, in the case of the earth, is believed to be when the planet was entirely covered by an ocean of molten rocks.

If on the other hand, as Harold Urey (1952) hypothesized, the accumulation of the earth was slower, then the earth must have formed relatively cold but still with no atmosphere. This is because the objects forming the earth were as small as the size of the moon and each one of them therefore would have lost whatever atmosphere they had had earlier in their history.

We know that life needs a relatively benign climate and the presence of liquid water to survive. It can be safely concluded that either because extreme climatic conditions prevailed during the first billion years, or because of the complete absence of an atmosphere, no life could exist or did exist on the surface of the planet.

Our first indication of a major climate change on earth comes from the fact that the oldest sedimentary rocks, now precisely dated back 3.8 billion years, contain evidence of the existence of primitive life and of the presence of liquid water on the surface. Both these observations imply that by that time the temperatures had fallen to less than 100°C, the boiling point of water at normal atmospheric pressure, and that the atmosphere contained molecules such as carbon dioxide, methane, nitrogen and water vapor which nature used to synthesize the first amino acids and complex organic molecules found in those old rocks. In order for this synthesis to have taken place, the atmosphere must have been devoid of free oxygen.

It is clear that, toward the end of the first billion years, the composition of the atmosphere was quite different from what it is today. However, the temperature had cooled down to approximately today's values. As we will see in the subsequent discussion, this was an important juncture in the history of life and climate because, starting from this point, the presence of liquid water and the subsequent evolution of life on the surface stabilized the climate of the earth to such an extent that during the next 3.5 billion years the average temperature of the earth as a whole has only oscillated in a narrow range of less than 50°C. This exceptional circumstance has provided not only continuity to the evolution of life on earth for such a long period of time but has molded our metabolism in such a way as to adapt it to the ecology of an interdependent climate-life system.

Uniqueness of Earth

But why did this only happen on earth and not on Venus and Mars? Venus is still sizzling at more than 450°C while Mars is frozen at sub-zero temperatures. The extreme heat of Venus and the extreme cold on Mars have condemned these planets to remain lifeless even though all the basic ingredients to produce life appear to be present on those planets. What is missing is water in liquid state to slowly stir and join the molecules into macrostructures, and clement temperatures for the thermodynamic reactions to proceed at a slow, deliberate pace. Neither of these two conditions appears to have been met at any other place in the solar system for any length of time, except on earth.

The crucial factors for determining whether liquid water accumulates at the surface and the temperature remains mild seem to be the distance from the sun and the size of the planet. One calculation (Rasool and de Bergh 1970) even suggests that if the earth was formed only 6% closer to the sun than where it was, conditions on earth today would be as severe as those on Venus, and life would not have appeared on our planet (Figure 1-1). With respect to Mars, on the other hand, if the size of the planet were larger, on the order of that of Venus or earth, it might have accumulated a heavier atmosphere which could have resulted in a larger greenhouse effect. Although Mars is much further away from the sun than the earth is, and therefore receives less than half the solar energy received by the earth, Pollack and Yung (1980) have argued that the increased greenhouse effect could have easily compensated for the lower solar illumination, and the ice that lies frozen at the poles of Mars could have very well flowed at the surface as rivers and

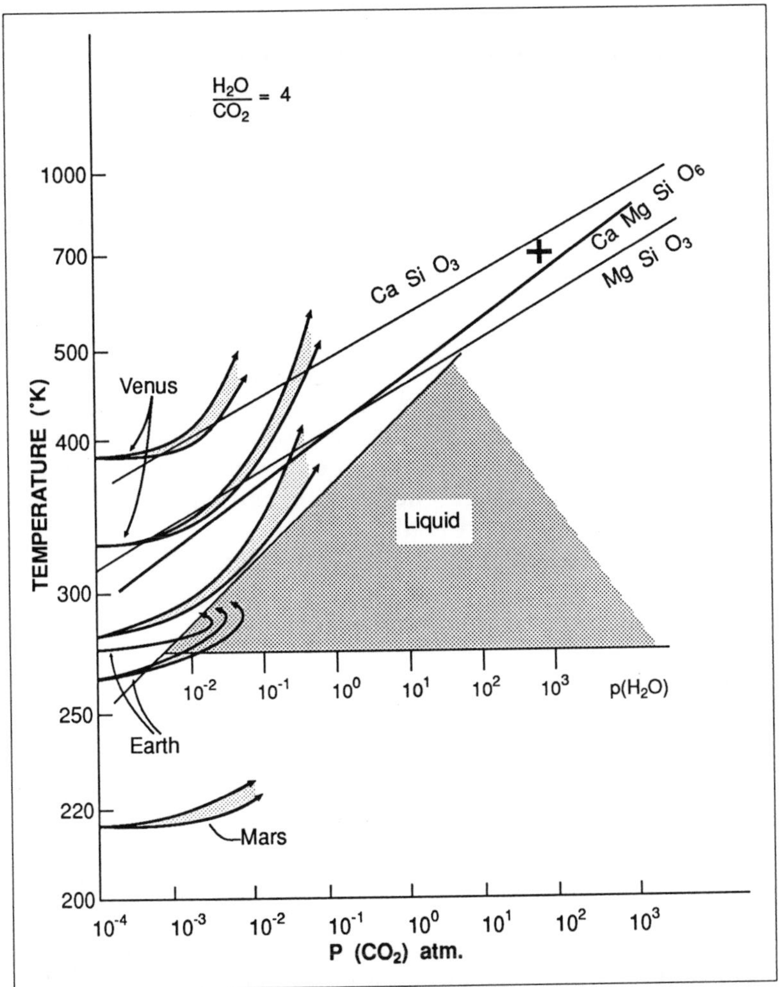

Figure 1-1: Plot of increase in surface temperatures on Venus, earth and Mars by the greenhouse effect on an H_2O-CO_2 atmosphere during the evolution of the three planets. The initial temperatures on these planets equal the effective temperature for a planetary albedo of 7%, and two different rates of rotation in the case of Venus. In the case of the earth, two values of the planetary albedo have been chosen (7% and 20%). The phase diagram for water is shown, and the region in which water can exist as liquid is represented by the hatched area. Also plotted are the equilibrium values of the partial pressures of CO_2 as a function of temperature for three different silicate reactions (Rasool and de Bergh 1970).

accumulated as seas and oceans of liquid water. Maybe at one point in the early history of Mars this did happen, because the images of Mars sent back by *Mariner* and *Viking* spacecraft do show evidence of ancient fluvial activity on the surface. However, Mars being smaller had two implications. First, it could not generate enough internal heat to outgas large quantities of atmosphere; second, whatever water came out from the interior either froze on the surface or "escaped" into space because of the planet's smaller gravitational pull.

It therefore appears that only on earth, because of its size and because it formed at a specific place in the solar system, have climatic conditions remained clement enough for life to evolve. It is a remarkable coincidence that the temperature extremes that occur on earth, between 0°C and 50°C, lie in the relatively narrow temperature range in which water is liquid. On other planets this is not the case and consequently they are either steaming hot or icy cold.

Figure 1-1 is an attempt to illustrate the paradigm that the position of the earth in the solar system has been the pacing factor in the origin of life on our planet.

Comparison with Venus

Why did two planets, nearly identical in size and weight, probably formed at the same time out of similar materials and situated at comparable distances from the sun, evolve so differently? Why does one planet offer an excellent climate for life while the other offers conditions hostile to terrestrial organisms? The answer to this problem requires the resolution of three other important questions: Why is the surface of Venus so hot? Why does its atmosphere contain such large quantities of carbon dioxide instead of N_2 and O_2 as on the earth? What happened to the oceans of water on Venus?

The measurement of the abundance of carbon dioxide on Venus is of great interest because it helps answer the first question: Why is Venus so hot? According to information radioed back to earth from spacecraft, the atmosphere of Venus consists primarily of a heavy layer of carbon dioxide, about 70,000 times more than is in the atmosphere of the earth. The dense atmosphere of carbon dioxide acts as an insulating blanket which seals in the planet's heat and prevents it from escaping into space. The trapped heat raises the surface to a far higher temperature than it would have otherwise. This effect is caused by the absorbing properties of a planetary atmosphere and can best be explained by taking the earth as an example.

The solar radiation reaching the earth has a value of 2 cal/cm^2/min. However, part of the energy (about 30%) is directly reflected back to space by the clouds present in the earth's atmosphere. Only 70% of the solar energy, therefore, penetrates through the atmosphere and reaches the surface. This energy is sufficient to heat the ground to a temperature of only -20°C. The earth's surface itself radiates, but since the temperature is not excessively high, the radiation is in the far infrared region of the electromagnetic spectrum—a dimly glowing object. The atmosphere of the earth, however, contains small quantities of water vapor, carbon dioxide and ozone. These gases have the property of absorbing far infrared radiation with great efficiency. As a matter of fact, only 10% of the infrared from the earth's surface actually gets through the earth's atmosphere. Having absorbed all this radiation, the atmosphere itself radiates in all directions, partly toward the surface and partly toward space. The radiation toward the surface increases the ground temperature by about 35°C, from -20°C to the observed value of +15°C. This phenomenon is called the "greenhouse effect" of the atmosphere, being an allusion to a greenhouse of plants where the glass cover acts like the atmosphere, transparent to solar radiation but opaque to radiation from the interior.

On Venus, an estimated greenhouse effect of about 500°C explains the observed temperature. Calculations based on the insulating properties of carbon dioxide (J.B. Pollack 1971) show that the temperature of Venus could easily be raised by 500°C as a result of the greenhouse effect of a very heavy layer of CO_2 as reported to be present on Venus, i.e., 70,000 times more than in the earth's atmosphere.

The high temperature on the surface of Venus can, therefore, be understood by the large abundance of carbon dioxide in the atmosphere. The question which one then asks is why carbon dioxide is so abundant on both Venus and Mars and not on earth.

Table 1-1: Surface Parameters and the Abundance of Major Volatiles on Venus, Earth and Mars

		Venus	*Earth*	*Mars*
Temperature		700°K	300°K	230°K
Pressure		75 atm	1 atm	0.01 atm
CO_2	atmosphere	70,000 g/cm^2	~ 1g/cm^2	~70 g/cm^2
	crust	?	70,000	?
N_2	atmosphere	<3000	800	<1
	crust	?	~2000?	?
H_2O	atmosphere	~ 100	~1	~0.01
	oceans	0	300,000	?
O_2	atmosphere	<10	200	~0.01
	crust	?	8 x10^6 total	?

Source: Rasool and de Bergh. 1970.

In this connection it is interesting to note that the amount of carbon dioxide on Venus—as measured by spacecraft experiments—is about the same as the amount of CO_2 that is today locked up in the earth's surface in the form of carbonates such as limestone (Table 1-1). Slowly, during the history of the earth, the carbon dioxide in the atmosphere reacted with calcium and magnesium silicates found in rocks to form carbonates that now lie buried in the crust. For this reaction to proceed rapidly two important factors are necessary: moderate atmospheric temperatures and the presence of liquid water. When the surface temperature is high and liquid water completely absent, as on Venus, this reaction becomes ineffective in removing carbon dioxide from the atmosphere, and its pressure builds up to very high values, as observed on Venus—an atmospheric pressure of 100 atm.

But, then, why is water scarce on Venus? The most probable explanation is that solar ultraviolet radiation has extensively dissociated Venus' water molecules into hydrogen and oxygen during the planet's history. Hydrogen, which is too light a gas to be held by the gravitational field of the planet, has escaped. The same process of dissociation and escape has occurred on the earth, but at a much lower rate, owing to three special circumstances.

First, the average temperature of the earth's surface is only 15°C: therefore water stays mainly in liquid form (in the oceans) and only a very small fraction of the total water (one part in 80,000) is in the atmosphere, in the form of water vapor. In order to be dissociated into hydrogen and oxygen by solar ultraviolet radiation, this water must rise through the atmosphere to its upper edge (an altitude of about 80 km), where it can be exposed to solar ultraviolet radiation. (This part of the sun's radiation does not penetrate down to the ground because molecules of oxygen and ozone absorb it high in the atmosphere.) But as the water vapor rises, 99.9% of it condenses out to form clouds before it gets to the altitude of 15 km. It then falls back to the ground as rain. The temperature of the earth's atmosphere decreases sharply with altitude; at 15 km (a level known as the "tropopause") it reaches a minimum of about -60°C. The colder the air, the less water vapor it can hold, and any excess amount immediately condenses out as drops of water or ice crystals. Because of this "cold trap" in the atmosphere, only an extremely minute amount of water vapor ever rises to the height where it is split apart by dissociation, and the hydrogen escapes. This is the second special circumstance that has inhibited the loss of oceans from the earth.

The third factor limiting water loss is the abundant presence of free oxygen in the atmosphere of the earth. As mentioned above, this gas absorbs the lethal ultraviolet rays and prevents them from penetrating to the lower levels of the atmosphere and to the earth's surface. In addition, the presence of free oxygen in the atmosphere gave rise to the formation of another molecule, namely ozone, which is even more effective in absorbing ultraviolet radiation. Today, for example, less than 1% of the relatively lethal ultraviolet reaches the surface, while more than 90% stays above the altitude of about 50 km. If it were not for this oxygen and ozone combination, the cold trap effect would be ineffective in limiting dissociation, because the solar ultraviolet would break up the water molecules near the earth's surface.

None of these three circumstances seems to exist on Venus. To begin with, Venus' surface temperature is so high that all its oceans should be in the form of water vapor. Then, the

Venusian cold trap is not as efficient as the earth's. The tropopause temperature on Venus as measured by spacecraft is a relatively warm -30°C, thus allowing about 1,000 times more water vapor to leak through to the upper atmosphere than on earth. Finally, the protective oxygen and ozone layer seems to be missing. Under these conditions, according to a recent calculation (Walker 1977), the rate of dissociation of water and the subsequent escape of hydrogen into space is so rapid that Venus could be losing about a million tons of water every day. This is approximately the rate at which water is being added to our oceans by hot springs, geysers and volcanoes, which bring water up from the earth's interior. In the last 4.5 billion years, enough water has accumulated from inside the earth to form our oceans. On Venus, it would appear that instead of accumulating, the water is dissociated, hydrogen lost to space and oxygen absorbed by the crust. The small amount of water that is now observed in the Venusian atmosphere (0.1%) may merely be in transit between the ground and the outer fringes of the atmosphere.

The scarcity of water and oxygen, and the abundance of carbon dioxide in the atmosphere resulting in extremely high surface temperatures, are all consequences of Venus' formation slightly closer to the sun than the earth. At the time of their birth, it seems likely that the earth's temperature was in the neighborhood of 5°C and Venus' was as high as 60°C. The difference in initial temperature was enough to cause the two planets to follow entirely different paths of evolution. One developed into a prolific haven for life, the other into a sterile, lifeless inferno.

Comparison with Mars

The recent measurements of the abundance of gases in the Martian atmosphere make it possible to discuss the processes that may have occurred on that planet in the context of the mechanisms of planetary formation. Among the newly established facts are:

- Organic molecules are very scarce on Mars at the two different locations studied.
- Water in the liquid phase has, at times, existed on Mars,

but not as abundantly as on earth and certainly not for the same length of time. Although this conclusion had already been reached from the orbital photographs of *Mariner* 9, some of the *Viking* pictures are particularly striking. (Figure 1-2).

• Water vapor is moderately abundant in the summer hemisphere, in confirmation of the difficult telescopic measurements over the past decade.

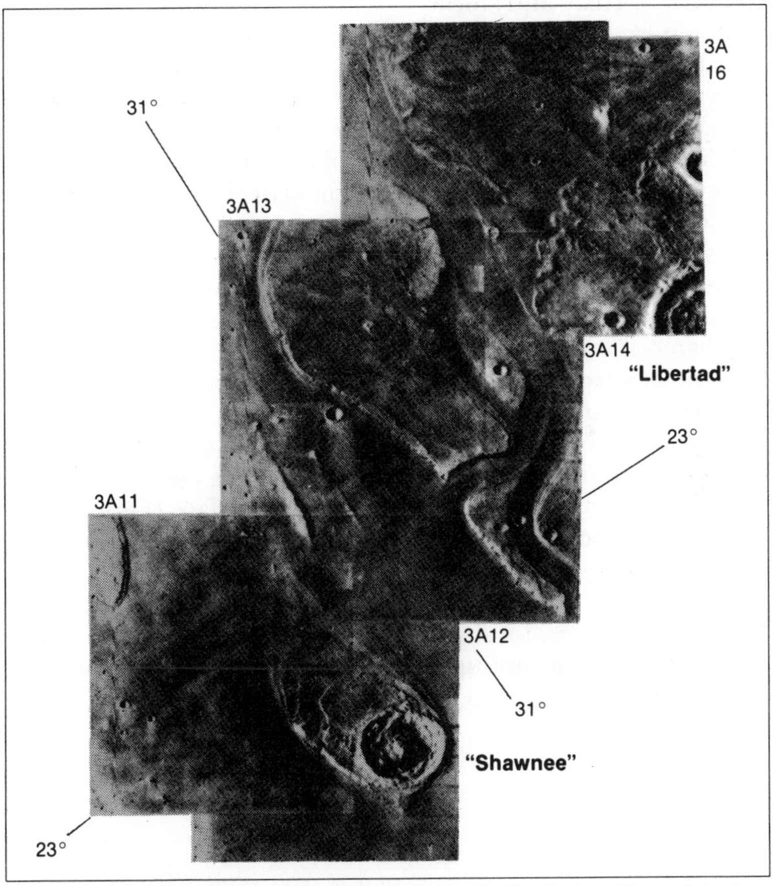

Figure 1-2: Meandering, intertwining channels flowing northward were vividly photographed by *Viking* in the Chryse region. Each frame is about 45 km across. NASA photograph n°76-H-481.

• *Mariner* 9 confirmed what had been known for some time, that ultraviolet radiation down to 2,000A reaches the surface.

Photochemical calculations based on these last two facts, and laboratory simulations, had already revealed that the surface environment must be highly oxidizing. The fundamental point is very simple: ultraviolet dissociates H_2O into H and OH at the surface. The latter is probably the strongest oxidant in existence. Further reactions lead to HO_2 and H_2O_2, both of which readily freeze out at Martian surface temperatures and make the surface rusty and sterile.

When we compare earth to Mars, it is tempting to suppose that the Martian atmosphere may always have been highly oxidizing and therefore highly unfavorable to the synthesis of prebiotic organic compounds. The surface, the water vapor and the short-wave ultraviolet are all present together. Growth of oxygen and ozone, which could shield the lower atmosphere, is also inhibited by the oxidants from water vapor photolysis. Mars does not have reservoirs of liquid water which make a planet more favorable for the preservation, accumulation and onward evolution of organic matter. Earth acquired relatively large amounts early in its history while Mars, being colder, has most of its water tied up in the frozen state, either at the poles or in the subsurface layers.

However, from *Viking* pictures it is also clear that major changes have taken place at some time in the past, that liquid water in abundance has flowed across the surface (Figure 1-2). Although these changes may be related to the astronomical cycles, there is evidence that the fluvial episode occurred in the remote past. Whenever it was, the atmospheric pressure must have been greater, for liquid water is not stable under present conditions. It is tempting to conclude that Mars had seas of water, but today it is in a deep ice age.

References

Lewis, J. (1990). In *Origins of the Universe* (S.F. Singer, editor). Paragon House Publishers, New York, N.Y.

Pollack, J. (1971). "A non-grey calculation of the runaway greenhouse: Implications for Venus' past and present." *Icarus* 14: 295–306.

Pollack, J. and Yung, Y. (1980). "Origin and evolution of planetary atmospheres." *Annual Review of Earth and Planetary Science* 8: 425–487.

Rasool, S. and de Bergh, C. (1970). "The runaway greenhouse and accumulation of CO_2 in the Venusian atmosphere." *Nature* 226: 1037–1039.

Urey, H. (1952). *The Planets: Their Origin and Development*. New Haven: Yale University Press.

Walker, J. (1977). *Evolution of the Atmosphere*. New York: Macmillan Publishing Company.

TWO

BIOGEOCHEMICAL CYCLES

Abraham Lerman

Introduction

The scientific concept of the cyclical nature of the processes in the surface environment of the earth emerged centuries ago from observations of such diverse phenomena as rainfall, the flow of rivers, the erosion of land and rocks, and the addition of new material to the earth's crust in the form of igneous rock (Gregor 1980). For water, rocks, and their mineral and chemical components, only a part of their cycle is observable, usually the part that is associated with the earth's surface. It is left to the observer's imagination and ingenuity to construct a conceptual model of a complete cycle, including in it the parts that are not immediately observable on the physical and temporal time scales of man.

An early scientific treatment of the geological and geochemical cycles that involve interactions with the living matter was due to the work of Alfred J. Lotka during the first quarter of this century. Lotka (1956) recognized the cyclic and interacting nature of many of the natural processes from the purely biological problems of population growth and predatory-prey relationships to the much more involved cycles of water and biologically important elements: carbon, nitrogen and phosphorus. Yet, despite the innovative mathematical and chemical approach to the cycles, Lotka was well aware that the concept of a natural cycle was as old as the Bible and the writings of the Greek philosophers. Today, much of the work on the biogeochemical cycles probes more and more (to use Lotka's words) "the fine details of material transformations revealed by the searchlight of modern chemistry."

What are the biogeochemical cycles? In a nutshell, they are the cycles of those materials involving inorganic and biological processes. The surface environment of the earth must have been a stage for interactions between the inorganic and organic worlds ever since life evolved on the planet. Organisms derive the energy needed for their life functions and reproduction from the environment, the energy of sunlight used in photosynthesis and the energy from a variety of chemical reactions in nature. The metabolic activity of organisms creates byproducts accumulating in the environment, and this process, to a greater or smaller extent, changes the chemical composition of the waters, soils and atmosphere. The emergence of photosynthetic organisms on earth resulted in the biological production of a new "pollutant" of the early terrestrial atmosphere—oxygen. In the course of the earth's long history, biological activity was responsible not only for the appearance of free oxygen gas in the atmosphere, but also for a great variety of chemical and physical changes in the environment. To name a few: the development of soils, the accumulation of fossil fuels, and the deposition of sediments made of calcium carbonates and of silica, both extracted by planktonic organisms from ocean water and transformed into their skeletons by a process known as *biomineralization*. The preceding examples also indicate the importance of the biological and chemical activity of photosynthetic organisms in the major fluxes of the materials on a global scale, among the reservoirs of land, water and the atmosphere.

The biogeochemical cycles of the elements build the environmental framework within which human and other animal species function. Understanding the cycles means understanding both the foundations of life on earth and the long-term evolution of the earth's surface environment.

This chapter discusses the basics of biogeochemical cycles that connect the biota to the inorganic world; it also summarizes the more important effects of biogeochemical activity on a global scale that helped shape the inorganic or geochemical conditions of the earth's surface today.

The Elements in Biogeochemical Cycles

The main chemical components of the living organic matter are the six elements: carbon, hydrogen and oxygen, and, less abundant but important, nitrogen, phosphorus and sulfur. The chemical composition of organic matter, written shorthand as CH_2O, is a product of the classic photosynthetic reaction between carbon dioxide and water:

$$CO_2 + H_2O \rightleftarrows CH_2O + O_2 \quad (1)$$

As can be seen, oxygen is another product of this reaction. The other chemical components of organic matter (nitrogen, phosphorus and sulfur) are omitted from the essentials of reaction (1). The reverse reaction—i.e., oxidation of CH_2O—is known as respiration.

In addition to the six elements—C, H, O, N, P, and S—many other less abundant and trace elements are important to the growth of organisms, from bacteria to mammals. The number certainly exceeds two dozen and includes the elements that are important nutrients to such groups as bacteria and algae, as well as some other elements (Cd, Ga, Hg, for example) whose role may be limited only to certain groups of aquatic organisms but which are known to be taken up by oceanic plankton. Experimental work on nutrient solutions, summarized by Bowen (1979), shows that the following eleven elements—all occurring as minor or trace elements in water and rock minerals—are important to the growth of bacteria, fungi, blue-green and green algae: B, Co, Cr, Cu, Fe, Mn, Mo, Ni, P, V, Zn.

These eleven elements serve as important nutrients to diverse groups of plants. Other elements, such as Si and Ca, are important in the building of the skeletal parts of planktonic plants and animals (diatoms, foraminifera, and coccoliths, for example).

Curious occurrences of different minerals in organs of the higher organisms and as components of the cells of the structurally less diversified groups, have been documented by Lowenstam (1980). The list of the biogenic minerals is long and includes such typically non-biological materials as gypsum ($CaSO_4 \cdot 2H_2O$), barite ($BaSO_4$), iron oxides, calcium fluoride, and several calcium phosphates. Among the biogenic minerals whose components are extracted from ocean water, only calcium carbonate ($CaCO_3$), silica (SiO_2) and calcium phosphate are quantitatively significant in the sedimentary record of the past.

The Limiting Nutrients

A nutrient element whose concentration in the environment is the lowest can serve to limit biological productivity. Among the main constituents of organic matter—C, H, O, N, P, S—the naturally abundant components are H_2O, carbon in the form of CO_2, nitrogen converted bacterially to nitrate (NO_{-3}), and sulfur occurring mostly in the oxidized state as sulfate ($SO_{4\text{-}2}$) in water. Phosphorus, however, is often a limiting nutrient element owing to its relatively low concentration in natural waters. The limiting-nutrient role of phosphorus is not unique, and an increase in phosphate concentration in a body of water may cause the biological productivity to become nitrogen-limited, rather than phosphorus-limited. Strong evidence for the limiting nutrient role of phosphorus comes from the seasonal changes in its concentration in the surface waters of lakes and the ocean. During the period of plankton growth, phosphorus concentrations in surface waters are driven almost to nil, to be restored only later by decomposition of the plankton settling through the deeper water, releasing phosphorus and other chemical species that would be carried upward by water mixing and advection.

The importance of phosphorus as a nutrient element in water and on land is best represented by the net chemical composition of the aquatic and terrestrial plants. Aquatic plankton is characterized by the relative abundances of carbon, nitrogen and phosphorus in a ratio C:N:P=106:16:1, whereas land plants are, on the average, characterized by the ratio C:N:P=882:9:1 (compiled in Lerman 1979, p. 23). The differences between the two ratios indicate that on land, much more carbon is being fixed in organic material for every atom of phosphorus than in the ocean and in fresh waters. By analogy

with the simplified photosynthesis reaction (1), the production of organic matter in water and on land can be written in the following form:
(2) In water:

$$106\ CO_2 + 16\ HNO_3 + H_3PO_4 + 122H_2O \rightarrow$$

$$\underset{\text{organic matter}}{C_{106}H_{263}O_{110}N_{16}P} + 138O_2$$

(3) On land:

$$882\ CO_2 + 9\ HNO_3 + H_3PO_4 + 891\ H_2O \rightarrow$$

$$\underset{\text{organic matter}}{C_{882}H_{1794}O_{886}N_9P} + 900\ O_2$$

The terms on the left-hand side of (2) and (3) are CO_2, nitrate and phosphate in solution (written in the form of HNO_3 and H_3PO_4 for reasons of stoichiometric balance), and water. On the right-hand side are the reaction products, organic matter and free oxygen. From a comparison of the two reactions, it follows that, on land, the process of oxygen production is much more efficient than in water; the ratio of oxygen produced to phosphorus consumed is about 900:1 on land, as compared to a lower value of 138:1 in water.

The global pool of available phosphorus, in soils and in the deep ocean, is sufficiently large, such that it is difficult to envisage interruption of its availablility to the biota on a long-term time scale. However, locally and for geologically short periods of time, low concentrations of phosphorus in sections of land surface and of the hydrosphere may become limiting to biological productivity.

The relative roles of phosphorus and ten other minor elements in limiting productivity can be examined from the data plotted in Figure 2-1. The horizontal coordinate shows the concentration values of each element that produces "healthy growth" in various group of bacteria, fungi and algae, grown in nutrient solutions. These are experimental data (Bowen 1979), the elemental concentrations needed for such "healthy growth" are usually much higher than the concentrations seen

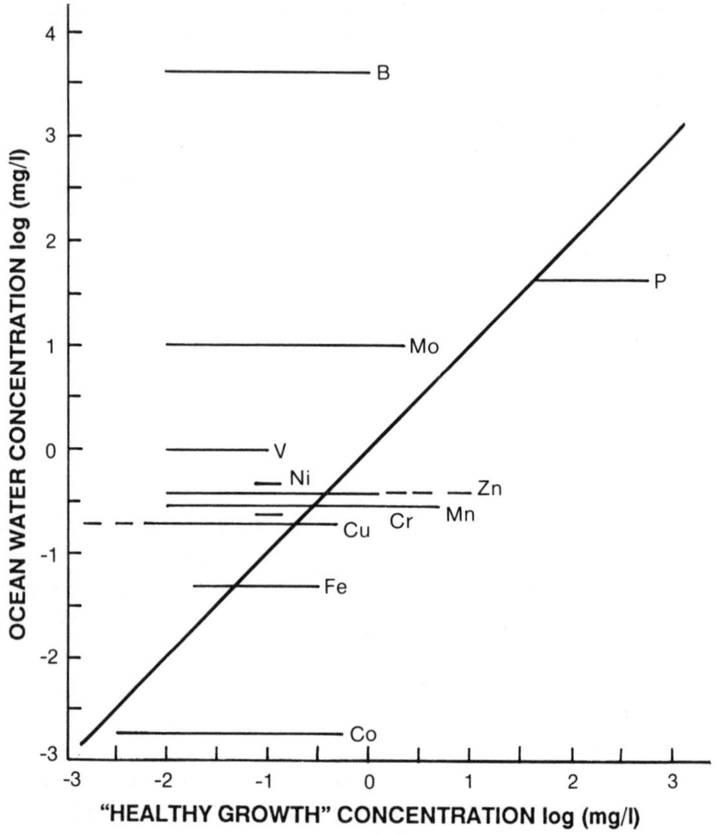

Figure 2-1: Concentration of eleven nutrient elements in ocean water and in nutrient solutions needed for "healthy growth" in different groups of bacteria, fungi, blue-green and green algae (from data in Bowen, 1979).

in ocean water, shown on the vertical coordinate. The empirical growth-requirement concentrations for the ten elements are roughly in the range of two to three orders of magnitude, from 10^{-2} to 10^{0} mg/1, whereas their mean concentrations in ocean water differ by several orders of magnitude. Compared with phosphorus, the abundance of nutrient elements in ocean waters falls in the order:

Mo>V>Ni>Zn>(Mn, Cr, Cu)>Fe>Co

If phosphorus is sufficiently abundant in water and does not limit the biological productivity, can any of the other elements, from B to Co (Figure 2-1), assume the role of the limiting nutrient? Or, could a change in the rate of supply of any one of the trace nutrient elements to the ocean cause major changes in the ecological structure of the existing communities, preserving such a change in the sedimentary record? At this time the two questions cannot be answered with a clear yes or no.

Removal of trace elements from river and ocean water by inorganic processes, such as chemical precipitation, adsorption and exchange on solid mineral surfaces (Goldberg 1965), can work against the availability of an element as a biological nutrient. Fast removal of a trace element from ocean water to sediments is reflected in a short residence time of the element in ocean water, on the order of 10^1–10^2 years. Such short residence times have been reported for suspended matter in the ocean (Lerman, Carder, Betzer 1977; Lal and Somayajulu 1977), and for iron in ocean water, as listed in Table 2-1, along with the residence times of the other nutrient trace elements. Another qualitative way to look at the residence times in ocean water is through a comparison of the trace element concentrations in river and ocean waters. An element whose concentration in river waters is significantly higher than in ocean water is obviously being removed from ocean water by some scavenging process(es). Conversely, a concentration value for ocean water much higher than for the rivers suggests a slow net removal rate or a long residence time. Figure 2-2 shows the river and ocean water concentrations plotted against each other: for B and Mo, the ocean water concentrations are much higher than the river water; for the metals Fe, Co, Cr, Ni, Mn, Cu, and Zn, scavenging from ocean water is indicated by lower concentration values than in rivers.

Although the roles of the trace metals as nutrient elements in natural waters are, as a whole, not known as well as the role of phosphorus, a glance at Figure 2-2 reveals a considerable global uniformity of the dissolved phosphorus concentration: the mean concentration in river water is about the same as in

Table 2-1: Residence Times in Ocean Water of Phosophorus and Ten Nutrient Trace and Minor Elements

	Element	*Residence time (years)*
P	phosphorus	6.9×10^4
B	boron	9.6×10^6
Co	cobalt	3.4×10^2
Cr	chromium	8.2×10^3
Cu	copper	9.7×10^2
Fe	iron	5.4×10^1
Mn	manganese	1.3×10^3
Mo	molybdenum	8.2×10^5
Ni	nickel	8.2×10^3
V	vanadium	4.5×10^4
Zn	zinc	5.1×10^2

Source: Broecker and Peng 1982, pp. 26-27.

the ocean. For those elements whose concentrations in the ocean are significantly lower than in river water, it is conceivable that their biological demand is met at low concentration levels, maintained by a combination of input from land via rivers and net removal from ocean water via sedimentation on the ocean floor.

Biogeochemical Cycle

The earth's crust, the hydrosphere, the atmosphere, and the biota are the main reservoirs of the biogeochemical cycles of the elements on the earth's surface. The main reservoirs are interconnected by fluxes transporting the materials among them, such as shown in a conceptual model of the biogeochemical cycle of carbon and sulfur in Figure 2-3.

The most important characteristic of our biogeochemical system is, perhaps, existence of three redox couples in the environment—three elements involved in oxidation and reduction reactions. The three elements are iron, sulfur and carbon, commonly occurring in the following oxidation states:

iron: Fe^{+2} and Fe^{+3}

sulfur: S^{-2}, S^{-1} and S^{+6}

carbon: C^0 and C^{+4}

Each of the three elements can also occur in other oxidation states in nature, but such occurrences are less common. For example, there exist metallic iron (Fe^0), elemental sulfur (S^0), and carbon in oxidation states other than 0 (designated for

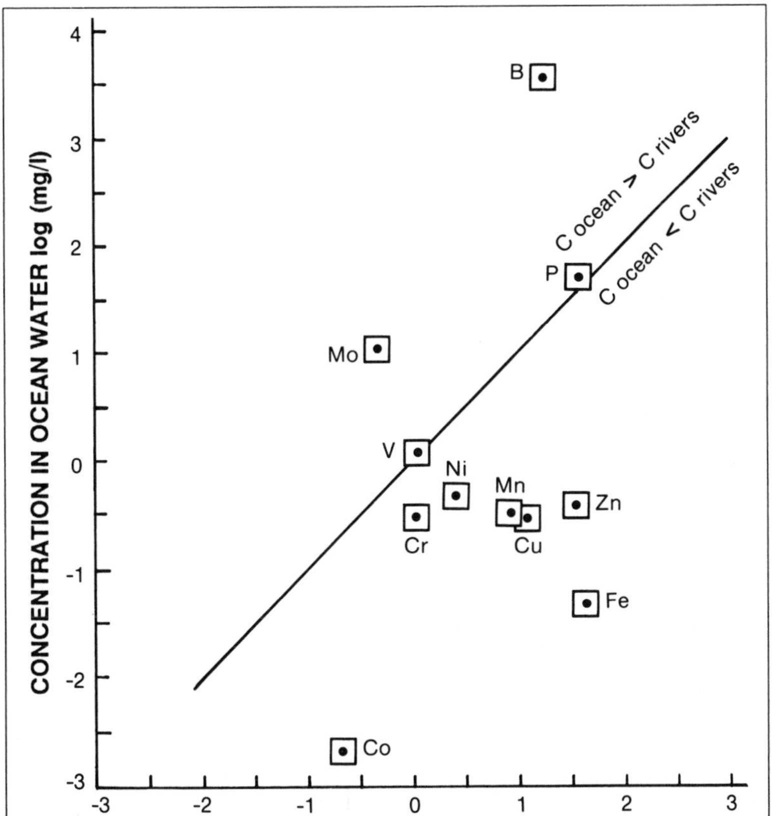

Figure 2-2: Concentration of eleven nutrient elements in rivers and in ocean water (from Bowen, 1979; Broecker and Peng, 1982).

organic carbon of CH_2O) and +4 (in carbon dioxide).

The main reservoirs of the oxidized and reduced carbon and sulfur in the surface environment are shown in Figure 2-3.

A study of the biogeochemical cycle of an element requires information on the sizes of the biogeochemical reservoirs, the magnitudes of fluxes between them, the residence times of the element within the individual reservoirs, and the processes capable of modifying the fluxes and the reservoirs in the course of time. At present, our knowledge of these parameters is very uneven: for some of the biologically important elements, such

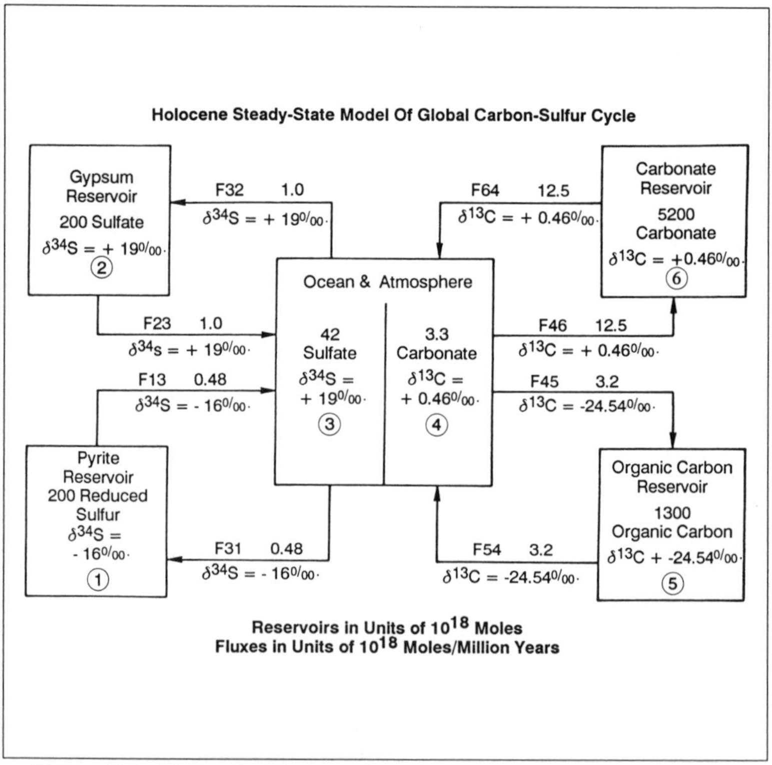

Figure 2-3: Biogeochemical model of the carbon and sulfur cycles showing four sedimentary reservoirs and the ocean plus atmosphere reservoir. Masses of sulfur and carbon, and the mean isotopic composition, is shown in each reservoir (Garrels and Lerman 1984).

as carbon, sulfur and oxygen, more is known than about other minor and trace elements. But even for the major building blocks of the living world, the quantitative information available is not of the highest precision. The chemical composition of the atmosphere and of ocean water, and the masses of the elements stored in each, are known. However, for the crustal and the sedimentary reservoirs that are much bigger than the ocean and atmosphere, the mass estimates of the individual components vary by more than one would like to see. For two of the main elements in the global biogeochemical cycles, carbon and sulfur, the estimates of their masses in the sedimentary rocks vary fairly widely, as Table 2-2 shows. The differences of up to a factor of two between the individual estimates of the masses translate into comparable differences in the magnitudes of other elements, such as oxygen and iron, that are bound to the oxidized and reduced sulfur in sediments.

Figure 2-3 diagrams a model of the global sulfur and carbon cycles. There are two sedimentary reservoirs of sulfur—oxidized sulfur, labeled gypsum reservoir, and reduced sulfur, labeled pyrite reservoir; and two of carbon—oxidized carbon, carbonate sediments, and reduced carbon, organic matter in sediments (see also Table 2-2). The reservoirs interact via the in and out fluxes with the ocean plus atmosphere reservoir. Fluxes from the sedimentary reservoirs to the ocean represent

Table 2-2: Estimates of the Size of the Sedimentary Reservoirs in the Carbon and Sulfur Cycles

Reservoir	*Estimated size range (10^{18} moles)*	*Size used in cycle model of Fig. 2-3*
Oxidized S (gypsum reservoir)	136 – 249	200
Reduced S (pyrite reservoir)	128 – 294	200
Oxidized C (carbonates)	3712 – 7034	5200
Reduced C (organic matter)	930 – 1292	1300

Sources from Garrels and Lerman 1984; see also Fig. 2-3.

weathering, and the fluxes from the ocean to the sedimentary reservoirs represent deposition. In a simplistic model such as the one shown in Figure 2-3, the cycle is at a steady state: the sum of the fluxes to each of the reservoirs is balanced by the sum of the fluxes out of it. For each of the reservoirs and fluxes, the figure gives the total masses of carbon and sulfur (for example, 200×10^{18} moles S in the gypsum reservoir), and the mean isotopic composition of S and C.

Coupling of the Biogeochemical Cycles

Incorporation of several of the chemical elements in living organic matter is an indication that the individual cycles of these elements are coupled one to another. The photosynthetic reactions (1)–(3) show in an abbreviated form that such coupling can be expected of carbon, nitrogen, phosphorus, and oxygen, all of which are involved in the production and respiration of photosynthetic plants.

The accumulation of organic matter in sediments is the result of an imperfectly functioning cycle of photosynthetic productivity and respiration. In a perfect cycle, all the organic matter produced from carbon dioxide and water reaction (1) would decay back to the original components. In an imperfect cycle, a small fraction of the organic matter is buried in sediments, and an equivalent fraction of oxygen produced by photosynthesis is at least temporarily prevented from recombining with the reduced sink of organic carbon. This left-over oxygen is in effect the free oxygen available to other chemical reactions on the earth's surface, such as oxidation of other reduced substances, iron and sulfur (Garrels and Perry 1974; Junge *et al.* 1977). From the data in Table 2-2, the mass of organic carbon stored in sediments is about 1300×10^{18} moles. An equal mass of oxygen, 1300×10^{18} moles O_2, must have been produced during the sedimentary history of the earth, but only 38×10^{18} moles oxygen are present in the earth's atmosphere, or 3% of the total net produced.

The net production of oxygen by burial of organic carbon in sediments and the production of oxygen by photosynthesis are two processes of strikingly different rates: recycling of atmospheric oxygen by photosynthesis and respiration in orders of magnitude faster than its net production rate over the geological history of the earth, as the following computation shows.

The primary photosynthetic productivity, as given in reaction (1) produces 3.3×10^{15} moles oxygen per year (Bolin and Cook 1983, p. 44). This corresponds to the renewal or residence time of oxygen in the atmosphere of about 11,000 years:

$$\text{Residence time} = \frac{3.8 \times 10^{19}\, moles\ O_2}{3.3 \times 10^{15}\, moles\ O_2 / yr} = 1.1 \times 10^4\, yr$$

For the geological record, the net rate of organic carbon storage in sediments has been estimated in the range from 3×10^{12} to 10×10^{12} moles C/yr (Holland 1978). Thus the residence time of oxygen in today's atmosphere with respect to its mean rate of production by carbon storage in sediments is between 4 and 10 million years:

$$\text{Residence time} = \frac{3.8 \times 10^{19}\, moles\ O_2}{(3 - 10) \times 10^{12}\, moles\ O_2 / yr} = 10 \times 10^6 - 4 \times 10^6\, yr$$

Clearly, if one addresses the biogeochemical cycle of carbon or oxygen on a time scale of human history, the net production of oxygen as evidenced by the occurrence of organic matter in old sediments is negligible, whereas the cycle of the primary productivity is of major importance. Conversely, the primary productivity and respiration are fast processes, such that any departures in the difference:

C stored in sediments = Productivity—Respiration

would exert an effect on the net production rate of oxygen only over a geologically long period of time.

An important point of the mass balance of the carbon-sulfur cycles should be noted: the mass of carbon present in the combined ocean and atmosphere (3.3 units) is very small in comparison to the masses in the sedimentary reservoirs (5,200 units in limestones and dolomites, and 1,300 in sedimentary organic matter). For sulfur, however, the mass of sulfur in the ocean is significant relative to the masses of the oxidized and reduced reservoirs: 40 units in the ocean and 200 units in each of the sedimentary reservoirs. These differences are reflected in the residence times of carbon and sulfur in the ocean, as shown in the figure: about 200,000 years for carbon and about 30 million years for sulfur. The main effect, however, on the carbon oceanic reservoir is that the isotopic composition of C in the ocean water carbonate is more susceptible to changes in the erosional and depositional rates of organic matter and sedimentary carbonate, as controlled by the fluxes in and out of the ocean.

In a closed cycle, such as the one shown in Figure 2-3, a higher rate of biological productivity in the ocean would result in a higher rate of storage of organic carbon in sediments (flux F_{45}), and this can come only at the expense of a reduced rate of deposition of carbonate in limestones (lower value of flux F_{46}). Strictly speaking, such a mutually reciprocal relationship between the depositional fluxes holds for an ocean of constant chemical composition, requiring that the masses of carbon and sulfur in the ocean remain constant through time. Substantial geochemical evidence for the constancy or near constancy of the chemical composition of the ocean at least during Phanerozoic time (the last 600 million years) has been discussed by Holland (1978).

By analogy with the carbon cycle, a higher rate of deposition of oxidized sulfur from the ocean in the form of $CaSO_4$ in sediments (flux F_{32}) must correlate with a lower rate of deposition of reduced sulfur in FeS_2 (flux F_{31}). When more organic carbon (CH_2O) is being stored in sediments, more oxygen becomes available for oxidation of other reduced substances. This excess oxygen may oxidize the reduced sulfur in the pyrite reservoir, causing a higher flux of sulfate ($SO_{4\text{-}2}$) to the ocean, wherefrom it can be removed as $CaSO_4$ into sediments. Thus, the simple coupling between the sulfur and carbon cycles implies that periods of higher storage rates of organic carbon in sediments should correlate on a geological time scale with periods of higher deposition rates of calcium sulfate in evaporites.

In this model, changes in the rate of biological productivity and, consequently, the net rate of burial of organic carbon in sediments, can be viewed as the driving forces behind the deposition rates in the three remaining sedimentary reservoirs.

The concept of such a "biological driving force" must be viewed discriminately. Changes in the rate of primary productivity in the ocean on a time scale of 10^6–10^7 years are likely to depend on the rates of delivery and the availability of the nutrient elements in ocean water. A higher rate of input of the nutrients to the ocean can be caused by a higher rate of erosion, which ultimately depends on the global tectonic forces producing changes in the relative elevation of the land masses and sea level. Thus, the role of the bioproductivity in the sedimentary cycle of carbon and sulfur is in itself conditioned by the global tectonic and weathering picture over a particular stretch of geological time. The organismal activity in the ocean, responding to an external perturbation, provides feedback that results in a modification of the sedimentary fluxes from the ocean into the carbon and sulfur reservoirs. Conversely, a geological period characterized by greater rates of deposition of evaporites ($CaSO_4$ reservoir in Figure 2-3) represents a tectonic perturbation of the carbon-sulfur system.

The broad picture of the coupling between the carbon and sulfur cycles, as originally proposed by Garrels and Perry (1974), is a global model for geological time. On a shorter time scale and smaller physical scale, such as, for example, in smaller sections of the ocean, there may be no evidence of a correlation between a higher rate of biological productivity and deposition of gypsum from ocean water in the same area. An analogous set of relationships comes to mind if one considers the living plant biomass and the dead organic matter (humus) on land. On a global scale, the standing plant biomass and the dead material formed from it interact with each other, either directly or indirectly via waters and atmosphere, and both are significant storage reservoirs of carbon in the terrestrial environment. However, the spatial distribution of forests and dead organic matter shows that in the areas of the greatest forest biomass—the tropical rain forest (Lieth and Whittaker 1975)—the amount of dead organic material preserved on the ground is much smaller than in the temperate zones, where conditions favor longer residence times for humus in the soils.

The main evidence for the coupling of the biogeochemical carbon and sulfur cycles during the last 600 million years is the negative correlation (Figure 2-4) between the isotopic composition of sulfur in sedimentary sulfates and the isotopic composition of carbon in sedimentary carbonates. During periods of greater storage of reduced organic carbon in sediments, the isotopic composition of C in ocean water carbonate shifts toward heavier values, as measured by ^{13}C. The reason for this is the preferential uptake of the lighter isotopes ^{12}C and ^{32}S by the organisms that reduce carbonate and sulfate to, respectively,

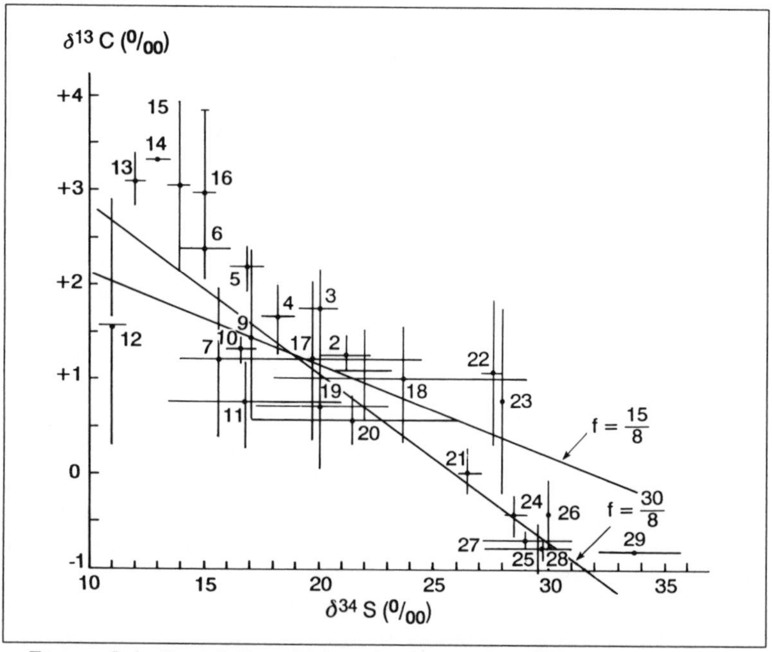

Figure 2-4: Correlation during the last 600 million years between isotopic composition of C in sedimentary carbonates ($\delta^{13}C$) and isotopic composition of S in sedimentary sulfates ($\delta^{34}S$) (From data of Veizer *et al.* 1980 and Veizer 1983).
Correlation equation: $\delta^{13}C = 1.27 + 0.92f - 0.049f\,(\delta^{34}S)$, where f is a factor relating the net rate of deposition of organic C (reservoir 5 in Fig. 2-3) to that of $CaSO_4$ (reservoir 2).
Point 1 is for time internal 0–20 million years; point 2 for 20–40 million years, and so on.

organic carbon and sulfide. $CaCO_3$ forming in the ocean (either by biogenic or inorganic processes) reflects the isotopic composition of C in ocean water carbonates; the latter becomes heavier during periods of greater carbonate storage. Similarly, periods of stronger reduction of $SO_{4\text{-}2}$ to $S_{\text{-}2}$ produce an isotopically heavier sulfate in ocean water, resulting in an isotopically heavier S in $CaSO_4$ forming during that time. The negative correlation between the isotopic composition of carbon in limestones and sulfur in sedimentary sulfates is thus an indication that higher rates of storage of organic carbon coincided on a geological time scale with the isotopically lighter sulfur in the ocean and its removal into the oxidized sedimentary sulfur reservoir $CaSO_4$.

Outlook on the Future

The overall stability of the biogeochemical cycles on a time scale of hundreds of millions of years does not imply that departures from a mean pattern did not take place, nor does it imply that perturbations of the cycles cannot take place on a shorter time scale in the future. What are the possible perturbations that might occur in the future and be of concern to humanity? Barring catastrophes of extraterrestrial or nuclear origin, the major focus of recent concern has been, and is, human activity causing an increase in the carbon dioxide content of the atmosphere and the potentially detrimental consequences of this change in one of the carbon reservoirs to the entire global cycle. Although one might argue that there were periods of higher carbon dioxide input to the atmosphere from volcanic activity in the geological past (Arthur *et al.* 1984), and that this extra carbon dioxide was eventually removed through a combination of chemical weathering and organic growth, there is little consolation to mankind in a salvation that may lie 10^5–10^6 years in the future. Another cause of perturbation in the biogeochemical cycle of carbon and phosphorus has been postulated to be related to the change in sea level at the end of the Wisconsin glaciation, approximately 120,000 years ago (Broecker 1982): a rise in sea level over the continental shelf resulted in removal of carbon and phosphorus in the organic matter that became buried in the continental shelf sediments, thereby withdrawing a significant fraction of the phosphate from the pool available to bioproductivity in the ocean.

As the main fluxes of materials in the biogeochemical cycles on the earth's surface are, generally, from the land to the ocean, it seems reasonable to anticipate changes that may take place in the biogeochemical reservoirs of elements with residence times comparable to the human historical time dimension, 10^1 to 10^3 years. A likely and pronounced change of this nature may be caused by changes in the rates of weathering and the rates of primary productivity on land. The mass of terrestrial biota, as measurable by the masses of carbon and phosphorus contained in it, is much greater than the mass of the oceanic biota (Bolin and Cook 1983). The oceanic biota draws its components from the surface ocean water, and the amounts of carbon and phosphorus in this latter reservoir are comparable to the amounts in standing crops on land and in some of the dead organic matter in soils. Thus, a faster release of nutrients from the terrestrial reservoirs of plants and soils would constitute a greater input of nutrients into the oceanic coastal waters, resulting in a higher rate of primary production in the coastal sections of the ocean. The possible causes for a higher rate of release from land may include such factors as a change in the type of vegetation (for example, a change from longer-living trees to shorter-living plants), faster rates of chemical weathering or faster rates of mechanical denudation.

Another flux that contributes to short-term perturbation of the biogeochemical cycles is the addition of fertilizers to soils. At present, the phosphorus added as fertilizer to soils is about 4 to 8 times greater than the amount of dissolved phosphorus brought by the world rivers to the ocean. The added fertilizer phosphorus is likely to stay in the soils for some time, however, thus producing a delayed effect in the release of this extra nutrient.

Various model computations on the behavior of the biogeochemical cycles of carbon and phosphorus on a time scale of a few hundred years indicate that an increased nutrient input into the coastal ocean waters can be a result of a global change in the residence times of these elements in the land biomass and in the soils. In other words, changes in the masses and rates of delivery may be expected to be reflected first in the coastal sections of the ocean and in their biota. According to the model analysis, an increase in the standing crop of the oceanic biota by a factor of as much as two could be a likely outcome of a major increase in the fluxes of the nutrients from the land biomass.

References

Arthur, M.A., W.E. Dean and S.O. Schlanger. 1984. "Global carbon cycle flux variations during the Mid-Cretaceous related to climate, volcanism and changes in atmospheric CO_2." Proc. Chapman Conf. on CO_2 and Climate, *Amer. Geophys. Union, Geophys. Mon.* 32: 504–529.

Bolin, B. and R.B. Cook (eds.). 1983. *The Major Biochemical Cycles and Their Interactions*. Wiley, New York.

Bowen, H.J.M. 1979. *Environmental Chemistry of the Elements*. Academic Press, Orlando, Florida.

Broecker, W.S. 1982. "Glacial to interglacial changes in ocean chemistry." *Progr. Oceanography* 11: 151–197.

Broecker, W.S. and T.-H. Peng. 1982. *Tracers in the Sea*. Lamont-Doherty Geological Observatory, Columbia Univ., Palisades, New York.

Garrels, R.M. and E.A. Perry. 1974. "Cycling of carbon, sulfur and oxygen through geologic time." in E.D. Goldberg (ed.), *The Sea*, 5: 303–336. Wiley, New York.

Garrels, R.M. and A. Lerman. 1981. "Phanerozoic cycles of sedimentary carbon and sulfur." *Proc. Nat. Acad. Sci.* 78 (8): 4652–4656.

Garrels, R.M. and A. Lerman. 1984. "Coupling of the sedimentary sulfur and carbon cycles—an improved model."*Am. J. Sci.* 284: 989–1007.

Goldberg, E. D. 1965. "Minor elements in sea water," in J.P. Riley and G. Skirrow (eds.), *Chemical Oceanography*, 1: 163–197. Academic Press, Orlando, Florida.

Gregor, C.B. 1980. "Weathering rates of sedimentary and crystaline rocks." *Proc. Konink. Nederl. Akad. Wetensch.*, ser. B, 83 (2): 173–181.

Holland, H.D. 1978. *The Chemistry of the Atmosphere and Oceans*. Wiley, New York.

Junge, C.E., M. Schinlowski, R. Eichmann, and H. Pietrek. 1977. "Model calculations for the terrestrial carbon cycle: Carbon isotope geochemistry and evolution of photosynthetic oxygen." *J. Geophys. Res.* 80: 4542–4552.

Lal, D. and B.L.K. Somayajulu. 1977. "Particulate transport of radionuclides C-14 and Fe-55 to deep waters in the Pacific Ocean." *Limnol. Oceanogr.* 22: 55–59.

Lerman, A. 1979. *Geochemical Processes*. Wiley, New York.

Lerman, A., K.L. Carder, and P.R. Betzer. 1977. "Elimination of fine suspensoids in the oceanic water column." *Earth Planet. Sci. Lett.* 37: 61–70.

Lieth, H. and R.H. Whittaker. 1975. *Primary Productivity of the Biosphere*. Springer-Verlag, New York.

Lotka, A.J. 1956. *Elements of Mathematical Biology*. Dover, New York.

Lowenstam, H.A. 1980. "Minerals formed by organisms." *Science* 211: 1126–1131.

Veizer, J., W.T. Holser, and C.K. Wilgus. 1980. "Correlation of $^{13}C/^{12}C$ and $^{34}S/^{32}S$ secular variations." *Geochim. Cosmochim. Acta.* 44: 579–587.

Veizer, J. 1983. "Trace elements and isotopes in sedimentary carbonates." *Min. Soc. Amer., Rev. Mineralogy* 11: 265.

THREE

LONG-TERM CLIMATE STABILITY

ENVIRONMENTAL SYSTEM STUDIES

Hans Oeschger

Introduction

In 1957 R. Revelle and H.E. Suess made the often-cited statement, that mankind is carrying out a large-scale geophysical experiment with the injection of enormous amounts of CO_2 into the atmosphere. If adequately documented, this may yield far-reaching insights into the processes determining weather and climate. In the meantime it has been observed that trace gases like CH_4, N_2O, etc. show rising concentrations in the atmosphere, too. Furthermore, the continuous emission of SO_2 and NO_x lead to acid precipitations observed over continental dimensions with negative impacts on the environment.

This situation inspired an international group of scientists from a broad spectrum of disciplines to improve our knowledge of environmental processes and the reactions of the natural systems to the rising anthropogenic impact.

In this paper a review of our knowledge of CO_2 and the climate systems is given. First, research methods and concepts are presented which have proved to be very successful during the last decades. Then the anthropogenic impact and its influence on climate is discussed. This leads to the state of the art of our knowledge on past climatic change. The long-term climatic change is probably mainly due to orbital parameter changes but short-term climatic changes are only partly understood today. The major role of the ocean regarding these phenomena is possibly reflected in a bistability of the climate system. Indications and recent results are discussed at the end of the paper.*

Concepts and Methods

The Environmental System (E.S.)

To illustrate the research in this field, a concept of the global environmental system is introduced. It is illustrated in Figure 3-1. It includes the entirety of physical, chemical and biological processes acting upon the earth's surface and in the atmosphere. The various parts of the system interact in various dynamic sequences and are in contact with the planetary and galactic systems. The E.S., as defined here, agrees largely with the climate system as it is generally defined, but stronger emphasis is given to chemical and biological processes. Special attention is drawn to those parameters which can be studied in natural archives and therefore enable the reconstruction of ancient system states.

The main components of the E.S. are the atmosphere, the hydrosphere, including the oceans and continental waters, the cryosphere, consisting of the polar ice sheets, sea ice and mountain glaciers, the biosphere, containing marine and continental living organisms, and the lithosphere, with bedrock and sediments which interface with the hydrosphere.

The energy of the sun drives the dynamic processes in the

---

* See also the chapters by Kraus and Ellsaesser (this volume) and the discussion in Singer (1989).

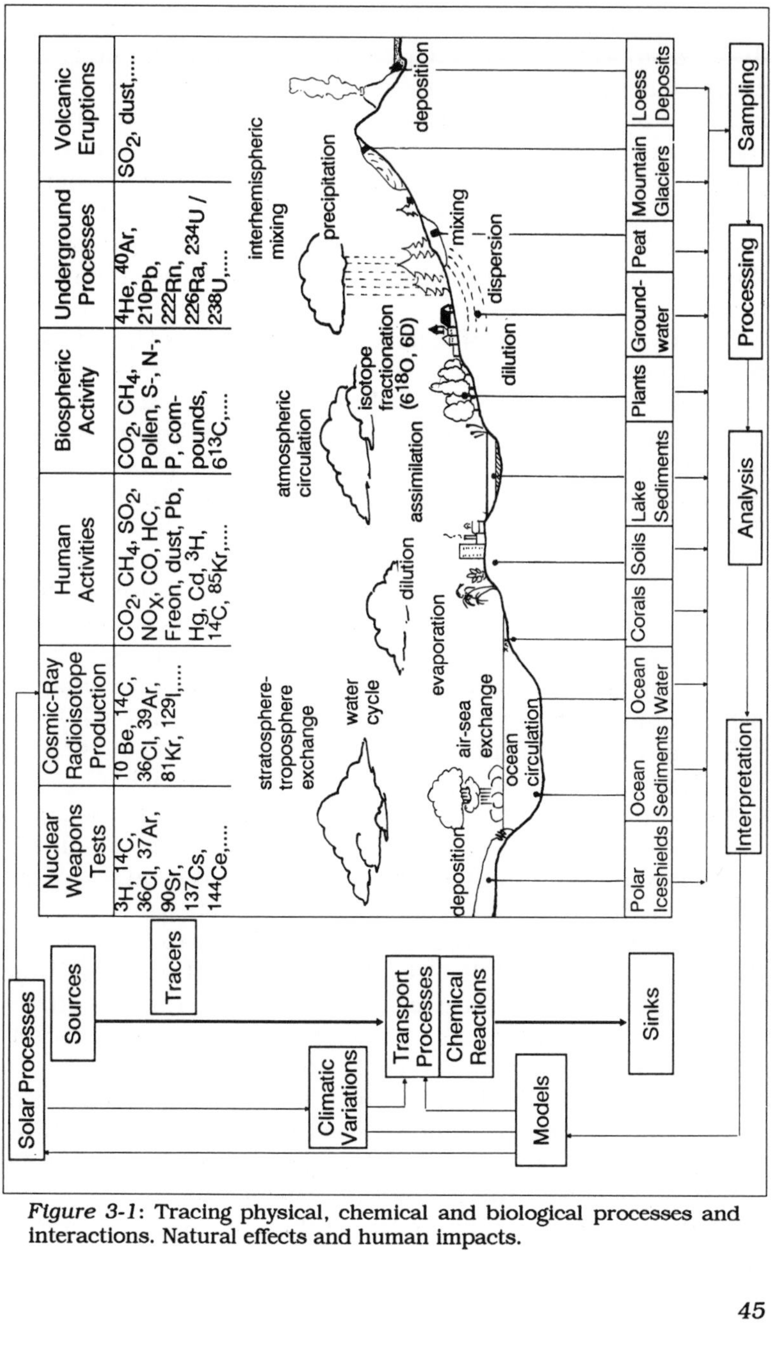

Figure 3-1: Tracing physical, chemical and biological processes and interactions. Natural effects and human impacts.

E.S. It causes atmospheric circulation and oceanic mixing, and due to evaporation and precipitation, the cycling of water. The energy balance determines the climatic conditions at individual locations on the earth's surface. It is affected by scattering and reflection of short wavelength solar radiation in the atmosphere and on the earth's surface, and the infrared radiation emission absorption and reemission by the surface and by water vapor and gases (CO_2, O_3,...) in the atmosphere, together with the transfer of latent and sensible heat into the atmosphere and ocean.

The dynamic cycles of some elements, such as C, N and O, play an important role which is regulated by biospheric activity, chemical reactions, and physical exchange processes.

Dust particles and aerosols are injected into the atmosphere by wind action, volcanic eruptions, biospheric processes and human activities. They reappear on the earth's surface by dry fallout or wet deposition.

Of special interest for our approach to the understanding of the E.S. processes are the radioactive and stable isotopes which constitute ideal tracers for a variety of processes and their dynamics. Radioactive isotopes have different origins:

a) They are formed by the interaction of cosmic radiation with atoms in the upper atmosphere (^{10}Be, ^{14}C, ^{36}Cl, ^{39}Ar, ^{81}Kr, ...). This cosmic production is modulated by the changing shields of solar plasma and the earth's magnetic field.

b) They are also introduced to the E.S. as a result of society's use of nuclear fusion and fission (^{3}H, ^{37}Ar, ^{85}Kr, ...), and finally

c) They are released from the earth's crust as products of the natural decay series of U and Th (^{222}Rn, ^{210}Pb,...).

Since half lives vary from days (^{37}Ar, ^{133}Xe) to hundreds of thousands of years (^{10}Be, ^{36}Cl, ^{81}Kr), information about time constants of natural processes over a very wide range is attainable. Each isotope has its characteristic field of applications which may reach far beyond that of merely dating.

Stable isotopes (^{2}H, ^{13}C, ^{18}O) are other important sources of information. Phase transitions, chemical reactions and diffusion processes produce small changes in the natural isotope ratios. They reflect the conditions at which the processes occurred. Elements originating from different natural reservoirs can often be distinguished based on their different isotopic composition. Samples of air, water and ice, and organic materials and sediments, taken from many parts of the E.S., contain information on its static characteristics, like the partitioning of water between atmosphere, cryosphere and ocean, but also its dynamic characteristics, like mixing and circulation and exchange processes in and between the different system components. This and other information can be derived from the isotopic ratios, from the concentration levels of chemical elements and molecules, pollen and dust. A complete set of these parameters defines the state of the E.S. As "fingerprint parameters" they are continuously recorded in the natural archives, as in polar ice sheets, mountain glaciers, ocean and lake sediments, and organic materials like tree-rings or peat and coral deposits. Analyses of sequential samples allow the reconstruction of the historical evolution of the E.S.

The overall objective of investigating the E.S. is a consistent and systematic description of its complex processes and an understanding of the mechanisms controlling them.

Mathematical models play an important role in this research. The models are based on the fundamental physical, chemical and biological knowledge. Since the various processes are very complex, it is often necessary to simplify the equations and to use empirical procedures to arrive at conclusions. Of course the models should produce system responses to various perturbations which closely agree with observations. Man's impact upon the environment is an example of a perturbation. Past system perturbations and responses are revealed from the natural archives. Figure 3-2 illustrates the process of model development. Such an analysis leads to increasing confidence in the models which also are used to predict future natural or anthropogenic environmental changes.

The Climate System

The average global energy balance on the earth's surface is given by:

(1) $S\pi R^2(1\text{-}A) = 4\pi R^2 \sigma T_S^4(1\text{-}B)$

with

S = solar constant
R = radius of earth
A = albedo (reflected fraction of solar irradiation)
σ = Stefan-Boltzmann constant
B = fraction of infrared radiation (emitted from surface), absorbed in atmosphere and reemitted back to surface
T_S = surface temperature

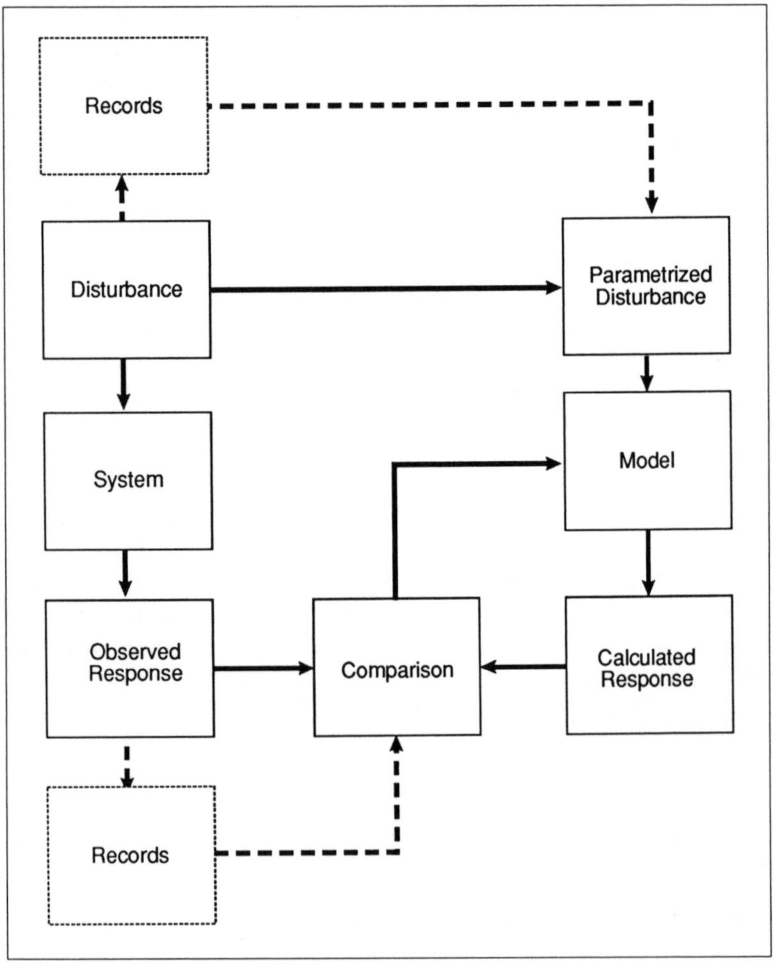

Figure 3-2: Flow of environmental processes.

Variations of the parameters S, A and B lead to changes in the passive parameter T_S, the earth's surface temperature. Information on all of these four parameters are recorded in natural archives. The varying emission of solar plasma leads to changes in the magnetic shielding of galactic cosmic radiation in the inner part of the solar system. This produces variations in the cosmic ray flux reaching the earth. These are reflected as variations in the production of radioactive nuclei in the earth's atmosphere. The changes in the production rate are recorded in tree-rings as $^{14}C/^{12}C$ ratio changes and in precipitation, as changes in the cosmogonic radioisotopes ^{10}Be and ^{36}Cl. Other solar properties like luminosity and ultraviolet emission might also influence climate. If they are related to the solar plasma emission—which seems to be plausible—changes in the ^{10}Be content in ancient deposited snowfalls therefore reflect changes in solar parameters (like S) which influence climate.

Atmospheric turbidity alters the earth surface's albedo (A). It is influenced by volcanic eruptions which lead to stratospheric dust layers. Solid electrical conductivity measurements on ice cores enable the identification of volcanic dust and therefore contribute to the reconstruction of the history of atmospheric turbidity.

Ice seems to be the only natural archive in which essentially undisturbed air samples from the ancient atmosphere are stored. Measurements of gas composition reveal variations of the contents of infrared active gases like CO_2 and CH_4, which influence parameter B.

Variations in the $^{18}O/^{16}O$ ratio in precipitations reflect changes in temperature (T_S). Relative to seawater, cold periods are strongly depleted in ^{18}O, in warm periods the depletion is less. Ancient precipitation is stored in cold glacier ice. Under favorable conditions, the high resolution of isotopic information in ice-cores enables even the reconstruction of seasonal ^{18}O variations as far back as 10,000 years.

The Global Carbon Cycle

The chemical element carbon plays an important role in all biological processes, where carbon compounds are formed, modified, or decomposed.

In the sea and in lakes, debris of organisms forms sediment layers which consist to a large part of carbonate and organic carbon. A tiny fraction of those sediments, reduced carbon compounds in concentrated form, are our most important energy source as coal, oil, and natural gas.

In the atmosphere, the CO_2 content significantly influences the terrestrial radiation balance.

Roughly, exchanging carbon (Figure 3-3) can be divided into the four main reservoirs. For a direct comparison all amounts are given by the equivalent mass of pure carbon:

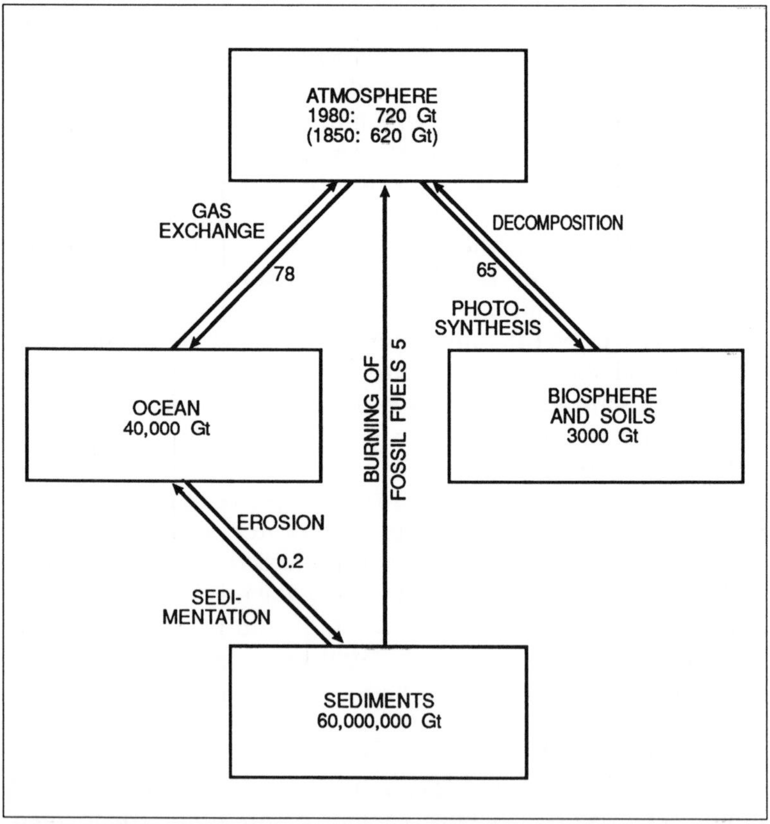

Figure 3-3: Global carbon system. 1 Gt (gigaton) = 10^{15} gram.

The *atmosphere* contains at present some *700Gt* (1Gt = 1 gigaton = 10^{12} kg) carbon in the form of CO_2. Its concentration has been increasing since 1958 by about 1.5 ppm per year on the average to a value of 340 ppm in 1981.

The *ocean* contains roughly *40,000 Gt* which equals 60 times the atmosphere amount. Carbon here is present as dissolved CO_2 (1%), as bicarbonate (85%) and carbonate ions (10%), and also as dissolved organic carbon compounds (3%). The size of the *land biosphere* is difficult to estimate because of large regional differences in plants, humus and soils. The values range between *2000 and 3000 Gt* or 3 to 4 times the amount of the atmosphere.

In *sediments*, carbon is stored in huge amounts, estimated at *60 million Gt.*

Of course, each of these main reservoirs represents itself a very complicated system and may be subdivided further.

Carbon is exchanged between the different reservoirs. The exchange fluxes try to bring the system to an equilibrium state. In each reservoir the influxes compensate the losses. For the study of the fate of CO_2, released due to human activity, it is very important to know the size of the different exchange fluxes.

The biospheric fluxes, CO_2 assimilation and release of CO_2 by decomposition of organic matter, can be estimated based on ecological data. The annual cycle of vegetation is reflected in the CO_2 record shown in Figure 3-4. During the growing season the removal of CO_2 from the atmosphere exceeds the production by decay of organic matter and the CO_2 level decreases by several ppm. In winter, when biological productivity comes to a rest but decomposition continues, the CO_2 concentration increases again. This effect is dependent on the geographical site of the observation. Neglecting human interference and possible natural changes in vegetation, on an annual mean, the total biomass remains constant, so that the biosphere represents neither a sink nor a source of CO_2.

Natural Ice as Archive of the History of the Environmental System

Natural ice has unique properties as an archive of information on E.S. processes: During the past decades, ocean sediments had been the main source of information on the

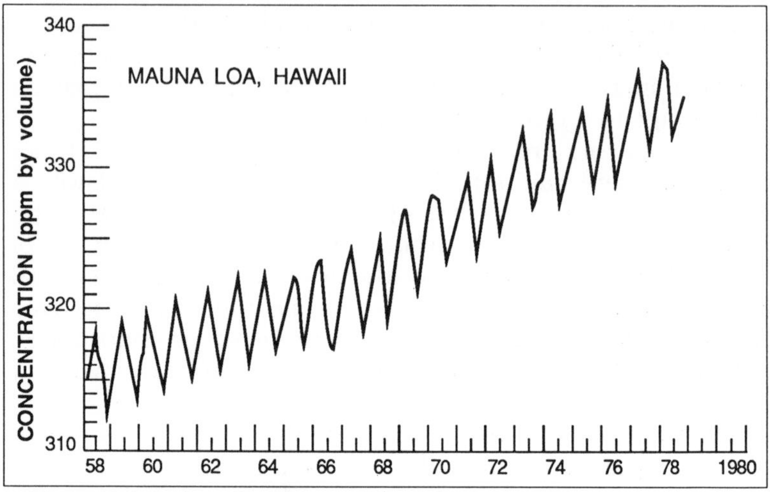

Figure 3-4: Carbon dioxide growth trend.

response of the climate system to perturbations like varying orbital parameters of the earth. In the last few years new information, also on short-term climatic variations, has been obtained by the study of information recorded in ice cores, obtained by drilling into polar ice caps and alpine glaciers.

Particles of different origins suspended in the air serve as condensation nuclei for water vapor. At temperatures below freezing, snow flakes are formed. During their fall and in the surface layers of snow, additional particles and chemical compounds are absorbed. Under the load of subsequently deposited snowfall, the annual layers sink to greater depth, get compressed and thinner. At depths of 50 to 70 m in Greenland, the sintering of the firn (neve) grains encloses atmospheric air in void spaces. Thus, the air bubbles in old glacier ice constitute physically occluded samples of the atmospheric gases at the time of pore close-off.

In the upper ice layers the time resolution is high, enabling the identification of single precipitation events or at least of seasonal variations. The thickness of annual layers thins with depth, and allows one to study the information recorded during longer time periods. So far, ice cores cover up to approximately

135,000 y but at some locations, e.g. in Central Greenland or East Antarctica, much older ice should be recoverable at the bedrock. But the limited amount of sample material calls for new high sensitivity analytical tools.

Accelerator Mass Spectrometry (AMS)

Up to now, cosmic ray-produced radio isotopes, like ^{14}C, ^{10}Be, ^{36}Cl and others, have been measured exclusively via counting the number of radioactive decays in a given sample. Due to the relatively long half life of these isotopes during a measuring period, only a very small fraction of the radioactive nuclei decays. Thus relatively large samples have been required, e.g., for the measurement of ^{10}Be in precipitation, several tons of rain or snow have been needed. Very intriguing scientific projects, like the reconstruction of the history of radioisotope production in the atmosphere by the measurement of ^{10}Be and ^{36}Cl in polar ice cores therefore had been virtually impossible.

In 1977 the situation changed drastically when groups in Berkeley and Rochester successfully showed that accelerators, as used in low energy nuclear research, enable one to detect 10^4 or 10^6 atoms of isotope, even if 10^{15} to 10^{18} atoms of the neighbor isotopes are present in the sample. Instead of huge samples, ice samples of only 1 kg in the case of ^{10}Be and ^{36}Cl are sufficient for a reliable measurement with AMS.

For a few decades, these accelerators had served on the frontier of fundamental nuclear physics research. Today much higher energies and therefore much larger accelerators are needed to study elementary particles. The old accelerators are an important tool in interdisciplinary environmental research. We see here a fascinating example demonstrating the unity of science: instruments originally developed for basic research in a highly specialized scientific field today provide most valuable information for earth scientists, archaeologists, palaeobotanists, climatologists and space and solar scientists.

At this place we especially would like to point out the raising of this technique to a very high standard by a group at the ETH in Zurich. All accelerator measurements discussed in this article were performed in collaboration with this group.

The Environmental Impact of Man

The CO_2 and Trace Gas Problem

Acid rain and dying forests focus the attention of the public on an important ecological problem, but probably the most serious question of anthropogenic climate disturbances still remains in the background. In spite of their low concentrations in atmosphere, CO_2 and trace gases like O_3, CH_4, N_2O, etc. considerably influence the radiation balance on the earth's surface (Kellogg 1989). Without atmospheric CO_2 the global temperature would be lower by approximately 10°C. A CO_2 doubling would lead in the long term to a global temperature increase by 1.5 to 4.5°C. Extrapolations indicate that the atmospheric CO_2 concentration might double in the second half of the next century. During the last years it has been observed that also the concentrations of trace gases like CH_4, N_2O, and freons are increasing (e.g. CH_4, by about 50% since the last world war). This augments the expected temperature increase and might enhance the effect of the CO_2 rise by ⅓ to ⅔. A series of questions are posed to a broad spectrum of sciences.

The first group of questions concerns the global carbon system: How is the atmospheric CO_2 concentration determined? What is the capacity for the uptake of CO_2 emitted into the atmosphere? What was the pre-industrial atmospheric CO_2 concentration and have there been CO_2 concentration variations in the past? Other questions concern the changes of climate provoked by higher atmospheric CO_2 and trace gas levels and their consequences for the environment.

The Present Increase of CO_2, its Preindustrial Value and Natural Variation during the Last 1000 Years

Mainly due to fossil-fuel consumption, the atmospheric CO_2 concentration is increasing monotonously since 1958 (Figure 3-4). The carbon flux of 5 Gt/y from fossil fuel sources into the atmosphere is relatively small compared to the natural exchange fluxes between the main carbon reservoirs (Figure 3-3). Why then does this minor disturbance create such a significant increase in atmospheric CO_2? This is an often-posed question. Is there another reason for the increase or is it just accidental?

The answer lies in the reconstruction of the natural (preindustrial) variations of atmospheric CO_2 and the understanding of the partitioning of excess CO_2 in the carbon-exchanging reservoirs.

Atmospheric CO_2 concentration measurements prior to 1958, the beginning of the Mauna Loa and South Pole measurements, are affected with uncertainties. The most precise information can be obtained from the analysis of the CO_2 concentration of air occluded in dated polar ice cores. Recently developed procedures give astonishingly precise values which are presented in Figure 3-5. The CO_2 concentrations are measured on 500 g samples from an ice core drilled at the South Pole. The long axis of the ellipses correspond to the enclosure time period, and the short axis gives the standard deviations of the single measurements. The preindustrial CO_2 concentration, as concluded from these measurements, was in the range of 280 æ 5 ppm and therefore significantly below the values observed during the last decades. Additional information on atmospheric CO_2 is available from a newly recovered ice core from Antarctica which covers the time span from 1800 till 1970: In the overlapping period from 1960 to 1970 the CO_2 data

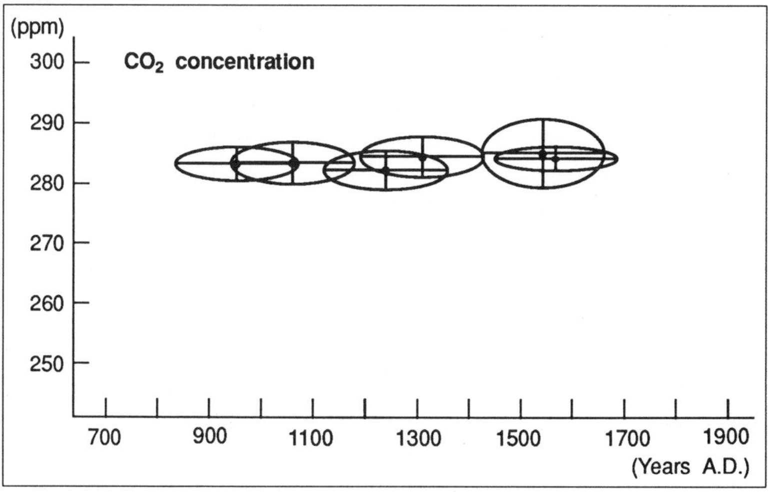

Figure 3-5: CO_2 concentration South Pole.

from the ice core agree within error limits with the precise atmospheric measurements. The data also show that the CO_2 increase had started already in the early nineteenth century, prior to intensive fossil-fuel consumption. The latter fact can be explained by deforestation and land urbanization.

The Partitioning of Excess CO_2 and the Delay of Warming

The comparison of estimates of anthropogenic CO_2 emissions with the actually observed atmospheric CO_2 increase shows that under present conditions approximately 50 to 60% of the emitted CO_2 remains in the atmosphere. To estimate the uptake by the two other reservoirs, the ocean and the biosphere, a number of physical, chemical, and biological phenomena have to be considered:

Uptake by the biota is probably relatively small. It should be visible, for example, in increasing tree-ring width due to a higher photosynthetic rate resulting from CO_2 fertilization.

However, the assimilation rate is determined also by other nutrients besides CO_2 and by the climatic conditions. Stress on the plants by anthropogenic effects like acid rain has to be considered, too. In many regions of the northern hemisphere we observe the phenomenon of dying woods which seems to indicate that CO_2 fertilization is not able to counteract these stress factors. The main sink for anthropogenic CO_2 is the ocean. We have to find out if their atmospheric interaction and internal mixing can withdraw the missing part of the excess CO_2 balance from the atmosphere.

For this purpose carbon cycle simulation models are developed. A simple example is shown in Figure 3-6.

In this model, the atmosphere, the biosphere, and the oceanic surface layer are considered to be well-mixed reservoirs; and first-order kinetics are used to simulate the exchange. Subsurface oceanic mixing and circulation are simulated by eddy diffusion. The exchange coefficients are determined from the specific ^{14}C activity in the different reservoirs. As a first approximation we assume that its production, transport, and decay in the carbon system is in steady state. The specific activity of carbon (as CO_2) in the atmosphere is normalized to 100%. Due to radioactive decay its value is lower (95%) in the dissolved

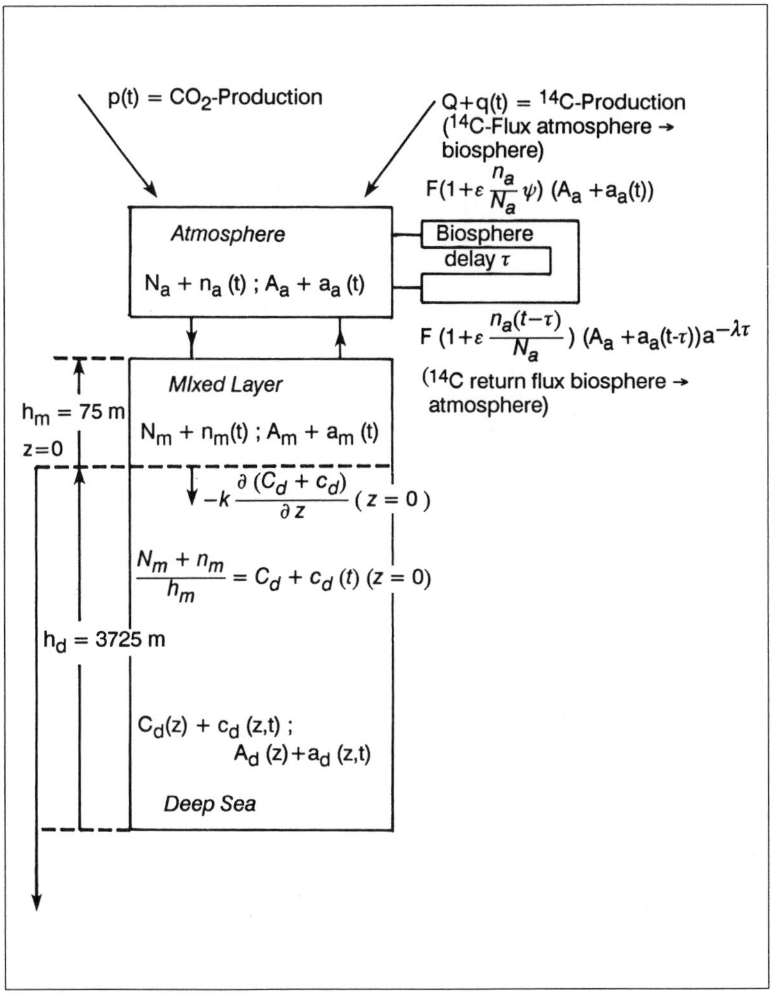

Figure 3-6: **A Carbon Cycle Simulation Model.**

carbon of the surface ocean (as CO_2, HCO_3- or CO_3^{-2}) and the subsurface ocean with an average of 84%.

Based on these ^{14}C activities and the CO_2 content of the different reservoirs, the exchange coefficients and the eddy diffusion coefficient for the subsurface ocean can be derived. With this type model one calculates that about 40% of the emitted fossil CO_2 is taken up by the ocean, which is in fair agreement with the observed airborne fraction of 50 to 60%. The essential result of these investigations is the observation that for atmospheric disturbances exponentially increasing with e-folding times of 20 to 30 years, roughly 10% of the ocean water is in physical and chemical equilibrium with the atmosphere. This is not only important for calculating the uptake of excess CO_2 by the ocean, it also enables us to estimate the delay of expected CO_2 induced warming, due to the heat capacity of the ocean-surface layer. If a quasi-exponential change of the energy balance on the earth's surface is assumed, calculations indicate that the actual warming lags behind the equilibrium values by about 20 years.

To check the validity of the model, the determination of the distribution of ^{14}C, as produced by nuclear weapons tests in the atmosphere-ocean system, is an excellent possibility.

The ^{14}C - ^{10}Be Experiment

In the discussion of environmental problems it is generally assumed that in the future the systems will behave as they did in the past. We will now discuss an experiment which nature is continuously performing. The new AMS made it possible to study it. Recently obtained data give insight into the dynamics of the carbon system during the last 6000 years. ^{14}C measurements on tree-rings show that the atmospheric $^{14}C/C$ ratio was not constant in the past. Figure 3-7 shows a data set obtained for the last ca. 8000 y. Two types of variations are visible: a long-term sinusoidal trend and short-term sawtooth-like excursions of about 2% lasting for about 200 years. There are essentially two possible causes for such variations: fluctuations in ^{14}C production, due to solar or geomagnetic modulation of galactic cosmic radiation, or fluctuations in the carbon cycle and its exchange dynamics. In the first case we can speak of an external forcing of the carbon system which continues to operate in a constant mode. In the second case we assume that ^{14}C production was constant but that the carbon system changed its mode of operation. The reason may be a release of CO_2 from

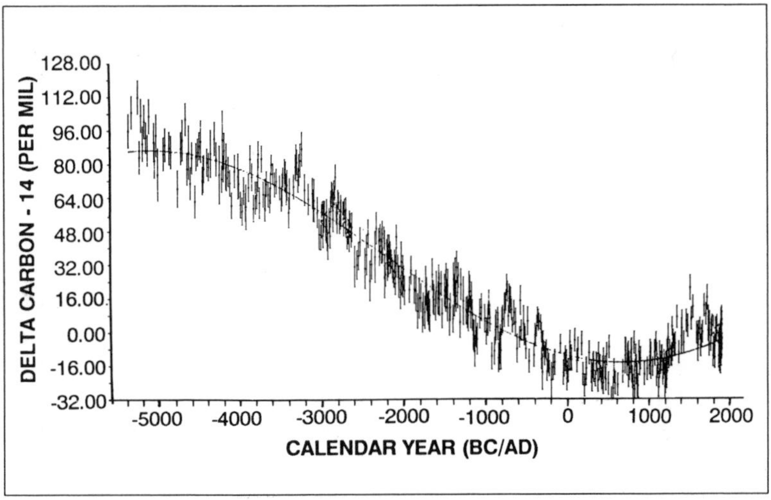

Figure 3-7: Measurements on tree rings.

the ocean into the atmosphere or a slowing down or speeding up of the oceanic circulation.

The question regarding the cause of the ^{14}C variations can be solved by the measurement of ^{10}Be, another cosmic ray-produced isotope with a different geochemical behavior. It is produced similarly to ^{14}C and should show proportional production rate variations. Unlike ^{14}C it is attached to aerosol particles and deposited with precipitation on the ground.

The residence time of ^{10}Be in the atmosphere is relatively short, on the order of months to a few years. Changes in its production rate are therefore almost unattenuated and reflected with good time resolution in glacier deposits. ^{10}Be measurements from ice core samples correlate well with sunspot numbers. Periods with low solar activity correspond to periods with high ^{10}Be concentrations in the ice. These results are in agreement with direct observations made by neutron monitors during the last few solar cycles. It was shown by the monitors that low solar activity means less shielding from the galactic component of cosmic radiation reaching the inner part of the solar system; and thus the production rate of radio isotopes in the earth's atmosphere is higher. During periods of high solar activity, the ^{10}Be concentrations were correspondingly lower. During the period of the quiet sun from 1645 to 1715 A.D., the so-called Maunder Minimum of solar activity, the ^{10}Be concentration was a factor of 1.6 higher (Figure 3-8). This parallels an increase of the $^{14}C/^{12}C$ ratio found in tree-rings. Assuming proportional production variations of ^{14}C and ^{10}Be, the expected ^{14}C variation can be predicted by carbon cycle model calculations. For the Maunder Minimum period and the last 800 y in general, the calculated ^{14}C variations agree well with the measured values. This suggests that the short-term ^{14}C variations are induced by production variations and that the carbon cycle model yields correct attenuations and phase shifts in the frequency band of short-term solar modulation. The carbon cycle dynamics of the last 1000 years seem to be understood.

Completely different is the situation in the long-term trend covering the last 5000 years. ^{10}Be concentrations in samples from a Greenland ice core do not show the increase we would expect from ^{14}C measurements on tree-rings. Though we cannot exclude completely that a climate with higher precipitation dilutes the ^{10}Be concentration of ice and thus simulates a lower production rate, there is a high probability that the long-term ^{14}C trend is caused by an internal change in the carbon system. One explanation could be a speeding-up of ocean circulation since the end of the last glaciation which reduced the ^{14}C difference between the surface ocean and the deep sea. As a consequence, the atmospheric $^{14}C/C$ ratio decreased, which would lead to the observed results.

We now discuss the variability of climate and will meet similar examples of changes caused by both external and internal forcing of the system.

Past Climatic Change

Variations of the Orbital Parameters of the Earth and the Glacial Cycles

Even for constant solar luminosity the intensity of solar radiation reaching the earth's surface can undergo changes due to variations in the geometry of the earth's orbit around

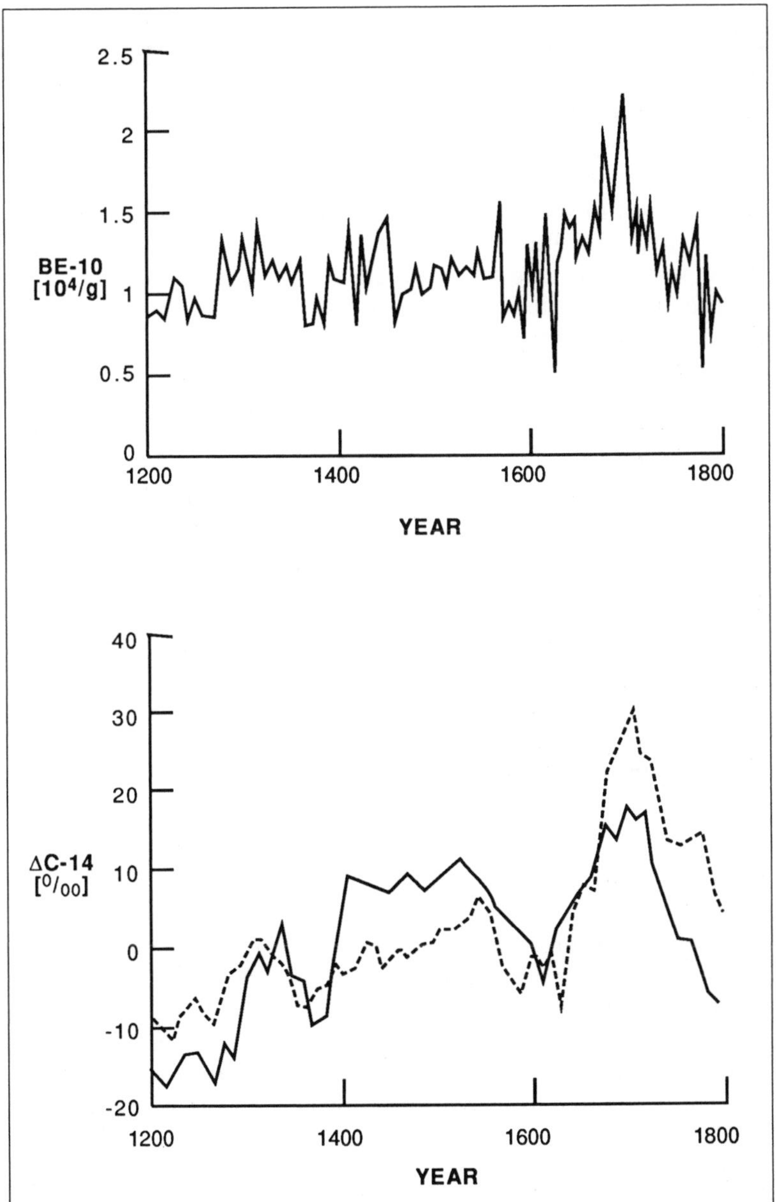

Figure 3-8: History of ^{14}C and ^{10}Be concentrations.

the sun. These changes, a result of gravitational interaction in the planetary system, involve the eccentricity of the orbit and the obliquity and the precession of the earth's axis. They produce significant changes in the pattern of incoming radiation on time scales from several thousand to several hundred thousand years. These changes can be calculated many hundred thousand years back into the past and can also be extrapolated into the future. Milankovitch proposed in 1930 that these variations might have caused the glacial periods. The averaged irradiation over the globe is not much changed by these orbital variations. The important effect is the modulation of the seasonal cycle. Summer insolation varied by as much as 5% at the latitudes at which continental ice sheets existed during glacial periods. The history of continental ice extent is reflected in the foraminifera of deep-sea cores. A comparison of the northern summer insolation history and the ice mass record shows that periods of rapid ice disappearance coincide with peaks of higher summer insolation. Furthermore, frequency analyses of the sedimentary oxygen isotope record reveal the characteristic frequencies of the orbital changes. It is widely accepted today that orbital changes are the primary cause of glacial cycles.

Short-term Variations: Information from Polar Ice Cores and Lake Sediments

Superimposed on the long-term glacial cycles, there are rather drastic short-term climatic changes. An example is the so-called little ice age in the period from the middle of the sixteenth to the middle of the nineteenth century, followed by a significant temperature increase, leading, e.g., in Central Europe, to a strong retreat of the Alpine glaciers. Information on short-term climatic changes is not available from deep-sea sediment cores because bioturbation leads to a continuous mixing of the uppermost sediment layers; and low accumulation rates do not allow sufficient time resolution. More detailed climatic information is stored in ice cores and lake sediments. In Figure 3-9 the $\delta^{18}O$ record is clearly visible. This not only holds for the glacial-postglacial transition 10,000 years ago but also for most of the pronounced $\delta^{18}O$ oscillations in the ice from

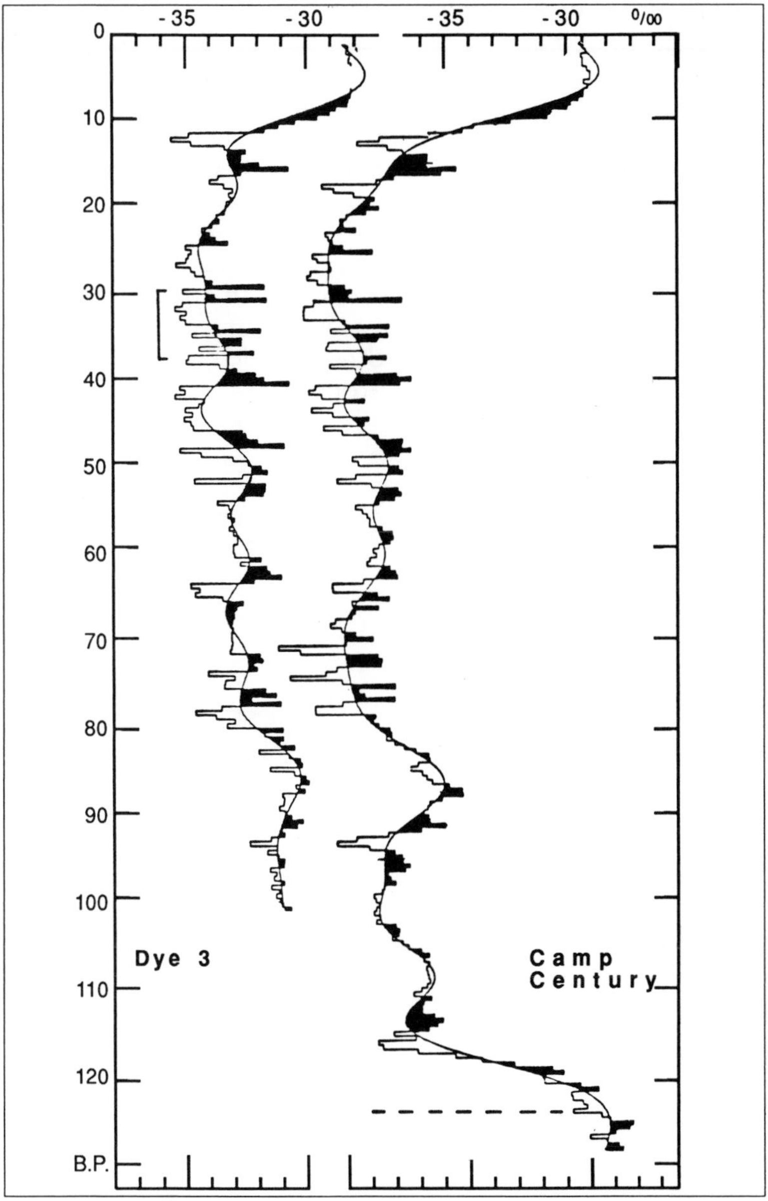

Figure 3-9: ^{18}O profiles Copenhagen. The time is given in millennia before present (B.P.).

the Wisconsin stage. The shifts of ^{18}O at the transition to the Holocene 15,000 and 10,000 years B.P. are also recorded in carbonate deposits of Central European lakes. Figure 3-10 demonstrates the excellent correlation. The rapid ^{18}O oscillations reflect relatively warm periods in the generally cold Wisconsin stage. Some of them may have their counterparts in pollen profiles of peat bogs or lake sediments from Central Europe. Such pronounced correlations are not found in climatic records from the North American continent. Ruddiman and McIntyre (1981) found evidence in North Atlantic sediment cores for changes of the North Atlantic polar front. This would lead to a deviation of the Gulf Stream which then caused the climatic variations in Central Europe.

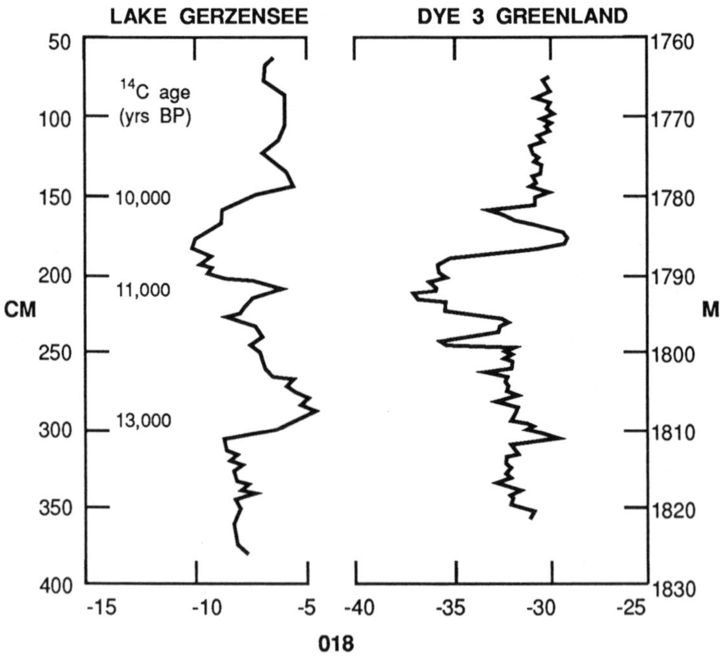

Figure 3-10: Lake Gerzensee/Dye 3 Greenland.

Ice Core Parameters during the Wisconsin and at the Wisconsin/Holocene Transition

In the discussion of experimental evidence on the carbon cycle, we mentioned that during the last thousand years the atmospheric CO_2 concentration has been essentially constant in the range 280 ±5 ppm. But does this hold for periods of major climatic change? It is one of the most exciting observations on ice cores that at the end of the Wisconsin period the CO_2 concentration ranged between 180–200 ppm and then increased parallel to the ^{18}O to values of 260 to 300 ppm. Measurements on the Dye 3 ice core confirm this observation (Figure 3-11). It seems to be a relatively rapid transition during the first warming period around 13,000 BP.

Another example is the high CO_2 concentration at 1890 m depth corresponding to an age of approximately 40,000 BP. This value coincides with one of the high $\delta^{18}O$ periods during the Wisconsin. Figure 3-12 shows the result of a detailed study of the $\delta^{18}O$–CO_2 relationship in the 30,000 to 40,000 years old section of the Dye 3 core. All the rapid $\delta^{18}O$ oscillations are accompanied by simultaneous, perfectly correlated CO_2 oscillations. Though the observation of rapid atmospheric CO_2 concentration changes during the Wisconsin needs further confirmation by measurements on other ice cores to exclude artifacts due to melt-layers or interaction with the impurities in the ice lattice, these experimental results have inspired the discussion of mechanisms which might produce atmospheric CO_2 changes of the observed extent.

Other parameters have been observed to vary in a similar fashion over this same interval. Dansgaard and his colleagues have shown that microparticle concentrations as measured by light scattering show strong $\delta^{18}O$ correlated variations (Hammer *et al.* 1985). Concentrations of particles are more than a factor of six higher during cold periods than during warm. Findel and Langway have observed that Cl-, NO_{-3} and SO_{4-2} concentrations all showed significant variations which correlated with the measured $\delta^{18}O$ shifts (Findel and Langway 1973). The cold/warm ratios are about 1.5 for Cl- and NO_{-3} and about 4 for SO_{4-2}. Beer has observed similar $\delta^{18}O$ correlated variations in ^{10}Be at the same depths (Figure 3-13) (Beer *et al.*

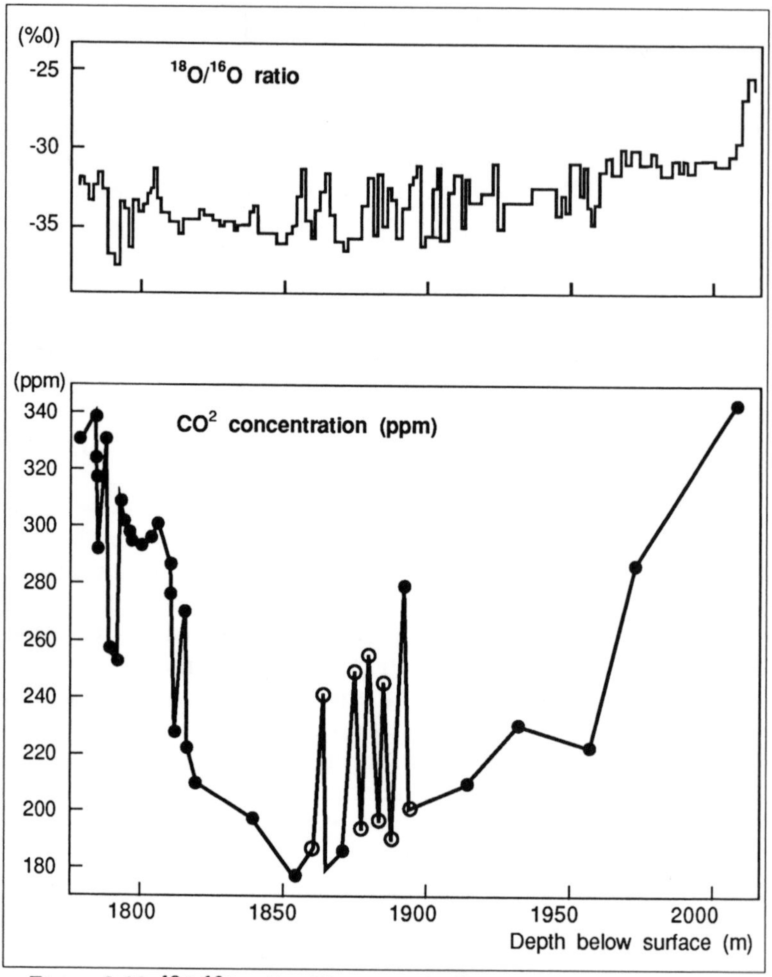

Figure 3-11: $^{18}O/^{16}O$ ratio; CO_2 concentration.

1984). Because of the larger sample requirements for the ^{10}Be analyses, measurements could not be made with the same resolution as for the other species. ^{10}Be is also more concentrated, by about a factor of 2.5, during periods of low $\delta^{18}O$ as compared to periods of high $\delta^{18}O$.

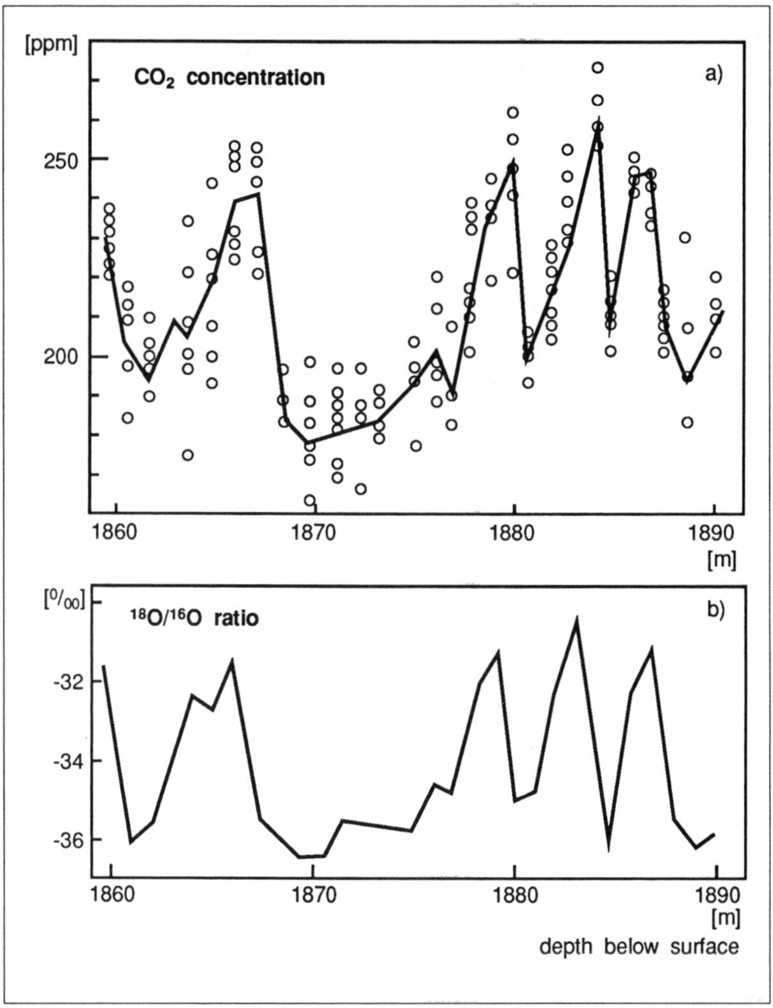

Figure 3-12: CO_2 concentration; $^{18}O/^{16}O$ ratio.

It is too far reaching to try explanations for these phenomena in this context. However, because the relative concentration shifts are not the same for all species, the variations cannot be the result of a simple dilution modulation of a constant impurity flux by a variable water-flux system.

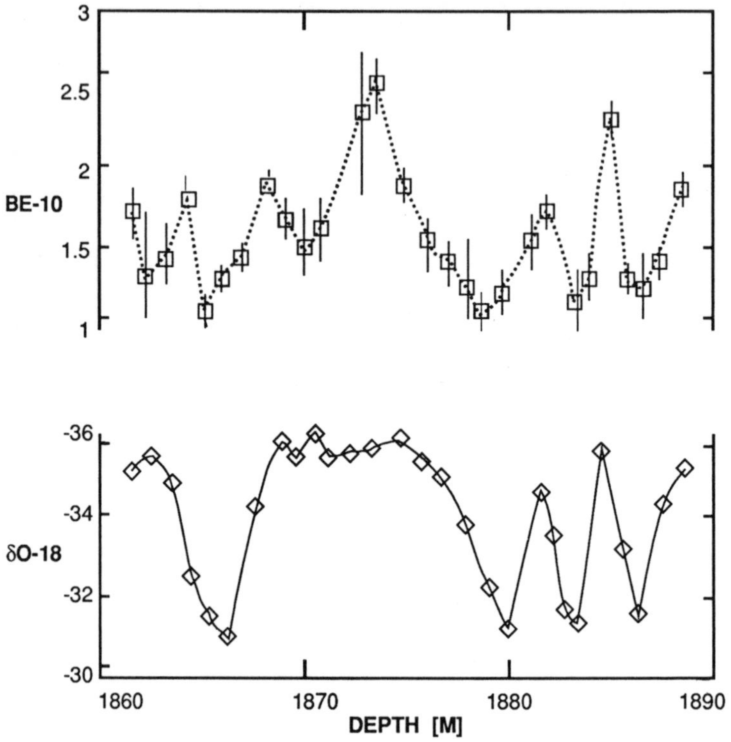

Figure 3-13: ^{10}Be concentration *vs.* depth.

The Bistable Climatic System

Not much is known for sure about the mechanisms determining the state and the stability of the climate system.

The most remarkable thing in the data set from the Dye 3 core is the apparent bistable nature of the observed variations. Cold and warm-period values of all parameters tend to occur in narrow bands relative to the difference between these bands. The correlated variation of the parameter sets suggests the existence of a bistable climate system during the Wisconsin, one set describing the warm and the other the cold-climate state.

The rapid climatic oscillations during the Wisconsin are probably internally forced changes of the climate system. During the time span of 1000 years, the essential external parameters and boundary conditions like the insolation pattern, sea level, and continental ice cover probably changed in a very limited range. It seems therefore possible that, for a given set of boundary conditions, the atmosphere-ocean system has more than one mode of operation. After a period of one to two thousand years, the stabilizing mechanisms of one mode of operation seem to become ineffective, and the system organizes itself in a new mode. Based on the $\delta^{18}O$ recorded, one gets the impression that during the ice age essentially two separated climatic modes existed. From this point of view, the transition to the postglacial is the end of the possibility for the system to switch back into the cold state. Based on European continental climatic information, we know that around 13,000 B.P. almost Holocene climatic conditions existed. Around 11,000 B.P. the system switched back for the last time to the cold mode, leading to almost glacial conditions in Europe. After the transition to the warm state around 10,000 B.P., the stability was already so high that a return to the cold state was impossible. Since then the system has remained essentially in the warm state; and it is important to note that, during the Holocene, the climate, as reconstructed by $\delta^{18}O$, was much more quiet than during the Wisconsin. It seems that the large amounts of continental ice played an important role in the pronounced variability of the climate system during the last glaciation.

Climate and Ocean

The role of the ocean in climate is not restricted to physical processes. For example, the atmospheric CO_2 concentration is determined by the CO_2 partial pressure in ocean surface water.

According to Broecker, the difference in $^{13}C/^{12}C$ ratios in total CO_2 between surface and deep ocean water should reflect atmospheric CO_2 concentration. A recent study from Shackleton and Pisias (1985) on carbonates from Pacific sediment cores provided a record of ice volume based on their $\delta^{18}O$ values and from the difference in the $^{13}C/^{12}C$ ratios in surface and in deep ocean dwelling foraminifera, they derived CO_2 partial pressure changes in ocean surface waters. Thus they could confirm the low CO_2 concentrations at the end of the last glaciation as measured in ice cores. A spectral analysis of the CO_2 variation showed significant amplitudes for the Milankovitch frequencies of the changing orbital parameters. These studies show that both CO_2 and ice volume lag behind orbital changes. And there is most exciting evidence—which should be confirmed by additional measurements—that the changes of CO_2 seem to lead those in ice volume by a few thousand years. A possible explanation for the apparent effect of orbital changes on atmospheric CO_2 lies in oceanic biological activity which controls the partial pressure of CO_2 in surface waters: The varying solar irradiation at high latitudes influences deep-water formation and ocean circulation in general. Most probably, the chemical conditions of the surface ocean are not the result of an alteration in the nutrient element chemistry of the ocean as a whole. The rapidity of the atmospheric CO_2 variation, as deduced from ice core studies, points at changes effecting the surface ocean only. The climatic bistability during the Wisconsin may reflect the switching of deep-water formations between the North Atlantic and the North Pacific oceans, as Broecker proposed recently.

Conclusions

Variations of the earth's orbital parameters through latitudinal insolation changes provide the boundary conditions for the cyclic variations of glacial and interglacial periods. In addition, recent discoveries indicate that they are responsible for CO_2 fluctuations due to ocean circulation and biological activity changes.

Recently available high-resolution records from polar ice and lake sediments reveal the existence of additional short-term climatic changes. The most prominent example is the climate in Europe between 13,000 and 10,000 B.P.: During a century or less it switched back and forth between glacial and Holocene conditions.

The knowledge of the physical, chemical and biological behavior of the ocean allows one to estimate the response to a higher atmospheric CO_2 level and resulting higher infrared backradiation. However, such disturbances may induce nonlinear effects which can hardly be predicted yet. As we have seen from the ^{10}Be–^{14}C comparison, several thousand years ago the mixing between the surface and deep ocean probably was slower than today.

It is our task to predict the consequences of our impact on the environment. Long-term basic research is necessary, rather than the concentration on single narrow questions of pressing importance, neglecting the complex interactions in the climate and environmental systems. There is not much reason to believe that they in general have developed a resilience which automatically keeps the consequences of human interferences limited in time and space and prevents us from negative consequences. The potential magnitude of human impact is illustrated in Figure 3-14 which draws the average climatic trend of the last 100,000 years into the future. The superimposed global warming, as expected from the CO_2 and trace gas

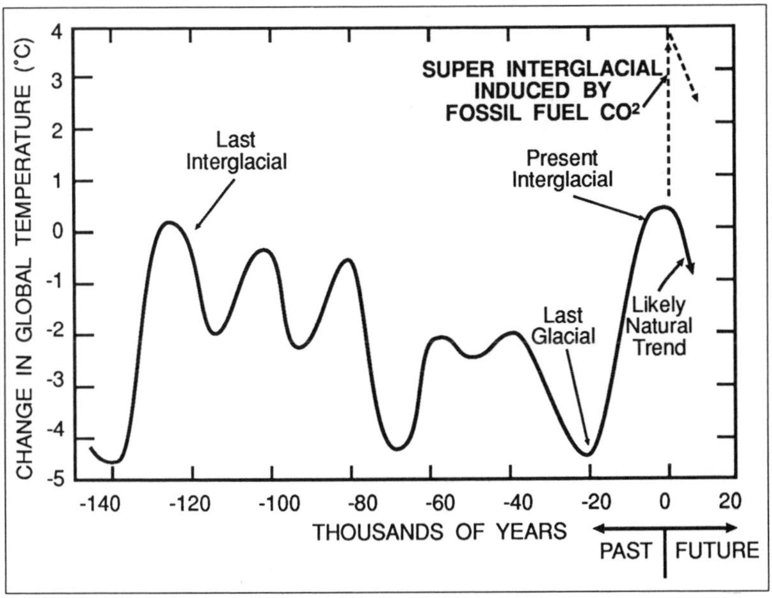

Figure 3-14: Average climatic trend of the last 100,000 years into the future.

increase, is on the order of the transition from a glacial to an interglacial period.

Human society has to be aware of the possibility of such a rapid warming within a few generations and must learn to react adequately.

Acknowledgment

I would like to thank U. Schotterer for valuable discussions and his assistance in the final version of this paper.

References

Beer, J., M. Andree, H. Oeschger, B. Stauffer, R. Balzer, G. Bonani, Ch. Stoller, M. Suter, W. Wolfli, and R. Finkel. (1983). "Temporal ^{10}Be variations in ice." *Radiocarbon* 25: 269–278.

Beer, J., U. Siegenthaler, H. Oeschger, M. Andree, G. Bonani, M. Suter, W. Wolfli, R.C. Finkel, and C.C. Langway, Jr. (1983). "Temporal ^{10}Be variations." Cosmic Ray Conference, Bangalore.

Beer, J., H. Oeschger, M. Andree, G. Bonani, M. Suter, W. Wolfli, and C.C. Langway, Jr. (1984). "Temporal variation in the ^{10}Be concentration levels found in the dye 3 ice core, Greenland." *Annals of Glaciology* 5: 16–17.

Berner, W., H. Oeschger, and B. Stauffer. (1980). "Information on the CO_2 cycle from ice core studies." *Radiocarbon* 22: 227–235.

Broecker, W.S. (1982). "Ocean chemistry during glacial time." *Geochimica et Cosmoschimica Acta* 46: 1689–1705.

Broecker, W.S. (1983). "The Ocean." *Scientific American*, 100–112, Sept., 1983.

Broecker, W.S. (1984). "New Program for Critical Year-Round Data on Ocean Uptake of Industrial CO_2." *Lamont Newsletter*, Lamont-Doherty Geological Observatory of Columbia University, Spring 1984, p. 2.

Campbell, P. (1984). "Carbon cycle; new data upset ice age theories." *Nature* 307: 688–689.

Dansgaard, W., H.B. Clausen, N. Gundestrup, C.U. Hammer, S.F. Johnson, P.M. Kristinsdottir, and N. Reeh. (1982). "A new Greenland deep ice core." 218: 1273–1277.

Delmas, R.J., J.M. Ascencio, and M. Legrand. (1980). "Polar ice evidence that atmospheric CO_2 20,000 BP was 50% of present." *Nature* 284: 155–157.

Duplessy, J.C., G. Delibrias, J.L. Turon, C. Pujol, and J. Duprat. (1981). "Deglacial warming of the northeastern North Atlantic Ocean: correlation with the palaeo-climatic evolution of the European continent." *Palaeogeogr., Palaeoclimat. Palaeoecol.* 35: 121–144.

Finkel, R.C. and C.C. Langway, Jr. (1985). "Global and local influences on the chemical composition of snowfall at Dye 3, Greenland: the record between 20 ka BP and 40 ka BP." *Earth and Planetary Science Letters* 73: 196–206.

Hammer, C.U., H.B. Clausen, W. Dansgaard, A. Neftel, P. Kristinsdottir, and E. Johnson. (1985). "Continuous impurity analysis along the Dye 3 deep core." American Geophysical Union, *Geophysical Monograph* 33: 90–94.

Imbrie, J. (1985). "A theoretical framework for the pleistocene ice ages." to be published in the *Quarterly Journal Geol. Soc.* London.

Kellogg, W., (1989). "Carbon Dioxide and Climate Changes: Implications for Mankind's Future." In Singer (1989).

Langway, C.C., Jr. (1970). "Stratigraphic analysis of a deep core from Greenland." *Geol. Soc. Am., Special Paper* 125, 186 pp.

Langway, C.C., Jr., H. Oeschger, and W. Dansgaard. (1985). "The Greenland ice sheet in perspective." In: The Greenland Ice Sheet Program, *Geophys. Monogr. Ser.*, edited by C.C. Langway *et al.*, AGU, Washington, D.C., in press.

Neftel, A., H. Oeschger, and H.E. Suess. (1981). "Secular non-random variations of cosmogonic carbon-14 in the terrestrial atmosphere." *Earth and Planetary Science Letters* 56, 127pp.

Neftel, A., H. Oeschger, J. Schwander, B. Stauffer, and R. Zumbrunn. (1982). "Ice core sample measurements give atmospheric CO_2 content during the past 40,000 y." *Nature* 295: 220–223.

Oeschger, H., U. Siegenthaler, U. Schotterer, and A. Gugelmann. (1975). "A box diffusion model to study the carbon dioxide exchange in nature." *Tellus* 27: 168–192.

Oeschger, H. (1982). "The contribution of radioactive and chemical dating to the understanding of the environmental system" In: "Nuclear and Chemical Dating Techniques: Interpreting the Environmental

Record." L.A. Currie (Ed.), *American Chemical Society Symposium Series* 176: 5–42, 1982.

Oeschger, H., J. Beer, U. Siegenthaler, B. Stauffer, W. Dansgaard, and C.C. Langway (1984). "Late glacial climate history from ice cores." In: "Climate Processes and Climate Sensitivity." Amer. Geophys. Union, *Geophysical Monograph* 29: 299–306.

Oeschger, H., B. Stauffer, R. Finkel, and C.C. Langway, Jr. (1985). "Variations of the CO_2 concentration of occluded air and of anions and dust in polar ice cores." In: "Natural Variations in Carbon Dioxide and the Carbon Cycle." *Geophys. Monogr. Ser.*, AGU, Washington, D.C., in press.

Revelle, R. (1982). "Carbon dioxide and world climate." *Scientific American* 47, No. 2, 35–43.

Ruddiman, W.F., and A. McIntyre. (1981). "The North Atlantic during the last deglaciation." *Palaeoecol.* 35: 145–214.

Shackleton, N.J., and N.G. Pisias (1985). "Atmospheric carbon dioxide orbital forcing and climate." Paper presented at Chapman Conf. on Natural Variations in Carbon Dioxide and the Carbon Cycle, Tarpon Springs, FL., January 9–13, 1984, in press.

Singer, S. Fred (1989). *Global Climate Change: Human and Natural Influences*. Paragon House Publishers, New York, N.Y.

Stauffer, B., H. Hofer, H. Oeschger, J. Schwander, and U. Siegenthaler. (1984). "Atmospheric CO_2 concentration during the last glaciation." *Annals of Glaciology* 5: 160–164.

Stuiver, M., and P.D. Quay. (1980). "Changes in atmospheric carbon-14 attributed to a variable sun." *Science* 207: 11–19.

Suess, H.E. (1980). "The radiocarbon record in tree-rings of the last 8000 years." *Radiocarbon* 22 : 200–209.

US National Academy of Sciences. (1983). *Changing Climate*. National Academy Press, Washington, D.C.

FOUR

COMMENTARY On OESCHGER'S PAPER

Joel Gat

In his excellent review, Hans Oeschger describes the global scale climate changes and discusses probable causes for their occurrence. Much of the evidence stems from the detailed information obtained from Arctic and Antarctic ice cores.

The aim of the following comments is to draw attention to the relationship between global and local climate changes. These, surprisingly, are not strictly synchronous, nor is the sense of local and global changes necessarily in the same direction.

In the early literature relating to the Pleistocene, during which time the transitions between glacial and interglacial regimes dominate the scene, it was assumed that the changes from pluvial to arid conditions which occurred in the past in (present day) desert areas, paralleled the glacial, i.e., the buildup and dissipation of glaciers. Closer perusal of the paleo-climate evidence, however, casts serious doubt whether this parallelism indeed holds in detail, and whether climate changes in different areas are in phase one with another.

Let us consider specifically the mid-latitude desert belt which extends from Northern Africa to Arabia and which includes the Mediterranean lands and the Middle East, addressing ourselves to the transition from the glacial stages of the Pleistocene to a warmer Holocene climate (which occurred some 10,000 years ago) and to climate changes in the early Holocene until the (relative) stabilization of the arid situation some 3,000 years ago. As was discussed by Gat and Magaritz (1980), the evidence seems to disprove the longstanding notion of pluvial conditions coinciding with periods of glaciation. Apparently the period of the last glacial maximum (about 18,000 BP) actually was a rather dry era in the area of the desert belt. A transition to more humid conditions started during the final stages of the Pleistocene, but the sharp boundary in the glacial record some 10,000 years ago (which formally marks the end of the Pleistocene and coincides with the eustatic rise in ocean levels) has no clear parallel in this area; the transition from the dry phase of the Pleistocene to the more humid Early Holocene is noted at different times in various areas, anytime between 13,000 to 9,000 BP. Indeed the whole period up to about 6,000 BP is quite changeable climatically speaking and inhomogeneous from the spatial and temporal point of view.

One will have to decide about apparent differences in the climate record of various areas, be they differences in the time of the onset of wet or dry phases, or inconsistencies in the very nature of the phenomena, such as a high-water stand in lakes when other evidence points to arid conditions in the same region (as is the case with Lake Lisan, the Pleistocene precursor of the Dead Sea; Neev and Emery 1966). Is there indeed as great a variability in climate pattern in time or space as indicated by these data or is much of this variability an artifact introduced by the nature for the evidence on which we base our findings?

The glacial record by its very nature is cumulative and continuous and literally "frozen in." It thus provides a fairly reliable data base for as long as the record is available. Deep-ocean cores, under optimal conditions, also provide a fairly uninterrupted chain of evidence from which certain paleoclimatic information (such as surface temperatures) can be inferred. The assignment of absolute temperature to the record, however, depends on calibrations based on the present day geophysical situation, which may not be applicable at a time when a different climate prevailed. The very fact of the occurrence of a change can, however, be established unequivocally.

The major problem of the arid zone paleoclimate reconstruction is, in contrast to the above-mentioned cases, the lack of a continuous depositional record. During dry-climate phases, lakes tend to dry up, wind erosion denudes the landscape, human habitations are abandoned, and even stalactite growth in caves may be interrupted. Rather indirect evidence from the stratigraphic column, such as paleo-soils (whose formation signifies a wetter climate), or fossil snails, in whose shell an isotopic memory is embedded (Magaritz and Heller 1980), are used to glean paleoclimate information which is semi-quantitative at best and, as explained, sketchy in time. One could think to use the sedimentological record in marine basins adjacent to the arid zone, such as in cores formed under the Mediterranean or Red Seas, or offshore of the Western Sahara. Indeed loess-type layers in such cores have been interpreted as indicative of dry (arid) periods (Sarntheim and Koopmann 1979). But we find that major transitions in the marine record are related to global changes, especially sea-level changes, which in turn are controlled by the volume of ice in the glacier fields, rather than to the local climate. Furthermore, freshening of surface waters in the Mediterranean, which gave rise to the so-called sapropel layers in the sedimentary column (Maldonado and Stanley 1978), are obviously timed by the discharge of freshwater from the European continent (possibly including a lot of melt water) rather than by any pluviality in the eastern Mediterranean Sea region.

Another factor to consider is that even when events are identified in the paleoclimate reconstruction scheme, it is their absolute dating which often is the weakest link in the chain of evidence. For the time period considered, the major dating tools are the ^{14}C content and uranium series disequilibria measurements. Materials suitable for reliable dating by these methods (such as organic matter, charcoal, etc.) may be hard to find. Thus what appears to be a phase shift between climate records at two sites could be an artifact of the dating procedure.

Unreliability of the dating procedures makes one wonder whether all of the apparent phase shifts between different zones are real; this doubt is reinforced by the fact that the events in the more recent past are better synchronized. On the other hand, the region discussed here is exposed to a variety of meteorological regimes, namely monsoons, Atlantic disturbances and cyclogenesis in the Mediterranean air space. Local climate is a result of the interplay or combined effect of all of these, and each one may influence one or another part of the region in a way which is not necessarily in phase with the glacial cycles or with one another.

The various meteorological regimes differ in the nature of the rain associated with them: monsoonal rains are predominantly summer rains of high intensity. The storms originating from depressions over the Atlantic Ocean are year-round events producing rain which is of a predominant continental character, of the type occurring today in Europe. The "Mediterranean-generated" precipitation, on the other hand, as already stated, is a winter phenomenon with relatively intense showers.

A marked climate change in this area can be caused simply by a shift in the area of influence of one or the other of the meteorological regimes. Such shifts can then have far-reaching effects on the hydrological balance and ecological pattern and a change will then also be registered by our climate monitors. An example is the "once in a hundred year" flood which took place in the Sinai in 1974 and whose origin was traced by both synoptic and isotopic evidence to a northward intrusion of a tropical (monsoonal) air mass into the "Mediterranean climate" region.

The late Pleistocene and Holocene climate fluctuations are interpreted as due to such shifts in the influence of weather patterns. The rather dry period during the last glacial maximum would be related, on the one hand, to the diversion of the monsoons from the Indian and Arabian subcontinents and also to the deactivation of the cyclogenesis in the Mediterranean, possible as a result of the lower winter temperature in the northern part of the sea. The onset of more plentiful rain towards the end of the Pleistocene and Early Holocene might be explained by the reactivation of the monsoonal and Mediterranean mechanisms, respectively.

The overall impression gained on analysis of local and global climate changes is that these are interrelated, with feedbacks operating between them. However, the complex response of the atmospheric system to stimuli and changes in the boundary conditions prevents a simple one to one correlation in the climatic pattern of various regions.

The position of the arid-zone boundary in the Levant is very sensitive even to minor shifts in the meteorological pattern because of the dependence of the Mediterranean climate on the coupling between the movement of cyclonic disturbances over Europe and the local condition of the sea.

Monitoring of this and other climate transition zones is thus the most efficient tool for "feeling" an impending change in climate.

References

Gat, J.R. and M. Magaritz 1980. "Climatic variation in the Eastern Mediterranean Sea area." *Naturwissenschaften* 67: 80–87.

Magaritz, M. and J. Heller 1980. "A desert migration indicator—oxygen isotopic composition of land snail shells." *Paleogeography, Paleoclimatology* 32: 153–162.

Maldonado, A. and D.J. Stanley 1978. In *Canyons, Fans and Trenches*, (Stanley and Kerllugs, eds.). Dowden Hutchison and Ross Publications.

Neev, D. and K.O. Emery 1966. "The Dead Sea." *Science Journal*, December 1966: 2–7.

Sarntheim, M. and B. Koopmann 1979. "Late quaternary deep sea record on the North West African wind circulation." Symposium on Sahara and Surrounding Seas in Sediments and Climate Changes, Mainz.

FIVE

COMMENTARY On OESCHGER'S PAPER

Roger G. Barry

A variety of ocean-climate interactions take place on widely differing time scales. The longest geological time scale involves major changes in ocean configuration and circulation arising from continental drift. For example, the separation of Australia from Antarctica and the opening of the Drake Passage between South America and the Antarctic Peninsula resulted in the establishment of a circumglobal deepwater circulation in the Southern Ocean about 23 million years ago (MYA). This displacement and its consequences may have contributed to the steady cooling of Southern Ocean surface water that began about 40 MYA (Eocene) and gave rise to the formation of Antarctic bottom water with near-freezing temperatures. Early traces of glaciation are apparent in Antarctica by 38 MYA (Oligocene) with significant ice buildup between 14 and 10 MYA (Miocene). In the northern hemisphere, the final closure of the Panama Isthmus about 3.5 MYA strengthened the Gulf Stream current in the North Atlantic Ocean and, together with the renewed link between the Mediterranean Sea and the Atlantic which increased the salinity of the North Atlantic, appears to have favored the onset of glaciation on the northern continents.

The details of these major shifts in global climate are still being traced in ocean sediment records; but they are important to understanding the relative roles of continental locations, ocean circulation, ocean temperatures, and other effects in setting up a global climatic state that is evidently close to the threshold for an oscillating glacial/interglacial regime. Seventeen glacial/interglacial cycles have been distinguished during the last 1.7 MY, but only the last of these cycles has been examined closely in the context of global climate. The CLIMAP Project (1976) has constructed maps of estimated summer and winter sea-surface temperatures over the world oceans for the last glacial maximum, 18,000 years before the present (BP) and a more limited analysis has been carried out for 125,000 BP (the last interglacial maximum), when global temperatures were slightly higher than at present.

Some key questions emerge from these studies. *If* the reconstructions are reliable, the glacial age sea surface in the subtropical gyres showed no cooling, whereas the mean ocean cooling was 2.3°C, with maximum depressions of 10° to 15°C in the northern North Atlantic. The nature of the slow north-south circulations is the ocean at this time and the temperature characteristics of the ocean deep water remain problematic. Models calling for warm deep water during the glacials have been contradicted in the North Atlantic by temperature estimates from oxygen isotope measurements on the remains of bottom-dwelling foraminifera (Duplessy *et al.* 1980).

The patterns of temperature change during the last glacial cycle in the North Atlantic show many striking features. For example, the oceanic front between polar and subpolar water masses shifts between its extreme glacial and interglacial positions within less than 5 to 10 thousand years and between mean glacial and interglacial conditions in less than 2,000 years (Ruddiman and McIntyre 1977). Nevertheless, several ocean sediment records indicate lags of the order of 2,000–3,000 years between changes in surface and bottom waters, implying slow vertical circulations (Pisias *et al.* 1975). Another impressive feature is that over the last 450,000 years, the warm Norwegian Current appears to have been present only during the last 10,000 years and during the last interglacial, i.e., a total of 10,000 years (Kellogg 1977). This implies significant displacements of the present locus of deep North Atlantic water formation in high latitudes during long-term intervals. Perhaps the cold bottom water during the glacial regime was formed as a result of coastal freezing, or freezing along the marginal ice zone in winter.

A key to understanding ocean-climate interactions is the asynchronous nature of their respective temperature oscillations. The persistence of warm surface waters in the northern oceans, during the onset phase of a glacial cooling cycle, appears to provide the necessary moisture source for rapid growth of continental ice sheets about 75,000 years ago (Ruddiman *et al.* 1980). There is a corresponding lag of about 5,000 years in the post-glacial warming of the oceans, influenced by the great input of meltwaters and direct iceberg calving. The role of such thermohaline forcing of ocean circulation on short and long time scales is reviewed by Rooth (1982).

Further major ocean changes occurred between glacials and interglacials with respect to world sea level. As a result of the waxing and waning of continental ice sheets, sea level was lowered by some 120 to 160 m at 18,000 years BP and rose about 6 m above present at 125,000 years BP. It is thought that the higher sea level in the last interglacial may reflect a collapse of the West Antarctic ice sheet, which is substantially grounded below sea level and therefore vulnerable to changes in temperature regime or a sea-level rise induced elsewhere (Mercer 1978). The ice in East Antarctica also may not be wholly immune to such effects (Alley and Whillan 1984). The exposure of continental shelf areas during glacial times had limited climatic effects, mainly on a regional scale, although phenomena such as the land bridges in the Bering Sea and the Torres Strait had significant impact on the spread of plants, animals, and people. More significance is attached to considerations of sea-level change in the context of the possible effects of a global warming, due to increased atmospheric CO_2 levels. Polar regions may experience a temperature rise two to three times greater than the global average effect and thereby cause ice melt similar to that during the last interglacial interval. The flooding of coastal lowlands that would result from a collapse of the West Antarctic ice sheet (or its equivalent) has been described by Schneider and Chen (1980). However, should it occur, the time scale of such an event is considered to be a few hundred years.

It has been suggested also that the cyclical exposure and flooding of continental shelves, as a result of glacial-interglacial sea level changes, had large effects on oceanic phosphate content (via burial on the shelves as the sea level rose) and consequently on nutrients and the carbon cycle (Broecker 1982). Model calculations (Keir and Berger 1983) indicate that this effect could account for up to half of the lowering (about 70 ppm) of *atmospheric* CO_2 content during the last glaciation identified in ice cores. Other remarkable fluctuations in these records, on the order of 50–70 ppm within a few hundred years, could reflect changes in ocean temperatures, sea-ice extent, upwelling and biological processes according to Oeschger (1985). An air temperature change of approximately 10°C would be needed to produce a factor of 1.4 change in CO_2 concentration, effectively ruling this out. It has been hypothesized that changes in the productivity of high-latitude (primarily Antarctic) surface waters, and/or in thermohaline overturning, could account for these CO_2 fluctuations (Sarniento and Toggweiler 1984; Siegenthaler and Wenk 1984). A further factor may be sea-ice extent, which appears to contribute to modulations of the seasonal CO_2 cycle. There are, however, few data on actual CO_2 fluxes in high latitudes. In the Arctic, open leads in winter are apparently a CO_2 source with an ocean surface-atmosphere difference (P_{CO_2}) of 120 ppm (Kelley and Gosink 1984). In contrast, there is a P_{CO_2} of -110 ppm over the Barents Sea in summer, and it may also remain a CO_2 sink in winter (P_{CO_2} of -20 to -40 ppm). The areal extent of leads in winter is approximately 1–3 percent of the Arctic Ocean.

It is interesting that the Arctic Ocean appears to have had a permanent sea-ice cover for at least the last 700,000 years and possibly throughout the last 2 million years (the Quaternary) (Clark 1982). However, there is some indirect evidence for slightly more temperate intervals in the Arctic, with at least more mobile ice (Boyd *et al.* 1984). These periods of more mobile ice would account for Siberian timbers occurring as driftwood in Spitsbergen and elsewhere across the Arctic. In a future, warmer world, the Arctic and Antarctic Sea ice covers could contract considerably (Barry 1983).

These topics illustrate some of the wide interdisciplinary interest in ocean-climate research and their relevance to understanding our present climatic state and its potential vulnerability, or otherwise, to perturbations in the global-climate system.

References

Alley, R. and Whillan, I. 1984. "Response of the East Antarctica ice sheets to sea-level rise." *Journal of Geophysical Research* 89: 6487–6493.

Barry, R. 1983. "Arctic Ocean ice and climate: perspectives on a century of polar research." *Annals, Association of American Geographers* 73: 485–501.

Boyd, R.; Clark, D.; Jones, G.; Ruddiman, W.; McIntyre, A.; and Pisias, N. 1984. "Central Arctic Ocean response to Pleistocene orbital variations." *Quaternary Research* 22: 121–128.

Broecker, W. 1982. "Glacial to interglacial changes in ocean chemistry." *Progress in Oceanography* 11: 151–197.

Clark, D. 1982. "Origin, nature and world climate effect of Arctic Ocean ice cover." *Nature* 300: 321–325.

CLIMAP Project Members 1976. "The climate of the ice age earth." *Science* 191: 1131–1166.

Duplessy, J.; Moyes, J.; Puyol, C. 1980. "Deep water formation in the North Atlantic during the last ice age." *Nature* 286: 479–498.

Keir, R.; Berger, W. 1983. "Atmospheric CO_2 content in the last 120,000 years: The phosphate extraction model." *Journal of Geophysical Research* 88: 6027–6038.

Kelley, J. and Gosink, T. 1984. "Carbon dioxide in the Arctic atmosphere: Air-sea and air-land interaction." *The Potential Effects of Carbon Dioxide-Induced Climatic Changes in Alaska*. Edited by McBeath, J., University of Alaska School of Agriculture, Fairbanks, pp. 40–68.

Kellogg, T. 1977. "Paleoclimatology and Paleo-oceanography of the Norwegian and Greenland Seas: The last 450,000 years." *Marine Micropaleontology* 2: 235–249.

Mercer, J. 1978. "West Antarctic ice sheet and CO_2 greenhouse effect: A threat of disaster." *Nature* 271: 321–325.

Oeschger, H. 1985. "Long-term climate stability." This Volume.

Pisias, N.; Heath, G.; and Moore, T. 1975. "Lag time for oceanic responses to climatic change." *Nature* 256: 716–717.

Rooth, C. 1982. "Hydrology and ocean circulation." *Progress in Oceanography* 11: 131–149.

Ruddiman, W.; McIntyre, A. 1977. "Late Quarternary surface ocean kinematics and climate change in the high-latitude North Atlantic." *Journal of Geophysical Research* 13: 3877–3888.

Ruddiman, W., *et al.*, 1980. "Oceanic evidence for the mechanism of rapid northern hemisphere glaciation." *Quarternary Research* 13: 33–64.

Sarniento, J. and Toggweiler, J. 1984. "A new model for the role of the oceans in determining atmospheric CO_2." *Nature* 308: 624–626.

Schneider, S. and Chen, R. 1980. "Carbon dioxide warming and coastline flooding: Physical factors and climatic impact." *Annual Reviews of Energy* 5: 107–140.

Schnitker, D. 1980. "Global paleoceanography and its deep water linkage to the Antarctic glaciation." *Earth Science Reviews* 16: 1–20.

Siegenthaler, U. and Wenk, T. 1984. "Rapid atmospheric CO_2 variations and ocean circulation." *Nature* 308: 624–626.

SIX

The ROLE Of The OCEAN In CLIMATE FLUCTUATIONS

Eric B. Kraus

Abstract

Through its role in interannual climate fluctuations, the state of the world ocean affects almost every aspect of human affairs—including food production, health, transport, communication, energy use, defense—in developed countries and in the Third World. During the last two decades millions of people died because the monsoon winds, which carry rains from the South Atlantic into Africa south of the Sahara, failed to sweep as far north and east as in good years. Changing conditions in the oceans affected not only the supply of life-giving moisture to the air, but also the pattern of winds which carries this moisture into the continents.

The environmental effects of oceanic temperature changes depend on the duration, extent, and location of the change.

These are a function in turn of the internal ocean dynamics and of the atmospheric forcing fields. Changes in the temperature of the tropical sea surface tend to have a larger, more immediate effect upon the global climate than corresponding changes in temperate latitudes. The adjustment of the climate to the anthropomorphic injection of carbon dioxide into the atmosphere depends partly upon the redistribution of heat in the deep ocean which has a time scale of several centuries.

Significant climate changes have been observed directly and quantitatively only during the last hundred years. This period is too short for the statistical deduction of causes and effects. Computer models are therefore an essential tool for the student of atmospheric and oceanic climate changes. It is shown that deductions from these models involve inevitably an unpredictable, random component. At best, they can provide forecasts with a known, quantitative probability. This raises the problem of the role of such probability forecasts in human affairs.

Introduction

Earth receives energy in the form of directed radiation from the sun. It radiates the same mean amount of energy at a lower frequency into all directions of space. This degradation of energy is the earth's main contribution to the production of entropy in the universe. It also constitutes an integral constraint on almost all physical and biological processes on the surface of the globe.

The local rates of entropy production are highly non-uniform. In fact, entropy is decreased locally in some developing physical structures and in growing organisms. However, the global integral of the difference between the entropies of the outgoing and the incoming radiation is always positive. It cannot vary by a large fraction; though it does become somewhat larger—in other words, energy is used more efficiently by the planet—if temperature contrasts between latitudes and seasons are relatively small. This happened apparently during the Cretaceous, when water covered a larger fraction of the earth's surface and when the difference between equatorial and polar surface temperatures was less than half its present value.

The ocean contributes directly to the planetary entropy production, by the storage of heat during summer which is then released during winter and by the transport of energy from the tropics into higher latitudes. It also contributes indirectly through its participation in the hydrological cycle which involves a poleward—that is, down-gradient—transport of latent heat by the atmosphere. Together, these processes were responsible for the persistence of an equitable terrestrial climate and for the creation of an environment which was and is conducive to the development and the diversification of life.

Being heated at its lower boundary and cooled partially at higher elevations under lower pressures, the atmosphere is more efficient as a heat engine than the ocean. Kinetic energy is mainly generated there. Ocean currents are largely driven by winds. With its great mass and even larger heat capacity, the ocean is truly the flywheel of the climate system.

The development of locally unstable perturbations is inevitable in an open system with non-linear interactions. Rather soon after their appearance, the growth of perturbations in the ocean/atmosphere system is inhibited, however, by the disparate thermal and dynamic inertia of the two media. Perturbations grow at different rates over areas of different extent and this interferes with their development both in the air and in the sea. The terrestrial climate is relatively stable, because almost all internal feedbacks are negative. A storm of global dimension and many weeks duration, as occurred on Mars a few years ago, could not develop on earth.

The ocean acts not only as a physical but also as a chemical buffer. For example, partly through the intermediary of marine organisms, it has absorbed and then precipitated most of the carbon dioxide outgassed by volcanoes during the planet's lifetime. This produced our chalk and dolomite mountains. It also prevented the development of a run-away greenhouse atmosphere of the Venus type, which would have inhibited the colonization of the surface by living organisms. Today, the same buffering role of the ocean has limited the increase in atmospheric CO_2 concentration and the resulting climatic impact, which might have been caused otherwise by our burning of fossil fuel.

Oceanic Variability on Different Scales of Space and Time

The energy of a geophysical fluid such as the ocean varies in space and time. These variations can be associated with:

1. Internal readjustments,
2. Changes in external mechanical forcing,
3. Changes in thermal forcing and
4. Changes in the boundary configuration.
5. The last type of change is imposed upon the oceans by continental drift and other long-term morphological transformations which will not be considered in this article.

Just like radiation, the distribution of energy in the ocean can be associated with a spectrum of perturbations with different wave lengths and frequencies. Unlike solar radiation, the spectra of oceanic or atmospheric energy fluctuations are neither homogeneous nor stationary; in other words they have a different character at different places and dates. Essentially this is due to a mismatch between the extent or the duration of the internal readjustment processes and the external forcing. The study of climate changes is essentially the study of these inhomogeneities and nonstationaries. For the present purpose, we are concerned particularly with the thermal perturbation spectrum and with the associated variations in sea temperature.

Internal Dynamic Readjustments

The readjustment of a geophysical fluid to forcing changes generally involves the generation of turbulence and waves. The division is somewhat artificial. We view turbulence as a process in which energy dissipation and entropy production play an essential role. In wave dynamics, dissipation is neglected or plays a minor role. This permits waves to transmit energy and information through the ocean.

Both waves and two-dimensional, geophysical turbulence occur in a variety of modes. In the external or barotropic mode, the horizontal velocity does not vary with depth; and the dynamical restoring force is associated with sea-level changes. Climatologically more important are the internal or baroclinic modes, particularly the so-called first mode which involves horizontal mass transports in the shallow layer above the thermocline that are equal and opposite to those in the much deeper layer below. All baroclinic modes involve transient, horizontal density changes in the ocean interior without change in sea level.

The Rossby Radius of deformation is the horizontal scale or distance beyond which rotational effects become more important than buoyancy effects. Formally it is determined by the ratio between the velocity of gravity waves and the local value of the Coriolis parameter. The relevant waves are tides or tsunami for the barotropic radius of deformation and long internal gravity waves for the baroclinic radius.

For the atmosphere, a typical mid-latitude value of the baroclinic Rossby Radius is about 1,000 km which is equivalent to the "synoptic" scale of transient cyclones and anticyclones. The length of the corresponding oceanic deformation radius is only about 10–30 km. Geostrophic ocean eddies are therefore about 50 times smaller than their atmospheric synoptic counterparts. On the other hand, their lifetime is counted in months, while that of atmospheric perturbations is counted in days.

Geostrophic turbulence is a collective name for cyclones and countercylones in the atmosphere or for the corresponding ocean eddies. Mechanical energy in the mid-latitude oceans varies predominantly on the eddy scale. The spectral power of these fluctuations is considerably larger than that associated with large-scale ocean currents like the Gulf Stream. The associated changes in sea surface temperature are observable from satellites, though they are small compared to seasonal changes.

Waves are distinguished from geophysical turbulence by their role as telecommunication agents within the ocean. Two important wave forms in climate studies are Rossby or Planetary Waves and Kelvin or Edge Waves. Both involve essentially the rotation of the earth; in other words, their wave length or scale length is necessarily longer than the deformation radius.

Planetary waves always propagate against the direction of rotation: they therefore propagate from east to west through the surrounding fluid. The speed of propagation increases with the deformation radius and with the cosine of the latitude. Both these factors decrease from the equator towards the poles. The speed of Rossby Waves decreases therefore rather strongly with latitude. An equatorial Rossby wave can traverse any of the ocean basins from east to west in less than a year. At subtropical latitudes it would need several years to cover the same distance.

The crest of a Kelvin wave extends only over a limited distance which corresponds to the deformation radius. The wave length—that is, the distance between crests—can be much larger. Kelvin waves are also called Edge waves because they propagate around the edge of ocean basins, clockwise in the southern hemisphere and counterclockwise in the northern. They can cause relatively large changes in vertical velocity or upwelling along the continental coasts. Kelvin waves cannot traverse the ocean interior, except along the equator from west to east. Their propagation speed there tends to be at least three times faster than that of Rossby waves which travel in the opposite direction.

Wind-forced Perturbations of the Temperature Field

Ocean kinetic energy is mainly derived from the wind. The wind stress can affect the temperature field locally and directly by moving water in a direction parallel to the horizontal temperature gradient, by displacing water vertically and by stirring an initially stratified water column. It can affect the temperature field indirectly through the adjustment process, which generally involves the emission of Rossby or Kelvin waves. When these waves are absorbed again, they can produce temperature changes in regions which are far away from their origin.

Outside the equatorial region, the wind stress tends to drive the near-surface water towards the right in the northern hemisphere and toward the left in the southern. This transport of water at a right angle to the wind stress is known as the Ekman drift. Under the trades, the Ekman drift transports the heated surface waters poleward. The compensating flow towards the equator at lower depths carries much colder water. The process contributes, therefore, directly to the poleward heat transport. By contrast, the stress exerted by the westerlies at higher latitudes drives the surface water away from the poles and therefore diminishes the role of the oceans in the meridional transport of heat.

Wind stress can induce vertical motion in the water. Under a cyclone, the Ekman transport is always directed outward away from the center of cyclonic activity. The outflow of surface water is compensated by an upwelling of colder water from below. The passage of a hurricane therefore leaves a cold wake behind. Upwelling occurs also when the wind stress drives the surface water away from a coast. In regions of countercyclonic wind stress curl—notably in the broad belt between the core of the trades and the westerlies—the Ekman transport is convergent. The surface water column is therefore stretched vertically, and heat is transported downward there.

Squalls and breaking waves stir the upper ocean. This tends to be associated with the entrainment of cold water from below into roiled surface layers. The process lifts the center of mass and increases therefore the potential energy. It also contributes to the lowering of the sea-surface temperature in the region of hurricanes and cyclonic storms.

Waves disperse the available potential energy associated with local, wind-generated density anomalies. The energy which is radiated westward by Rossby waves is partly absorbed by the so-called western boundary currents, the Gulf Stream, the Kuroshio, the Brazil current and the Agulhas current off the east coast of South Africa. The supply of energy to the western boundary currents is essentially an integral, averaging process. The spectrum of baroclinic Rossby waves comprises waves of many different lengths which move with different speeds; they all need many seasons or years to reach the western boundary. The effect of individual or short-term wind stress fluctuations is therefore smoothed and becomes unobservable. This accentuates the flywheel role of the western boundary currents and the associated great ocean gyres in the dynamic system.

The flywheel effect becomes much weaker as one approaches the equator. The reduction of rotational constraints and the resultant increased speed of equatorial waves facilitates a much faster transmission of energy together with relatively large vertical displacements. For example, the seasonal reversal of the Somali current can be associated with equatorial Rossby waves that move fast enough to transmit the effect of seasonal monsoon wind changes from the interior of the Indian Ocean towards the East African coast. In the Pacific, large anomalous surface warmings along the South American coast known as El Niños are believed to be caused by the arrival of equatorial Kelvin waves which were generated by wind changes far to the West in Melanesia.

The amplitude and rapid growth of temperature anomalies in the equatorial sea surface layers is enhanced by the large vertical temperature gradient. Compared to higher latitudes, the potential temperature changes more slowly with height in the tropical atmosphere; it changes more rapidly with depth in the tropical ocean. Relatively small vertical displacements therefore cause large local temperature changes in the upper ocean.

Thermally Forced Perturbations

Depending on the turbidity of the water, most of the incoming solar radiation is absorbed within ten meters of the surface. The upper ocean is stirred not only by winds and by breaking waves, but also by convection associated with the evaporative and radiational cooling of the surface molecular strata. Together these processes tend to distribute heat more or less uniformly through a layer of limited depth, the so-called surface mixed layer.

The depth of the mixed layer is determined by the ratio of mechanical and convective stirring to the stabilizing effects of solar heating. In spring and early summer, when the heating is large and storms relatively infrequent, the mixed layer becomes shallow and warm. As its depth decreases it leaves partly heated water strata below, and these form the seasonal thermocline. The waters of the seasonal thermocline are again entrained into the deepening mixed layer during fall and winter when stirring becomes once more the dominant process.

The ocean-mixed layer and the troposphere owe their genesis to analogous processes, but the former contains only about 1% of all the water while the latter contains about 80% of the air. In spite of their relatively small fractional mass, mixed layers and seasonal thermoclines have sufficient thermal inertia to inhibit the large seasonal temperature excursion which would be forced otherwise by the annual change in irradiation.

The heat content of the upper ocean and the sea surface temperature reach their highest local values in late summer. They are coldest and the mixed layer tends to reach its greatest depth at the end of the cooling season in March. This contributes to the familiar six-week lag of the seasons behind the astronomic calendar even on the continents.

The difference between summer and winter is the dominant signal in sea-surface temperature records outside the equatorial zone. Fluctuations between years tend to be smaller than annual changes, but they are less predictable and we may be economically more sensitive to them. Ocean dynamics do not appear to play a major active role in the genesis of these extratropical, interannual surface-temperature fluctuations. Their existence is due mainly to random or systematic air-sea interaction changes.

Random changes are associated with gales, rain storms, air temperature and humidity fluctuations, changes in cloudiness and so forth. On the ocean time scale, the succession of atmospheric perturbations can be viewed simply as a high frequency white noise. In the long run, such a random white noise input can produce large, low-frequency departures from the statistical equilibrium. The principle is familiar to physicists from the phenomenon of Brownian motion, the random walk of a heavy molecule in a gas mixture which can lead to arbitrary large departures from its initial position. It is applied routinely by hydrologists who know that large, long-period fluctuations in the level of a reservoir can be caused by a random succession of minor storms. In the ocean the same principle can produce large and persistent anomalies in the sea surface and mixed layer temperature or salinity. In the very long run, the amplitude of these anomalies is limited only by the always present statistical energy constraints and negative feedbacks.

Systematic changes in the energy flux through the sea surface can be due also to a variety of causes: persistent vacillations in the pattern of the atmospheric general circulation, natural or man-made changes in air turbidity and transmissivity, solar irradiation changes caused by orbital variations, etc. These processes can produce large, low-frequency changes in the ocean climate. The associated changes in the ocean temperature which could occur as a result during periods of a few years or decades are, however, very much smaller than those associated with annual or random input changes. Their diagnosis is therefore difficult. The problem is compounded by the unstationariness of statistics of short-term fluctuations, i.e., the local frequency of storms and other random perturbations is likely to be affected by systematic changes in the state of the atmosphere at large.

The depth of the mixed-layer changes not only with the season but also with latitude. It tends to be less than 50 meters in the tropics and becomes at least 200 meters deep during winter in mid-latitudes. It may reach down to the ocean bottom during periods of intermittent penetrating winter convection in parts of the Norwegian, Labrador and Weddell Seas. The water masses which occupy the lower two-thirds of all the ocean basins are produced episodically in these very limited areas, which play the same role in the world ocean as do areas of deep tropical and continental summer convection in the atmosphere.

The process of convection in the polar seas is limited mainly by the salinity stratification. Sea ice contains little or no salt. Partial melting in spring forms a surface layer of relatively fresh water which is separated by a halocline from the saltier, denser water below. In the arctic basin, the halocline is strengthened by fresh water discharge from the Siberian and Canadian rivers. It isolates the surface layers from the deep ocean reservoir of heat, and this facilitates the maintenance of the arctic ice cover. It also causes a larger meridional temperature contrast and therefore a reduced entropy production. During the onset of the last glacial age, the growing continental ice sheets reduced the fresh water discharge. As pointed out by Rooth (1982), convection was less inhibited as a result and the sea surface layers were kept relatively ice free by allowing them to draw heat from deeper strata. The efficiency of oceanic meridional heat transport was therefore increased, and a local source of moisture was made available for the growing continental ice sheets. The proposed diversion of the Siberian rivers into Central Asia could push the climate in a similar direction.

Environmental Effects of Oceanic Variability

Cells in the human body are conditioned by the whole organism, which is affected in turn by their functioning. The cells interact with viruses and with organic molecules, while the individual interacts also with a wider physical and social environment. There are analogies between such a system and a turbulent, thermodynamically active, geophysical fluid. No part is entirely independent in these complex entities and nothing can be isolated without penalty. Our ability to discern the effect of changes in the ocean upon the climate is limited by the inherent uncertainty of environmental developments.

Classical physicists liked to deal with processes which could be isolated. When confronted with complex phenomena, they endeavored to explain the behavior of the whole from the character and the behavior of its parts, which was expected to be governed in turn by well-defined universal laws. The rigorous application of this approach was never quite as successful in meteorology or oceanography as in some other branches of physics.

Oceans and atmospheres are open systems that cannot be reduced to an assembly of independent parts. Like living organisms, they involve different levels of scale and organization. Information propagates up and down between these levels along intricate, nonlinear pathways. Energetic exchanges with a wider environment protects these systems from entropic decay, but the same throughput of energy also generates unpredictable instabilities and prevents the attainment of a static equilibrium. The enduring character of the system—or the organism—is preserved only by negative feedbacks which suppress the indefinite growth of these instabilities.

Circulation patterns in geophysical fluids are not determined uniquely by external constraints. They vary incessantly. The character of the global atmospheric circulation can be changed in the aftermath of a single hurricane. The appearance of this hurricane at a particular place and time may have been due to a chance clustering of a few cumulus clouds. The development of these clouds was perhaps stimulated by a small hot spot on the sea surface which in turn may have been caused by quite local turbidity, and so on down to smaller and smaller scales.

The search for exact causes of environmental developments leads us inevitably to details which are beyond the scope of our observational and analytical capabilities. We can not specify the present state of an extensive turbulent fluid exactly. The resulting uncertainty inevitably grows with time. Studies by Phil Thompson (1957), Ed Lorenz (1965) and others after them indicate that two states of the atmosphere, which could not be distinguished initially by observations, will evolve into two completely unrelated, large-scale patterns in less than two weeks. This period represents therefore the limit of mechanistic weather predictability.

It is essentially impossible for us to extend predictions into the indefinite future, because we cannot know exactly what is going on at this moment. This limitation applies not only to environmental forecasting, but also to our ability to predict the stock market or our personal and social future. Like Heisenberg's Uncertainty Principle for the subatomic world, it is an inescapable limitation which is rooted in our inherently inadequate knowledge of the present and the past. I believe that the elaboration and quantification of this insight by meteorologists will come to be recognized as a major contribution to the modern view of the world.

Changes in sea-surface temperature will almost certainly favor specific atmospheric responses. However, the actual development will be influenced also in different ways by innumerable other factors which cannot all be observed and analyzed. A particular surface temperature anomaly can coexist therefore with a de facto infinite number of different weather patterns. The anomaly can be associated only with a "tendency" for the development of certain atmospheric configurations.

Perhaps we shall learn to represent these "tendencies" with some confidence by numerical probability values. The operational usefulness of such a technique is by no means certain. To take a hypothetical case, consider a large sea-surface temperature anomaly which tends to recur about once in five years. Assume that this anomaly tends also to induce the development of certain specific winter weather patterns over the Mississippi valley with a relatively high probability of 30%. Many other patterns are possible but their probability would be much smaller. For a statistician this may seem very significant, but a farmer may require a lifetime to capitalize on the information.

The Effect of Interannual Sea-Surface Temperature Changes

It is convenient to distinguish between equatorial temperature changes and those in other latitudes. The equatorial ocean plays a special role in the climate system. Small changes in sea surface temperature there translate into relatively large changes in the saturation vapor and in the latent heat supply to the atmosphere. The hydrostatic stability of the atmosphere is weak near the equator; its whole depth there can be affected by convective adjustment to small surface temperature changes. Such a local adjustment in depth is generally not possible in higher latitudes. Perhaps most important, however, is the fact that the dynamic response time of the equatorial oceans is better matched to forcing changes on the seasonal and interannual time scales, than is the case at higher latitudes.

A combination of these effects probably causes the so-called ENSO (El Niño/Southern Oscillation) cycle to be the largest and possibly the only statistically significant signal which recurs in climate time series with a period between the annual and the secular scale. El Niños are episodes of abnormally warm surface waters in the eastern equatorial Pacific, which tend to appear at intervals of about 3–7 years near Christmas, hence the name El Niño, the child. The associated phase of the Southern Oscillation involves relatively low barometric pressures over the eastern subtropical South Pacific and a corresponding excess of air pressure in the west over the Australian/Indonesian region.

The ENSO literature is large and growing. Surveys by Philander (1983) and others suggest that during the years between El Niños, the subtropical South Pacific countercyclone is strong, and warm surface water is piled up by the trades against the western boundary of the equatorial Pacific. The sea surface is relatively cold off the South American coast and along the equator in the east because the wind stress there causes upwelling from intermediate depths and also advection from higher southern latitudes.

At some stage, for reasons unknown, the South Pacific countercyclone weakens and the equatorial trades relax. This allows the piled up warm water in the west to slosh back eastward as an equatorial Kelvin wave. The arrival of this wave at the coast of Ecuador coincides with onset of the El Niño. Part of the wave is reflected west again as an equatorial Rossby wave which can produce further surface warming in the mid-Pacific. The remainder propagates north and south as two coastal Kelvin or Edge waves which tend to interfere with normal coastal upwelling processes off California and off the South American west coast. The excessively high sea-surface temperatures cause anomalous atmospheric convection over the eastern and central equatorial Pacific. The warm air ascending there is replaced partly by an inflow of surface air along the equator from the west. This further weakens or reverses the already weakened equatorial trades and therefore amplifies the development.

The theories which describe these equatorial developments do not address the basic problem of existence to the Southern Oscillation. Why does the South Pacific countercyclone become weaker, and why do the trades relax every few years? What causes the termination of the episode? Whatever the answer to these questions, there can be little doubt that the phenomenon involves the atmosphere and the equatorial ocean in an interactive manner and that it has global climatological and economic implications.

The anomalously warm waters cause fish kills and a severe drop in the yield of commercial fisheries off the South American coast. Birds which live on fish also die. Abnormal rainfalls over the adjacent, normally arid coastal areas interfere with agriculture and damage roads, bridges and other public facilities. At the other side of the Pacific, over Australia and Indonesia, the same phase of the ENSO cycle causes abnormally high barometric pressures, suppression of rainfall, catastrophic droughts, and bush fires like the one which devastated parts of Australia during the 1982 El Niño.

The climatological repercussions of the ENSO cycle outside the area of the tropical Pacific are less well established. The evidence suggests—but does not prove—that El Niños are associated with anomalous droughts and famines along the equatorial margins of the African deserts. Much has been written about the fact that southern Russia also was afflicted by severe drought and harvest failures during the 1972 El Niño episode, but this may have been a coincidence. The relationship between the ENSO cycle and the weather pattern over North America is equally problematic. The 1982/83 El Niño has been variously charged with having caused conditions which varied all the way from extreme hot to extreme cold in the central US. Whether or not it was guilty of these charges remains uncertain.

A theory developed by Hoskins and Karoly (1981) suggests that the concentration of convection over anomalously warm areas of the equatorial Pacific should give rise to wave perturbations in the upper atmosphere. These can transmit the effect to higher latitudes, affecting the atmospheric circulation there. The theory has found suggestive—but by no means conclusive—support in observations. The problem lies with the inherent noisiness of atmospheric development. With El Niños occurring only about twenty times in a century, it may take considerable time before observations allow us to assess their effect upon the North American weather pattern with any degree of confidence. In the meantime we can rely only upon numerical simulations.

The possible influence of extratropical sea surface temperature anomalies upon the climate is even more problematical. The amplitude of these anomalies tends to be small, not only compared to seasonal changes, but also compared to the land/sea temperature contrast and—what is even more important—compared to synoptic-scale temperature fluctuations in the air above. Short-term variations in the energy flux across the sea surface are determined almost exclusively by these atmospheric perturbations. The effect of sea-surface temperature anomalies can manifest itself only in the long run. Even then, it is probably not observable locally because the hydrostatic stability of the extra-tropical marine atmosphere does not favor deep vertical convection. The influence of sea-surface temperature anomalies outside the tropics upon the atmospheric circulation is therefore difficult to diagnose even in numerical models. Their role in the climate system is certainly not known quantitatively.

Changes in sea-ice cover may play a more important role. Particularly in the southern hemisphere, the area of pack ice around Antarctica varies seasonally by a factor of five. Apparently it also experiences large interannual variations. The resulting changes in the atmospheric boundary conditions are so drastic that they are bound to have major effects upon the local and perhaps even global atmospheric circulation. As far as can be determined, the pattern of these circulation changes has not yet been established conclusively.

The General Circulation of the Ocean and CO_2 -Induced Climate Changes

Water which has a year-round temperature in excess of 12°C can be found only in a shallow equatorial layer or in large lens-shaped volumes, which extend in each ocean basin above the thermocline from the equatorial region to a latitude of about 40 degrees. Because of their countercyclonic circulation, these warm-water lenses are known as the great subtropical ocean gyres. Their narrow, poleward flowing branch is formed by the western-boundary currents. A water particle tends to circulate around a gyre within a few years. Its mean residence time within each warm-water lens appears to be less than about twenty years.

By contrast, the much larger mass of water which is colder than 4°C occupies an interconnected volume throughout the world ocean. Carbon dating suggests that water particles tend to remain about 500–1000 years within this volume. Long-term climate changes may be affected not only by the rate of replenishment of the deep-water reservoir by convection in high latitudes, but also by the way this water returns again to the upper ocean. Stommel (1956) suggested that this involves a distributed upwelling over most of the ocean interior. A quite different mechanism, considered among others by Rooth (1982), restricts the compensatory upwelling to the polar regions where the deep water had been produced in the first instance, though not necessarily in the same hemisphere.

One can raise awkward questions about either of these suggested mechanisms. The wind stress is countercyclonic, and the Ekman drift is convergent over the whole vast area of the subtropical gyres. Upwelling through the thermocline in the interior of these regions could be produced only by a density-driven "thermohaline" circulation. This implies some heating of the ascending water. The only possible source for this heat is conduction from the warm surface layer, but the value of the oceanic conductivity which is commonly accepted and which has been derived from fine-structure oceanographic measurements is far too small for this purpose. The mechanism which could entrain the lower water into the warm water lens of the upper ocean remains therefore unclear.

The same inhibition does not affect the return of the deep water to the surface in high latitudes. The wind stress is cyclonic on the polar side of the westerlies. Water is therefore sucked towards the surface by a divergent Ekman drift. It does not have to pass through a pronounced thermocline during its ascent. However, if all the vertical mass exchange occurs in high latitudes, one wonders how the huge deep-water reservoir in the rest of the world's ocean is being replenished within a few hundred years? The energy for the required horizontal mass transports in the ocean abyss would have to be obtained in some way indirectly from the wind, but the relevant mechanism is not well known.

The World Ocean Climate Experiment which is now being planned by the scientific community, and advances in modelling, may indicate an answer to these questions before the end of this century. The problem is not academic but affects the way in which our environment will respond to the systematic change in atmospheric infrared transmissivity which is caused by the consumption of fossil fuel and the associated rise in the atmospheric CO_2 concentration.

Dependent on economic and technical developments, the atmospheric CO_2 concentration may double within the next century. The ocean must affect the resulting environmental response through its capacity to store both carbon dioxide and heat. The solubility of CO_2 in sea water, which has prevented this gas from becoming the main component of the earth's atmosphere, has probably restrained also the rise in atmospheric CO_2 levels during the last hundred years from being about twice as fast as it might have been otherwise. The subtle role of the ocean heat storage capacity in the environmental development has been discussed recently by Bretherton (1982).

The well-known "greenhouse effect" is caused by the absorption and reemission of infrared radiation in the atmosphere. The main atmospheric constituent which produces this effect is water vapor, with ozone and carbon dioxide playing a very secondary role. The global atmospheric water content and with it the greenhouse effect and also the vigor of the atmospheric general circulation tends to change in the same sense as the globally averaged or more particularly the tropical sea surface temperature. Widespread aridity during the last ice age (Crowley 1983) when the surface was colder is in keeping with this tendency. Simultaneously, the general atmospheric circulation was presumably also weakened (Kraus 1973). On the other hand, when the sea surface is relatively warm for whatever reason, the increased atmospheric water vapor and greenhouse effect will tend to make it still warmer. The resulting amplification of sea-surface temperature variation is kept in bound ultimately by the evaporative cooling of the ocean and by changes in cloudiness.

A doubling of atmospheric CO_2 per se—without change in atmospheric humidity—would change the downward heat flux at the ocean surface only by about 3.5 Watt/m^2 (Ramanathan 1981). The resultant ocean-temperature change would be practically unobservable. The 2°C increase in the tropics and the 4°C increase in high latitudes which has been deduced from numerical models (see, e.g., Charney *et al.* 1979) are due almost entirely to the positive feedback and the amplification caused by water vapor.

If one wants to predict the environmental results of the CO_2 injection, one has to know how long it will take the ocean to reach a new thermal and hydrological equilibrium with a somewhat moister atmosphere. This depends on the amount of ocean water which is involved. If the temperature change is restricted to the top 50 meters—corresponding roughly to the depth of the mixed layer in the tropical half of the world ocean—the lag time would be only three years. This means climate changes would be practically in phase with the atmospheric CO_2 increase. On the other hand, if the ocean has to be warmed through its full depth, the lag would be many centuries and this would make the environmental problem of manmade CO_2 changes much less urgent. The actual response will probably be somewhere between these two extremes.

Bretherton (1982) argued that horizontal inequalities in the oceanic response would cause delay of at least 30 years and possibly one as long as 300 years. There are at least some areas where mixing reaches down to some considerable depth and where the heat capacity of the water column is therefore large. Even if these areas are relatively small they will continue to act as heat sinks in the system until thermal equilibrium has been reached. Compared to large areas of small virtual heat capacity, a few cold spots with large heat capacity can therefore exert an inordinately large influence upon the development.

The winter mixed layer in temperate regions is generally at least 200 m deep. It can communicate directly with the upper thermocline strata below the subtropical gyres. The heat capacity of the relevant water volume is therefore quite large. This fact alone would be sufficient to prolong the time which would be needed for the sea-surface temperature to come into equilibrium with a change in atmospheric CO_2 content, by a factor of 10 to about 30 years. The involvement of a relatively deep layer in the heating process is indicated by tritium observations. Tritium was injected into the system by bomb tests in the late 1950s and early 1960s. It is now mixed throughout the upper 500 m, even in the tropics. Presumably, an excess of heat would have been mixed down in a similar way.

Whether or not the lag time is actually even longer depends on the circulation of the deep water which has been discussed above. If this circulation is density-driven by meridional heating differences, it would be weakened by the CO_2 effect which particularly reduces the cooling in the polar regions. This would tend to restrict the oceanic temperature increase to the upper layers with a corresponding limitation of the lag time. Such a restriction would not apply to an essentially wind-driven deep water circulation which therefore may involve a thermal lag time of several centuries.

The preceding discussion was necessarily qualitative and conjectural. It does indicate, however, the important role of the oceanic general circulation in the evolution of initially CO_2 induced climate changes. The gathering of more reliable, quantitative information may have to wait for the development of new observation methods and much more sophisticated, interactive atmosphere-ocean models than are available now.

Models of the Atmosphere-Ocean System

We cannot experiment deliberately with the climate system. We cannot even observe its slow fluctuations in sufficient detail over an appropriately long period to make conclusive, quantitative deductions about its operation. The development of models becomes imperative in these circumstances.

Models always involve analogues. We can grasp analogues directly. The output of our digital models requires representation in terms of graphs, charts, and other analogue devices before it can be assimilated. The modeling of a sea-surface deformation as a group of harmonic waves is a mathematical abstraction, but it also involves a subtle appeal to a familiar visual analogue. Mach and other physicists of the positivist school maintained that truth could be found only in mathematical description and that attempts to represent subatomic phenomena, in particular, in terms of familiar images was misleading. This is true to some extent, but it did not stop Niels Bohr a few years later from representing the atom as a miniature solar system. In the end, the production of appropriate analogues is always the ultimate purpose of all modeling activity.

Models cannot represent all the intricate details of the real world. If they would do that, they would be useless. They involve deliberate simplifications which bring out the essential features of the process of concern. Some climate models can be very simple indeed. The effect of CO_2 changes, for example, can be simulated crudely by the exchanges between two or three differently sized reservoirs of the substance. Physical oceanographers have effectively used simple hydraulic analogues to simulate major features of the oceanic circulation. Most of the modern modeling effort is concentrated, however, in the field of numerical simulations.

The development of extensive numerical models had been pioneered by Richardson in the 1930s. It was a development in which meteorologists probably led the world. The advent of the modern electronic computer permitted use of the equations of motion, thermodynamics, and state for the prediction of changes in the velocity, density, temperature, and pressure fields. The computation of these changes inevitably involves small errors, because of the macroscopic uncertainty principle previously discussed. It is impossible to observe at one specific moment the relevant properties of all fluid particles in the ocean or their values at each point of an infinitesimally fine grid. Ultimately, any one fluid element can affect the fate of all the others, even those which were initially far away. The long term development is therefore unpredictable.

Even with the most powerful computer, we are forced to use a relatively coarse grid which can only provide a rather blurred representation of the real world. In the case of the atmosphere-ocean system, the matter is complicated further by the different time-and-space scales which characterize significant changes in the two fluids. The atmosphere fluctuates rapidly. Its evolution has to be represented in numerical models by snapshots which follow each other at relatively short-time intervals. Use of the same short-time steps for the simulation of the slowly evolving ocean would be very uneconomical in computer time. By contrast, the width of currents and the size of ocean eddies are governed by the oceanic deformation radius which is about 50 times smaller than its atmospheric counterpart. Mechanistic ocean models therefore require a much finer grid size than that required for an economical representation of the atmosphere.

The exchange of energy and momentum across the sea surface tends to be integrated in space by the atmosphere. It is integrated by the ocean in time. The ocean interacts essentially with statistical ensembles of many different atmospheric weather patterns. Conceivably, climate models could deal with this matter by repeated integrations of an atmospheric model with the same oceanic boundary, but with slightly different initial conditions. If done often enough, this would provide an ensemble of simulated weather patterns which are compatible with a particular oceanic configuration. The statistics of this ensemble could then be used to compute the character and probability of the resultant changes in the ocean. The next step would involve the computation of a new set of weather patterns which is compatible with the changed oceanic boundary, and so on.

Though feasible in principle, such an empirical approach would require very large resources in computing power, money, and time. It is also overkill, because one does not want the details of the various weather patterns for climate studies. A direct assessment of the relevant atmospheric statistics, without the laborious simulation of large numbers of weather patterns, would be much more convenient and satisfying. The theoretical foundations for such a stochastic approach to climate modeling have been considered by Hasselmann (1976), and more recently by Thompson (1985).

Stochastic climate models are a promising new venture; I shall therefore deal with them in some detail. In a numerical model of the atmosphere or the ocean, the fields of pressure, velocity, temperature, etc., can be represented by the value of these variables at a set of grid points. Alternatively, these fields can be approximated by a spectrum of Fourier components or waves. Either way, with M properties and N grid points or spectral functions, a set of $N \times M = K$ numbers is used in the model to approximate the actual state. From these K numbers listed in any arbitrary order as a sequence a_k ($k = 1,2....K$), one can reconstitute a "realization" or position vector, which has the a_k's as coordinates in a phase space of K dimensions. The state of the ocean may be specified in exactly the same way by a vector with components o_l in a domain of L dimensions.

The atmospheric or oceanic temperature and velocity fields change all the time. These changes are not arbitrary. They must satisfy various physical constraints, like conservation of mass, energy or momentum. This means that changes at any one point are likely to be influenced by conditions and events everywhere else in the fluid. They certainly will be affected almost immediately by the status at adjacent grid points or regions of the fluid. They also may be affected by solar heating and other external forces.

In phase space, the evolution of the system is represented by the trajectory or life line of the "realization point." The rate of evolution is specified by the change of the a_k coordinates during a short interval of time. This corresponds to a velocity in phase space with components da_k/dt, with t indicating time. Each of these components represents the rate of change of one property at one gridpoint. Because the local changes in geometric space depend on conditions throughout the fluid, each phase space velocity component tends to be a function f_k of all, or at least many, phase space position coordinates. It also may depend on the external force F_k. The evolution of the system is represented therefore by the K expressions

$$(1) \qquad da_k/dt = f_k(a_1, a_2, ...; o_1, o_2 ...; F_k)$$

Each of these K equations involves all the a_k's or at least a large subset of them, as well as ocean surface conditions, that is a subset of the o_l's. Analogous equations can be written for an oceanic domain.

Climate is characterized by more or less similar weather situations that tend to occur again and again. The corresponding trajectory or life line of the realization point passes therefore repeatedly through the same phase space region. Over a sufficiently long time period, the number of trajectory passes through a small volume element of the phase space, can be conceived as a continuous density of realizations p?(a_1, a_2...;t). The local value of p? in phase space then represents the probability of occurrence of some particular weather situation. As the trajectory had no end in time, the probability of its entering a small phase space volume element, must be equal to that of leaving it again. Thompson (1985) generalized this argument to a continuity condition for the evolution of the climate system in phase space.

$$(2) \qquad \delta \rho / \delta t + \sum_{k=1}^{K} \delta (\rho a_k)/\delta a_k = 0$$

In statistical mechanics (2) is known as the Liouville theorem.

The first term in (2) represents the change with time of the probability of recurrence of certain weather situations. This is tantamount to a change in climate. The second term represents the convergence of trajectories into the relevant volume element of the phase space. Introduction of the explicit form of the relations (1), into this continuity equation of realizations, suggests that it should be possible to calculate the probability distribution ρ of weather situations as a function of the phase space coordinates a_k. In principle, it may be possible to do that without the cumbersome specific simulation of a great number of weather situations, that would be needed otherwise to generate credible climate statistics.

The evolution of the weather involves inevitably an element of uncertainty. We cannot know exactly what the weather does just now. Its representation by a finite set of gridpoint values or spectral functions is approximate and rather coarse. The development is likely to be affected by unexpected random impulses, which come from the unresolved sub-grid scale interactions or from the truncated parts of the spectrum. In Thompson's approach, these random impulses can be represented as an additional stochastic forcing function R_k in the expressions (1). After introduction into the continuity equation (2), this yields a modified form of the Liouville equation, which is known as the Fokker-Planck equation. Solution of this equation requires that both the external forcing F_k and the stochastic forcing R_k can be expressed also as a function of the independent variables a_k.

The number of gridpoints or degrees of freedom K is arbitrary. In principle, the stochastic approach could be applied to anything from intricate general circulation models with many thousand degrees of freedom, to simple energy balance models for the planet which involve a two-dimensional phase space with one grid point for the whole globe and two properties, the planetary temperature and the albedo. Frankignoul (Frankignoul and Reynolds 1983) has used equation (2) in its stationary form ($\delta\rho/\delta t = 0$) for the determination of the changing ocean mixed layer temperature and depth as a function of stochastic atmospheric forcing.

The Fokker-Planck equation offers an elegant and promising approach towards the direct assessment of climate statistics in atmosphere-ocean models. To complete the picture, one has to know how the external and stochastic forcing functions F_k and R_k depend upon the internal state of the atmosphere or the ocean. This involves the parametric representation of local processes such as the absorption and emission of radiation, release of latent heat, transfer of momentum and energy across the sea surface, etc., as functions of the grid-scale averages of the temperature, the composition and the other field variables. The establishment and refinement of the relevant parameterizations requires viewpoints and modeling procedures which are very different from those used commonly in general circulation modeling. Essentially, the simulation of the atmosphere-ocean climate can be achieved only through an assembly of models, each of which is relevant only for a limited range of scales. It is of some interest that a similar view has been developed by some nuclear physicists for their very different field.

Summary and Outlook

Climate is a stochastic concept. It can be viewed as an ensemble of circulation patterns and temperature fields. The ensemble statistics are representative only for particular periods of time. They can be synthesized into four-dimensional wave number/frequency spectra. As climate studies are concerned mainly with horizontal variations, these spectra can be reduced to three dimensions, or even to two dimensions, if meridional changes only are taken into account.

Power is associated in the ocean perturbation spectrum particularly with wave numbers, which correspond on the one hand to the size of the ocean basins and on the other hand to the length of the baroclinic deformation radius. This length varies from about 100–250 km near the equator to something like 10 km near the pole. It tends to determine the width of ocean currents and size of the quasi-geostrophic eddies which are the most energetic features of two-dimensional turbulence in the oceans. Along the frequency axis, spectral power is concentrated in lines associated with astronomical forcing: the daily, annual and longer orbital frequencies. Geostrophic turbulence in the ocean involves a relatively broad frequency band, characterized by periods from one to two months to several years.

The corresponding atmospheric spectrum also has power at the annual frequency and at wave numbers which are determined by the size of the ocean basins or by the ocean/continent configuration. The identity of these scales in the ocean and in the atmosphere is responsible for the lag in the annual evolution of the climate behind the calendar. It also facilitates interaction between the two media in monsoon circulations. The size of mid-latitude atmospheric cyclones and counter-cyclones is, however, about 50 times larger than that of the corresponding quasi-geostrophic ocean eddies and their characteristic periods tend to be about 20 times shorter. Ocean eddies have apparently little direct influence upon conditions in the atmosphere, not only because the disparity in scales inhibits resonant developments, but also because the amplitude of surface temperature variations associated with them is considerably smaller than that associated with atmospheric perturbation.

Resonant dynamic interactions between the two media are possible apparently in the equatorial zone. The surface temperature manifestation of oceanic perturbations is relatively large in low latitudes. Near the equator, the dynamics of these perturbations is characterized by time scales which can match approximately the annual and semiannual scales. The amount of energy which can be transferred upward from a warm sea surface is also relatively large. Together, these processes give the equatorial ocean a specially important role in the global climate system.

The so-called ENSO-cycle is a large perturbation in the region of the equatorial Pacific. Its recurrence at intervals of approximately three to eight years is associated with a significant, though rather broad, peak in the wave number/frequency climate perturbation spectrum. The ENSO-cycle involves large climatic anomalies not only in and above the equatorial Pacific, but also in regions further south, as well as in western South America and Australia. Its genesis and possible influence in areas outside the Pacific basin is still uncertain, but may be significant.

Oceanic variability can also affect the climate at irregular intervals on time scales which can not be identified with peaks in the perturbation spectrum. In particular, relatively extensive sea-surface temperature anomalies can be produced at mid-latitudes by the cumulative effects of stochastic variations in the atmospheric inputs. These anomalies may influence the atmospheric circulation in turn. The existence of such a feedback mechanism has not yet been demonstrated quantitatively.

Another time scale of probable climatological importance is associated with the residence time of water particles, dissolved substances, and other tracers in the ocean as a whole and in specific sub-domains. In steady-state conditions, residence times are defined by the volume of the domain in question, divided by the volume inflow or discharge. The residence time of a particle in the warm subtropical gyres is about 20 years. Its residence time in the deep and bottom waters of the world ocean is about 500–1000 years. The lag in the response of the climate system to the historical man-induced injection of carbon dioxide depends upon the nature of the general ocean circulation and upon the involvement of deep water in the process.

The exact pattern of atmospheric responses to oceanic variations is inherently undeterminable and unpredictable. This is due to a macroscopic uncertainty principle, which is based on our inability to observe present or initial conditions in the real world in sufficient detail and extent. Predictions in space and time are associated inevitably with probability values which can approach but cannot equal unity.

The production of models is an essential component of climate studies. They are used for experimentation, sensitivity testing and for the condensation of the slow evolution of climate in time. Realistic numerical simulations of evolving circulation patterns involve relatively fine temporal resolution for the atmosphere and fine spatial resolution for the ocean. This makes experiments based upon the long-term integration of mechanistic ocean-atmosphere models difficult and very expensive. The use of stochastic models in climate studies is attractive because it can associate probability values with different solutions, at lower costs in computer time.

I shall venture to predict the development of atmosphere-ocean climate studies for the next 20 years. This prediction, like all predictions, must be associated with a probability which is smaller than unity—in the present case very much smaller than unity.

On the observational side, a much larger base of climatologically relevant data for the sea-surface and near-surface strata will accumulate from satellite observations and—in some regions at least—also from appropriately equipped commercial ships and from instrumented buoys. At lower levels in the oceans, more data will become available from stationary and drifting platforms and—more important perhaps—from the refinement and extension of acoustic-sounding methods. A good deal of money will almost certainly be spent over the next 20 years on observations from specially equipped oceanographic ships and aircraft. The sporadic nature of these observations is likely to limit their usefulness for climate purposes. On the whole, the value of the ocean-climate data base will depend on the maintenance of observation systems over periods which are commensurate with the duration of climate fluctuations. It cannot be expected that the required long-term commitments will become significantly more attractive to politicians and businessmen over the next 20 years.

An increasing number of reasonably realistic numerical ocean models will be developed probably over the next five to ten years. Mechanistic models of the atmosphere/ocean system will also appear in increasing number. The very large number of degrees of freedom in these models may make them rather indifferent tools for experimentation and meaningful sensitivity studies. For the same reason, it seems doubtful whether present and planned concentration of research into the ENSO phenomenon will in fact lead to significantly more useful climate forecasts for regions like North America. Stochastic models of the climate system are likely to attract increasing attention, but probably not as much as will continue to be dedicated to mechanistic simulations.

We cannot predict how people 20 years hence will evaluate all the research into the atmosphere-ocean system that is anticipated now. Ultimately their view is likely to depend upon any discernable change in the understanding of nature which may have resulted from the effort, and upon the social or economic benefits which it may have yielded. An assessment of such benefits is an altogether different story, which goes beyond the scope of the present article.

References

Bretherton, F. B. 1982. "Ocean climate modeling." *Progress in Oceanogr.* 11: 93–130.

Charney, J. *et al.* 1979. *Carbon dioxide and climate: A scientific assessment.* Climate Research Board, National Academy of Sciences.

Crowley, T.J. 1983. "The geological record of climatic change." *Rev. of Geophysics and Space Phys.* 21: 828–877.

Frankignoul, C. and R. W. Reynolds. 1983. "Testing a dynamical model for mid-latitude sea surface temperature anomalies." *J. Phys. Oceanogr.* 13: 1131–1145.

Hasselmann, K. 1976. "Stochastic climate models: Part I." *Tellus* 28: 473–485.

Hoskins, B. J. and D. Karoly. 1981. "The steady linear response of a spherical atmosphere to thermal and orographic forcing." *J. Atmos. Sc.* 38: 1179–1196.

Kraus, E. B. 1973. "Comparison between ice age and present general circulations." *Nature* 245: 129–133.

Lorenz, E. N. 1965. "Study of the predictability of a 28-variable atmospheric model." *Tellus* 17: 321–333.

Philander, S. G. H. 1983. "El Niño Southern Oscillation phenomena." *Nature* 302: 295–301.

Ramanathan, V. 1981. "The role of ocean-atmosphere interactions in the carbon dioxide climate problem." *J. Atmos. Sc.* 22: 267–272.

Rooth, C. 1982. "Hydrology and ocean circulation." *Progress in Oceanogr.* 11: 131–150.

Stommel, H. 1956. "A survey of ocean current theory." *Deep Sea Res.* 4: 149–184.

Thompson, P. D. 1984. "A statistical-hydrodynamical approach to problems of climate and its evolution." *Tellus* 37A: 1–13.

Thompson, P. C. 1957. "Uncertainty of initial state as a factor in the predictability of large-scale atmospheric flow patterns." *Tellus* 9: 275–295.

SEVEN

OCEANIC ROLE In TERRESTRIAL CLIMATE

A COMMENTARY

Hugh W. Ellsaesser

Introduction

Somewhat more than half of the received solar energy is absorbed at the planetary surface. The oceans, because of their greater area (71% of the global surface), lower albedo (0.05-0.10) and preponderance in low latitudes (76% of the area from 20°N to 20°S), account for over 75% of the surface absorption and thus approximately 55% of the solar energy absorbed by the earth-atmosphere system. Since only about 10% of this is reradiated directly to space, approximately 50% of the solar energy absorbed by the earth-atmosphere system is delivered to the atmosphere in the forms of sensible and latent heat and thermal radiation from the underlying ocean surface. The times, locations, forms and rates of delivery of this energy to the atmosphere are determined principally by the ocean-surface temperature, the surface wind speed, and the temperature and moisture gradients between the boundary layer of the atmosphere and the underlying ocean surface. This assures that the oceans play a dominant role in terrestrial climate.

In addition to the thermal role, water evaporated principally from the oceans returns as rainfall, averaging about 1 m per year globally. The river run-off to the oceans tells us how much of the precipitation was recently evaporated from the oceans—ultimately, it all was. Note that this role also makes possible the cryosphere, consisting of permafrost, snow cover, land glaciers and sea ice. While each of these leads to significant climatogenic atmospheric-oceanic interactions, with feedback loops on many time scales, there is not space to consider them here.

Statistically Obvious Oceanic Climatogenesis

A part of the climatogenic role of the oceans can be seen in Figure 7-1 showing the annual average incoming solar minus outgoing IR or net radiation. This clearly shows that the earth receives more radiation than it emits in low latitudes and radiates away more radiation that it receives in high latitudes. This is only possible if the low latitude excess is somehow transported to higher latitudes within the system. The transport is performed, of course, by both the atmosphere and the oceans, roughly 50–50 by current estimates. Note, however, that the zero (thickened) line is displaced poleward over the

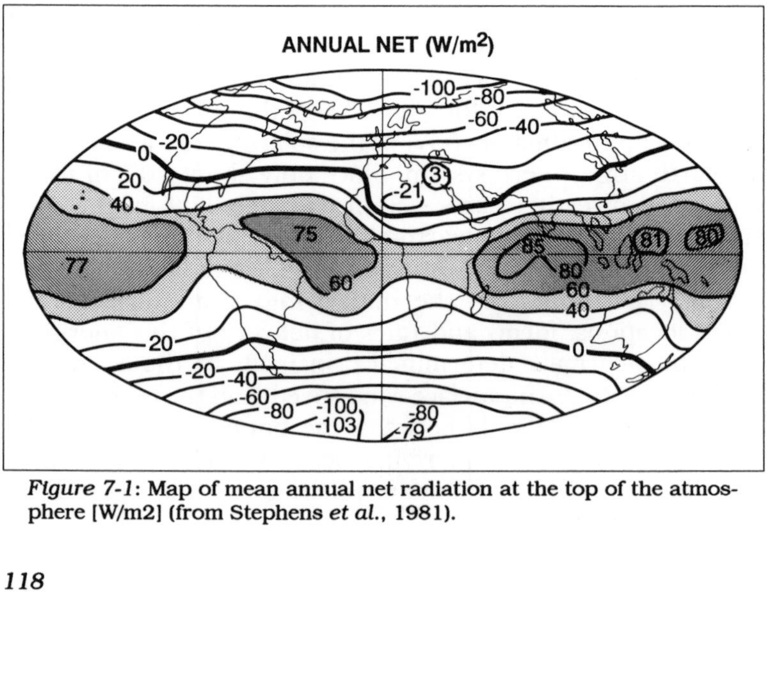

Figure 7-1: Map of mean annual net radiation at the top of the atmosphere [W/m2] (from Stephens *et al.*, 1981).

oceans and equatorward over the continents. This shows immediately that the presence of the oceans causes our planet to be warmer than it otherwise would be.

The tremendous impact of the oceans as a thermoregulator of terrestrial climate is more apparent in Figure 7-2, showing a map of the seasonal range in surface-air temperature. This map does not show continental outlines, but the locations of the individual continents are readily identifiable. Only over, and in proximity to, the continents and Arctic sea ice does the seasonal range in air temperature exceed 12°C—over Asia it reaches 56°C, North America 44°, Antarctica 36°, North Africa 24°, and elsewhere, no more than 16°C.

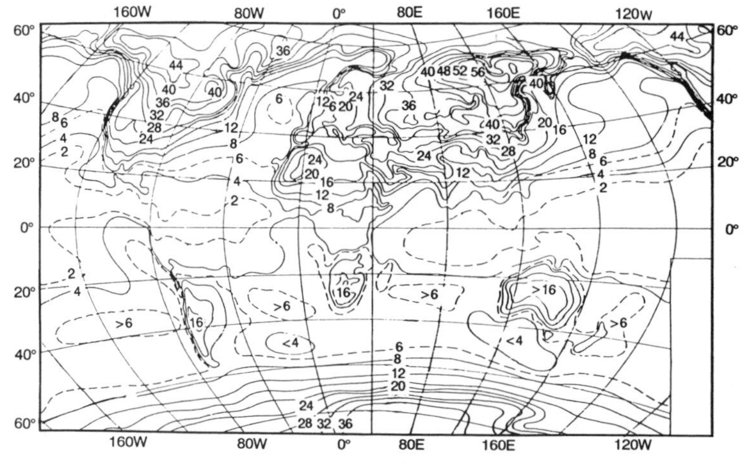

Figure 7-2: Map of seasonal range in surface-air temperature [°C] (adapted from Monin 1975).

When I first examined a map of this quality, I was surprised by the bands of relative minimum range over the oceans circa 50°–55°latitude—present in both hemispheres but far more obvious in the southern hemisphere (SH). However, their explanation is clear from Figure 7-3 which shows the seasonal range in surface-water temperature or sea-surface temperature (SST). The SST has a seasonal range of 1°-2°C at the equator, which increases poleward to bands of maximum range in mid-latitudes. The maximum seasonal range is both greater and somewhat farther poleward in the northern hemisphere (NH) (7°–15°C at 40°–50°N) than in the SH (4°–8°C at 30°–45°S).

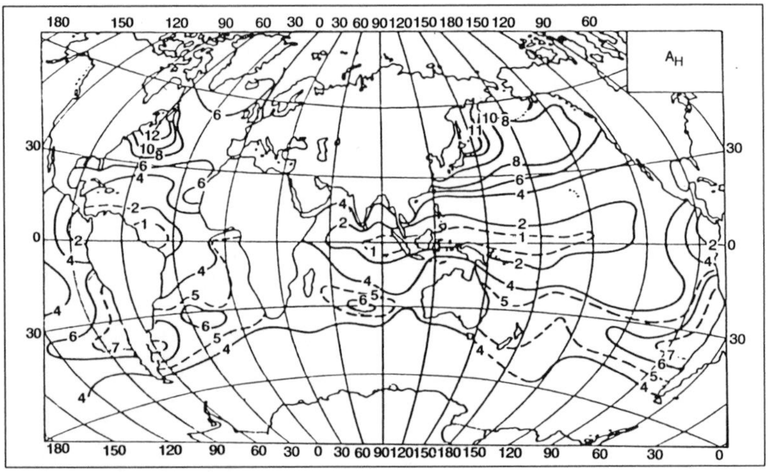

Figure 7-3: Map of seasonal range in SST(sea-surface temperature) [°C] (adapted from Panfilova, 1972).

Poleward of these bands the seasonal range in SST again decreases toward the data void areas at latitudes greater than 50°–55°. A little reflection reveals that the seasonal range in surface-water temperature must vanish at the summer ice boundary, since at each point on, and poleward, of this boundary the surface water is constrained to remain at the freezing point of the sea ice with which it is in contact throughout the year. Boundary layer air blowing off the continents is soon brought close to equilibrium with the SST, so is constrained to follow the seasonal range in SST far from land or sea ice. This accounts for the bands of minimum seasonal range of surface air temperature shown on Figure 7-2 near 50°–55°.

Figure 7-4 shows another example of oceanic control of climate. This is a map of the vector standard deviation of the 500-mb wind in winter. Kinetic energy generation and dissipation are roughly proportional to the cube of this quantity (Ellsaesser 1969). The centers of maximum over the oceans are indicative of centers of maximum transformation of potential to kinetic energy by cyclogenesis. Cyclogenesis is favored in these areas by the low frictional drag of the ocean surface, by strong thermal gradients developing along the downwind edge of nontropical continents and by the heat and moisture available from the warm western boundary currents of the oceans.

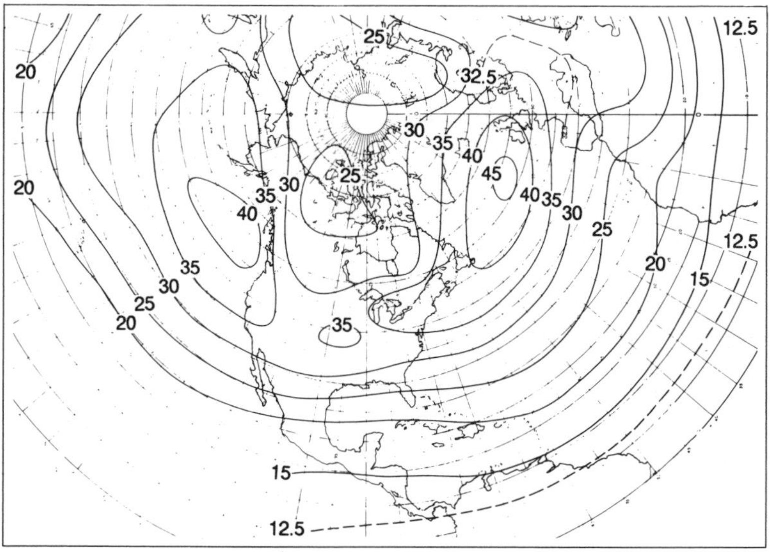

Figure 7-4: Vector standard deviation of the 500-mb wind [knots] in winter [Dec-Jan-Feb] (adapted from Crutcher 1959).

Operating Modes of Thermoregulatory Control

The low diurnal and seasonal range of SST gives evidence of the strong thermoregulatory control exerted by the oceans on terrestrial climate. This thermoregulatory control is quite complex and includes the capability, through atmosphere-ocean interaction, of changing the timing, locations, and modes of energy release to the atmosphere and transfers from one part of the atmosphere to another.

Thermal Reservoir Modes

A large degree of thermoregulatory control is provided simply by the large heat capacity of the mixed layer of the ocean in thermal contact with the atmosphere. This layer has an average thickness of about 70 m. Seventy meters of water has almost 30 times the heat capacity of the atmospheric column above it. At the average rate of absorption of solar energy at the earth's surface it would take almost 20 days to receive enough energy to warm such a layer 1°C. The oceans provide even larger thermal reservoirs against cooling in high latitudes and warming in low latitudes. Near the poles ocean surface cooling is reduced first by the release of latent heat through the freezing of sea water. Then, once an ice cover forms, evaporation is greatly reduced and heat lost is reduced by the low thermal conductivity of the ice which allows the upper surface of the ice to cool significantly below the temperature of the water below and thus to reduce the rate of loss of radiative energy to the overlying atmosphere and to space. As the SST increases in lower latitudes, a larger and larger fraction of the absorbed radiation (both solar and back IR from the atmosphere) is used to evaporate water rather than to raise its temperature. Under normally observed conditions, at ocean surface temperatures above .30°C, evaporation occurs at such a rate that it begins to draw sensible heat out of the atmosphere. (Ellsaesser 1984).

The Conveyer Belt Mode

Radiant energy, both solar and back IR from the atmosphere, absorbed by the mixed layer of the ocean, is transported elsewhere by the atmospherically driven ocean currents generally poleward and toward the eastern boundary of the ocean—before the energy is released back to the atmosphere. This effect accounts for the mild climate of the northeastern North Atlantic, for example. This mode is presumably controlled by the strength, scale, and constancy of the general circulation of the atmosphere. Similar but weaker cold currents occur along the eastern boundaries of the oceans.

The ITCZ-Hadley Cell Mode

Boundary layer air, warmed and moistened by contact with the tropical oceans, is swept by the trade winds into narrow bands of deep convection paralleling the equator, the so-called Intertropical Convergence Zones (ITCZ). Here both sensible and latent energy are quickly removed from the surface, carried up through the moist layer and spread laterally above most of the greenhouse effect of atmospheric water vapor, where the energy can more readily be reradiated to space. The two-dimensional Hadley circulation, thermally driven by the ITCZ convection, carries potential energy poleward where it is converted to sensible heat by later subsidence. This serves several thermoregulatory functions: it removes energy from the surface in the tropics at a much lower temperature than would be required to eject it radiatively; it transports heat from low to high latitudes; and over the tropics it significantly reduces the effectiveness of our principal greenhouse gas, water vapor. It reduces the water vapor greenhouse effect in two ways; it first circumvents it by physically transporting sensible and latent energy up through, and spreading it horizontally above, the moist layer; and second, it reduces the greenhouse effect directly by thinning the moist layer by the large scale subsidence which completes the downdraft legs of the Hadley circulation. This thermoregulatory mode is presumably controlled, not by the strength per se, but by the rate of convergence of the two trade-wind systems. Due to the rapid increase of water-vapor tension with temperature, it must also depend on tropical ocean-surface temperature. However, this effect may be inverse, since the greater the energy density of the rising currents, the smaller the volume required to remove energy from the surface at the constant rate at which it is received from the sun.

The Tropical Cyclone Mode

In this mode the warm, moist boundary air over the tropical oceans is swept into converging spiral bands of convection which can form only over the low-friction surface of the oceans, and displaced more than 5° latitude from the equator. The rapid transfer of latent and sensible heat through, and its spreading above, the moist layer occurs much the same as in ITCZ convection. However, the surrounding subsidence lacks zonal symmetry and presumably does not contribute to the Hadley circulation. On the other hand, since most tropical cyclones recurve into the westerlies, each carries a large pulse of both sensible and latent heat into higher latitudes. Thus, tropical cyclones accomplish all the same thermoregulatory actions as the Hadley circulation. In addition, they stir the mixed layer of the ocean, mixing heat down into the thermocline and bringing cooler water to the surface. This mode is presumably controlled by the degree to which the ocean surface temperature exceeds the 27°C threshold for tropical cyclone formation, and the depth, and the absence of vertical shear in the convectively unstable trade-wind currents.

The Thermohaline Circulation Modes

While the thermohaline circulation is planetary in scale, it is useful to think of it as having two distinct circulation cells; one which has a more-or-less globally uniform upwelling, and a separate one in which the upwelling is restricted to the areas of recognized surface upwelling. In both cases the downwelling (or bottom-water formation) occurs where there is rapid cooling of saline surface water and/or where dense water is produced when salt is forced out of newly formed sea ice in the North Atlantic and around Antarctica.

In the Uniform Thermohaline Mode the entire oceanic volume is filled by dense cold water sinking to the bottom near the winter poles. As newer bottom water is added, it forces the older water uniformly upward; and, where this meets heat diffusing down from the sun-warmed surface-mixed layer, creates the strong vertical temperature gradient identified as the thermocline. The loop of course is closed by surface flows of warm water toward the winter poles. This mode acts to transfer cold water from high to low and warm water from low to high latitudes and thus to moderate extremes of cold in high latitudes and heat in low latitudes. It is controlled by the rate of formation of bottom water which in turn would appear to be related to the volume of sea ice formed each year.

The Local Thermohaline Mode accomplishes the same role,

except that the cold water is identifiable where it returns to the surface in lower latitudes in favored locations recognized as areas of surface upwelling. As an example of this mode we will consider only the upwelling along the equator in the eastern Pacific and down along the coast of South America, the El Niño area. The El Niño phenomenon is part of the overall El Niño-Southern Oscillation event. The east-west seesaw of surface pressure in the equatorial and southern Pacific has been recognized since 1897 (Rasmussen and Carpenter 1982); but it was Bjerknes (1966) who linked it with the interannual SST fluctuations of the El Niño. The austral summer maximum in SST at Puerto Chicama, Peru rises above its normal maximum of I9°C by 1 to 4.5°C two or three consecutive years (Wyrtki 1975). In the usual case of two years, one of the warmings predominates, and the second occurs two to three months earlier than usual. However, some authors have reported periods of one and two years between El Niños, indicating nearly equivalent warmings in consecutive or alternate years of the cycle.

SST warmings extending northward from Peru to the equator and then westward to the dateline are now considered a more significant aspect of the El Niño. In this area, SST is normally cooled by upwelling by up to 6°C below that normally found at corresponding latitudes. Among other effects, this provides a thermal reservoir capable of accepting and storing a large amount of solar radiation—i.e., received solar radiation is converted into thermal energy remaining in the mixed layer, rather than being converted into latent heat that is released into the overlying atmosphere, as is done where the SST is at its normal equatorial value (Csanady 1984). This heat can then be carried in the surface-ocean currents to be released months to years later and thousands of kilometers from the point at which received. Occurrence of the El Niño interrupts this mode and causes the received solar energy to be returned with little delay to the overlying atmosphere, primarily as latent heat of water vapor (Ellsaesser 1984; Csanady 1984). This appears to enter and strengthen the Hadley circulation. That is, a pseudo-steady state is interrupted by a circulation mode which for 12–18 months accelerates the release of sensible heat over that portion of the atmosphere affected by the Hadley circulation originating from the El Niño area. However, this accelerated release of energy is largely injected above the greenhouse effect of water vapor where it can easily be radiated to space; and it is followed by periods of decelerated release, as solar energy is again stored in cold-surface water as the normal upwelling is renewed.

Remember that the solar energy that would have normally been stored in the upwelling cold water during the time of the El Niño was promptly lost from the ocean and is no longer available for return to the atmosphere during this part of the cycle. This seems to fit the studies of Angell and Korshover (1978a,b, 1983) which detect apparent warm pulses followed by cool pulses emanating from the El Niño area and propagating poleward and upward throughout most of the troposphere and stratosphere. Beyond the area of the SST anomaly itself, the cool pulses are the more apparent. Note that it appears highly possible that such El Niño cooling pulses have in the past been mistakenly attributed to the effect of stratospheric clouds created by strong volcanic eruptions (Ellsaesser 1983). The El Niño years since 1868 cited by Quinn *et al.* (1978) show a high degree of overlap with volcanic eruptions listed by Simkin *et al.* (1981).

This local thermohaline mode is presumably controlled by the strength of the surface winds driving the oceanic upwelling in the regions in question. For the El Niño, the strength of the southeast trades in the South Pacific would appear to be dominant. The CLIMAP (1976, 1981) studies tend to confirm this since they found SST cooling in the area significantly more extensive 18,000 BP when the zonal winds in the atmosphere were presumably stronger than now.

Potential Oceanic Climatogenesis

A global map of average January SST isotherms is shown in Figure 7-5. Note that in most areas these isotherms are nearly parallel to latitude circles. This is the pattern to be expected if SST were determined by processes other than advection under a pseudo-zonally uniform atmosphere. When the SST isolines depart from this pattern, we can be sure that oceanic advection of some type is involved; and since oceanic currents are driven

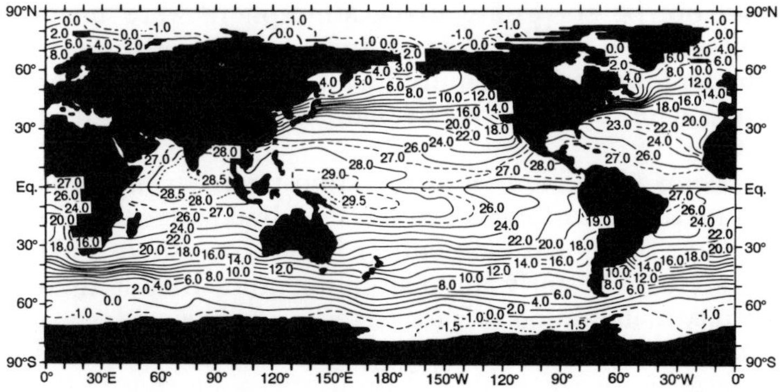

Figure 7-5: Global map of average SST isotherms for the month of January [°C] (from Levitus 1982).

primarily by atmospheric winds we can be equally certain that they are determined by some type of atmosphere-oceanic interaction. Since even a slight change in one partner of such interactions can lead to large changes before new equilibria are established, each area in which SST isotherms depart significantly from parallel east-west lines should be regarded as an area of potential climatogenesis. The two regions of Figure 7-5 showing the most marked departures from zonal SST isolines are the North Atlantic and the eastern South Pacific. Both are areas already diagnosed as having significant climatogenetic atmosphere-oceanic interaction. The El Niño-Southern Oscillation of the tropical Pacific has already been mentioned but it warrants further speculation.

It is well known that the atmosphere gains angular momentum from the nongaseous earth wherever there are easterly winds at the surface and returns it wherever there are surface westerlies. Also, the globally averaged angular momentum of the atmosphere undergoes an annual cycle with a maximum of westerly angular momentum in the boreal winter and a minimum in the austral winter (Rosen and Salstein 1983), due to domination by the seasonal cycle in winds of the NH. Due to the many other physical constraints on the atmosphere, it would not be surprising if the atmosphere were unable to maintain at all times the areas and strengths of surface easterlies and westerlies required to keep angular momentum flowing at just the right rate to follow its seasonal cycle in perfect "equilibrium."

It seems plausible that as the atmosphere strengthens and expands the area of surface easterlies to build up to the January maximum of angular momentum, it could overshoot and build up so much westerly angular momentum that it then has difficulty maintaining surface easterlies. As the westerly angular momentum is moved into higher latitudes and altitudes and the easterlies weaken, they drop to the point that the trade-wind-driven equatorial upwelling in the eastern Pacific cannot be maintained. Without the westward surface drag and resultant Coriolis-imposed divergence at the surface, both solar heating and hydrostatic readjustment within the ocean will cause the surface water to warm. Because it is the eastward component of the trades that is reduced—the equatorward component is actually increased (Quiroz 1983)—the warm SST leads to enhanced penetrative convection into the upper atmosphere, carrying air with little or no easterly component and, in the western Pacific, actual westerly components (Pazan and Meyers 1982). This represents a substantial addition of westerly momentum to the upper atmosphere compared to the air usually ascending in tropical convection. Here is a possible positive feedback mechanism, by which an atmosphere, with already excessive westerly momentum, develops an additional mechanism for generating more. Of course there remains the question as to whether the enhanced convection and Hadley circulation generate as much westerly momentum as would have the normal easterlies, whose weakening or absence brought the former into being. Suggestive confirmation is indicated by the tendency of the El Niño, once set in motion, to continue through at least two austral summers, and for the peak SST anomaly to be accompanied by a peak positive anomaly in the westerly angular momentum of the atmosphere (Stefanik 1982; Rosen *et al.*, 1984). Thus, The El Niño-Southern Oscillation appears to be an amplification of the normal annual cycle of angular momentum with a positive feedback mechanism providing an additional source of westerly angular momentum peaking in the austral summer. It appears to be initiated, or at least preceded, by a year or more of stronger than normal easterly trades giving higher sea level in the western Pacific and cooler SSTs due to stronger upwelling (Wyrtki 1975). This should show up as a negative anomaly in westerly angular momentum of the atmosphere and in turn lead to an above-normal rate of gain of westerly angular momentum from the earth. What terminates the self-amplifying cycle isn't clear, but the available data suggest two possibilities. First, in most El Niño for which we have data, the second amplified austral summer warming of SST off Peru occurs one to three months earlier than normal. This could allow the normal processes which build the austral summer southeast trades of the South Pacific to redevelop normally to bring the SSTs back to normal through upwelling. Second, the peak SST anomalies of the El Niño, and particularly that of the unusual El Niño of 1982–83, were accompanied by strong positive anomalies in westerly angular momentum of the atmosphere (Stefanick 1982; Rosen *et al.* 1984). Once this works its way back to the surface, frictional drag at the earth's surface will also be above normal and could bring the atmosphere back to its normal "equilibrium" position which again allows the easterly trades to develop normally and cool the SST by renewed upwelling. Atmosphere-ocean interactions in the North Atlantic appear both more probable and of more far-reaching consequences. We have heard of the North Atlantic seesaw since the time of Walker (1924); but this does not appear to be a very large perturbation. Of far greater consequences were the oscillations known as the Medieval Little Optimum and Little Ice Age, leading to the colonization of Greenland and its later abandonment, and the dramatic warming of the Arctic and northern North Atlantic from 1918 to 1938 known earlier as The Arctic Warming. These remain unexplained but are reasonable expectations for a slight shift in the North Atlantic polar front, the region of isotherm packing in the eastern North Atlantic in Figure 7-5.

Better documented are the shifts in this front since the peak of the last glacial, 18,000 BP. Figure 7-6 shows the most recent

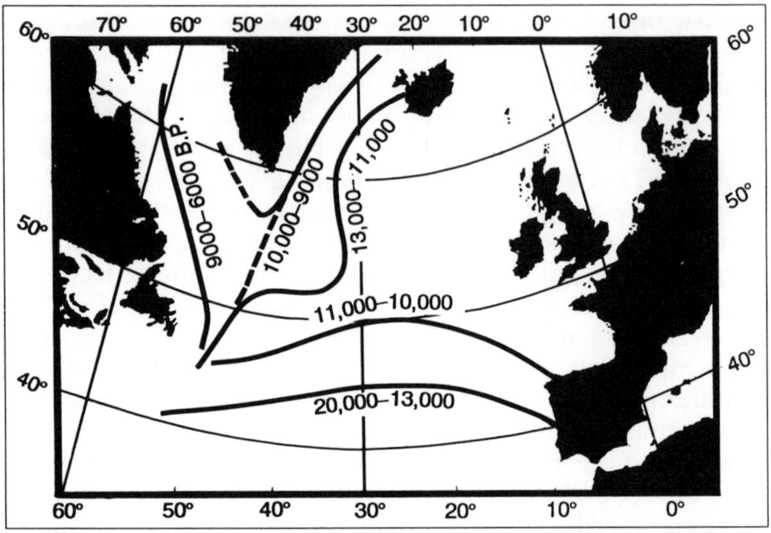

Figure 7-6: Locations of the polar front of the North Atlantic at various times during the most recent deglaciation as determined from ocean sediment cores (adapted from Ruddiman and McIntyre 1981).

positions as determined by Ruddiman and McIntyre (1981) from cores of sediment taken from the bottom of the North Atlantic. According to these studies, the North Atlantic polar front swung like a gate hinged southeast of Newfoundland. Also, the retreat from the southernmost position at the peak of the last glacial was not monotonic; from 13,000 to 11,000 BP the eastern end of the front readvanced thousands of kilometers to the south and then retreated again between 10,000 and 9,000 BP. This period of glacial readvance is well documented as the Younger Dryas cold period of northwestern Europe and Scandinavia (Ruddiman and McIntyre 1981).

If such swings of the North Atlantic polar front are possible in as short a period as 1,000 to 2,000 years, then smaller swings may account for the dramatic climate changes in this area now called the Medieval Little Optimum, The Little Ice Age, and The Arctic Warming. It is quite reasonable to expect that even slight shifts in the position of the North Atlantic polar front of the types shown in Figure 7-6 would lead to significant changes in mean annual temperatures over large areas of the North Atlantic, Eurasia, and even North America. From this and the paucity of evidence of any significant change in the volume of Antarctic glaciers (Burckle *et al.* 1982), it also appears plausible that the entire glacial-interglacial cycle could have occurred simply as a result of changes in the position of the North Atlantic polar front. What is not so obvious, of course, is whether changes in the polar-front position were the cause, or even preceded, the climatic changes. Ruddiman and McIntyre (1981) concluded that the bulk of the melt water from the Laurentide deglaciation occurred prior to 12,000 BP and thus before the final retreat of the polar front across the North Atlantic. A fundamental approach would appear to be to try to understand what physical processes cause the packed isotherms off Nova Scotia in Figure 7-5 to bend sharply left into the Labrador Sea. The SST isotherms of Figure 7-5 also show a large area of departure from an east-west orientation in the South Atlantic, suggesting the potential for interactive climatogenesis there as well. The fact that no significant climatic fluctuations have been reported for this area may be due simply to insufficient observational data or it might be due to the fact that the relatively narrow width of the South Atlantic does not allow sufficient variation in position or intensity of the anticyclone trapped there.

Summary

The oceans constitute a robust and multimodal thermoregulator of planetary surface temperature. In addition to the obvious thermal flywheel of the mixed layer averaging about 70 m in depth:

1. The latent heat of evaporation limits tropical temperature;
2. Both the latent heat of freezing and the insulation effect of sea ice limit planetary energy loss in high latitudes;
3. Both wind driven and thermohaline circulations transport warm water from low to high and cold water from high to low latitudes.

Both the low-frictional drag of the ocean surface and the inexhaustible supply of water for evaporation support the ITCZ-Hadley circulation and tropical cyclones which efficiently circumvent over the tropics our principal greenhouse gas, water vapor, by removing energy from the surface in low latitudes, convecting it through and spreading it horizontally above the moist layer for easier reradiation to space. In addition, these circulations transport energy to higher latitudes and directly reduce the greenhouse effect of water vapor by the drying effect of the broadscale subsidence which completes the downward legs of these convectively driven circulation cells. It is pointed out that departures of SST isotherms from parallel east-west lines show evidence of atmospheric-oceanic interactive transport and thus indicate areas of potential climatogenesis, since a slight perturbation can lead to large changes before new equilibria are established. The North Atlantic and the eastern tropical Pacific are the most outstanding areas in which this is observed. Important climatic fluctuations have been observed in both areas: El Niño in the Pacific and the Medieval Little Optimum, Little Ice Age, and The Arctic Warming of this century in the North Atlantic. Speculations are given as to the causes of these climatic fluctuations and the glacial-interglacial cycle.

Acknowledgments

This work was performed under the auspices of the Carbon Dioxide Research Division of the Office of Energy Research, US Department of Energy by the Lawrence Livermore National Laboratory, Livermore, California under Contract No. W-7405-Eng-48.

References

Angell, J. and J. Korshover. 1978. "Estimate of global temperature variations in the 100-30 mb layer between 1958 and 1977." *Monthly Weather Review* 106: 1422–1432.

______. 1978. "Global temperature variation, surface-100 mb: an update into 1977." *Monthly Weather Review* 106: 755–770.

______. 1983. "Global temperature variations in the troposphere and stratosphere, 1958–1982." *Monthly Weather Review* 111: 901–921.

Bjerknes, J. 1961. "El Niño study based on analyses of ocean surface temperatures, 1935–1957." *Bulletin of the Inter-American Tropical Tuna Commission* 5: 217–303.

______. 1966. "A possible response of the atmospheric Hadley circulation to equatorial anomalies of ocean temperature." *Tellus* 18: 820–829.

Burckle, L., D. Robinson and D. Cooke. 1982. "Reappraisal of sea-ice distribution in Atlantic and Pacific sectors of the southern ocean at 18,000 years BP." *Nature* 299: 435–437.

CLIMAP Project Members. 1976. "The surface of the ice-age earth." *Science* 191: 1131–1137.

______. 1981. "Seasonal reconstructions of the earth's surface at the last glacial maximum." *Geological Society of American Map and Chart Series* Number 36.

Crutcher, H. 1959. "Upper wind statistics charts of the northern hemisphere." NAVAER 50-IC-535, Volume 1. Ashville: Office of the Chief of Naval Operations.

Csanady, G. 1984. "Warm water mass formation." *Journal of Physical Oceanography* 14: 264–275.

Ellsaesser, H. 1969. "A climatology of epsilon (atmospheric dissipation)." *Monthly Weather Review* 97: 431–434.

______. 1983. "Isolating the climatogenic effects of volcanoes." *Lawrence Livermore National Laboratory Report* UCRL-89I6I. Livermore.

______. 1984. "The climatic effect of CO_2: a different view." *Atmospheric Environment* 18: 431–434.

______. 1989. "A different view of the climatic effects of CO_2—updated." *Atmosfera* (in press).

Levitus, S. 1982. "Climatologic atlas of the world ocean." *NOAA Professional Paper* 13, United States Government Printing Office, Washington, D.C.

Luther, D., D. Harrison and R. Know. 1983. "Zonal winds in the central equatorial Pacific and El Niño." *Science* 222: 327–330.

Monin, A. 1975. "The role of the oceans in climatic models." The Physical Basis of Climate and Climate modeling. GARP Publications Number 16: 201–205.

Panfilova, S. 1972. "Seasonal surface water temperature variations in the world ocean." *Oceonologia*. Union of Soviet Socialist Republic Academy of Science Oceanology 12: 333–344.

Pazan, S. and Meyers, G. 1982. "Interannual fluctuations of the tropical Pacific wind field and the southern oscillation." *Monthly Weather Review* 110: 587–600.

Quinn, W., D. Zopf, K. Short, and R. Kuo. 1978."Historical trends and statistics of the southern oscillation, El Niño and Indonesian droughts." *Fishery Bulletin* 76: 663–678.

Quiroz, R. I983. "The climate of the El Niño, winter of 1982–1983: a season of extraordinary climatic anomalies." *Monthly Weather Review* III: 1685–1706.

Rasmusson, E. and T. Carpenter. 1982. "Variations in tropical sea surface temperature and surface wind fields associated with the southern oscillation/El Niño." *Monthly Weather Review* 110: 354–384.

Rosen, R. and D. Salstein. 1983. "Variations in atmospheric angular momentum on global and regional scales and the length of day." *Journal of Geophysical Research* 88: 5451–5470.

Ruddiman, W. and A. McIntyre. 1981. "The North Atlantic ocean during the last deglaciation." *Palaeogeography Palaeoclimatology Palaeoecology* 35: 145–214.

Simkin, T., L. Seibert, L. McClelland, D. Bridge, C. Newhall and J. Latter. 1981. *Volcanoes of the world*. Stroudburg, PA.: Hutchinson Ross.

Stefanick, M. 1982. "Interannual atmospheric angular momentum variability 1963–1973 and the southern oscillation." *Journal of Geophysical Research* 87: 428–432.

Stephens, G., G. Campbell, and T. Vonder Haar. I98I. "Earth radiation budgets." *Journal of Geophysical Research* 86: 9739–9760.

Walker, G. 1924. "World Weather IX." *Memoirs Indian Meteorological Department* 24: 275–332.

Wyrtki, K. 1975. "El Niño, the dynamic response of the equatorial Pacific ocean to atmospheric forcing." *Journal of Physical Oceanography* 5: 572–584.

EIGHT

SIMPLE And COMPLEX OCEANIC INFLUENCES On CLIMATE

A COMMENTARY

Helmut E. Landsberg

The ocean is the great memory and control of terrestrial climate. It both reflects and influences climatic fluctuations. This is manifested by polar ice sheets and by sea-level changes. These two are intimately related and hence deserve some special attention. A distinguished ocean scientist put it this way (Revelle 1980):

> Sea ice variation is one of the strongest signals of variations in climate, both in the ocean and the atmosphere, because a very slight variation in meridional heat transport from south to north in the polar regions causes variations in the extent of sea ice and there is a positive feedback relationship. If the sea ice extends, the albedo increases, less radiation is received, the air and the water are cooled and therefore the sea ice extends further.

There is little question that sea ice is a major factor in the earth's albedo, together with cloud cover, both strongly under oceanic control—and both poorly represented in models. Russian determinations of albedo of Arctic sea ice have shown notable variations with latitude, ranging by 23% from the pole to the southern edge of the ice (Yefimova 1980). The importance of this portion of the earth's albedo has been stressed by Henderson and Hughes (1982). Only in recent years have satellites provided adequate global coverage to assess their fluctuations. A decade or two is a short time interval, climatically speaking. So far these observations show only the strong climatic "noise" but no changes, as reported at the 1984 COSPAR meeting, for both polar areas (Anderson *et al.* 1984, Cavalieri and Zwally 1984). But present satellite data yield only areal extent of sea ice and albedo data. Thickness data, which are equally important, are restricted to sporadic observations.

One cannot stress too much the complexity of the interactions of the wind field, radiative components, heat transport on sea-surface temperatures and sea ice. The work of Reiter (1980) in the North Pacific demonstrates this, and his analysis of 15 years of data shows the considerable variability of the controlling diabatic forcing functions. For the Atlantic Ocean from 70N to 20S latitude, Lamb (1981) has presented a table for the uncertainties in estimates of the annual meridianal heat transport that in the decisive tropical and subtropical latitudes of the northern hemisphere runs between about 20 and 40% of the average. The interannual variation can be gauged from Bunker's (1980) time series for the Atlantic. All this is, of course, reflected in the sea-surface temperature data, covering 120 years in parts of the Atlantic. And according to Cayan (1980), sea-surface temperatures and surface-air temperatures show approximately the same variance. All this, and uncertain time scales of the deep-ocean circulations (Watts and Hayder 1983), bode ill for reliance on any of the present models for long-term climatic predictions. Smagorinsky (1983) stated it quite succinctly:

> However, the mechanistic links are not well enough understood for a physically-based modelling approach which can deal deterministically with the prediction problem of month-to-month, season-to-season, and year-to-year anomalies. There are still fundamental observational facts to be gotten, particularly in the ocean.

The problems have been very extensively discussed, but progress is likely to be slow. In the meantime, semi-empirically and statistically based forecasts for months or seasons are the best available now (Namias and Cayan 1981). Teleconnections still seem to offer some reasonable prospects for these short-term predictions. The venerable Southern Oscillation (Walker 1928) and the more recent studies of El Niño seem to bear this out; this seems to be especially true for the Asiatic monsoon areas (Joseph 1983; Wang 1984).

The question of sea-level changes has also been extensively bandied about as an index of climatic change. It seems necessary to scrutinize it closely, especially since the public has been flooded with estimates of sea-level rises expected as results of anthropogenic increases in atmospheric carbon dioxide. Just what are the facts? There is reasonable agreement that during the last century, starting in 1880, a rise in sea level of 10 to 12 cm has taken place (Gornitz *et al.* 1982). This is based on measurements of tide gauges at coastal stations on various coast lines. There is some spread in the indications which introduces some uncertainty about the actual value. This trend is apparently composed of two components. The first is the thermal expansion of the sea water due to the simultaneous global temperature rise of about 0.5°C. The other is attributed to the melting of sea ice and runoff from glaciated continental regions. It is this latter component that has been indicted as the sign of climatic change, possibly of anthropogenic origin.

There have been extensive reviews of the history of sea-level changes as the result of deglaciation after the last ice age. These have been substantial and amount to several decameters. They certainly reflect the notable global climatic change of 5° to 7°C (Allison 1981). There have been some speculations that the current trend of sea level includes a signal of the warming attributed by many to rising CO_2 (Etkins and Epstein 1982). While warnings of dire consequences if CO_2 continues to rise have been voiced, recently there have been more sober appraisals and the evil day of CO_2-doubling has been postponed by decades far into the next century. There have also been new appraisals of the sea-level rise which looked at biases in the data and question the facile explanations offered for the small rise

(Barnett 1983). Monitoring sea level will, of course, remain an important task. It will stay in the inventory of climatic indices, but one can hope that the coastal tide gauges will be superseded by geodetic satellite measurements.

From the human point of view, far more acute than long-term climatic changes are the tropical storms and their frequency, which show large variations from year to year. Their occurrence is closely tied to the features of the general circulation (Ding and Reiter 1983). Should there be a global temperature rise, their numbers will increase. The reason for this is the increase in water vapor in the atmosphere that is seasonally adjusted by the tropical storms (Landsberg 1960). They are at present principally a feature of Northern Hemisphere weather with the average annual number about 50. In the North Atlantic about six per year were observed in the mean of the last half century. Over the eastern North Pacific 15, and over the western North Pacific 29 per year are the averages. These tropical storms, through their copious rainfalls reduce the atmospheric water vapor, which rises during the northern summer to its winter values. The hemispheric difference in precipitable water, evaporated from the ocean, is about 15 mm. The argument for assigning the balancing act to tropical storms is the fact that they occur mostly in late summer and autumn. That is also the season for maximum rainfall on the coasts affected by the storms. Thus, for example, 731 mm of rain falls in Tokyo from July to October or 47% of the annual average precipitation of 1,563 mm. In Miami the July to October rainfall is 53% of the annual total of 1,520 mm. A simple calculation based on average size, path length, and rain amount of tropical storms, and the excess of precipitation over evaporation in the affected areas, shows that they eliminate about 70% of the summer water-vapor surplus. Actually in many regions this rainfall from the ocean-borne storms is a benefit for both water supplies and vegetation. Yet on the other hand these same storms are one of the major meteorological menaces. They cause floods, wipe out coastal communities by accompanying storm surges and destructive gales.

In most countries affected by tropical storms timely weather warnings, aided greatly in recent years by satellite observations, have reduced the death toll. But the history is grim. In the US, the Galveston disaster of September 1900, with over 6,000 deaths, has not been repeated. But the catastrophe in Bangladesh of November 1970, when a Bay of Bengal tropical storm killed at least 50,000 persons, is extremely recent. The year 1974 saw 3,800 Hondurans wiped out in September. That the southern hemisphere is not immune was shown by the fate of Darwin, Australia, in December of that year. A tropical storm left the town in shambles and required evacuation of 10,000 people. Short-range weather forecasting can nowadays predict tropical storms with considerable precision, but in many areas of the world communications for warnings are still inadequate. Even if warnings reach the people, timely evacuation may fail. Evacuation problems have become acutely important with the rapid increase of offshore platforms for fossil-fuel recovery.

Manifestly much of the risk could be avoided by improved land-use decisions. Also prevalent structural damage could be materially reduced by use of the existing climatological information. High winds and wind-driven water are the main hazards along the shores afflicted by tropical storms. Dangers to structures increase exponentially with increasing peak gusts. In hurricanes and typhoons these can reach 210 km hr^{-1} (130 mi hr^{-1}). It is quite possible to predict on a probabilistic basis the occurrence of extreme wind speeds. This is, based on past observations fitted by a suitable statistical distribution for extreme values, a forecast without date. It indicates what the probable highest wind speed will be once in 50 or 100 years. Such values can then be incorporated into building codes and designs. Similarly, the characteristics of past tropical storms passing near or crossing the shore line can be used to estimate the highest storm surge to be expected. This information can be used to plan further land use in coastal areas and to map evacuation routes for existing settlements.

In all, the ocean remains a benign influence on climate, its fluctuations, and its potential changes. The existing climatological knowledge should be used to moderate its menaces, and oceanic research should replace ignorance by knowledge.

References

Allison, I., editor, 1981. "Sea level, ice and climatic change," International Association of Hydrological Sciences, Publication number 134. *Proceedings of Canberra Symposium,* December, 1979: 471.

Anderson, M., R. Crane, and R. Barry. 1984. "Characteristics of Arctic Ocean ice determined from SMMR data for 1979." *Committee on Space Research, Twenty Fifth Meeting, Graz,* June–July, 1984, Abstracts, 92.

Barnett, T. 1983. "Recent changes in sea level and their possible causes." *Climate Change* 5: 15–38.

Bunker, A. 1980. "Trends of variables and energy fluxes over the Atlantic Ocean from 1948–1972." *Mon. Wea. Rev.* 108: 720–732.

Cavalieri, D. and H. Zwally. 1984. "Satellite observations of sea ice." *Committee on Space Research, Twenty Fifth Meeting, Graz,* June 25–July 7, 1984, Abstracts, 91.

Cayan, D. 1980. "Large-scale relationships between sea-surface temperature and surface air temperature." *Mon. Wea. Rev.* 108: 1293–1301.

Ding, Y. and E. Reiter. 1983. "Large-scale hemispheric teleconnections with the frequency of tropical cyclone formation over the Northwest Pacific and North Atlantic Oceans." *Arch. Met. Geoph. Biocl.* Ser. A. 32: 311–337.

Etkins, R., and E. Epstein. 1982. "The rise of global mean sea level as an indication of climatic change." *Science* 215: 287–289.

Gornitz, V., S. Lebedeff, and J. Hansen. 1982. "Global sea level trend in the past century." *Science* 215: 1611–1614.

Henderson, A. and N. Hughes. 1982. "Albedo and its importance in climate theory." *Progress in Physical Geograph* 6: 1–44.

Joseph, P. 1983. *Inter-annual variability of Indian summer monsoon rainfall.* University of Poona Ph.D dissertation, Pune (India), Typescript p. 106 and charts.

Lamb, P. 1981. "Estimate of annual variation of Atlantic heat transport." *Nature* 290: 766–768.

Landsberg, H. 1960. "Do tropical storms play a role in the water balance of the northern hemisphere?" *Journal of Geophysical Research* 65: 1305–1307.

Namias, J. and D. Cayan. 1981. "Large-scale air-sea interaction and short-period climatic fluctuations." *Science* 214: 869–876.

Reiter, E. 1980. Air-sea interactions and climatic variations. *Das Klima-Analysen und-Modelle, Geschichte und Zukunft*. Edited by Oeschger, H., B. Messerli and M. Soilar. Berlin: Springer-Verlag, 275–285.

Revelle, R. 1980. "Climate and the Oceans." *EDIS* 11: 3–8.

Smagorinsky, J. 1983. "The problem of climate and climate variations, World Meteorological Organization." *World Climate Program* 72: 14.

Walker, G. 1928. "World Weather." *Qu. J. Roy. Meteorol. Soc.* 54: 79–87.

Wang, S. 1984. "El Niño and summer temperatures in north-east China, 1860–1980." *Tropical Ocean-Atmosphere Newsletter*. Seattle: University of Washington, number 25: 4.

Watts, R. and M. Hayden. 1983. "Climatic fluctuations due to deep ocean circulation." *Science* 219: 187–188.

Yefimova, N. 1980. "Effects of change in albedo of earth's surface on the earth's thermal regime" (translated title). *Meteorologiya i Gidrologiya* 7: 50–56.

PART TWO:

EXPLORATION TECHNOLOGY

NINE

The ROLE Of SATELLITES In OCEAN SCIENCE And TECHNOLOGY

Robert B. Abel

An Elementary Overview

To someone whose days as an active seagoing oceanographer ended a couple of decades ago, recent developments in the theory and practice of oceanography make Rip Van Winkle's feat seem like a catnap. This is particularly true with respect to the emergence of satellites as integral tools to the science.

My personal introduction to the concept of satellite use was at a lecture given in Washington about three decades ago (before *Sputnik*) on the subject of "A Minimal Orbital Unmanned Satellite of Earth," i.e., Project MOUSE. The lecture was given by an articulate—if somewhat way-out—professor from the University of Maryland named S. Fred Singer. Although he was technologically miles ahead of his audience, the nature and technique of his delivery sparked an intensive, almost frenzied, audience response. And America's satellite program escalated at a rate exceeding the dreams of even its most dedicated proponents.

Any overview of satellite oceanography confronts the problem of how to report the state-of-the-art. This relates not only to the pace of developments within a given technology, but to the proliferation of the technologies themselves, as the vista of satellite utilization expands at a rate almost as great as the vehicles themselves. Accordingly, this article will be categorized as much by mission as technology. It will include navigation technology, communications, oceanographic observations, and a discussion of a special application in the interests of inter-country cooperation. This will focus on the implications of satellite oceanography for human affairs.

Navigation Technology

Perhaps the development of navigation technology was inevitable as an initial, obvious utilization of satellites. In any case, it was certainly fortuitous as oceanographic observational techniques became so highly refined that minute differences in characteristics of a given mass of ocean water became evident over distances of meters as opposed to hundreds of kilometers in an earlier generation of oceanographic field activity. In the early days of shipboard oceanography, positioning at sea within a mile or two was quite permissible because the observable parameters themselves would not change measurably within this distance. Not so today. The Navstar Global Positioning System is as central a tool to the modern oceanographer as were the sextant and chronometer to his grandfather.

The TRANSIT satellite navigation system, in use for some time now, is reasonably accurate. It is limited however, to such times when a ship is in view of one of the satellites in the system. A system is projected for inauguration in 1991–1992 in which 24 satellites will provide global, continuous, and even more accurate ship positioning. It will be called, appropriately, the Global Positioning System (GPS) (Baker 1984).

The French ARGOS system provides ship-positioning information with an accuracy of about 1 km. An improved version is under design now.

Communications

The story of satellite communications is largely the same as that of navigation technology. Oceanographic observations are conducted today in a network theme in which ships and platforms at sea are tied to one another and with their respective shore installations. The installations in turn are closely linked (Heitman 1983).

The most important stimulus to maritime communications has probably been the offshore petroleum development industry. Undoubtedly, well over half of all of the traffic handled by maritime satellite communications systems is devoted to one or another feature of offshore exploration, drilling, and production.

Once upon a time the finances of international airlines were measurably affected by couriers zooming back and forth between some of the world's most exotic outposts and various Texas computer centers. When an exploration vessel working off South America can transmit to Texas in real time, utilizing satellites with 56 kilobit data transmission capabilities, the airlines must look for new sources of passenger traffic to replace those couriers. It is estimated that a new generation of satellites will come on line sometime around 1988 offering 1,500 kilobit service which would presumably totally replace all present forms of human conveyance.

After all, only a decade ago radio offered the only feasible method of communicating ship-to-shore. Commercial use was limited to high frequency and very high frequency, both limited in performance. High-frequency transmission is vulnerable to solar interference, and very high-frequency radio would be subject to range limitations. Further, the supply/demand problem has become increasingly serious as the need for bands has escalated, particularly in major shipping areas.

In 1976, the National Aeronautics and Space Administration (NASA) launched the first satellite (MERISAT) to handle marine traffic over the Atlantic Ocean. Within five years, over half of the seismic exploration vessels in the world were equipped with MERISAT terminals. Three years later, a number of nations got together to form the International Maritime Satellite Organization (INMARSAT). Now consisting of about forty country members, INMARSAT manages the global system developed by MERISAT. By the end of 1984, about two dozen earth stations will have been established handling about a half a dozen INMARSAT satellites. Newer satellites feature improved coverage and higher-channel capacity (Baker 1984). For instance, as seismic data are observed and recorded aboard ship, they are simultaneously being forwarded automatically to onshore terminals where the tapes are written out to duplicate their shipboard origination. The effectiveness of data rates, peak efficiency and relay times have escalated astronomically over the recent years.

In 1983 the system got a significant boost when the MARECKS A satellite was launched over the Atlantic. This satellite, developed by the European Space Agency, now covers the entire Gulf of Mexico. Operating telephone capacity was increased from eight to fifteen circuits, and the satellite apparently has a maximum capacity of about 40 coast-earth stations and about 2,000 ship-earth stations. MARECKS B, successor to MARECKS A, failed in launch owing to a misfire of the carrying rocket. It would have duplicated in the Pacific the increased capacity provided by MARECKS A in the Atlantic.

While the United State has, of course, enjoyed prominence in development of satellite communications systems for geophysics, the technology is hardly limited to the industrial nations; stations are also located, for instance, in Singapore, Kuwait, and Brazil. Terminals are manufactured in the United States, Norway, Germany, England, and France.

While discussion has necessarily emphasized geophysics, owing to the dominance of the petroleum industry overall, other uses are planned. The ship-earth stations now in use are called standard A systems. A second system, B, will use advanced communications techniques, including digital voice. This will reduce the antenna size. A third system, C, will use a still smaller antenna and will offer low-capacity services. These more recent types of stations would be planned mainly to accommodate other than geophysical exploration vessels, e.g., cargo carriers, pleasure craft, and fishing boats. Furthermore, they would cost much less than the standard A station. Most of these stations, however, will require a further generation of satellites, currently scheduled for initiation about 1988 (Lazanoff 1983).

In spite of the fast-moving technology overall, and increased participation by many countries and industries, the primary fear is that advancing recognition of the value and potential of these systems will accelerate demand faster than the supply can keep up. In order to upgrade planning to insure a balance between supply and demand, the United States representative to INMATSAT, COMSAT, has been collaborating with the National Ocean Industries Association. The latter group represents the most successful alliance of oceanographic and related enterprises, and most clearly and effectively represents American industry in the ocean. For instance, it is expected that the greater power and versatility of the newer satellites, e.g., INTELSAT IV and MARECKS, with design lifetimes of about seven years, will permit the phasing out of the initial MERISAT satellites. MARECKS, for instance, can provide more than 40 voice channels, nearly three times the capacity of MERISAT. Once all of the first generation satellites are in place, each of the three major oceans will be serviced by an operational satellite, plus a backup to assure the continuity of the service.

A spinoff of geophysical communications satellite technology relates to distress communication. Over the past two years, scientists and engineers from several nations have been testing a number of designs for emergency position indicating beacons. A number of systems have been developed, each one employing a different technique which would transmit distress signals to search and rescue teams via the aforementioned satellites. Since hundreds of lives are lost each year through accidents at sea, development of a satellite-operating distress signal will significantly influence the maritime and aquatic recreation industries (Heitman 1983).

In summary, diehards may bemoan the passing of signal flags, semaphores, and radios, but in the new era instantaneous transmission of observational data would advance oceanography and related sciences by light-years.

Oceanography

Oceanographic observational capabilities of satellites are breathtaking in scope, variety, and precision. In addition to their previously mentioned navigational and communications powers, satellites are capable of the following observations:

1. Large changes in salinity, occasioned through changes in reflectivity,
2. Temperature changes, through infrared imagery,
3. Currents, through high resolution photography,
4. Biological productivity, through the same technique, and
5. Movement of sediments by currents and their pollution effects.

SEASAT

Over a decade ago the LANDSAT satellite pioneered the era of observing the earth through satellites. It provided 18 pictures a day, i.e., every 103 minutes, in an 800 km polar orbit. Accordingly, every 18 days, the satellite passed over every location on earth at the same time of day. The successful LANDSAT, in part, inspired development of a later generation satellite, SEASAT, by the Jet Propulsion Laboratory of the National Aeronautics and Space Administration. The purpose of SEASAT was to assess the value of microwave sensors for remote sensing of the oceans and their major characteristics.

SEASAT was intended and planned as a conveyance for the following gear:

1. A radar altimeter capable of measuring wave height to within a meter as well as changes in the earth characteristics caused by gravity variations;
2. A microwave radar scatterometer;
3. A microwave radiometer;
4. A visible and infrared spectrum radiometer;
5. (and most intriguing) Synthetic Aperature Radar (SAR).

SEASAT was launched on June 27, 1978. While it lasted only 106 days, that period of time witnessed perfect operation and production of an enormous amount of data. In fact, it has been suggested that had the flow of data continued at its original rate, it would have exhausted every sensing, processing, and evaluating routine on the face of our planet. Unfortunately, only one ground station in America received the data telemetry. Since there was no onboard storage, the United States received data only when the satellite was on our side of our planet. Of course, none of this precluded the Soviets, British,

French, and West Germans receiving data of equal interest (Apel 1982).

One of SEASAT's outstanding achievements was elucidation of worldwide undersea features produced from the Satellite Radar Altimeter. In fact, this technique disclosed for the first time a discontinuous chain of sea mounts running southeast of the Tonga-Kermadec Trench, in the South Pacific. While large sea mounts were detected immediately from the incoming data, matched filtering, using automated techniques, later revealed even the small sea mounts, as well.

One of the most dramatic examples of SEASAT's power related to sea-surface observations from satellites, i.e., is measurement of ocean waves by Synthetic Aperture Radar (SAR). The theory and physics of this sophisticated apparatus are beyond the scope of this article; suffice it to say that it operates from a moving platform, i.e., an aircraft or satellite and obtains high resolution (on the order of tens of meters) radar images of the earth's surface. Operating from SEASAT, SAR eyed the sea for a width of about 100 km along the flightpath by scanning from side to side. The beam is differently reflected by the varying roughness of the surface below. The SAR image consists of a map of the radar-reflecting properties of the surface image. During its operation in mid-1978, the SEASAT satellite collected approximately 100 million km2 of SAR images. Practitioners expect that improved measurements of ocean waves will come with increased understanding of the physical mechanism which allows the SAR to image ocean waves. High spatial resolution is obtained by identifying each reflector according to its measure range and Doppler shift in frequency associated with spacecraft motion.

As far back as the mid-1960s, the Gemini manned flight program yielded pictures of internal waves through photography in the visible wave-length spectrum under favorable light angle conditions. The SAR data interpretations permitted the processing of signatures of both shallow and deep-water internal waves with much greater precision.

The success of SAR in detecting and measuring internal waves has led scientists to wonder whether the technique could not be equally effective in detecting submarine wakes.

Part of the beauty of SAR is its ability to show waves and winds in detail, operating to the surface of the ocean, regardless of weather or cloud cover. It is unfortunate that inclusion of SAR in U.S. technology is unlikely for at least the next five years. However, the Europeans and the Japanese will both launch satellites in 1985, carrying this precious equipment.

Fisheries

Owing to dominance of food considerations among the applications of oceanography, the use of satellites in fisheries will be covered in somewhat greater detail than the other sectors of this article.

In the early 1970s, high-resolution sensors aboard polar orbiting satellites began to send infrared data which provided a far better picture of the ocean's surface-thermal structure than had ever been obtained before, with particular respect to detail. In 1974, a very high-resolution radiometer aboard the NOAA-3 polar-orbiting satellite produced such excellent data that the scientific community was forced to recognize satellites as potential displacers of conventional shipboard detection techniques. In 1975, a number of commercial fishermen got together in California to study infrared imagery of sea-surface temperatures along the California coast. The data were exceptionally useful in portraying thermal boundaries which the fishermen knew from experience often coincide with concentrations of bait fish, i.e., the fish that commercially valuable fish seek for sustenance.

As a result of these meetings, the satellite Field Services Field Station in Redwood City, California provided a thermal analysis covering the Pacific Northwest in Seattle. From that point the program was expanded to include a popular fisheries area northwest of Midway Island, at the specific request of albacore fishermen.

Satellite imagery has particular application for fisheries along the West Coast, owing to the importance of temperature and temperature changes in fisheries technology. The normal flow of the ocean's surface along the West Coast of the United States is predominately southward. This is the California current. It is extremely cold, coming from Alaska. Current patterns on the

West Coast, however, also feature large-scale coastal upwellings, referring to the process whereby subsurface waters a few hundred meters below the surface are brought to the surface through the action of coastal winds. Surface stress imparted by the prevailing winds along the coast, together with the deflecting influence of the Coriolis force, caused the water to be driven from the shore seaward.

Water is brought to the surface from deeper depths to compensate for the transport of the surface water away from that particular area. This vertical motion, even though it may be less than a meter per day, is extremely important, because it causes recycling of nutrients from greater depths. Microscopic organisms depend for growth on these nutrients. The small grazers depend, in turn, on the microscopic organisms, and the fish in turn depend upon the grazers for their survival.

The intensity of the upwelling is dependent upon the direction of the wind, its speed, and duration, as well as the orientation of the coastline. Since the surface winds off the West Coast are predominantly from the north and the northwest during the summer, they cause upwelling almost on a continuous basis. This upwelling is normally accompanied by fog. Peak upwelling activity along the West Coast progresses generally northward during the summer months. As the upwelling water moving offshore meets and interacts with the warmer waters of the California current, ocean fronts occur, which become the scenes of high concentrations of fish. The edges of the upwelling water systems show as thermal boundaries at the surface, becoming detectable in infrared satellite imagery. Along such fronts, as boundaries separating two water masses emerge, salinity and/or temperature may change. Owing to its dependence on temperature, density may change quite rapidly in such areas. Other changes which take place relate to the distribution of dissolved and suspended particles and marine life.

Residents of the trophic levels in any marine ecosystem are sensitive to temperature and its variations. Keeping in mind the overall dependence of larger fish on the abundance and distribution of the lower trophic levels, a number of authors have identified interrelationships between movements of schools of selected species and existing temperature patterns (Montgomery 1983).

The program under discussion has been projected to several species of tuna and salmon. To a lesser extent, swordfish, crab, and shrimp have also been studied. The classic studies of Flitner, Laurs and Lynn (1963) were made of the albacore across the Pacific and to the West Coast. Owing to the fidelity with which albacore adhere to a customary thermal structure, and the historic commercial importance of this stock, the project has had significant importance to the fishing industry. 18°C is the optimal temperature for albacore, and they seldom reside below 16°C or above 20°C. On the other hand, Pacific salmon prefer much lower temperatures than tuna, commonly between 11°C and 13°C; such temperatures are usually found within the zone of coastal upwelling, rather than outside it.

Lest the foregoing imply that prediction of schools is simple, a hasty demurral is in order. Referring to lower trophic levels and their preferences also for various thermal patterns, it must be realized that the existence and movement of prey may be almost as important as temperature in controlling the movement of the larger fish. These fish may pursue their traditional prey even outside their normal temperature range of acceptability—or they may not. If the local temperatures are well beyond those acceptable to food-fish stocks, most species will not penetrate such regions, even if the food is available. Recent observations have indicated that ocean frontal activity appears to coincide with periods of intense upwelling, and that local increases in most organisms take place at the same time. Thus, the stage would appear to be set for a large-scale application of any system which can provide rapid, broad-range, and reasonably precise temperature information.

It was in this view that NASA determined to utilize two of their polar-orbiting satellite systems: a second-generation Improved TIROS Operational Satellite (ITOS) and the third-generation Polar Orbital Satellite System, called TIROS-N. This latter is a two-satellite system. The two satellites were launched in 1975 and 1976 respectively. They follow a near-polar orbit which is synchronous. Their approximate altitude is 850 km. At this altitude, ground coverage encompasses a circular area of about 6,200 km in diameter.

The TIROS-N spacecraft contain six sensors. The only one utilized by the system under discussion, however, is the advanced Very High Resolution Sensor (AVHRR). It is a multi-spectral apparatus sensitive to reflected radiation in the visual portion of the electromagnetic spectrum and to emitted radiation in the infrared region. The spectral widths of bands numbers 3 and 4 are 3.55–3.93 and 10.5–11.5 microns, respectively. These are directly applicable to earth-surface temperatures. Since the 10.5–112.5 microns bandwidth is subject to short-wave solar contamination during daylight hours, it can only be used at night. On the other hand, it is less subject to undesirable atmospheric efforts than the other bands. Because of the high-thermal resolution of a radiometer (about 0.2°C) and its high resolution of scan, data are transmitted to ground at a great rate of speed. This, in turn, required highly sophisticated receiving and processing electronics at the ground station. The NOAA facility at Redwood City, California processes the data at a thermal resolution of about 0°C (Squires and Krumboltz 1981).

In addition to the ground station at Redwood City, similar facilities at Gillmore Creek, Alaska, and Wallops Island, Virginia, also are equipped to receive and process data from the radiometer. In other words, they are set up for satellite tracking, signal reception and processing, image display, and data storage. A mini-computer handles ground-station data processing. They are also equipped with software to remove panoramic distortion for digital enlargement and for image enhancement in processing the image. The images are then produced on high-quality facsimile recorders and stored on magnetic tape for any additional data processing.

Since this particular project is typical of the important and specific applications of satellite oceanography and very typical of the kinds of systems already in use and/or planning, it is described in detail as an appendix to this report, with particular reference to the construction and processing of the image.

Ocean Forecasting

In the 1950s, using forecasting techniques developed at New York University (Pierson, Neumann, and James 1955), scientists at the U.S. Naval Oceanographic (then Hydrographic)

Office developed an operational program to forecast ocean conditions, with particular reference to wave, ice, and sonar conditions. At the same time, a few private entrepreneurs took advantage of the developing technology to design and execute private ocean-forecasting services, mainly for private passenger and cargo lines. The principal impediment to precise, dependable long-range forecasting related to frequency and acquisition of synoptic data. The emergence of satellites and satellite technology offered promise of solutions to the dilemma.

As far back as 1952, the American President Lines asked Howard Kaster, chief meteorologist for United Airlines in San Francisco, to provide forecasts, in more detail than government predictions, for the American President Lines ships operating on Northern Pacific Ocean routes (Bascom 1981). Mr. Kaster was asked at the time to recommend routes to avoid the worst storms. This was terribly important; statistically, the North Pacific is the second worst ocean sector in the world for weather. The impact of weather on conveyance of both cargo and passengers is highly important. Louis Allen Inc., Ocean Routes Inc. and Pacific Weather Analysis Corporation emerged in the late 1950s to provide the same service. They were followed in the early 1960s by Bendix Marine Science Services in Teterboro, New Jersey. A number of organizations now provide these same services.

The principal aim of weather routing is to help the ship to the safest and most economical route to a given destination. These companies supply their clients with a complete synopsis of the weather for each voyage, accompanied by a recommended route to avoid the worst weather conditions. While such diversions often may increase the length of the voyage geographically, their avoidance of adverse winds and seas frequently save quite a bit of money, to say nothing of the advantages respecting safety of the crew and reductions in damage to the ships. More recently, fuel savings have become the most important consideration in these programs. Thus wind and sea-surface conditions are particularly amenable to satellite measurement. The principal apparatus for this is the scatterometer. This microwave radar measures back scattered radiation from a broad area of sea surface. Measurements made with two or more antennas viewing the surface from different directions allow determination of both wind speed and direction.

Overview of Sensors

Environmental satellite sensing has occasioned the development of sensors which constitute an almost completely new technology. This, in turn, has generated an almost completely new industry (Malay *et al.* 1983). Tables 1-4, on the following pages, showing respectively available domestic remote sensors, available remote sensor technologies, developmental domestic remote sensors, and developing sensor technologies, demonstrate the already significant catalog of gear either in present use or in various stages of development which ultimately may make the satellite the most powerful tool available to the oceanographic community (reprinted by permission of the authors, Malay, Brown and McCandless 1983). As the authors themselves point out, the most obvious shortcoming of this array of apparatus is its inability to measure subsurface temperatures and thus to be able to depict the vertical temperature profile of the ocean.

The Navy is possibly the single organization making the largest scale use—now or in the future—of satellite oceanography. The reasons include: a spectrum of obvious applications and missions; a string of in-house laboratories and contractors to develop new gear as needed and to translate observations into practical information; and the wherewithal, attendant upon the increased military budget.

Last year the Oceanographer of the Navy commissioned a group to assess existing and planned capabilities within the context of Navy requirements. As identified in the study they include (regardless of priority):

1. Ocean Temperature Structure (Three dimensional)
   a. Horizontal Structure (Sea-surface temperature)
   b. Vertical Structure (Temperature profiles)
2. Sea/Swell (Waves)
   a. Amplitude (Significant wave height)
   b. Period
   c. Direction (Spectra)
3. Coastal Processes

Table 9-1: Available Domestic Remote Sensors

Sensors	*Name*	*Sponsor/Developer*	*Salient Characteristic*
Visible & IR	VAS GOES	NOAA Hughes Aircraft, Culver City, CA	Surface & cloud images, atmos. sounding
	AVHRR NDAA	MOAA ITT Fort Wayne, Inc.	Surface & cloud images
	OLS DNSP	Air Force Westinghouse, Balt, MD	Surface & cloud images
	MIRS 2 NDAA	NDAA ITT Fort Wayne, ID	Temp. water vapor, ozone profile
	SSI MDAA	NDAA	Stratospheric sounding
	SSM DMSP	Air Force	Vertical profile
	CZCS MINBUS 7	NASA Ball Bros. Res., Bould. CO	High-resolution multispectral ocean images
	MSS LANDSAT 4	NASA Hughes	MSS (7DM, 3DM) multispectral images
Microwave	MSU NDA	NDAA Jet Propulsion Laboratory	All weather atmos. sounding
	SSM/T DMSP	Air Force - Aerojet General, Azuza, CA	Atmospheric sounding
	SSM/1 DMSP	Air Force - Hughes Aircraft	Surface temperature images
	SMMR NIMBUS 7 SEASAT	NASA Jet Propulsion Laboratory	Multichannel sounding & surface images
Altimeter	Radar Altimeter-Seasat	NASA Applied Physics Laboratory	K-Band, sea state, topography
Imaging Radar	SAR Seasat	NASA Jet Propulsion Laboratory	L-Band 20° look angle surface mapping
	SIR A Shuttle	NASA Jet Propulsion Laboratory	L-Band 47° look angle surface mapping
Scatterometer	Radar Scatterometer-Seasat	NASA General Electric Valley Forge, PA	K-Band, wind speed and direction

Table 9-2: Available Remote Sensor Technologies

Target Parameters	*Imaging & Sounding Parameters*			*Short Pulse Imaging*		
	Visible	*Thermal*	*IR Microwave*	*Alti-meter*	*Radar*	*Scatter-ometer*
1. Ocean Temp. Structure Horizontal, Vertical and Color	H (Color) C (true)	H	H			
2. Waves - Amplitude Period, Direction, Spectra	P. D			A	P. D	
3. Coastal Processes surface & Bathymetry	S. B (Clear Water)		B (Sea Mounts)		S. B	
4. Sea-Surface Structure Roughness, Currents Topography, Fronts and Eddies	R. C	F. C	R.F	R.C.T	R.C.F	R
5. Cloud Cover	C	C				
6. Sea Ice - Extent Thickness, Navigability	E. N	E. T N	E. T	E. T	E. T. N	
7. Visibility	V	V				
8. Precipitation	P	P	P			P
9. Winds - Surface (Speed & Direct. Upper Atmosphere)	U	U	S	S		S. D

Notes:

1. Letters used in each column above denote the specific parameter to be measured from the target parameters in the first column (sample in above: U. Upper atmosphere. S. Speed. and D. Direction.
2. O denotes inferred measurement (ice thickness inferred from roughness and age).
3. . denotes that observation requires clear weather.
4. Many imaging measurements such as wave period ice navigability and other fine scale measurements require good (5–100 m) resolution.

Reprinted by permission of the authors, J.T. Maloy, D.N. Brown, & S.W. McCandless, Jr.

Table 9-3: Development Domestic Remote Sensors

Sensors	*Name*	*Developer/Time Frame*	*Salient Characteristic*
Visible & IR	MLA.Sensor	NASA Hughes, Kodak, Honeywell Ball Brothers; 1990	Early telescope and focal plane designs and test units.
	Wind Sensor Lidar	NDAA Wave Propagation Lab 1995	
	Ocean Sensor Lidar	NASA AVCO, RCA, 1995	
Microwave	LAMMR Sensor	NASA GSFC, G.E., Hughes; 1990	Design Studies for 94 GHZ, 140 GHZ Imager
	Millimeter Imager	Navy NRL; 1987	
Altimeter	Wave Spectra Sensor	NASA GSFC, Fred Jackson; 1990	Experimental Aircraft Tests
	GEOSAT A	Navy APL; 1985	Improved Topographic Accuracy
	TOPEX	NASA JPL; 1988	Improved Geold
Imaging Radar	SIR B Shuttle	NASA JPL; 1984	Variable incidence L band Imager digital data
	SIR C Shuttle	NASA JPL; 1987	
	Pressure Sounder	JPL; 1995	Experimental Laboratory and aircraft tests
	Wave Spectrometer	Navy NRL; 1990	Experimental aircraft tests 10 GHZ wave spectra
	Surface Contour Radar	NASA /GSFC ED Walch; 1990	Aircraft Tests 35 GHZ
Scatterometer	Wave Spectra Sensor	NASA; 1990	2 Frequency

Table 9-4: Developing Sensor Technologies

Target Parameters	*Imaging & Sounding Parameters*			*Short Pulse Imaging*		
	Visible	*Thermal*	*IR Microwave*	*Alti-meter*	*Radar*	*Scat-ter-ometer*
1. Ocean Temp. Structure Horizontal & Vertical	V-LIDAR Active Laser					
2. Waves - Amplitude Period, Direction, Spectra				A. P. D	A. P. D	A. P. D 2 Freq.
3. Coastal Processes Surface & Bathymetry	Im-proved S. B			B		Im-proved S. B
4. Sea-Surface Structure, Roughness, Currents Topography, Fronts and Eddies				F	Im-proved R.C.F	
5. Cloud Cover	Im-proved	Im-proved				
6. Sea Ice - Extent Thickness, Navigability			Improved Spatial Resolution	Sounder for thickness		
7. Visibility	Haze Discrimination Albedo Measurements					
8. Precipitation			P Improved		P	P
9. Atmospheric Temp. and Humidity, Profiles		Im-proved T. H.	H. T- Improved			
10. Winds - Surface (Speed & Direct. Upper Atmosphere)	U-Lidar Active Laser				S. D	

Notes:
1) Letters used in each column above denote the specific parameter to be measured from the target parameters in the first column. Example in 10 above: U Upper atmosphere. S. Speed, and D. Direction.
2) . denotes that observation requires clear weather.
3) Many imaging measurements such as wave period ice navigability and other fine-scale measurements require good (5–100 m) resolution.

   a. Surf
   b. Bathymetry
4. Sea Surface Structure
   a. Roughness (Texture)
   b. Currents
   c. Topography (Includes the marine geoid and mesoscale variations)
   d. Fronts and eddies
5. Cloud Cover (surface expression)
6. Sea Ice
   a. Extent
   b. Thickness
   c. Navigability
7. Visibility
8. Precipitation
9. Atmospheric Profiles
   a. Temperature
   b. Humidity
10. Winds (speed and direction)
   a. Surface
   b. Upper Atmosphere

Workshops to intercompare satellite measurements and to evaluate their global accuracies against each other and in turn against ship and buoy measurements, were designed and conducted in January 1983, June 1983, and in early 1984 (Burne 1983).

Surface temperature and anomaly maps were produced for all sensors by subtracting interpolated climatology from the satellite area surface temperatures prior to forming the monthly 2° latitude/longitude averages.

Additional comparisons between the data sets were performed by collocating individual retrievals and *in situ* data using a time-distance window of appropriate size, and performing monthly averaged fields by binning data into 2°C latitude/longitude cells. As noted by the scientists from the Jet Propulsion Laboratory (NJOKU 1983), agreement in the North Atlantic was remarkable; the extent of warm and cold-water regions was virtually identical. In the North Pacific the patterns again were similar, except that data from the Advanced Very

High Resolution Sensor proved to be about 0.5°C colder than that shown by the ships which were obtaining ground-truth data.

Reckoning from surface sea-temperature point comparisons, the Advanced Very High Resolution Sensor showed better agreement with the bathythermograph information.

The conclusions drawn from the workshops (held at the Jet Propulsion Laboratory) were that: AVHRR data are more accurate (less noisy) than the data radioed to the Fleet Numerical Oceanography Center from ships, in point comparisons with high-quality bathythermograph information. Thus MMR measurements are better than ships but less accurate than AVHRR in point comparisons with bathythermograph data. The SMMR sea-surface temperature anomaly fields do not show good similarity with AVHRR and ships (Barnett *et al.* 1979).

International Relations

The recently agreed-upon Law of the Sea Treaty (to which the USA is not a signatory) restricts access to a large part of the coastal ocean that is responsible for more than 25% of the ocean's primary productivity and more than 95% of the estimated fishery yield. It also limits access to vast areas of the deep ocean contiguous to islands.

Remote sensing by satellite is a recently acquired technique—actually the only feasible way—of circumventing local restrictions and individual national jurisdictions.

Furthermore, joint use of a given satellite system by several nations could grant this new technology a friend-making role perhaps unanticipated by its many creators and early practitioners. This is the mechanism which ties into the title of *The Ocean in Human Affairs*.

I would therefore like to relate a little of a program which is unique. There is nothing like it elsewhere in the world. I refer to a Cooperative Technology Program between Egypt and Israel. Two dozen laboratories in those two countries and the United States are currently cooperating in a program of marine-based technologies, including fisheries and aquaculture, management of lakes, protection of the shoreline, and (fundamental to the whole program) determination of the biological productivity of the Southeastern Mediterranean Sea (Abel *et al.* 1984).

Construction of the Aswan High Dam in 1964 had various effects on the physical, chemical, geological, and biological oceanography of the southeastern Mediterranean Sea, not the least of which was the significant decline in the commercial marine fish landings in Egypt. The decreased primary productivity of the Egyptian coastal waters resulted from the abrupt curtailment of the Nile River's flow of nutrient-rich waters into the sea following completion of the dam in the mid-1960s.

The catastrophe apparently occurred in two stages, the first being an immediate decline in the catch of *Sardinella Aurita*, a planktivorous fish which had an annual feeding migration to the Nile delta region during the pre-dam flood period. The cessation of the autumnal final plankton outburst in the post-dam period has most likely resulted in an altered migration of the species to feeding grounds other than the Nile Delta.

The second state (in addition to the immediate influence on the *Sardinella*) related to the decline in demersal fish landings following in the late 1960s. While, clearly, the dam has had a greater effect on the fisheries of the delta area than elsewhere, there is also evidence of abrupt changes in Israel's *Sardinella* stocks since 1966. There is strong likelihood, therefore, that other, more gradual, processes operate towards a trophic equilibrium. The cooperating Egyptian, Israeli, and American scientists decided that the *Sardinella* studies would be a good starting place toward the objective of relating primary production of the southeast Mediterranean to fisheries abundance. Not only is this species the dominant fish in the eastern Mediterranean, but it feeds on lower trophic levels from detritus through zooplankton to postlarval fish.

At the start of the program, little information was available concerning the distribution, recruitment and nutrition of the ichthyoplankton stocks in the eastern Mediterranean. There appears to be more bio-mass produced in the high trophic levels than would be justified by the measured primary productivity. To resolve the paradox requires a better understanding of the carbon flux between the major trophic levels in these ecosystems. Among other objectives, it was decided to use selected data from the Coastal Zone Color Scanner on NIMBUS-7 to determine the width and structural features of the coastal areas as they pertain to total phytoplankton pigment concentration.

During a series of cruises in 1981 and 1982 the scientists measured Secci disc depths ranging from 33–46 meters, diffuse downwelling attenuation coefficients from 1.031 to 0.046 m-1, and near-surface chlorophylls from 0.026 to 0.069 mg/L. Images from the coastal Zone Color Scanner on board the NIMBUS-7 satellite confirmed that these low chlorophyll concentrations were characteristic for the pelagic region (Berman *et al.* 1984).

A sharp frontal feature about 10.5 km long was observed in the data collected from the Coastal Zone Color Scanner in July 1979. This front was distinguished by both sharp thermal and chlorophyll discontinuities. That is, the nearshore water mass was warmer than the adjacent offshore waters, and surface chlorophyll concentrations were quite sharply delineated, with higher values corresponding to the warmer waters.

In this project, the distribution and abundance of phytoplankton in terms of total pigment concentration are related to ocean color measured by the Coastal Zone Color Scanner on the NIMBUS-7 earth-orbiting satellite. The structure and extent of thermal and color fronts which are ultimately responsible for the distribution and productivity of commercially important fish species are interpreted from this data. Selected images are analyzed, and total pigment images are generated.

The cooperating institutions include the Department of Oceanography of the University of Alexandria (Egypt), the Institute for Oceanographic and Limnological Research Ltd, (Haifa, Israel), The Department of Oceanography at Texas A&M University (College Station, Texas), and the Bigelow Laboratories (Booth Bay Harbor, Maine). While the American institutions initially bore responsibility for the satellite imagery portion of the project, all of the institutions ultimately will cooperate in this phase, and the Israelis and Egyptians have primary responsibility for conducting the cruises supplementing the satellite imagery with ground-truth observations. The Egyptian and Israeli institutions plan the cruises together in order that their respective ships conduct complementary tractlines. It can now be reported that the first representative of the Israeli institution recently joined the Egyptians on their ship for their portion of the cruise program.

As a major objective of the program the participants hope to establish an ichthioplankton laboratory equipped with necessary microscopes and sophisticated instruments with a view toward building a regional ichthyoplankton research center, the first of its kind in the Middle East. It is currently contemplated that this would be established in Alexandria, where, among other things, satellite imagery would be processed for all laboratories in the Middle East.

Philosophically, it is hard to conceive of anything less political than a satellite winging its way around the earth, available for any and all to use for measurement purposes. In the program just mentioned, however, data processing is accomplished in a truly cooperative manner among countries which have not been traditional friends. They share objectives, planning, and project execution. One hopes this cooperative spirit can be extended to other programs involving satellite observations and data processing, to say nothing of the communications possibilities derived therefrom.

Predictions of Satellite Uses and Their Future

In summary, it might be interesting to compare the visions of satellite oceanography as conveyed by the myriad examinations and reports of the National Oceanographic Program that have taken place in the last two decades. It has been said that oceanography has been the most examined, analyzed, evaluated, and assessed of all of our country's programs. It is quite likely that the ratio of words to deeds is the highest of any technology employed in the United States of America. Of the two dozen major evaluations of our marine activities, three might be considered typical landmarks: Effective Use of the Sea, prepared by the President's Science Advisory Committee in 1966; Our Nation and the Sea, the report of the Commission on Marine Science Engineering and Resources enacted by Congress in 1969; and Toward Fulfillment of a National Ocean Commitment prepared under the auspices of the Marine Board of the National Academy of Engineering in 1972.

The President's Science Advisory Committee did not even list satellites in its report. In 1966 it may not have been considered realistic to advocate regular global observations of the surface temperatures and currents of the ocean. Three years later the Commission on Marine Science and Resources, chaired by Julius Stratton, noted the promise of satellites and urged the techniques then being tested with aircraft over the ocean be adapted for satellites. The Marine Board, in its more conservative report, made little reference to satellites in proposing instrumentation for surveying and studying the ocean (Bascom 1981).

Given the rapid rate of development in the 1970s and the alacrity with which the ocean community accepted and embraced the use of satellites, what of the future? In 1982 the National Academy of Sciences formed a panel, under the leadership of Willard Bascom, to consider the past, present, and future of satellite oceanography. The panel developed a set of objectives for the next decade which has never been published; thus, with Dr. Bascom's kind permission, this will be their report's first outing.

1. Develop the capability to measure sea level on a routine basis to an accuracy of æ2 cm relative to the geoid. The ocean's major currents relate to variations in the topography of the sea surface of from 10–1000 cm. If the elevation of the sea surface relative to the geoid were determined to about æ2 cm, it would be possible to define medium size and small eddies encompassed within the major currents. A serendipitous spinoff of this technique would be greater insight into the various causes and effects of tides.

2. Develop the capability to measure sea-surface wind vectors with increased accuracy. Current satellite technology enables observation of wind to within æcm/sec. Precision of at least four times this factor is desired.

3. Develop the capability to describe distribution, age, and thickness of sea ice. This particular objective has largely been obtained over the past year through the large-scale international arctic project involving six countries and 250 scientists.

4. Develop the capabilities to describe the distribution of sea-surface temperature to an accuracy of 0.5°C or better. At the time the panel met precisions of æ1.5°C were obtained.

Significant increases in accuracy have been obtained since then.

5. Develop methods that will allow a reliable estimation of primary productivity. In one sense, this could be the most important strength of satellite oceanography to the degree that it may provide a useful picture of parameters in and under the ocean which in turn determine the fisheries potentials in various sectors of the sea.

6. Develop methods for assessing secondary and higher trophic-level production. This is directly linked to the previous objective.

7. Develop buoys specifically for use with satellites that make supportive measurements of the upper-ocean water and the lower atmosphere. This type of development would provide at least an extra dimension to satellite oceanography allowing the use of the enormously greater precision made available through *in situ* measurements from the buoys. Almost every known parameter is now measurable from buoys; use of the satellites for interrogation and information transmission will mark an enormous step forward, particularly when lower-cost buoys are developed, enabling vast networks of placement.

8. Provide higher resolution of sea-surface temperature and color measurements for coastal regions of special interest. Observation of features intimately connected with man's activities such as small upwelling areas, plankton patches, river runoff effects, pollution distribution, and nearshore sand transport would be of infinite use to agencies charged with appropriate jurisdiction and industries which must operate within defined environmental limits.

9. Develop means for measuring certain chemicals in or on the sea, such as salinity, nutrients, and oil. The utility of such techniques is self-evident.

10. Develop an improved system for supporting and confirming satellite data with data from ships and buoys. Such improvement is constantly going on, particularly with respect to the Navy ships wherein a little more funding is available.

11. Provide and process data on wind waves and temperature on a near-real-time basis to scientists and industrial users who need them. This will be of value to fishermen, directing their efforts more efficiently, and to scientists who would be able to

change the nature, direction, and quantity of their observations according to observed perimeters.

12. Provide navigational capability to position research vessels and buoys within 10 meters. It is understood that such a capability has been attained since Dr. Bascom's report was written.

Conclusion

Today, the technical ability to achieve worldwide measurement of at least the surface of the ocean and of many of the processes in the atmosphere that are strongly coupled to the ocean have been well demonstrated. In terms of coverage, the possibilities for satellite oceanography are almost limitless. The needed refinements relate to increased precision of surface measurements and our ability to penetrate the surface to obtain vertical profiles.

And finally, as a humorist once remarked, the oceans will ultimately do more for satellites than satellites for the oceans, by providing their final resting place.

Appendix A

A Special Project, Utilizing Satellite Imagery to Locate Particular Fish Stocks

The use of the TIROS Satellite System to locate fish stocks has just been described. Construction of the images and treatment of the images received and translation into usable information is as sophisticated a technology as that of the imaging apparatus itself.

As received from the sensors, the images are constructed line by line, each line corresponding to one rotation of a mirror located within the optics of the radiometers. In the AVHRR, this mirror scans lines over the earth normal to the motion of the spacecraft at a rate which produces contiguous scan lines. Each scan line contains a sequence of instantaneous use of the earth which forms adjacent picture elements called pixels. Since each scan line from the AVHRR contains over 2,000 pixels, and each image contains about 2,000 scan lines, one image contains more than 10 million bits of data.

Image enlargement is useful and utilized especially where relatively small areas within an image are of interest. Image processing also includes gray-shade enhancement. This produces an image which is easier to interpret. Image enhancement is very helpful in working with sea-surface temperatures which include small gradients.

The Redwood City facility corrects the image for earth curvature and commences a chain of activities, including image processing, ocean feature identification, image coding, transfer of cartographic projection, and the final dissemination of the product to the fishermen.

To avoid conveying a sense of ease and simplicity in this particular type of satellite oceanography, it might be useful to identify some of the limitations. It is first necessary to identify areas covered by clouds, and inspection of visual imagery taken over the same area is often helpful, when available. Second, radiance temperatures of fog and stratus are often nearly identical to sea-surface temperatures, thus making it practically impossible to make a distinction on the basis of infrared temperatures alone. Sometimes it is possible to determine the presence of fog and/or stratus along the coast by the manner in which they tend to obscure the coastline.

Sea-surface temperature patterns may occasionally persist for a week or longer, although distorted during that period. However, when surface winds change abruptly, the frontal patterns may be quickly destroyed. Once cloud-free areas have been identified, frontal activity is usually quite easy to identify in a properly enhanced image.

Once the fronts have been identified, it is then necessary to code the fronts which have been selected. This consists of tracing the selected features directly onto the imagery. The Redwood City facility indicates the apparent relative intensity of the various fronts by using a sequence of dots. The spacing of dots along the front indicates its apparent strength. Under the condition of a sharp or intense front, the dots would practically touch one another. This whole process requires a high degree of quality control. In the encoding process cloud edges are indicated by scalloping. The Redwood City facility also uses appropriate symbols to identify ocean areas which appear to be especially cold or warm. (The process of front identification is important. Since satellite imagery is incapable of penetrating the surface waters, detection of all except surface-swimming fish must be dependent upon implicit, rather than explicit, methods.)

After the image has been coded, the information is transferred to a suitable base chart, since the image itself does not correspond to any standard cartographic projection. The data transfer from a coded image to the map projection is accomplished with an optical device called a Zoom Transfer Scope produced by Bausch & Lomb. This device consists of a series of lenses and a half-silvered mirror which allows one to optically superimpose an image on a base map. Through various adjustments, the image can be enlarged and warped to fit the map. Once satisfactory alignment has been achieved, it is a simple matter to trace the coded features from the image directly onto the base chart. These base charts include altitude and longitude markings for navigation.

The chart has now been completed, and the next and final step is circulating the product to the clientele, the fishermen. The Sea Grant Extension service has been extremely useful in this regard. Since the chart is no better than the weather and ocean system that it portrays, it must be made available to the user almost in real time. Dissemination techniques include the National Weather Service Radio Facsimile, telecopiers, and sometimes the US Mail. Although boats equipped with radio facsimile receivers and recorders receive excellent chart coverage, this equipment is often too expensive for many small boat owners.

Redwood City produces charts approximately weekly during the winter, but seldom during the summer. They provide distribution for the California chart via telephone telecopier. While US Mail is sometimes employed, it is a poor method, because by the time the fishermen receive the chart, it may no longer be representative of actual conditions (Squires and Krumboltz 1981).

This system is sophisticated overall but quite serviceable to fishermen who have used these charts. They are apparently able to spend less time at sea and consume less fuel to produce a given catch using these charts.

The Jet Propulsion Laboratory has been using the Coastal Zone Color Scanner in league with the Scripps Institution of Oceanography to provide better images with additional parameter senses (Montgomery 1983). The Coastal Zone Color Scanner is the only sensor operated from satellites specifically designed for measuring phytoplankton biomass. It accomplishes this by measuring the upwelling radiant energy, in four visible bands which are back-scattered from the near-surface waters of the ocean. The ocean's biota, mainly the phytoplankton (or microscopic marine plants), are the principal cause of color in the ocean. Pigments absorb strongly in the blue and red regions of the visible light spectrum and cause the back-scattered solar radiation of 0.443 microns to decrease rapidly as the chlorophyll concentration increases. Since the fundamental color of water is blue, the effect of the biomass is to change this to various shades of green.

Changes in radiance can be observed very dramatically over several orders of magnitude in chlorophyll concentrations. The sensitivity at 0.443 microns enables the discrimination between water masses of high and low chlorophyll content and between water masses of low but different chlorophyll MIA concentrations. The coastal zone color scanner makes use of microwaves. Chlorophyll A absorbs the back-scattered radiation at 0.443 microns, and this change can be compared with back-scatter at 0.520 microns which is unaffected, thus giving a sense of the amount of chlorophyll and plankton present. Chlorophyll can be measured over a wide range of concentrations (0.1 to 7.0 mg/L), assuming that corrections can be made for atmospheric conditions. The average horizontal resolution ranges from 800 meters to 1.2 km over a 1,500 km swath (Montgomery 1983).

Thus, the instrumentation used at two levels of science, so to speak, enables the following: First, the estimation of primary productivity of the oceans and then the forecasting of schools of valuable fish stocks. Representatives of the Jet Propulsion Laboratory have been exploring, with officials of the New York/New Jersey Port Authority and the sea grant offices in New York and in New Jersey, the possibilities of rendering a similar but expanded service to East Coast fishermen.

Until recently, the use of radio facsimile on the East and Gulf Coasts has been limited by available lower-quality products. Collaboration between the Sea Grant Extension Service and National Weather Service has upgraded the frequency, quality, and choice of atmospheric and oceanographic radio facsimile transmission. New broadcast stations in Slidel, Louisiana and Boston, Massachusetts, (with two more planned) will accelerate acceptance of satellite imagery as a tool for the communications industry.

References

Abel, R., S. El Sayed, C. Serruya and A. Bayoumi, 1984. "Progress Report II of the Cooperative Marine Technology Program for the Middle East." Submitted to the Agency for International Development, May 1984. Ft. Hancock: Available from the office of the New Jersey Marine Sciences Consortium.

Apel, J. 1982. "Some recent scientific results from the SEASAT altimeter." *Sea Technology*, October 1982, Volume 23: 21.

Baker, J. 1984. "Oceanography from space—a research strategy for the decade 1985–1995." Washington, D.C.: Report by the Joint Oceanographic Institutions, Incorporated.

Barnett, T., W. Patzert, S. Webb and B. Bean, 1979. "Climatological usefulness of satellite determined sea-surface temperatures in the tropical Pacific." *Bulletin of American Meteor Society* 60: 197–205.

Bascom, W. 1981. "Satellites and Oceanography." Unpublished paper, in the National Academy of Sciences, Washington, D.C., October 1981.

Berman, T., D. Townsend, S. El Sayed, C. Trees and Y. Azov, 1984. "Optical transparency, chlorophyll, and primary productivity in the Eastern Mediterranean near the Israeli coast." *Oceanologica Acta* 7.

Byrne, H. 1983. "Review summary of U.R.I. satellite sea-surface temperature workshop, September 1982." Proceedings of the Marine Technology Society, Oceans 1983, 8/29–9/1. Washington, D.C.: Available from the M.T.S. Office, Volume I: 338.

Flimlin, G. 1983. "Gulf stream eddies: formation, monitoring, and application." *New Jersey Sea Grant Extension Service Bulletin*, July 1, 1983. Ft. Hancock: Available from New Jersey Marine Sciences Consortium.

Flittner, Glen, B. Lars and R.J. Lynn, 1963. "Review of seasonal movements of albacore tuna off the Pacific coast." *Comm. Fisheries Rev.* April: 7–13.

————. 1969. "Sea Surface Temperatures." *World Met. Org. Tech. Note* 103:37–66. In *Earth Temperature Structure and Its Relation to US Tuna Fisheries in the Eastern Pacific Ocean*. New York: U.N. Library.

Heitman, L. 1983. "Marine satellite communications update." *Sea Technology* 34: 11.

Maley, J., D. Brown and S. McCandless, 1983. "Spaced-based ocean remote sensing-capabilities and deficiencies in the 1980s." Proceedings of the Marine Technology Society, Oceans 1983. Washington, D.C.: Available from the Marine Technology Office, Volume I: 326.

Montgomery, D. 1983. "The Use of Satellite Observations of the Ocean Surface in Commercial Fishing Operations." Paper presented at the New York/New Jersey Port Authority. Pasadena: Available from Jet Propulsion Laboratory.

Njoku, E. 1983. "Satellite-Derived Sea-Surface Temperatures." Workshops I May, 1983. Jet Propulsion Laboratory of the California Institute of Technology.

1984. "Oceanography from space: an update." An editorial summary in *Sea Technology Magazine* 25.

Pierson, W.J., G. Neuman, and R.W. James. 1955. "Practical methods for observing and forecasting ocean waves by means of wave spectra and statistics." H.O., Pub. 603, US Navy Hydrographic Office, Washington, D.C.

Squires, J. and H. Krumboltz. 1981. "Profiling pelagic fish schools using optical lasers and other remote sensing techniques." *Journal of Marine Technology Society* 15: 10–15.

Vasecky, J., S. Durden, D. Napolitano and M. Smith. 1983. "Theory and practice of ocean wave measurement by synthetic aperture radar." Proceedings of the Marine Technology Society, Oceans 1983. Washington, D.C.: Available from Marine Technology Society Office, Volume I: 331.

The President. 1966. President's Science Advisory Committee. *Effective Use of the Sea.* US Government Printing Office, Washington, D.C.

The President. 1969. President's Commission on Marine Science, Engineering, and Resources. *Our Nation and the Sea.* Washington, D.C. US Government Printing Office.

National Academy of Engineering. 1972. "Toward Fulfillment of a National Ocean Commitment." National Academy of Sciences Press. Washington, D.C.

TEN

SOME REFLECTIONS On OCEAN OBSERVATIONS

Gunnar Kullenberg

Introduction

Technological developments of advanced instrumentation for oceanic observations have played a major role in the recent development of oceanography. It can be said that each important new discovery about conditions in the oceans has been associated with a technological innovation which has been applied to ocean instrumentation (IOC/UNESCO 1984). Examples can be given from laboratory stúdies, e.g., the surge of developments in analytical techniques in chemistry (Grasshoff *et al.* 1983), which have made it possible to obtain reliable data on concentration levels of inorganic and organic substances in the sea, resulting in major revisions of the levels compared to results obtained before about 1975. The possibility of determining very low levels of decaying substances accurately (e.g., radioactive and certain gases like freons), has given oceanographers new tools in studies of air-sea exchange, deep and bottom-water formations, oceanic circulation, and oceanic ventilation. This, of course, is extremely important in relation to climate studies and the problems associated with the increase of CO_2 in the atmosphere.

Examples of *in situ* techniques are the automatic recording current meters which can be reliably moored for extended intervals (several months), making it possible to obtain time series of data; the continuous profiling instruments for measuring the conductivity (salinity) and temperature with high accuracy and vertical resolution; the various forms of towed bodies which make it possible to obtain information from different depths continuously with high-spatial resolution. These devices include the deep-sea towing systems to study bottom formations and conditions on the bottom at great depths with very high resolution.

A serious drawback is the lack of synoptical observations from ships and fixed or drifting buoys. Almost simultaneous observations of large areas of the ocean surface can be obtained by means of remote sensing from satellites. This has made it possible to study surface conditions of, e.g., temperature, ice, and color over large areas repeatedly. Thus, a time series of seasonal temperature or ice conditions can be obtained and shown for instance, in the form of a film.

The surge of various kinds of obtained data has, of course, stimulated theoretical work. Developments of models of the circulation on various scales have been made possible through computer advancement; and testing of such models is being made possible through the increasing amounts of data. Without this kind of development, the gradual understanding of the physical conditions in the oceans that is emerging would remain concealed in the abyss.

However, an imbalance can be noticed when comparing the recent development within different disciplines of marine science. Very noticeable advancements have occurred in physics and in geology. In chemistry, the analytical techniques have advanced strongly, but marine chemistry is only beginning to thrive on this. The technical development for biological studies is still relatively far behind. In particular, there is a lack of reliable *in situ* techniques for several important biological parameters, e.g., the size distribution of particles and plankton, the separation or identification of various types of plankton, and the determination of productivity.

The requirements of observations defined by the necessity of protecting the environment against unacceptable contamination and pollution also have strong implications for observational programs. The environment is of global concern, and data on contamination or concentration levels must be intercomparable between different regions. This requires intercalibrations of methods of sampling and analysis. Monitoring of environmental conditions in selected areas and of selected species requires international cooperation, as do baseline studies designed to give a broad brush picture of contamination levels in biota, sediments, and water on a regional basis. Technological and personnel capacities should ideally be on a similar level in the countries bordering the region.

There is still a great need for ocean observations, but to a large extent in selected areas or in specific parts of the water column. The observations usually also have to be tailored to different types of programs having different aims as requirements: process oriented studies, time series, model testing, and monitoring for human or environmental health protection.

Some specific types and concerns of ocean observations will be addressed in the following, with no claim of completeness.

Satellites

Satellites can be used for observations, for communication and data transmission, and for navigational purposes. All these uses are very essential for oceanography, as fully discussed in Dr. Abel's article. The data-transmission aspect is growing in importance along with the increasing use of drifting buoys tracked by satellites, as well as in connection with a growing need for real-time data, i.e., data delivered to the user almost directly after the measurements are made. Off-shore industry, shipping, and environmental monitoring are increasingly demanding real-time data. These can be surface observations obtained by satellite sensors or *in situ* measurements from sensors mounted on moored or drifting buoys and transmitted to the satellite. Real-time data are also increasingly used in ocean experiments to direct the participating ships to relevant areas of observation, for instance an eddy, a front, or a river plume. Without remote sensing information on such features, the ships will operate more or less "blind."

The large amounts of data can only be stored in a few world or regional data centers. From there the users must be able to obtain the relevant data directly, which can only be accomplished through a satellite-based telecommunication system.

On the measurement side, a very prominent part of satellite oceanography is its synoptic nature, which can only be obtained through airborne remote sensing. The synoptic data make it possible to look at large areas simultaneously; a global view can be achieved. Variability on various space scales may then be reliably investigated and spectra of variance determined.

The greatest weakness of satellite observations is the fact that they only cover the surface or the near-surface part of the water column. Thus the data must be supplemented by *in situ* observations of conditions in the water column. For calibration purposes, sea-truth data from the surface layer are also required.

On the physical side, the continued development of increasingly accurate surface altimetry measurements, giving the absolute elevation of the sea surface, is probably at present the most significant one. Altimetry measurements are envisaged to be a very important part of the world-ocean circulation experiments included in the coordinated climate-research program. A supplementary important development of satellite measurements relates to the possibility of determining the wind-induced surface stress (see, e.g., NASA 1982). On the biological side, the possibility of obtaining ocean-wide measurements of the primary productivity is a very important development. This can now be accomplished for the open ocean, where disturbances due to inorganic particulate matter and humic substances from land runoff are negligible. In coastal waters, these disturbances often make a unique interpretation of the satellite signal impossible. Furthermore, the ocean color measurements by satellite are very sensitive to meteorological and atmospheric conditions; cloud cover cannot be penetrated.

The European community is participating in the satellite development of geophysics through the European Space Agency (see, e.g., ESA 1980), and through cooperation with NASA.

Coupling Between Environmental Compartments

Much of the action in the oceans is associated with ocean boundaries: the land-sea, atmosphere-ocean, and sediment-water interfaces, across which exchanges and interactions with other parts of our environment also take place. In relation to environmental problems it is necessary to consider also the coupling and cycling between the compartments: land-freshwater-sea-atmosphere. Processes at the interfaces often determine the rates of exchange. In order to determine the fluxes it is necessary to measure the gradients across the interfaces, which requires high precision and micro-sensors. These are now being developed for the sediment-water interface (Caldwell and Chriss 1979). The observations have shown the existence of large micro-scale gradients in physical and chemical properties. The same is true of the air-sea interface. Great problems are associated with investigations of the land-sea interface. In practice, we may also refer to this as the coastal zone, which can be loosely defined as the coastal boundary layer, e.g., defined by the internal Rossby radius of deformation

$$R_i = \sqrt{\frac{g\,h\,\delta\rho}{\rho_0}}$$

where h is a representative depth, $\delta\rho$ the vertical density difference, r0 the average density, and g the acceleration of gravity. An essential problem is to determine the flux of substances from the land through the coastal zone to, or into, the open ocean. This requires determination of inputs from the land and atmosphere, observations of particulate and dissolved forms in the water column, sedimentation, and exchanges across the sediment-water interface and the open-sea boundary. Interdisciplinary teams for observations and analysis are necessary to achieve the goal. Oceanography was, for a period, shy of working in the coastal zone, but, during the last couple of years, there has been a clear tendency to direct considerable efforts to the coastal zone (see, e.g., UNESCO 1981; ICES 1985; Saetre and Mork 1981). This is obviously related to the environmental problems of, or concerns for, the coastal zone (see, e.g., GESAMP 1982).

Integrators: Tracers

During the last decade there has been a very great increase in the application of tracer technology in oceanography. This is associated with the development of analytical capabilities, development of proper sampling methods and the discovery of a series of suitable transient tracers. These include the following: radioactive substances injected from atmospheric bomb tests and through nuclear power production activities (the latter now dominate, constituting well-defined point sources); gases from the atmosphere like freons, krypton, and injection of helium from the sea bottom through thermal vents or fracture zones. Other types of tracers are the classical ones, like the conservative salinity and non-conservative temperature, oxygen and nutrients (phosphate, nitrate, silicate). Humus-like substances, end-products from decomposition of organic matter, and mainly brought to the sea from river runoff, are often useful tracers in the coastal zone. Suspended particulate matter can also be used in various areas. The latter (humus, particles) are suitably recorded by means of *in situ* optical methods (e.g., Jerlov 1976).

Observations of tracer distributions give integrated measurements in the sense that the influence on the distributions of various processes is inherently included in the observations. An interpretation of several tracer distributions simultaneously should thus make it possible to determine, within certain limits, the relative importance of the different processes, like advection and mixing, in diagnostic models. This is currently being attempted in relation to the CO_2 problem (Bolin *et al.* 1983). Observations of the distribution of tracers released from European nuclear power plants have given a picture of the transport along the coastal boundary currents in the northern parts of the North Atlantic and an estimate of the passage time between different regions (Aarkrog *et al.* 1983).

The existing tracer observations need to be supplemented, especially in remote areas. Combinations of modeling and observations will yield the most fruitful use of this powerful technique.

Time Series Observations

Probably, the most important task in oceanography at present is to elucidate the role of the oceans in climate changes. This includes part of the anthropogenic CO_2 problem. Conditions in the high latitudes are a focus of great interest in this connection. Observations there are a challenge, and currently great efforts are devoted to these regions. Technological developments there include upward-looking sonars for determination of ice thickness; buoy sensors placed in the ice for measuring temperature and melting; satellite remote sensing of ice and temperature; special moorings for ice and low-temperature conditions; and telemetering moorings which can be discarded after use. Satellite communication is a necessity.

Long-time series of observations are of particular importance in climate studies. Gradually time series are emerging of such a length that the variance distributions of current, temperature, and salinity fluctuations can be determined. This is, of course, also of great relevance in relation to ecological variability. The marine environment is characterized by an increasing variance of increasing time scales (red noise), at least up to periods of several decades.

Time series are obtained from moorings and from shipborne observations at selected stations or in sections (e.g., WCP/WCRP 1983). The oceanic weather ships have played a very important role here, and the loss of several such platforms without any substitutes is now becoming noticeable (see, e.g., ICES 1984/85). From shipborne observations large temperature variabilities have been established, e.g., in the North Atlantic, north to northwest of Iceland (Malmberg 1984), west of Greenland (Buch 1984), and in the North Pacific (e.g., Tabata 1984).

Salinity time series are available from the early 1900s and onwards, showing large negative salinity anomalies before the 1920s and in the mid-1970s (e.g., Dickson *et al.* 1984). It is obvious that it is of extreme importance to have access to such time series observations. Efforts must be directed towards maintaining selected long-time series. The selection should be done in consultation with theoretical results and modeling. On a historical time perspective, the significance of time series of data is demonstrated by the results on temperature, acidity and CO_2 content in the ice cores from Greenland and Antarctica (see Oeschger, this volume). The geological perspective is of course seen in the sediment cores. However, the interpretation of these observations is certainly not straightforward. This aspect again identifies a need for time series on present conditions which can be coupled to ice and sediment records, and help toward an interpretation of these.

Environmental changes are presently due both to natural fluctuations and anthropogenic factors. In order to properly identify the causalities it is necessary to be able to distinguish between natural and man-induced changes and fluctuations. Time-series observations are again of crucial importance. However, these should be designed in the proper way, so that frequency of the observations, space resolution, siting, and parameters are as appropriate as possible. Monitoring without proper design and proper tribute to the requirement of understanding governing processes will only be a waste of effort and time.

An example of a region where long-time series of data on several properties (S, T, oxygen and nutrients) exist is the Baltic Sea. In relation to the deterioration of the oxygen conditions in the Baltic bottom and deep waters during this century, such time series of data are clearly of the utmost importance (e.g., Kullenberg 1983; Voipoi 1983).

Satellites can be used to obtain synoptic type observations to study variance in both time and space. The latter will yield information on the variability as a function of wave number for the surface or near-surface layer. Satellites can provide such information on physical and biological parameters simultaneously, which is of great importance when investigating the interactions, and which is often neglected in shipborne work. Satellites give a great amount of valuable information on coastal boundary conditions, e.g., through mapping of the distribution of runoff and through positioning of various frontal zones.

Synoptic-type information on space variability below the surface can be obtained through the use of tomography, which is gradually developing in oceanography.

Concluding Remarks

The development of marine science is very closely related to the development of observational techniques making it possible to obtain continuous-type measurements underwater over extended periods of time. Special requirements must be met by the instrumentation as regards rigidity, sampling volume, and structure (e.g., weight and flow resistance). The technological developments tied to space research have also found many applications in oceanography. Also from this point of view, satellites are of importance to the oceans.

References

Aarkrog, A., H. Dahlgaard, L. Hallstadius, H. Hansen, and E. Holem. 1983. "Radiocaesium from Sellafield effluents in Greenland waters." *Nature* 304 (5921): 49–51.

Bolin, B., A. Bjorkstrom, K. Holmin, and B. Moore 1983. "The simultaneous use of tracers for ocean circulation studies." *Tellus* 35B: 206–236.

Buch, E. 1984. "Time series of temperature and salinity from West Greenland fishing banks." ICES C.M. 1984/C:25, mimeo. 23 p.

Caldwell, D.R. and T.M. Chriss. 1979. "The viscous sublayer at the sea floor." *Science* 205: 1131–1132.

Dickson, R.R., S.-A. Malmberg, S.R. Jones and A.J. Lee. 1984. "An investigation of the earlier Great Salinity Anomaly of 1910–1914 in waters west of the British Isles." ICES C.M. 1984/GEM: 4, mimeo, 30 p.

ESA. 1980. CHARM: Proceedings of an ESA Workshop on: Climatology, Hydrology, Atmospheric Research, and Meteorology from Space, ESA SP-150, 220 p.

GESAMP. 1982. "The review of the health of the oceans." Reports and studies 15, UNESCO. 108 p.

Grasshoff, K., M. Ehrhardt, K. Kremling (editors). 1983. *Methods of Seawater Analysis,* second, revised and extended edition. Verlag Chemie, Weinheim, 419 p.

ICES. 1984–85: "Proces-Verbal de la Reunion 1984". *Palaegade* 2–4, 1261 Copenhagen K, Denmark.

ICES. 1985. "Proceedings of the Nantes Symposium on the Contaminant Fluxes through the Coastal Zone." Rapports et Proces-Verbaux des Reunions, in press.

IOC/UNESCO. 1984. "Ocean science for the year 2000." UNESCO 7, Place de Fontenly, 75700 Paris, France, 95 p.

Jerlov, N.G. 1976. "Marine Optics." *Elsevier Oceanography* 14: Amsterdam.

Kullenberg, G. 1983. "The Baltic Sea." In: *Estuaries and Enclosed Seas,* editor B.H. Ketchum, pp. 309–335, Elsevier, Amsterdam.

NASA. 1982. "Scientific opportunities using satellite surface wind stress measurements over the ocean," rep. by Satellite Surface Stress Working Group (ed. J.J. O'Brien). Nova University/N.Y.I.T. Press, Fort Lauderdale, 153 p.

Saetre, R. and M. Mork (editors). 1981. *The Norwegian Coastal Current,* Volumes 1 and 2, University of Bergen, 795 p.

Tabata, S. 1984. "Anomalously warm water off the Pacific Coast of Canada during the 1982–83 El Niño." Tropical Ocean-Atmosphere Newsletter Number 24, p. 7–9.

UNESCO. 1981. "River inputs to ocean systems (R.I.O.S.)," Proceedings of a Workshop, Rome, March 1979. United Nations, New York.

Voipio, A. (Editor). 1981. "The Baltic Sea." *Elsevier Oceanography 30*: 418. Amsterdam.

World Climate Program, WCRP. 1983. Symposium on time series in oceanography. Tokyo 1982. WMO, Geneva.

ELEVEN

The EXPLORATION Of INNER SPACE

MAN AND MACHINE IN THE SEA

Don Walsh

This article gives a historical perspective to the development of man's present ability to explore and work in the oceans' depths. The history of this development is remarkably long, rich, and varied. However, the purpose is not to simply write a history of man in the sea; too much has been left out in this brief account. The intent is to trace technical and scientific progress, as driven by man's curiosity and material needs, since the dawn of history.

The complementary and interdependent development paths of man in the sea as a diver or in submarines continue to the present. In the past decade and a half, unmanned robotic vehicles have evolved as a third development path. Today the diver, submarine and unmanned submersible offer a broad spectrum of effective capabilities for work in the sea.

Early Man in the Sea: Some Fragments of Recorded History

The history of manned exploration of the sea is in fact at least 5,000 years old. Drawings made as early as 900 B.C. depict the Assyrians using inflated goat stomachs as air bladders for brief underwater excursions.

Greek sponge divers first practiced their trade before the 6th century, B.C., diving to depths of less than 100 feet. This business continues today, with only slightly more modern equipment. Their basic mode of operation was to sight the sponges from the surface, possibly using some sort of underwater window, or viewing box. Taking a large breath of air and holding a stone as a diving weight they would plunge to the bottom, quickly cut sponges loose and return to the surface. Sponge diving and fishing were the first ocean businesses.

In 500 B.C. the Greek historian Herodotus recorded that the Persian King, Xerxes, used divers to salvage valuable treasures from the sea floor. Later, Thucydides reported that the Athenians used divers to clear away underwater obstacles during the attack on Syracuse in 414 B.C.

In the 300s B.C., legend relates that Alexander the Great (356–323 B.C.) had himself lowered into the sea in a cask-like container fitted with primitive viewing ports. Alexander's report on what he saw has come forward in the historical records of several cultures from the ancient world. However the several illustrations of the event all seem to date from the Middle Ages. Nevertheless, as with all such persistent legends, there is probably some truth to it. Aristotle also reported that Alexander used teams of underwater swimmers to remove obstructions to his ships and troops during the siege of Tyre in 334.

Eighteen hundred years later, during the 16th century, the great Renaissance genius Leonardo da Vinci was reported to have submerged in the sea to a depth of 10 feet. There is no clear historical record of this, but it sounds like something he would eagerly attempt. His famous sketchbooks show an understanding of the basic principles for undersea devices such as the diving suit, diver fins, snorkel breathing tubes and submarines.

The 18th and 19th Centuries: The Dawn of Practical Undersea Systems

By the 18th century, practical (for the time), working diving systems were in limited service, mostly for salvage tasks. These were diving bells made of wood, leather, and iron. Lowered from the surface, they carried a small crew of salvage divers who would enter or leave the air-filled bell by swimming down and under the lower lip of the inverted cup. Working by feel or through the use of primitive goggles, the divers would attach lifting lines to objects to be salvaged. The diving time of these bells was usually limited to the size and quality of the air bubble trapped in the bell. Work periods of a few hours were not uncommon. In cold waters the unheated bell made human cold tolerance the limiting factor.

An early inventor of such practical devices was the famous astronomer and physician, Sir Edmund Halley. In 1690 he devised a truly remarkable bell which enabled divers to work at depths of up to 60 feet for periods of up to two hours. Halley invented a means for replenishing the air supply under pressure in the bell. He also devised one of the first bell-supplied air systems for diving helmets. In this way divers could make excursions from the bell wearing helmets (miniature bells over their heads) to operate more effectively and safely in their work tasks.

Not content to be simply an inventor and witness to events, Halley spent four hours of his 65th birthday, with four friends, in his bell at a depth of 65 feet on the bottom of the Thames River!

In 1776, during the American Revolutionary War, an American named David Bushnell developed a small one-man submersible designed to attack British ships at anchor. Called the "Turtle," it looked more like an egg. The "Turtle" made an attack on HMS *Eagle*, the flagship of the British fleet blockading New York harbor. The pilot was unable to attach the explosive charge since the vessel was sheathed in copper. But the result was the desired one; the British fleet got underway and moved to avoid additional submarine attacks. Although the "Turtle" never went to war again, this was the first combatant use of a submarine.

By the end of the 18th century the English were the best and most successful salvage divers in the world. British supremacy of the seas had brought with it a high level of related technical skills in many maritime areas.

In the 19th century undersea work capabilities were greatly advanced through the development of the first practical diving suit permitting greater working depths, longer work times, and increased safety. The most successful design was developed by an Englishman, Augustus Siebe, in 1837. It was based on earlier (1823) concepts developed by Siebe's countrymen John and Charles Deane. Siebe's design was the great-grandfather of the present deep sea diving dress whose appearance and principles of operation have not changed much in a century and a half.

In France in 1866, Rouguayrol and Denayrouze designed and tested a self-contained air supply system for divers. The inventors were looking for ways to free the undersea worker and explorer from bulky air hoses used to send compressed air down from a vessel at the surface. The self-contained system gave the diver freedom from the surface, greater mobility, and was less expensive than surface-supported systems. Unfortunately, the ideas of Rouguayrol and Denayrouze did not find acceptance. It would be more than a half century later before self-contained underwater breathing apparatus came into use as a practical alternative to surface-supported diving systems.

This century saw the design, development, and construction of the first practical submarines. Although Robert Fulton is best known as the inventor of the first practical steamship, The *Cleremont*, he actually built a military submarine first. This was the *Nautilus*, which was completed in 1800. The US government was not interested in his submarine. Fulton eventually demonstrated it in the Seine River to Emperor Napoleon, but the French did not adopt it either. In 1806, Fulton demonstrated a larger model to the British Navy. Again, there was no interest. Fulton's submarine worked, but it was not until late in this century that the true military submarine would be adopted by a major navy.

In the US Civil War, the Confederate Navy used a submarine named the CSS *Hunley* to attack an anchored Federal warship which was blockading Charleston Harbor. The attack, on February 17, 1864, was successful, and the new US Navy corvette, *Housatonic*, was sunk at her anchorage. Although the blast sank the *Hunley* with the loss of her crew, this was the first successful submarine attack in the history of naval warfare.

By the second half of the 19th century there were a great number of large-scale experiments with submarine craft. Some remarkably modern design features were seen in military submarines developed by the US and major European navies.

The trend in man-in-the-sea activities during this century was the divergence between the man-carrying submarine and the diver. Up to this point the man-carrying device (mostly the diving bell) took the diver to the work site, with the diver then accomplishing the work task. This was a "man-machine system," and an idea that was not to be repeated for nearly another 100 years.

Through all the history of man in the sea, up to the beginning of the 20th century, undersea systems were intended to do either work or military tasks. There was little consideration given to undersea research and exploration possibilities. However, fiction writers such as Jules Verne, who wrote the classic *Twenty Thousand Leagues Under the Sea* (published in 1869), did speculate on the possibilities. There is a modern-day parallel seen in the work of early space science fiction writers. It was they who first told us about how man would enter and live in space in accounts that seem quite believable today.

The several interlocking factors of imagination, genius, scientific and technical knowhow, and new engineering materials combined to help advance man's capability in inner space long before there was man (or any of his satellite surrogates) in outer space. But, unlike space exploration, the evolution in the oceans was painfully slow. Compared to exploration and technology advances on land and at the sea surface, the undersea world got relatively little attention as the end of the 19th century marked over 2,000 years of gradual increase in capability.

The 20th Century: Man Conquers and Uses Innerspace

The 20th century has provided the greatest thrust in the history of mankind in science and technological development. This has been true in the undersea area as well. In the early

1900s, the American inventors John Holland, Simon Lake and George Baker (all of whom began their work in the late 1800s) perfected the first submarines that could be produced in quantity. Holland and Lake submarines were built and sold to many navies throughout the world. Lake even built a special submarine, fitted with giant wheels, which was used in some unsuccessful attempts to recover bulk ship cargoes (for example, coal) from harbor bottoms.

By World War I the submarine had become an important, though tactically misunderstood, component of most major navies. In the 15 years since the early designs of Holland and Lake, submarine design had advanced to the point where the basic design concepts remained almost unchanged until the advent of the nuclear-powered submarine in the mid-1950s.

The "man-in-the-sea" side did not develop as quickly. Diving equipment and capabilities improved through evolution rather than through the "revolution" that characterized submarine development. Until 1910, Navy divers rarely went deeper than 60 feet. By the 1920s, the extensive experimental test programs permitted dives to depths of over 300 feet. Also in the late 1920s, work began with mixed-gas breathing mixtures of helium and air to permit greater depths with increased safety.

Even though progress in diving seemed slow, it should be noted that a 300-foot-dive exceeded the maximum diving depth of most military submarines of the time. Progress resulted from the need to do work at greater depths in the sea, not the least of which was the need to be able to rescue crewmembers of submarines bottomed in waters less than their crush depth.

The 20th century brought a major growth in submarine fleets. It also saw several situations where submarines were lost during both peacetime and wartime operations. In several cases they were in salvageable depths and some people on board remained alive, but trapped on the seafloor. Surface ships equipped to carry submarine-rescue systems were developed and perfected. However, all of them were diver-dependent. In several cases these systems were successful in rescuing some personnel from their downed submarines. This application of divers' abilities greatly helped to advance deep-sea diving, salvage and work techniques. Paralleling this development were significant advances in high-pressure (hyperbaric) medicine. This work was primarily sponsored by navies, however, the scientific and technical advances helped improve the welfare of all types of commercial diving.

The navies of the world trained great numbers of divers. This training also became a principal source of divers for the commercial world. This manpower pool was especially important in the post-World War II days when the offshore oil industry first began to develop throughout the world.

The 1920s also saw the beginnings of recreational diving as we know it today. The focus of much of this early activity was in the south of France, the Caribbean and southern California. Underwater sports enthusiasts learned how to fashion elementary goggles and swim fins suitable for free (breath-holding) diving. The simple light-weight and low-cost underwater breathing devices would not be available until the late 1940s.

The 20th Century Deep Divers: Bathyspheres and Bathyscaphes

It was in the late 1920s that the first real deep diving scientific explorations were made possible through the development of the "bathysphere." Its name was derived from two Greek words, "bathy," meaning deep and "sphere," meaning ball. It was not a free-swimming submersible, but was tethered by a cable to a surface vessel.

This machine was conceived, designed, and built by Otis Barton, an American engineer who wanted to put man into the deep ocean to make direct scientific observations. Barton teamed with Professor William Beebe, who became the chief scientist and director of the program, to use this new tool for ocean research.

Barton built the small (4.5 feet in diameter) manned submersible during 1929–1930. The two-man crew would enter the sphere on deck, seal the hatch, and, once pre-dive checkouts were completed, they would be lowered into the sea.

The 2.5 ton, cast-iron sphere contained a hatch for crew access and three windows, made of quartz, for viewing while submerged. One of the three ports was for a fixed still camera to permit continuous photography of marine life without the scientists having to give up their positions at their viewing ports. A modest life-support system provided oxygen and absorbed the carbon dioxide in the cabin's atmosphere. Electrical power and communications to the surface ship/barge were via a set of electrical wires which passed through the hull of the sphere and were fastened to the lifting cable.

After the bathysphere's launching in 1930, with the backing of the New York Zoological Society, the National Geographic Society and the Explorers Club, it commenced a series of increasingly deeper test and scientific dives beginning in June 1930. The first manned dive was to 790 feet, and, by August 1934, Beebe and Otis Barton had dived the small submersible to a depth of 3,028 feet. This dive (number 32 in the series) took place near Nonsuch Island, Bermuda. Professor Beebe and engineer Barton had achieved a depth that exceeded by nearly 10 times the existing capability in commercial or military diving. His world's depth record was not to be broken until nearly two decades later.

Beebe's illustrated account of his work was contained in his book, *Half Mile Down*, a classic in the literature of ocean exploration. Even today it still makes excellent, exciting reading.

At about this same time, a Belgian physicist, August Piccard, was achieving considerable fame as an explorer using high altitude balloons. With sponsorship from the Belgium *Fonds National pour la Recherche Scientific* (FNRS), he pursued his studies of cosmic rays entering the earth's atmosphere. Earlier he had tried climbing to high altitudes in the Alps with his instruments. But he did not get the quality of data that he sought since the earth's atmosphere acts as a partial shield for these particles. Thus, the use of a balloon to get even higher was the next logical step for Professor Piccard. Ever the good scientist, he used the balloon merely for the platform needed to place himself in the optimum position for his data gathering. Setting world-altitude records was secondary to the pursuit of good science.

Remarkably, as a young student in Zurich's Polytechnic School, Auguste Piccard had first dreamed of constructing an underwater-balloon system for deep-research work in the oceans.

Many years later, aware of Beebe's work, he revived his underwater balloon concept, believing this would work much better than the surface-lowered bathysphere.

The Beebe submersible had several inherent limitations. The first was sensitivity to motion of the mother ship, since it was connected by cable to the ship. If there were large surface waves, the mother ship's motion would become the motion of the sphere as well. Attempting to do science while moving up and down several feet could be very difficult, especially if you were working at the seafloor.

A second problem dealt with the dynamics of the cable and the weight of the sphere. Just as ice skaters can develop considerable forces in "cracking the whip" maneuvers, the sphere at the end of the cable could be subject to similar violent motions if sea motion, length of cable, and weight of the sphere all coincided to produce the critical condition. Since sea motion and cable length were variable, careful attention had to be paid to make sure the operating crew did not accidentally set up such a situation.

Finally, the lifting cable has weight; that is, a half mile length weighs much more than a hundred foot length. Therefore, there was a practical depth limit as to how deep a surface-tended submersible could go before the cable would pull apart from its own weight.

Piccard's idea was to free the submersible from the surface, making it free-swimming. Thus the major limitations in the bathysphere design could be avoided. Theoretically, there would be no depth limit for the machine he called "bathyscaphe"—deep ship.

Professor Piccard presented his idea to the FNRS in the early 1930s. Funding support was approved and the first design was completed. Model tests were made and actual construction was begun before World War II. However the war prevented completion. The Piccard bathyscaphe "FNRS 2" (his last balloon was FNRS 1) would have to wait until 1945 for the work to resume.

As with World War I, the tragic events of World War II had the effect of rapidly advancing undersea technology for the navies involved in the conflict. In military submarines, depth capability increased from about 200 feet (US) at the beginning of the war to nearly 700 feet (German) at its end. Major components such as power systems, batteries, sonar, electrical systems, electronics, etc., all showed rapid engineering progress. New and improved materials for hulls, piping and paints were developed, providing basic technological building blocks for the future.

No comparable increases in depth capability were achieved in diving, with about 600 feet remaining the maximum feasible depth for the deep sea diver using the helium-oxygen breathing mixture. However, there was considerable development of new and better work tools for the diver. The field of diving medicine enjoyed rapid expansion in both knowledge and in available trained manpower.

The war also saw the development of combat swimmer groups in most of the major navies. While Alexander the Great had used such units in the siege of Tyre, there is little historical evidence that they were used very much since that time. In World War II these specialized groups actually conducted pre-invasion beach surveys, removal of obstacles, covert entry into enemy facilities for sabotage, and destruction of ships at anchor.

Since this was essentially a new area of diving technique, many new concepts and technologies had to be developed. Underwater, self-contained rebreathing devices permitted the combat swimmers to carry a closed circuit air supply with them in order to remain completely submerged during their missions. By making the breathing unit closed circuit, there would be no tell-tale surface bubble stream to show the diver's locations as he approached his target. But these units limited the diver to relatively shallow depths (less than 35 feet) and could be unsafe if not carefully used. However, this did represent the first successful means for the submerged diver to operate without the need for elaborate surface support for air lines, communications, etc.

Midget submersible "taxis" to deliver divers to their work site were perfected by several navies. These vehicles were free-flooding and were generally capable of carrying combat swimmers and their equipment for considerable distances.

Other specialized submersibles were developed for attack against enemy shipping in his harbors. These midget submarines were used with good results by the British, Italian and Japanese navies.

In the early 1940s two Frenchmen, Jacques Cousteau and Emil Gagnan, finally perfected the first practical open circuit self-contained underwater breathing apparatus, or SCUBA, a unit much simpler and safer than the military rebreather systems. At the naval base in Toulon in April 1942, they made the first dive with the device and thus launched the technology that was to make "SCUBA diving" a common term among military, commercial, sport, and scientific divers. While World War II and the German occupation of France delayed the full implementation of this invention, it did not take long after the war to see it gain an almost universal acceptance among those who needed to work or relax in the sea. Now the trained mind and eyes could go to the site of interest. Finally the marine biologist and geologist could enjoy the same direct, field observation abilities as their dry-land counterparts enjoyed.

The post-World War II years found many positive elements in place to help begin an era of real progress in the exploration of inner space. The scientific manpower pool had been developed along with a supporting base of seagoing vessels and equipment. SCUBA equipment now permitted the average scientist to be trained as a diver with little risk for depths down to 150 feet. The appeal of such systems for the marine recreation market helped to provide the incentive for many manufacturers to enter this market, thus bringing choice and quality up while keeping the price down.

Military submarine technology and production had developed skilled design and construction personnel. Engineering materials, systems, and components were now available to help undersea work system designers to build efficient machines for the environment. Also military developments in harbor works and forward area seaports helped provide a knowledge and capability to build structures that could withstand the forces of the marine environment.

The bathysphere concept was briefly resurrected in the late 1940s by Otis Barton, who had been with the original Beebe group in Bermuda. He designed and built the Benthoscope and in 1948 he was lowered to a depth of 4,484 feet off the coast of Southern California. Otis Barton had broken his 1934 world depth record, and it remained his for another five years until the Piccards took it away with their bathyscaphe.

In 1946, Professor Piccard, now joined by his son Jacques, resumed his work on the FNRS-2 bathyscaphe with renewed support from the FNRS. The submersible consisted of two major assemblies: the float (or balloon) and the cabin. The balloon was to be filled with a liquid hydrocarbon, such as aviation gasoline, which would be lighter than water, thus giving lift to the bathyscaphe. The cabin suspended below the balloon would be pressure resistant and have sufficient room for a two-man crew in relative comfort.

To make this underwater balloon submerge, it was necessary to make it heavier than water. This was accomplished by the use of ballast tanks which were dry during surface operations, being flooded only at the time of submergence.

To control the rate of descent, to stop and to return to the surface required the removal of weight. This was done through a ballast system that contained steel shot, or pellets. The shot was held in large containers which had an opening at the bottom. Surrounding the opening was an electromagnet. When the magnet was energized, the shot was magnetized and could not fall through the opening. But, when the electrical current was turned off, the shot was free to flow, thus releasing weight from the bathyscaphe. In case of emergencies the entire shot container could be dropped immediately for a rapid return to the surface.

The two-man cabin was only about six-and-a-half feet in diameter and contained an entrance hatch with a viewport at the back and a single plastic viewing port at the front. Controls in the cabin permitted the bathyscaphe pilot to monitor and control all systems, since the submersible was completely independent from surface support while submerged.

Small thruster motors provided limited vertical, horizontal, and turning mobility. Essentially a balloon, the bathyscaphe made most of its movement due to ocean currents. The small motors only permitted small adjustments of position while on or near the sea floor. Outside lights and camera provided the crew with the ability to make and record direct observations during the dive.

The FNRS-2 made its first and last dives in October and November 1948. The second dive was an unmanned test prior to putting a crew aboard. While the bathyscaphe dove successfully to a depth of 4,485 feet, it was seriously damaged during its recovery due to high seas and surface handling problems. Instead of repairing the damage and resuming the test dive series it was decided to redesign the submersible to make it more sea-worthy. The FNRS agreed to provide additional support, asking that the work be done in cooperation with the French Navy at the Toulon naval shipyard.

Of the original FNRS-2, the only major part that was saved was the cabin. A new float was designed and constructed at Toulon as this component was where the major problems occurred. In addition, other improvements were added reflecting the lessons learned in the design, construction and brief operations of the FNRS-2.

In March 1952, the Piccards decided to leave the program with the French Navy in order to build their own bathyscaphe based on even newer design concepts. Their idea was to go to Italy and through the support of various sponsors in Europe build the new submersible. This new bathyscaphe, the *Trieste* (named after the city where the float was constructed) was placed into service in August 1953.

Due to limited operating funds the Piccards operated the *Trieste* mainly in the waters surrounding Italy. Involved in a wide variety of scientific and technical research activities, the *Trieste* proved to be a very reliable design.

In August 1953, on their fourth dive in the *Trieste,* the Piccards surpassed Professor Beebe's 1931 record dive. Later, in September 1953, the Piccards made a dive to a depth of 10,330 feet in the Tyrrhenian Sea in the Mediterranean, breaking their own earlier record of 3,500 feet and taking the record away from Otis Barton's Benthoscope.

The FNRS-3 was put into service at Toulon in June 1953. It was operated by a new French Navy group which would specialize in bathyscaphe operations. After an extensive test-dive program, the FNRS-3 proved to be an excellent research submersible. It served in a variety of undersea tasks in support of the French Navy and marine scientific research. On February 14, 1954, a French Navy team dove in the Atlantic to a depth of 13,700 feet. This depth, which is about the average depth of the whole world ocean, established a record which was not to be broken for five years.

The Trieste Joins the US Navy: A 26-Year Enlistment

The Piccards operated the *Trieste* during the summer of 1957 for the US Navy's Office of Naval Research (ONR). They had been considering finding a major sponsor for the submersible who would either lease it or purchase it outright. The ONR-sponsored series of dives was designed to expose this new research technique to US scientists representing a number of different marine science disciplines.

At the conclusion of these sample dives in the Mediterranean it was the judgment of the scientific group that the US Navy should purchase the *Trieste* and bring it to the US to support advanced marine research. The Navy Department agreed; and, in the summer of 1958, the *Trieste* was disassembled and packed into a freighter for the long trip to San Diego, California, its new home port.

The *Trieste* arrived at the Navy Electronics Laboratory in San Diego on August 15, 1958. Thus began a 26-year era of *Trieste* (various models) operations in the US Navy.

On December 15, 1958, the reassembled *Trieste* made its first dive for the US Navy. During the winter of 1958–1959 the *Trieste* made several more training and orientation dives off San Diego. The project team's major activity, though, was the planning for a dive to the deepest place in the ocean.

Deep-ocean seafloor surveys conducted in the 1950s by the British, US and the Soviet Union, all agreed on the location and depth of the deepest place in the world ocean. This place is the Challenger Deep in the Marianas Trench, some 250 miles southwest of the island of Guam, in the Western Pacific. The water depth is about 36,000 feet, nearly seven miles.

With some reluctance the Navy approved the project for 1959–1960 and authorized the necessary funding as well as the support of the Navy command on the island of Guam. The name for this program would be "Project Nekton."

For the *Trieste* to attempt such a feat required several modifications of the basic submersible. The float (balloon) needed to be lengthened to hold more aviation gasoline for increased buoyancy at the greater depths, where sea pressure would be in the order of eight tons per square inch. The capacity of the ballast system for the steel shot also needed to be increased to provide for more reserve at great depths.

The original Italian-made cabin was only designed for operating depths of 20,000 feet. Therefore, a new cabin had to be designed and built. This was done by the Krupp Steel Company in Germany, resulting in a two-man cabin with an entrance hatch (with a viewport) and another viewport in front. The cabin walls were nearly five inches thick, increasing to seven inches in the vicinity of the hatch and windows. The plastic viewing port was in the shape of a truncated (sawed off) cone with the large diameter on the outside of the hull. It was seven inches thick.

Other systems on the *Trieste* were upgraded and modified. In addition, new lights, cameras, and instruments were added to the submersible. Since few of these items were "off the shelf," the *Trieste* team was kept busy designing, modifying, and building specialized equipment.

On April 12, 1959, the modified *Trieste* was launched at the Navy Ship Repair Facility in San Diego. On the 25th of that month it made its first dive in the new configuration. After a brief series of test dives in the San Diego area, the *Trieste* was disassembled, put aboard a ship, and sent to the US naval base at Apra Harbor, Guam. That would be the *Trieste*'s home for the next nine months.

Meanwhile, the French Navy's bathyscaphe group continued their work with FNRS-3. They were also now working on the design of a completely new bathyscaphe to be called *Archimede*, after the Greek scholar Archimedes. *Archimede*, like the newly modified *Trieste*, would have the capability to dive to the deepest point of the world ocean. The race for the deep was now on; it was estimated, however, that this new bathyscaphe would not be ready until 1962. *Trieste*'s planned goal was to reach the deepest point in early 1960.

The early summer of 1959 found the US Navy military and civilian *Trieste* team hard at work at Guam reassembling the *Trieste* in preparation for a progressively deeper test dive series. Jacques Piccard, who had come to the US as consultant and advisor when the *Trieste* was purchased by the Navy, also joined the Project Nekton team at Guam.

In August 1959, the *Trieste* made its first test dive to a depth of 112 feet in Apra Harbor, Guam. In quick succession additional ocean test dives were undertaken, culminating in a dive to 18,000 feet on November 15, 1959. This broke the French record set in 1954 and brought the world's depth record back to the United States.

The 1960s: Deep Submergence Era Begins

On January 14, 1960, the *Trieste* broke its own record by diving to 23,500 feet in the Nero Deep in the Marianas Trench. Finally, on January 23, 1960, the final goal of Project Nekton was achieved. On a nine-hour dive, the *Trieste* successfully dove seven miles (35,800 feet), into the deepest place in the world ocean.

After the deep dive, the *Trieste* worked at Guam for another six months in the follow-up Project Nekton II. The deepest dive of that series was 20,000 feet.

In the early 1960s, in addition to the U.S. Navy's *Trieste*, there was a great deal of new activity in the sea. New submersibles were designed and constructed, while diving technique began to exhibit bold new advances. In France, Jacques Cousteau began operations of his "Souscoupe Sousmarin," or undersea saucer, the first of the modern deep submersibles. Its small ellipsoidal hull contained modest space for its three-man crew, but its displacement was sufficient to provide the necessary buoyancy without the need for the gasoline-filled balloon. Its maximum operating depth was a respectable 3,000 feet and it was an advanced design for the time. A whole generation of deep submersibles that would follow would use similar design features.

Meanwhile, in Florida, businessman John Perry was evolving his famous series of manned submersibles. Beginning with swimmer-delivery vehicles which simply provided streamlined, free-flooding, underwater transportation for sport divers, Perry soon developed his first real submersible, the *Cubmarine*. While it only had a modest depth capability, it was the first in a series of over 30 submersibles built by his company, Perry Oceanographics, over the next 20 years. The majority of the Perry submarines went to work in offshore oil and gas development, especially in the North Sea. There they gained a reputation for rugged reliability and safety. Ultimately their depth capability would reach 3000 feet, which was wholly sufficient for the offshore industry.

One of the most unusual phenomena during the 1960s was the movement of aerospace companies into the undersea field. This was not a broad-front movement. It was almost exclusively concentrated on the deep submersible. Companies such as Lockheed, General Dynamics, Grumman, Boeing, Northrup and Douglas either built submersibles or had design groups seriously at work on them. In addition, other major defense-oriented firms such as General Motors, General Mills, Westinghouse, Litton Industries and Reynolds Aluminum built submersibles.

What was the reason for all of this? Certainly it was not due to any requirements generated by the US Navy; as there were not any at that time, although the Navy had ordered two vehicles from General Dynamics, the *Sea Cliff* and the *Turtle*, as well as the *Alvin* which the Navy had purchased and assigned to the Woods Hole Oceanographic Institution.

The real reason appears to be a self-generated perception by these aerospace and defense companies that the Navy would have to move in this direction in the future. They believed the Navy's initiative to acquire the *Trieste* and dive it to the deepest part of the ocean signaled an expanded Navy effort in this area. Unfortunately this logic was faulty. The negative signals were not seen and the companies, hyped up by their own publicity and that of their competitors, forged ahead; the result was an amazing array of different submersible designs. Most went to sea and worked for very brief periods of time, but by the end of the decade, they and their companies were out of the exploration of inner space.

The submersible *Alvin* deserves special mention. Built by the US Navy's Office of Naval Research (ONR) in 1964, the *Alvin* had a 6,000 foot depth capability. ONR assigned it to the Woods Hole Oceanographic Institution to support deep-ocean scientific research. For the next two decades this research tool would make thousands of dives into the Atlantic and Pacific Oceans, taking hundreds of scientists to their work sites. Many of her voyages of discovery have been shared with millions of people via National Geographic television special programs. Without a doubt, the *Alvin* is the best-known submersible in the history of man in the sea.

At no time in the history of undersea technology had such a burst of activity resulted in so much new design and technology associated with a single focus, the deep submersible. Unfortunately they were "answers" looking for "the question" and the whole effort was bound to face a severe retrenchment.

In the 1960s diving not only saw the continuing rapid increase of sport and scientific diving through the use of the SCUBA device (made by an even greater number of companies), but it also saw the advent of practical saturation diving.

Saturation meant the diver could reach physiological equilibrium with respect to dilution of his breathing mixture throughout his body's bloodstream and tissues. Once in equilibrium you could work at depth for prolonged periods of time, as long as you allowed for this time through use of decompression procedures in the return to sea-level pressure. This suggested that if houses, or habitats, could be constructed to be placed on the seabed, then the divers could remain under pressure continuously while at the work site. The dry habitat would be maintained at the same pressure as the surrounding waters so the diver could enjoy his work/rest cycle without the need to return to the surface.

Pioneers in saturation diving were Americans Edwin Link and Captain (Dr.) George Bond, US Navy, and Frenchman Jacques Cousteau. Their early experiments made it possible for the advanced saturation dive systems that are now commonplace in the offshore oil and gas industry.

A few hundred feet (200 to 600) was the depth frontier in the early days of saturation diving. Today the technique has advanced to the point where working operational capabilities to beyond 1,500 feet are offered by the larger commercial diving companies that support offshore development. The sea floor habitat is no longer very useful in commercial work. Instead the habitat is located aboard the diving support ship. This permits the diving team to be maintained at working depth pressure around the clock until their work is completed. Again, as in the early years of this century, the diver in his suit approaches, or exceeds, the depth capability of many modern submarines.

As with the earlier development of submarine rescue equipment, tragic losses of submarines in the 1960s forced the development of advanced submarine rescue systems. In April 1963, the US Navy nuclear submarine *Thresher* was lost with all hands near Boston in over 8,000 feet of water. In combination with other research systems, which had located the wreckage, the venerable *Trieste* dove to inspect the debris, hoping to learn something about how the tragedy occurred. After this final mission in its logbook, *Trieste* was retired by the Navy. It had been in service for 10 years. In 1964, a new version of the *Trieste*, *Trieste II*, built by the US Navy, went back to the *Thresher* site to continue the investigation.

As a result of the *Thresher* loss, the Navy founded the Deep Sea Systems Project (DSSP). This program was initially assigned the task of finding a means to rescue downed submarine crews at greater depths than existing surface-lowered bell-rescue systems. This would not have helped in the case of the *Thresher*. She went down in water depths greater than her crush depth. But the incident served to focus attention on a potential problem should these deep-diving submarines be stranded on the sea floor at depths less-than-crush depth.

The result of the DSSP's first major program was the development of the Deep Submergence Rescue Vehicle (DSRV). Two of them were built by Lockheed and put into service in the early 1970s. They have a depth capability of 5,000 feet and are capable of rescuing submarine crews by joining with the downed submarine's hatches and transferring crew members into the passenger section of the submersible. Despite their size and complexity, they are air transportable to permit rapid mobilization to any point in the world. At the nearest seaport the DSRVs could be put on board a variety of ships or even loaded piggyback on a nuclear submarine to make the trip to the accident site. Both DSRV's have their home port at the Naval Air Station in San Diego, California.

The undersea technology surge of the 1960s also saw the beginning of a new undersea system that would eventually take over some work from both divers and manned submersibles. This was the remotely operated vehicle (ROV). These tethered vehicles were controlled by umbilical cables from a surface vessel. The vehicle pilot would sit before a console controlling vehicle motions while looking out of the vehicle through the use of a television camera mounted on the vehicle far below. Note that in using the ROV the human was still in the control loop, just as in the manned submersible. The difference was in where the man was located. Thus the term "unmanned" for these vehicles is not entirely correct.

There were only a few such systems designed in the 1960s, mostly by or for the Navy. But they were to be part of the wave of the future.

At the end of the decade tragedy would again strike the US Submarine Force. The submarine *Scorpion* was lost in the eastern Atlantic near the Azores. The *Trieste II* was used to make the investigation. And again the water depth was too great for the DSRVs to have been of help.

The decade of the 1960s was a period of perhaps the greatest advancement yet experienced in undersea systems design, construction and operation. While much of this progress took place in the US, there were significant parallel advances in Canada and Europe.

Of special interest were the two submersibles developed by Jacques Piccard. The first, the *Auguste Piccard,* was used at the Swiss National Fair (1964 –1965) to take 49 paying passengers on a deep (1,000 feet) tour of Lake Geneva. During the Fair, over 32,000 passengers were carried during a series of over 1,100 dives. At peak times the *Auguste Piccard* made nine dives a day.

Later, in 1968, Piccard worked with the Grumman Aircraft Corporation to build another large submersible, the *Ben*

Franklin. This submersible achieved fame when Piccard and a crew of five piloted it on a 30-day submerged research mission in the Gulf Stream off the East Coast of the United States.

Progress in undersea capability evolved over a broad front. The value of advanced dive systems use was not hard to sell to the offshore industry. It took this industry longer to understand the advantages of manned submersibles and where they could actually be more efficient than the diver. The eventual acceptance of manned submersibles offshore was largely due to the rigors of operating in the newly developing North Sea oil and gas fields.

The Navy, within its research laboratories such as the Naval Undersea Center (NUC) at San Diego, was developing a family of bold new designs to take advantage of advanced materials and technologies. Much of the new knowledge was borrowed from aerospace (a bit of irony for the aerospace companies who had tried earlier to get into this field).

Of special emphasis were advanced hull materials such as acrylic plastic and glass. The Navy built and tested several pressure hulls of acrylic, installing them in two submersibles, the *Nemo* and the *Makahiki*. Another Navy submersible, the *Deep View*, used a massive borosilicate (pyrex) glass hemisphere as one end of its cylindrical hull. The view from these submersibles was spectacular. Many of those who had experienced dives in these vehicles called them "people bowls"—the fish outside looked into the bowl at the people. While the massive glass program did not lead to large-scale adoption of this material, the plastic hull program did. Today acrylic hemispheres and even full spheres are quite common.

Since the submersible is intended to take the trained mind and eye to the work site, the more viewing area the better. Thus it is not hard to understand the wide acceptance of these new concepts.

The veteran Navy submersible *Alvin* benefited from a Navy program to develop a new structural material, titanium, for pressure hulls. In 1973, the *Alvin* received a titanium hull, which increased her operating depth from 6,000 feet to 12,400 feet, the average depth of the world ocean.

Concurrently, improved sensor systems such as cameras,

instruments, sonars, etc., helped make the submersible even more efficient in underwater tasks.

Another important development was the remote controlled arm, or manipulator. These mechanical hands had become available to submersibles in the mid-1960s, permitting the crew inside the submarine to do work tasks and recover objects. By the end of the decade they were becoming reliable and easy to operate.

Perhaps the most ambitious submersible ever built was constructed by the Navy at this time. This was the nuclear-powered deep submersible, NR-1. Most of its operational characteristics are still classified. However, we do know that it has the ability to take its crew to great depths for prolonged periods of time, since its nuclear reactor provides unlimited power. The only real limitation appears to be how much food and other provisions it could carry to sustain a mission. Several marine scientists have had the opportunity to use the NR-1. Their reports have been very positive about its capabilities for deep-ocean research. However, most of NR-1's work has been associated with Navy project requirements. The very high cost of such a system makes it unlikely that more will be built.

Although much of the preceding has dealt with US Navy work, it is not an unfair accounting. The US Navy did, in fact, represent the major technical force in the development of new undersea capability. Also, very little of this advancement was put under the cloak of secrecy, so technological advances were very quickly made available to civil users. Unfortunately, the late 1960s found a new style of management in the Pentagon, which emphasized "mission-oriented" research and technology within the Defense Department. It was often difficult initially to see the direct mission relationship on any other basis than intuition and hunch. This was not good enough for the senior policy people, and the former aggressive push of science and technology was replaced by cautious conservatism. In the face of being told not to do things that appeared not to be "mission-oriented," the Navy trimmed its sails and began to lose its momentum as a major force in pushing undersea technology. The cap was put on the whole business when the increasing resource demands of the Vietnam War resulted in funding being diverted from research and development associated with ocean science and technology.

The 1970s brought a period of reduced funding, a Navy program that was losing its technology thrust and the birth of the nation's first civil ocean agency, the National Oceanic and Atmospheric Administration (NOAA). But it was also a time for useful consolidation and shake-out of the marginal performers among private companies and government agencies.

Mr. Perry continued to build his small submarines, mainly for the offshore industry, and in the process began to make money as the largest producer of small submersibles in the world.

Also in Florida at this time, Edwin Link and Seward Johnson began a partnership that was to lead to the development of the largest private, non-profit marine research institution developed in the US since the Woods Hole Institution was founded half a century before. This was the Harbor Branch Foundation, endowed by both Link and Johnson. Link's interest in undersea systems and diving was evident as he designed a new manned submersible, the *Johnson Sea-Link*. Made primarily of aluminum and acrylic plastic, it placed the pilot and co-pilot inside an enormous plastic bubble—an infinite window for efficient viewing of the subsea environment. The *Johnson Sea-Link* was given a depth capability of 2,000 feet and the mission to operate in support of marine science. In the late 1970s, a second submersible of the same design was added to Harbor Branch's fleet. Careful conversion of a vessel to a mother ship for these submersibles has provided needed mobility to do ocean research at considerable distances from Link Port at Fort Pierce, Florida.

By the mid-decade, the ROV had joined the manned submersible as an accepted tool for offshore work. In 1975 there were some 24 ROVs and 86 manned submersibles available. Growth was rapid. At the end of that decade there were 235 ROVs and 144 manned vehicles.

As an undersea work tool the ROV could be used in routine tasks to replace the more expensive manned systems, whether diver or submersible. In addition, the ROV was ideally suited for vital tasks where the risk to a man was great. More and more off-shore diving services companies began to acquire diver-alternative systems in the form of manned submersibles and ROV's.

The 1970s boom in undersea work systems was driven by the rapid expansion of the offshore oil and gas industry. The technological advances and additions of new undersea equipment were not through the navies, as in the 1960s, but through the demands of the oil companies to get the job done safely and efficiently.

Even with this increased tempo of operations worldwide, there were few serious accidents involving manned submersibles. Less than a half dozen people have lost their lives in these machines in 25 years, a tribute to their inherently safe design and careful operating procedures.

In the diving world, the statistics were more unfortunate. The cost of pushing the operational frontier even deeper into the oceans was quite high. Massive overhauling of training, safety, and qualification standards with direct government supervision and enforcement have helped to reduce the rate of injuries.

One means to reduce the cost of diving services and improve safety for undersea work operations was through the development of the one-atmosphere diving system (ADS). Essentially this was a man-shaped diving suit which was pressure resistant. It gave the operator mobility similar to that of a diver but with the one-atmosphere comfort of a manned submersible. In this way it is possible to get individual diver performance at the work site in a low-cost vehicle system, but without the high cost of having to decompress the man after each operation. The ADS combines the best features of diver and submersible; it is a real convergence point in the evolution of both man in the sea capabilities.

Actually, the idea was not that new. In 1937, the Roberto Galeazzi Company in Italy developed such a diving suit and over the years sold about 50 of them. These units had a depth capability of about 600 feet. A major advance in ADS technology came with the development of the JIM Suit in 1973. These "submersible suits" had a 1,300 foot diving capability and were immediately put to work in the offshore oil and gas service industry. Oceaneering, a major US diving company, and one of the largest in the world, bought 17 JIM Suits for this kind of work. To date, about 24 have been built, including some new models for the US Navy which can dive to 2,400 feet, deeper than most current military submarines.

More advanced ADS designs now offer limited propulsion mobility, along with better visibility and ease of movement. A British company, OSEL, has built and sold several of its Wasp and Mantis ADS units.

Of course, the ROV does not have the problems of hazards to man. But the early models were often unreliable and hard to maintain. Inexperienced operators (pilots) put them into situations where frequent losses occurred, due to severing or fouling of the umbilical line. But these problems were worked out and today many offshore drilling companies expect to continue the use of both ROVs and divers. The undersea work system that has suffered the most loss of business from the advent of an efficient ROV is the manned submersible.

The 1980s: The Present and Prelude to the Future

In the evolution of man in the sea, the 1960s were the period of rapid growth and innovation; the 1970s were the period of consolidation and nationalization; the present appears to be a time of maturity. Undersea work-system options are now regarded as a complementary set of capabilities. As noted earlier the offshore services operator will probably have these capabilities in at least two of three areas. Many have all three.

In the 1980s, the world experienced a major economic recession which, combined with a worldwide oil glut, greatly depressed the level of industrial activity offshore. Nevertheless, by 1984, the vehicle count, worldwide, was 280 ROVs and 176 manned submersibles. Of interest is the fact that over eight nations now operate submersibles that are dedicated to marine scientific research.

May 1984, saw the world's last bathyscaphe retired when the US Navy's *Trieste II* was decommissioned at San Diego, California. The development of new construction materials, such as titanium and buoyant hard plastic foams, provided the deep submersible designer with capabilities that made the old gasoline-filled balloon of the bathyscaphes obsolete. The *Trieste II* was retired in favor of the completely rebuilt Navy submersible; the *Sea Cliff*'s operating depth was increased from 6,500 feet to 20,000 feet.

An ability to dive to 20,000 feet is significant. This permits diving to 98% of the ocean floor. Only 2% of the oceans' depth is between 20,000 and 35,800 feet.

The government of France has built a 20,000 foot-capable submersible, the *Nautile*. It completed its deep-dive tests in 1985 and is now operational. In Japan, the government has authorized the funding for a submersible with similar depth capability. It should be operational by 1989. Finally, the USSR Academy of Sciences has also been planning a similar program; however, no construction has yet begun.

The rapid progress in the evolution of the ROV continues, even though its primary employment is in support of offshore oil and gas development. There are large new ROV operations, with some of them operating as many as 30. In 1984, a major new development occurred in this area, with the introduction of the low-cost ROV (LCROV). The LCROV aims at a cost range from $20,000 to $40,000, which may sound high, but the previous lowest cost systems were on the order of $150,000. The LCROV's will be able to undertake many simple tasks where a "swimming eyeball" is all that is necessary to make an inspection. The low cost now makes ROV technology available to a much wider band of users, such as small diving companies, fishermen, merchant ship operators, police departments, etc. One designer is even working on a $5,000 LCROV that will be offered to the recreational boating community.

As the recession eases and world energy demand begins to climb again, we will see a new surge of interest in advanced undersea systems. Most of this will be driven by commercial applications and military requirements. As always, the advancement of marine scientific research technique will reap the benefits from all sources.

As for the future, it is clear that man will still be involved in direct work in the sea, even as the ROV takes over many of the tasks formerly done by divers and submersibles. It really is the case of an expanding universe of things to be done. The inquiring mind of man, and his eyes, will continue to dwell at the edge of the far frontier of the oceans' inner space.

Acknowledgment

Over the last 31 years it was my good fortune to have participated in many of the recent events mentioned in this account. It's for this reason that I insist that it is not so much a history of man in the sea as it is a personal view. Due to reasonable limits of space for this contribution, much has been left out. The full story would be a book-length treatment. With these imperfections in mind it is, nevertheless, a useful overview of an important enterprise: man in the sea.

I would like to make a special acknowledgment for the assistance and helpful suggestions made by Dr. Jacques Piccard. Dr. Piccard was my colleague in the early US Navy dives of the bathyscaphe, *Trieste*, when I was the Navy commander of that submersible. It was good to work with him again at this conference. However I must state that all errors and omissions in this article are mine alone.

General References

Beebe, W. 1934. *Half Mile Down*. New York: Harcourt Brace

Busby, R. 1976. "Manned Submersibles." *Office of the Oceanography of the Navy*. Washington, D.C.: United States Government Printing Office.

Busby, R. 1985. *Undersea Vehicle Directory*. Arlington: Busby Associates.

Earle, S. and A. Giddings. 1980. *Exploring the Deep Frontier: The Adventure of Man in the Sea*. Washington, D.C.: National Geographic Society.

Geyer, R. 1977. *Submersibles and Their Use in Oceanography and Ocean Engineering*. New York: Elseiver.

Piccard, J. 1961. *Seven Miles Down*. New York: G.P. Putnam.

________, 1971. *The Sun Beneath the Sea*. New York: Scribners.

Sweeney, J. 1970. *A Pictorial History of Oceanographic Submersibles*. New York: Crown.

Talkington, H. 1981. *Undersea Work Systems*. New York: Marcel Dekker.

Selected References

Beebe, William. 1934. *Half Mile Down*. Harcourt Brace, New York.

Busby, R.F. 1976. *Manned Submersibles*. Published by the Office of the Oceanographer of the Navy. US Government Printing Office, Washington.

Busby, R. F. 1985. *Undersea Vehicle Directory*, 1985 Edition, Busby Associates, Arlington, Virginia.

Earle, Sylvia A. and Al Giddings. 1980. *Exploring the Deep Frontier—The Adventure of Man in the Sea*. National Geographic Society, Washington.

Geyer, Richard A. 1977. *Submersibles and Their Use in Oceanography and Ocean Engineering*. Elseiver, New York.

Piccard, Auguste. 1956. *Earth, Sky and Sea*. Oxford University Press, New York.

Piccard, Jacques. 1961. *Seven Miles Down*. G.P. Putnam, New York.

Piccard, Jacques. 1971. *The Sun Beneath the Sea*. Scribners, New York.

Sweeney, James B. 1970. *A Pictorial History of Oceanographic Submersibles*. Crown, New York. 1970.

Talkington, Howard R. 1981. *Undersea Work Systems*. Marcel Dekker, New York.

Terry, Richard. 1966. *The Deep Submersible*. Western Periodicals, Los Angeles.

Trillo, Robert L. 1977. *Janes Ocean Technology, 1976–77*. Last year of publication. Franklin Watts, New York.

Walsh, Don. 1960. "Our Seven Mile Dive to the Bottom." *Life Magazine*, 7 February, 1960.

Walsh, Don. 1985. "The Conquest of Inner Space." US Naval Institute Proceedings, January, 1985

PART THREE:

OCEAN RESOURCES

TWELVE

OCEAN RESOURCES

Kurt Stehling

The oceans cover about 70% of the earth's surface. Within that enormous mass of about 350 million cubic miles (over one billion km^3) of sea water are trillions of tons of dissolved elemental compounds, mostly those of sodium, magnesium, potassium, and chlorine. All 92 of nature's elements are dissolved in the oceans in one form or another and in varying concentrations with the lighter elements (as above) predominant. Besides the dissolved elements (or "minerals"), there are known or suspected colossal deposits of inorganic metallic and other minerals on, or under, the sea bottom. Furthermore, plentiful non-living organic resources in the forms of petroleum and natural gas occur on or near about 30% of the world's coast or "shelf" areas.

The above resources can be called "non-living." But the oceans' water column and many shallower bottom areas (less than 600 feet) also contain the biomass, or "living" resources—mostly resident within the water's upper 600 ft (180 meters) or so. The most obvious of these living resources are, of course, fish and shellfish. Extracting (i.e., fishing) these food sources has been an historic activity; with increasing world population the fishing or "harvesting" (e.g., finding, catching and transporting the food to port) and even cultivation of marine food species will become increasingly important. Despite the disappearance or serious depletion (from over-fishing) of many species, only about 15% of the total biomass (flora and fauna) are presently harvested.

Living Resources

About 70 million metric tons of fin-fish, shellfish, (and other crustaceans) whales, other sea mammals—such as seals, walrus, etc.—were harvested throughout the world in 1983. Much of this catch is obtained by industrial nations (Japan, Western Europe).

The 70 million ton harvest represents about 10% of total animal protein production. These gross figures conceal, however, the very real economic and social significance of marine fishery products, regionally and nationally. For some nations, food from the sea represents an indispensable source of animal protein, without which currently deficient diets would become disastrously inadequate. Virtually all of Asia and Africa fall in this category. For others, high per capita consumption is not a matter of life, death, or even health, but rather a matter of strong preferences; the Scandinavian countries might be cited as an example. In still other nations food from the sea represents an important source not only of domestic protein but of foreign exchange as well. Both fish and fish meal are significant items of international commerce, and nations such as Iceland, Peru, and Norway are heavily dependent on exports of processed-fish products for stability in their balance of payments. For obvious reasons, fishing activities and the related processing and waterfront activities tend to be centered geographically in areas frequently deficient in other employment and investment opportunities.

In brief, the relatively small numbers associated with the world's marine fisheries, in comparison with other sources of food, should not conceal the fact that they are of very real economic importance; and efforts to improve the performance of these industries, whether by increasing output, reducing cost, or both, are increasingly important goals for developing countries.

The reasons for the demand for fish and shellfish include:

1. The level of personal income per capita;
2. Aggregate size and rate of growth of the population;
3. Tastes and preferences, including the influence of customs reflecting religious practices and national origin; and
4. Price and availability of closely substitutable products, of which meat and poultry are the most important.

The strength of world demand for protein food is evident in the rapid growth in production of marine seafoods during the past three decades. Landings of fin-fish and shellfish have been growing at a rate of more than 6% a year since the end of World War II. Total landings have jumped from about 20 million metric tons in 1950 to about 70 million tons in 1983, of which at least 65 million tons came from marine sources, and the rest from fish "ponds," etc. The areas of strongest demand spread across the entire spectrum of marine seafoods. Specialty processed fish and the more exotic forms of fin-fish and shellfish are among the highest-priced foods in the markets of the developed countries, and demand for low priced fish, though changing with respect to preferred forms of preparation, continues to expand equally rapidly in many of the less developed nations. A forecast of world population growth would, accordingly, provide a good indication of the minimum rate of growth expected in demand for marine food products.

The nature of this growing demand is of great interest in analyzing the kinds of markets that are emerging for living products of the sea. In the more highly developed nations there is a marked tendency for per capita direct consumption of seafoods to level off. As incomes increase beyond the level at which adequate caloric and nutritional need is assured, consumer demand reflects more and more heavily the desire for diversification as well as processing and marketing sources that make food products more convenient to handle and prepare.

Steady per capita demand for fin-fish and shellfish for direct consumption in the United States (and other nations such as Britain and Japan) conceals wide variations among species. In general, demand for products of unusually good flavor and texture, such as fresh and frozen salmon, shellfish, lake trout, and red snapper is sensitive to rising real incomes and has been very strong throughout the postwar period. Similarly, demand for species used to produce frozen sticks and portions and canned tuna, where a high degree of consumer convenience has been linked to effective merchandising programs, has been good throughout the period. On the other hand, there is a marked tendency for lower-income groups to shift away from cheaper fish, particularly in the United States (South) and in coastal areas, toward meat, poultry, and other preferred protein foods as their economic lot improves.

An important consideration for the future is the rapid growth in the demand for fish as an intermediate product. The per capita demand for fish in the developed countries must include the high and continuing increase in consumption of marine fish products in the form of fish meal. High quality protein meals have now become a standard element in feeding programs for poultry and meat producers. They are competitive in these uses with other sources of protein, such as soybean meal. However, they are continuing to expand their market position and will do so as long as the relative prices of fish meal remain favorable. Fish meal is produced from smaller fish, generally commanding much lower prices than those consumed directly by human beings, but its contribution to a varied and high-quality protein diet is real. There is no reason why the food industry should not use land animals as converters of forage fish rather than tuna or other predators in the sea.

There are certain common characteristics of the demand for marine seafoods in developing countries. The most striking is the strength of the demand for fish, not only for its important nutritional characteristics in areas subject to chronic protein and caloric deficiencies, but on grounds of tastes and preferences. Much has been made of the isolated cases in which protein deficiency exists side by side with abundant fish supplies because of religious or other taboos, but these are rare exceptions. In most of the countries with access to the sea, fish have always provided an important source of food. (The various Caribbean nations are only beginning to exploit this potential. Various shellfish and turtles are now being harvested to a limited extent.) Rising incomes, particularly in the rapidly growing urban areas oriented to international trade, have typically produced a striking increase in the demand for fish. Similarly, wherever technological developments have expanded sharply, i.e., satellite and aircraft surveys, improved acoustic detection of schools, better marine ecology and conservation, better harvesting gear, etc., the capacity of indigenous fisheries (or created new ones), the task of creating the necessary processing and marketing apparatus to distribute the increased landings has been, on the whole, much easier than expected because of the strength of demand for the products.

The demand for fish has also responded positively, and will continue to do so, to improvements in nutritional knowledge and in the quality and diversity of fish products. Even in areas where taboos against consumption of fish have been relatively strong, the use of fish as food in schools, hospitals, and other institutions, coupled with a rising literacy rate, has tended to break down the resistance to using marine resources. These, incidentally, are the areas of the world in which population is increasing most rapidly.

Interest in conserving the oceans' living resources is not new, and literature dealing with conservation and ocean resources dates well back into English history. Even in the early part of the 13th century, conservationists were pleading for restrictions on fishing techniques lest the coastal resources be depleted.

The vigor with which truly international fishery operations are being developed is indicated by the fact that 20 nations are now fishing off the southwest coast of Africa with modern long-range vessels. These include, among others, South Korea, Taiwan, Israel, Bulgaria, Rumania, Egypt, and Greece. The rapidly developing fisheries on the Continental Shelf of South America, south of the Rio de la Plata, are shared not only by South American nations but by Cubans, Spanish, Russians, Japanese, and others. There is already serious concern about declines in productivity on the major trawling grounds off the coast of Mauritania and Senegal, where more than 200 large, modern, oceangoing trawlers are now operating on a year-round basis. Rumanian vessels are active off the coast of New Zealand, and the Kuwaitis are involved in development of the shrimp fisheries off North Borneo. The pace of this development is such that unless some effective means of promoting the necessary scientific knowledge of yield potentials (and an adequate control mechanism to prevent exceeding these limits) is forthcoming, the economic effect of any improvement in technology or markets is likely to be vitiated by over-exploitation of existing stocks. This will occur unless technical breakthroughs produce a new era of wider ocean fishing and further diversification in exploiting shelf species.

It is of value to consider the relative utilization of major groups of marine species. The demersal fish forms (flounders, soles, cods, redfish), are probably the most fully exploited groups in terms of their total potential. The *National Marine Fisheries Report* for 1982 concluded that there are no large demersal fish stocks left unexploited in the northeastern Atlantic. In view of the rapid expansion of trawl fisheries in the eastern Pacific and the historically heavily exploited Asian stocks of demersals, there may be little increase in production of demersal fish in the northern hemisphere. This does not, however, preclude further development of local stocks in the Gulf of Alaska, the Gulf of Mexico, and several other areas. Very recent egg and larvae research suggests, however, that even in the North Atlantic very large populations of sand lance and blue whiting are being exploited at very low proportions of their potential yield.

The southern hemisphere does have under-utilized demersal stocks, particularly in the waters off both coasts of South America and New Zealand, and further development will occur off West Africa. This is tempered, however, by the fact that nearly 70% of the continental shelf areas of the world lie in the northern hemisphere, and most of these areas are rather intensively exploited. As a rough estimate, we might assume that demersal fish stocks are now providing about 60 to 80% of

Table 12-1: Seafood Estimated Possible Yields Maximum Exploitation (million metric tons)

Continent	*Estimated maximum production*	*1975 production*
Africa	9	3.0
North America	12	5.0
South America	15	9.0
Asia (except USSR)	23	20.0
Europe (except USSR)	9	11.0
Oceania	4	0.2
USSR	6	5.0
Total	78	53.2

their total potential, given present techniques and market preferences. The ultimate potential may be much greater.

Pelagic fish stocks (tuna, sardines, jacks, anchovies, hakes, etc.), have considerable potential for increased production. Anchovies are *already* a major sea food crop for Peru, where on average about 10,000 tons are processed each year. As with demersal fish, utilization is now most intensive in the northern hemisphere, and the potential for growth is greatest in the southern hemisphere and in the Arabian Sea. It is extremely difficult to fix the degree of utilization of pelagic forms in realistic terms, but obviously only a small percentage of the biological potential of pelagic fishes is being utilized, perhaps less than 5%.

Of the major shellfish and invertebrates, clams have been little touched. Oyster stocks are under considerable pressure, but shrimp, despite very strong market demands, are still capable of supporting much greater production.

If we look beyond present forms of fish considered marketable and present areas considered capable of supporting economically profitable operations, most of the world catch of marine fish comes from waters over the continental shelf at depths less than 200 fathoms. Only about 8% of the surface areas of the oceans may be classified as shelf areas. The remaining 92% encompasses the continental slopes and deep basin regions. About 90% of the world's catch is taken from the small area defined as continental shelf waters. As might be expected, on economic grounds, man's fishing efforts are centered on regions which are most accessible and where environmental conditions operate to concentrate fish.

On a per unit basis, waters beyond the shelf are producing only one-eightieth as much as the nutrient-rich self waters. The productivity of mid-ocean waters, at least of the forms now most useful to man, would be expected to be lower than over the shelf, of course. Very large parts of the high seas have primary productivity less than one-fifth that of the present fishing areas, and in many cases it is less than one-tenth. No primary production occurs below a depth of about of about 150 m. Nevertheless, the degree of utilization in the open oceans is even smaller than the expected availability of fish.

There are great quantities of squid, lantern fishes, pomfrets, bristle mouth, jacks, tuna-like fishes, etc., which inhabit open ocean regions, but effective utilization of many of these will call for development of new harvesting technology. Perhaps as much as 40 to 60% of estimated biological potential is tied up in fin-fish and shellfish inhabiting the open oceans. If fishing systems were stabilized at present efficiency levels there would be little hope of really major increases in the harvest of pelagic fishes in the open oceans (and of some pelagic forms which overlie the shelf as well). There are, however, some under-utilized and unused fish stocks which are available for harvest with conventional gear. Such potentials are available in varying degree in almost all areas of the world.

Present knowledge is admittedly not very definitive as to the areas and resources that will supply future catches. At the moment it seems likely that continued fisheries growth over the next decade will come largely from continued geographic expansion. Production will increase in the southern hemisphere as a result of greater efforts to utilize the hakes and sardine-like fish off Africa and the East and West coasts of South America, and pelagic fish off New Zealand and Australia.

There will be some expansion in demersal fisheries from these same waters, but the increase, relative to current production, will not be large. In the Indian Ocean (Arabian Sea) there is apparently a good possibility of expanding pelagic fish catches, and in the northeastern Pacific further increases in flounder catches are likely.

The following species and areas appear to have the greatest growth potential contingent on existing technology:

- *Herring-like fishes*: Arabian Sea, California, Chile, Argentina, Gulf of Alaska, Gulf of Mexico, Venezuela, northern Brazil, West Africa.
- *Hakes*: Chile, Peru, Mexico, Argentina, West Africa
- *Clams*: Worldwide
- *Flounders*: Northeast Pacific, Patagonian Shelf, New Zealand
- *Tuna, jacks and some saury*: New Zealand, Australia, mid-Pacific, Atlantic.

If we anticipate continued development of our ability to locate, concentrate, and harvest, the following marine forms might provide major increases in production:

- Squids
- Clams
- Pelagic ocean fishes, such as bristle mouth, saury, tuna, jacks, and pomfrets
- Redfish
- Smelts and herring-like fishes
- "Deep sea" forms (500–2,000 meters) (e.g., rattails).
- Krill—This species, a small shrimp-like "emphausiid" crustacean is assuming an increasingly important role as a seafood source, widely distributed in Antarctic waters.

Since there may be many hundreds of millions of tons of Krill present in the deep-cold Antarctic waters, the future potential harvest (without seriously depleting the renewable stock) may equal or surpass in *weight* (but not in value) the present world fish catch.

The Soviet Union, mainly, but increasingly the Japanese, are currently harvesting several million tons of krill per year, using special fine-mesh nets deployed like a trawl. Krill, being "lower" on the food chain, is converted into fishmeal and paste, rather than being used as a primary human food source.

Baleen whales consume krill as their main food source. Whether increased harvesting of the krill will affect the whale ecology has not yet been determined. The matter of baleen survival is, of course, connected with the larger problem of whale survival and management.

Various international treaties supported by the US, have tried to come to grips with whale preservation. The endangered species include the minke whale, while others such as the sperm are nearing extinction.

Despite steady violations by the Soviets and Japanese about catch size and type, some progress is being made in harvesting limitations. The US has a congressionally mandated obligation to "punish" whaling agreement transgressor nations by denying them—or reducing by at least 50%—their access to fishing stocks in the US "Exclusive Economic Zone" (EEZ) which extends 200 miles out from US shores.

The *controlled* growing and harvesting of marine species is called *aquaculture*. Fishery management is a form of aquaculture and is a logical first step toward farming at sea. Because the idea of farming the waters instead of randomly hunting the wild creatures growing in them has such great appeal, aquaculture has stimulated a great amount of visionary thinking. Intensive private aquaculture will first become practical when those products are grown that command high prices and ready markets.

Aquaculture resembles the shore-based livestock industry, in that animals either have to be permitted to forage for themselves in reasonably productive areas or, if they are closely confined, they must be fed.

Oysters and clams filter their food from the large volumes of water moving past with the tides and enough is now known of their biology to make their culture feasible. The fact that on the Atlantic and Gulf coasts tidal waters cannot be held privately is the principal obstacle to commercial culture. On the Pacific coast, where private ownership of appropriate water is permitted, the industry has begun. Provision is needed for shellfish producers to lease the bottom rights of water suitable for shellfish culture much as mineral rights are now granted.

The tremendous increase in oyster yields by raft cultivation, as opposed to bottom cultivation (16,000 to 84,000 pounds per acre for raft cultivation as opposed to 600 to 800 pounds per acre for bottom cultivation), illustrates the need for development of these techniques in United States fisheries.

A second fishery where culture techniques are well-advanced is salmon and steelhead. Eggs from selected mature fish are hatched in trays and the young are reared in troughs and ponds until they reach a size suitable for seasonable migration. Upon liberation, they migrate to the sea where they forage and grow for two to four years. Finally they return to the ponds of their birth where most are harvested and some are selected for spawning. In fact, over half the silver salmon running up the Columbia River have been raised in this manner in government hatcheries. Again, however, commercial enterprise is presently frustrated by the fact that the fish are fair game for anyone while at sea and while they are returning upstream. Unless a private producer can be reasonably certain of harvesting his fish, investment is discouraged.

In order to increase the economic attractiveness of aquaculture, besides the problems of a producer's control over his "livestock," there is an immediate need for more knowledge of life cycles, the breeding of faster growing and tougher varieties of stock, improved diets, better control of disease and parasites, and better facilities for feeding, harvesting, and confining fish. In particular, more biological knowledge is necessary for the culture of shrimp and lobsters, while there is still much to be done to improve the production of oysters, clams, and salmon. Here, also, the fishing industry is in no position to undertake the research and development on the scale that is desirable; thus, it is a proper area for government support.

The Japanese, with a limited arable land area for food crops have, not only the world's largest fish harvest per capita, but also have the most extensive and varied aquaculture program. In 1982 they raised almost 700,000 tons of prawns, smaller shrimp, crabs and other shellfish besides dorsal fish in estuarine and other coastal areas. Also, they harvested about 50,000 tons of seaweed and various marine algae for animal and human consumption. Other nations (e.g., Australia "grows" about 90 million oysters annually in the brackish estuaries of New South Wales) are also studying and practicing controlled growth of marine seafood. Several Caribbean islands are experimenting with sea turtle cultivation. The People's Republic of China has an ambitious program planned or underway, for raising approximately 2 million tons of ocean sea food and seaweed per year along its shore line.

Most aquaculture will probably, for the near future, concentrate on high density, high-value shellfish, and maybe turtles. Other species of seafood do not yet fetch the prices needed to recover the expense of aquaculture installations, control, marketing, etc. The flora (mostly seaweed) have uses as food additives or garnish. Whatever means are used to produce or harvest the oceans' living resources, there is no doubt that the potential exists for expansion of sea food recovery—at least for the next 50 years or so—provided that international conservation and control efforts, buttressed by treaties (when these are observed!) permit an orderly exploitation, instead of a self-defeating international free-for-all.

Non-Living Mineral Resources

It is becoming apparent to geologists and geophysicists that the tremendous area beneath the seas has considerable potential for the extraction of mineral resources.

The development of submarine non-living or mineral assets is becoming especially important for the United States, whose oil, gas and metallic ore reserves are shrinking rapidly. Marine mineral explorations and exploitation is even more important for such industrialized countries as Japan which have almost no indigenous industrially important solid mineral or hydrocarbon (HC) deposits.

The formation and evidence of possible ore deposits on the ocean bottom differs markedly from that which has occurred on dry land, where such deposits have been exposed to discovery and extraction by the actions of weathering and erosion over geologic ages. Such actions are usually lacking in the marine environments. Thus, the *known* and *deep* mid-ocean bottoms have not yet shown *obvious* ore deposits, which, if they exist, would be covered by layers of mud and silt.

Yet, there are other bottom areas where the peculiarities of such geological anomalies as tectonic crustal spreading and upwelling in, or near, the Northern Pacific Coastal Zone (for example) have shown deposits of various metallic sulfide minerals. Furthermore, one of the most remarkable evidences of the peculiar functioning of oceanic processes is the creation of metallic "nodules," mostly manganese, which are deposited on the abyssal sea bottom. These deposits, more fully described later, are unlike anything found on land. Also, the continental shelves, which seem to be extensions of drowned continental margins, may contain ore bodies similar to those of the adjacent continental land mass. Most shelf areas are "newly" formed, compared with the abyssal ocean floor; therefore ore bodies, if any, may not have been heavily covered with sediments, thus making them accessible to marine mining operations.

If economic recovery and profitable marketing are the criteria, then proved reserves of most ocean minerals are relatively small. However, changing economic conditions (e.g., greater demand and land resource depletion), coupled with improved mineral exploration and recovery technologies, may result in the exploitation of very large (suspected) ore-body reserves even in mid-ocean floor areas.

Some examples of undersea HC and mineral resources and their actual, or probable, locations and distribution follow:

HC-petroleum and gas-recovery from drilled coastal shelf bottom wells accounted for about 95%, in 1984, of the total value of undersea mineral production. Most wells are drilled in relatively shallow waters, less than 1,000 feet deep. However, as the pressure for off-shore HC recovery increases, test drilling has been done to depths as great as 6000 feet. As deep ocean exploitation technology advances, sizeable HC (almost entirely petroleum) recovery may become routine.

Considering the present state of sub-sea geophysical exploitation technology, it is impossible to estimate firmly and completely the world's undersea HC resources. However, tentative global estimates, partly extrapolated from extant and proven HC deposits, indicate that about 13-billion barrels of petroleum and the equivalent of 35-billion m^3 of natural gas may be available for future recovery.

Almost every coastal nation seems to have off-shore areas favorable for the occurrence of HC and other mineral resources. To protect their resources, most nations have now established a 200-mile "Exclusive Economic Zone" (EEZ). Living resources are included. Intensive geophysical exploration has been underway for over a decade (motivated by the petroleum "crises" of the 1970s) off the coast of more than 80 countries. Substantial new petroleum reserves are suspected off the coasts of China, Pakistan, the Bay of Bengal, Guyana, Nigeria, the North Sea, and South Africa, to name just a few. In the US, the North Alaskan Slope oil recoveries are going full blast; however, expectations of new finds off the northeastern US coast and Newfoundland have been reduced. Major drilling efforts in the "Baltimore Canyon," for example, have yet to reveal major "strikes." Other actual or planned drillings off the New England coast have been thwarted by environmentalists' resistance, while geophysical and drilling tests were disappointing. Nevertheless, new US fields may yet be found and exploited in the future, even in such "worked-over" areas as the Gulf of Mexico, Alaska, and the shelf areas near Santa Barbara, California.

Thus the seas, both shallow and deep, may yet displace present land areas as future HC (mainly oil) sources. Natural gas is not so economical to search for, or exploit, although few countries would ignore the exploitation of easily accessible off-shore fields. Natural gas is more valuable to industrialized countries and several—Holland, the Soviet Union, Italy, New Zealand, Britain, and other countries—either use, or plan to use, hundreds of millions of cubic feet of off-shore gas for metallurgical industries, chemical plants, power generation and even as sources of liquid fuel for automobiles by complex chemical conversion.

Other Mineral Resources

The inorganic (non-HC) minerals shown in Table 12-2 are being either recovered commercially, or may someday be recoverable in commercial quantities and prices competitive with land-derived minerals.

The rocks beneath deep ocean floors are believed to be principally basic and ultra-basic rocks of igneous origin. Therefore the types of mineral deposits that might be found in this environment are restricted to those commonly associated with the same kinds of rocks on land. Chromite and nickel appear the most likely. Soviet oceanographers have found pure chromite in sea floor rifts in the Indian Ocean. Deposits of the Red Sea type are also likely in certain areas.

Copper, zinc, silver, lead, tin, and gold have been found to occur in significant quantities in hot brines and metal-rich sediment in one of the deeps of the Red Sea. Subsequent studies have revealed similar deposits in two other deeps. One of these, the Atlantic II deep, has been estimated to contain the following concentrations in the upper 10 m. of sediment:

Percent by Weight

Copper	Zinc	Silver	Lead	Tin	Gold
0.90	2.6	0.008	0.10	0.0002	0.0001

Iron and manganese are also present in large quantities. These metals, along with barium (in barite) and mercury (in cinnabar) are among the metals that in some deposits are

Table 12-2: Recovery of Inorganic Minerals

Substance Sold	*Recovery location*	*Availability & Promise*
Gold & other metals	Off-shore "placer" deposits, e.g., off W. Alaskan coast	Small quantities have been dredged. Moderate amounts recoverable in future.
Sea-water chemicals: * gypsum * sodium chloride * potash * magnesium * calcium salts	Many warmer coastal areas (India, Caribbean, Mediterranean, etc.)	"Salt" has been recovered from on-shore solar sea water evaporation for a long time; gypsum, potash & magnesium salts & other chemicals are also recoverable by evaporation as well as from near-shore deposits which can be dredged or mined.
Sulfur	About 20% of US sulfur production comes from off-shore deposits. Few other undersea deposits are known.	Obtained by drilling & pumping with hot water. Demand presently level. Supply almost inexhaustible.
Metallic nodules	These "nodules" formed by some, as yet poorly understood, water-solution precipitation process litter the deep ocean floors, mostly in the Pacific Ocean at depths 10,000–15,000 feet (3,000–4,000 meters).	It is estimated that many billions of tons of such nodules rest on the deep Pacific floor (some deposits may occur in other marine regions). Their composition is usually 85–90% manganese, with the rest nickel, copper & cobalt. Recovery and refining technology—such as suction pipes and seaborne smelters—is still primitive; no commercial recovery as yet, due to the early technology, international legal squabbling ("Law of the Sea"), other legal restraints & no urgent markets.
Sand, gravel calciferous mud (sea shell derived)	Most coastal areas of world; S.E. US coast, Alaskan coast, St. Lawrence River Estuary, other estuaries (Chesapeake, etc.)	Several millions of tons recovered annually for construction industry, etc. Supply limitless.

thought to have a hot springs origin. It seems likely that a variety of metalliferous deposits may be found on the ocean bottoms in association with submarine hot springs.

Such deposits of hot brine and metalliferous muds also seem to occur on US continental shelves and slopes.

Summary

The HC and solid mineral resources of the oceans have only been moderately exploited. HC recovery is the basis of a sizeable ($2 billion in 1983) undersea exploration diving, drilling and pipe construction industry, as well as at least $1–2 billion for ocean drilling platforms. The Persian Gulf, Gulf of Mexico, Northern Alaskan shore areas, and the North Sea are the prime producers. Estimated ocean reserves may, when developed, partially supply world demand at the present rate of consumption until the mid-21st century. Certain currently untapped minerals, such as phosphorite, may become future commercial possibilities. As the various off-shore mineral deposits are depleted, recoveries will be attempted to depths of at least 3,000 feet. Manganese nodules will, once technical and

Table 12-3: Summary of Global Off-Shore Mining Operations

Minerals		*Estimated Value (In Millions)*
Minerals dissolved in Seawater	Sodium Magnesium Calcium Bromine Diamonds Gold Heavy Minerals Sands	$200
Mineral Deposits	Iron Sands Tin Sands Lime Shells Sand and Gravel	250
Sub-seabed Mineral Deposits	Iron Ore Coal Sulphur	410
Total		$860

legal problems are resolved, become important supplements to shrinking land resources.

The most important ocean resource of all, fresh or potable water, may, within a decade or two, become a powerful resource for the world's arid lands, via irrigation. However, the cost, in terms of energy needed for extracting the salts from seawater, is considerable. New technologies, such as osmosis, ion exchange, flash-freezing, etc., coupled with (say) "cheap" solar or nuclear (fusion?) energy, will make water desalinization an economical proposition for countries such as Israel, Egypt, India, Saudi Arabia, some parts of Western Africa, the Caribbean islands, etc. The desalinization will produce enormous quantities of "sea salts" whose commercial use and disposition will pose a considerable challenge to future scientists, engineers and economists.

Some peripheral ocean "resources" include the salvage of wrecks containing valuable cargo such as nickel ingots and marine archaeology, a subject of great interest to the public and one which inserts a romantic note into the often prosaic nature of resource recovery activities. The virtues of tidal power are frequently touted and interests and activities in that subject come and go like the tides. Small experimental power stations have been built in France, Scotland, Maine and elsewhere but little electrical power (in terms of a nation's overall power output) has been produced. The Canadians have proposed a bizarre scheme to "harness" the Bay of Fundy tides. It would not produce electrical power more economically (probably less) than that produced by a "standard" coal, gas, or even a nuclear facility. It might, in fact, prove to be an ecological and environmental disaster.

General References

Pirie, G. 1975. *Oceanography*. Oxford: University of Oxford Press.

______. 1984. *Fisheries of the United States*. National Marine Fisheries Service.

______. 1982. Annual Report—Fisheries Statistics. National Marine Fisheries Service.

______. 1985 Annual Report: The Dept. of the Interior, "US Geological Survey."

THIRTEEN

COMPETING USES Of The OCEAN

Edward D. Goldberg

Introduction

The oceans provide many resources for higher living standards—food, recreation, transportation, aesthetics, and waste disposal sites. Each of these uses can impact upon others. Thus, the protection of all ocean space depends upon the identification of any insulting forces. Further, the resolution of use conflicts is the key to successful exploitation of ocean resources.

Ocean space, much like land real estate, has a spectrum of values. Coastal areas can be compared to land in central Tokyo, very costly. On the other hand, some deep ocean waters relate more closely to the Sahara Desert, clearly of lesser worth. To much of the world's citizenry, the beaches of the marine shorelines will be the most desirable resource, providing a site for a variety of social and leisure activities. To more restricted groups, industrial and maricultural pursuits will place a high economic value on the coastal region.

Herein I will consider some possible changes and problems in the utilization of ocean space over the next decades. I will consider potential developments in mariculture, recreation, waste heat and waste material disposal, and transportation.

Waste Disposal*

Following the development of environmental movements in the 1970s, a view developed that all ocean space is equal in value and should remain inviolate with respect to receiving societal wastes. The marine scientific and engineering communities, on the other hand, have in general a different view. They argue that complete assessments of waste disposal processes must be carried out to make an optimal choice among land, air, and sea options (NAS, 1984). A recent US workshop concluded that the waste capacity of US coastal waters is not fully utilized (NOAA, 1979). A consensus emerged that there is a scientific basis for regulating pollutant discharges to both coastal and open ocean waters. But further, foreclosure of the marine option can jeopardize the quality of the environment, especially the domain of the terrestrial fresh waters, through leakages of toxic substances from waste disposal sites.

Estuarine and other coastal waters receive today the greatest amount of domestic and industrial wastes introduced to the marine environment. As a consequence, a variety of impacts have been observed, such as increasing areas of anoxia; human morbidities from exposure to microbial pathogens in beach areas and from the consumption of tainted fish and shellfish; and coastal zones littered with plastics, metals, and paper. A recent US survey (OTA, 1987) of the role of the oceans in waste management predicts further degradation of coastal waters. It is therefore crucial that a continuing surveillance of coastal waters for unacceptable waste discharges be carried out by appropriate governmental agencies.

The OTA study found little degradation of the open ocean, primarily because little waste disposal takes place there today. In principle, the open ocean sites do offer the promise of waste space. The last remaining US open ocean site, Deepwater Dumpsite 106, is located on the continental slope off New Jersey. It has been only modestly investigated with respect to

---

* For a more detailed discussion of problems of ocean pollution, see, e.g., Park (1989).

impacts from the industrial and domestic disposal occurring over the last two decades. Still, using present day knowledge, its assimilative capacity for wastes can be roughly calculated (NOAA, 1979). The limiting factor for industrial waste discharge will be the impact upon the biota in the surface waters. Some preliminary data on the effects of typical wastes discharged there (wastes from titanium dioxide production and from the manufacture of organic chemicals) upon zooplankton are not disturbing (Capuzzo and Lancaster, 1985). Sub-lethal effects were noted in the waste plumes at the site; they appeared to involve only a very small percentage of the organisms in the water mass. At the rates of dumping in the early 1980s, long-term consequences are minimal, according to these investigators. Dumpsite-106 is being phased out in 1991 for both domestic and industrial wastes by the US Congress. The action seems to be an emotional and political response to a disturbed public.

Domestic and Industrial Wastes

Comparison of land and sea disposal options can be made rationally. A group of 55 social and natural scientists applied a variety of criteria to consider two disposal problems: municipal sewage sludge, and industrial acid waste from titanium dioxide production (NAS, 1984).

The latter case involved options of (1) ocean disposal and (2) acid neutralization of the wastes with limestone, followed by the disposal of the iron sludge to land and the effluents to a stream. The assessment of the alternatives required data about potential impacts upon human health, property, ecosystems, aesthetics, recreation, noise, and odors. Institutional considerations involved community attitudes, services, economy, and safety.

The environmental and economic factors favored ocean discharge, whereas the institutional parameters were less inclined toward this alternative.

In the case of the sewage sludge disposal, public perceptions, regulatory considerations, available technology, environmental risks, and economics did not bias a conclusion toward either option. But what is important in this study is that ocean disposal was at least as attractive as land disposal to the assembled group of scholars.

Hazardous Wastes

A simple definition of a hazardous waste is a disposed material that can jeopardize the vitality of living organisms. The production of hazardous wastes throughout the world is startling. In the United States there is a generation of about one ton per capita annually, most of it coming from industry—chemical plants, petroleum refineries, and manufacturers. The companies are responsible for the disposition of these wastes. Arguments to reduce their amounts and to recycle them are continually made. Still, their production will continue to be high in the foreseeable future. Some in principle can be burned; some are maintained at hazardous waste disposal sites.

The concept of hazardous waste disposal in ocean waters today would horrify the citizenry of the developed world so conditioned to the concept of a sacrosanct ocean. Still, seawaters in the past have successfully accommodated deliberately introduced hazardous wastes.

A case in point is the 1970 disposal of around 67 tons of nerve agents held in projectiles (Linnenbom, 1971). The munitions were placed in steel-encased concrete vaults which were loaded aboard an obsolete World War II Liberty ship. The vessel was towed to a site about 400 kilometers east of Cape Kennedy, Florida, and sunk in 5000 meters of water. The ship did not break up upon hitting the bottom and there was no evidence that the marine biota were subsequently affected by any leakages of the nerve agents. The nerve gas, isopropyl methylphosphonofluoridate (GB), rapidly decomposes in water with an estimated half-life of 30 minutes (Epstein, 1970). An effective discharge of the wastes was carried out.

Although today there may be preferable techniques for disposing of this type of military weaponry (freezing the projectiles, cutting them up into smaller pieces, and incinerating the toxic materials), still a combination of environmental, technological, and economic concerns may in the future direct some hazardous wastes to the sea. An interdisciplinary assessment by scholars today might still favor the sea disposal of nerve gas.

Radioactive wastes constitute another collective of materials that have posed great problems. The fine-grained sediments of the deep sea floor have been proposed as a site in which radioactive wastes might be disposed (Hollister *et al.*, 1981). The areas of such deposits cover about 20% of the earth's surface. The radioactive wastes, placed into a chemically stable solid form, would be encased in canisters and introduced into the sediments either gravitationally or by a boosting system which would be activated when the wastes were just above the sediment/water interface. Economic and social considerations will guide the potential use of such systems. Still, the feasibility of ocean disposal of radioactive wastes merits continued discussion in the face of the tremendous problems associated with the identification of acceptable terrestrial sites.

Waste Exportation

The inability of developed countries to husband their domestic and industrial wastes within their own confines has led to some exportation to the developing world. For example, notifications of intent to export, filed with the US EPA, rose from 12 in 1980 to 465 in 1987 (French, 1988). Most of these shipments are to other developed countries; but the developing countries are receiving an increasing share.

There has been an unpleasant, but justifiable response from some developing countries. For example, Sidiki Kone (1988), Chief of the Division for the Preservation of Nature and Human Environment of the Ministry of Natural Resources and the Environment of Guinea states: "[Developing world countries]...must refuse to import foreign wastes, no matter how much money we are offered; otherwise we risk turning our continent into the garbage dump of the world."

The developed countries are running out of terrestrial waste sites. They have given up ocean disposal for the present. A partial solution to this unpleasant dilemma is to utilize scientifically and economically justifiable ocean space for waste disposal.

Transportation

Over recorded history the oceans have been used for the transport of goods from one place to another. With the varying abilities of countries to produce products of commerce, be they agricultural, industrial, medical, etc., the interdependence of national economies emphasizes the need for ready trade. The increasing world population is demanding more materials and energy to achieve higher standards of living than now enjoyed. For those countries producing or requiring as imports high-volume, low-cost commodities, such as coal, oil, timber, and wheat, large bulk ocean-traversing carriers (150,000 dwt or more) appear to be essential.

The vessels require deep-water ports for berthing (water depths up to 55 feet or more), facilities often not available. A recent US report (NAS, 1985) poses the problem for the United States—is the expense of altering harbor space through dredging a rational path to take? But perhaps of greater importance are the assumptions used in the replies: what will be the mix of materials the US will import and export and how will the US relate to the future world economy.

Changes in the US trade situation over the past half century can be seen in the dollar differences between exports and imports (Table 13-1). High-technology products and coal, grains, and timber presently constitute most of the exports. Forecasting the amounts of future exports is wrought with uncertainty. Still,

Table 13-1: US Import/Export Balance.
Exports Minus Imports in Millions of Dollars

Year	1930	1937	1947	1960	1970	1973	1981
Agricultural Goods	-459	-459	1604	857	558	8023	24308
Fuels and Lubricants	433	395	1013	-739	-1384	-6359	-71333
Chemicals	3	22	553	1128	2216	3137	11995
Capital Goods	518	486	3144	4949	10557	13928	45680
Consumer Goods	-92	-38	958	-505	-4834	-8481	-22864
Automotive Goods	282	353	1147	633	-2242	-4543	-11750
Military Goods	7	22	174	804	1230	1385	3608
Other	-271	-184	890	-1226	-3163	-5854	-11325
Total	782	265	9530	5528	3303	1863	-27566

Source: W.H. Branson, cited in NAS, 1985.

the NAS Report concludes the US should act expeditiously to increase its deep-port facilities.

Present assessments suggest that North America (Canada and the US) will be major exporters of grains in the future, primarily to Asia (Brown, 1988). Asia has become a major importing region as a consequence of a small and shrinking cropland area per person (Table 13-2), whereas agricultural technologies promise to maintain North American countries as producers. Such statistics provide compelling economic arguments for deep-water ports. Still, the costs of increasing the physical capabilities of ports must be balanced against the gains from more competitive exports and the lesser costs for landing imports.

Major federal dredging projects take on the order of 22 years (NAS, 1985). Uncertainties in market changes, which may take place over much shorter times, emphasize the risk factor in any assessment of deep-port needs.

There can be unacceptable environmental impacts as a consequence of the dredging operations and the disposal of the spoils. The former seems to be the more serious. The changes in the geometry of the harbor can affect its hydraulic regime. Circulation patterns can be altered, with disturbances to the prevailing compositions of the seawater. The biological productivity of the harbor can be significantly altered. Problems with the disposal of dredged materials are in general small.

Table 13-2: World Grain Trade by Region[1] (Million metric tons), 1950–1988[2]

	1950	*1960*	*1970*	*1980*	*1988*
N. America	23	39	56	131	119
L. America	1	0	4	-10	-11
W. Europe	-22	-25	-30	-16	22
E. Eur/USSR	0	0	0	-46	-27
Africa	0	-2	-5	-15	-28
Asia	-6	-17	-37	-63	-89
Aust./NZ	3	6	12	19	14

1. No sign indicates net exports, minus sign net imports.
2. Estimates.
Source: Brown, 1988.

However, if they contain toxic materials, there is the potential for adverse effects.

There are few examples in literature treating the seriousness of toxic materials in dredged spoils; however, with conventional wisdom the concerns can be addressed before sediments are moved. For example, Crystal Mountain Workshop (NOAA, 1979) considered the problem of cadmium in dredged materials and the consequential transfer to humans through the consumption of shellfish, such as clams and oysters, known concentrators of the metal. For the worst possible case scenario, oysters living in the spoil region could accumulate cadmium to levels higher than those deemed acceptable by the US Food and Drug Administration.

On the other hand, in some cases the dredged materials can be considered a resource for use as construction aggregate, sanitary landfill, beach replenishment, and the creation or enhancement of wetlands.

Recreation

Increasing time for leisure activities, coupled with an increasing population, is making public beaches more and more attractive to tourists and to residents of a given region. Yet, their use is being challenged in both the developed and developing world by the increasing entry of enteric bacteria and viruses to coastal waters through domestic waste disposal. There are both economic and social facets to the problem. For countries seeking a more secure financial footing, the loss of tourist revenue on the short term must be weighed against the output of revenue for improved sanitation facilities. For the developed nations, the recreational amenity must be broached in the political arena.

Two challenges to public health arise from the disposition of the pathogens in the coastal zone. First, there is the risk of disease through exposure in the waters or on the beaches. Swimmers swallow water; they also take it up through body cavities. However, most information about morbidities from such exposures is anecdotal rather than epidemiological. Still, there is a flux of reports to international agencies concerned, strongly relating ear, nose, and throat disorders, respiratory infections, and gastrointestinal infections to micro-organisms of the coastal zone.

On the other hand, there is a substantial data base relating illnesses and even mortalities to the consumption of seafoods contaminated with toxic viruses and bacteria. Most diseases are related to the consumption of molluscs; fish and crabs are less frequently the carriers of these micro-organisms. The viruses are dominant over the bacteria in inducing illnesses. Both cholera and viral hepatitis have been associated with the consumption of uncooked or poorly cooked seafoods taken from contaminated areas.

Both residents and tourists look to coastal areas as a source of rest and recreation as well as seafoods. They will be directed away from such regions where their health might be endangered.

Ranching and Farming

Farming and ranching the organisms of the sea are explosively expanding in both the developed and developing world. Aquaculture, including seaweeds, is estimated to account for 10% of the world's fishery landings in 1985 (Rhodes, 1988). The regional productions are given in Table 13-3. In marine farming, the organisms are maintained in enclosures of one type or another, whereas in marine ranching, the young fish are introduced into rivers or estuaries. Later, the adult fish return for spawning. As Lowe (1988) points out, the difference in techniques depends upon who feeds the fish. In ranching, naturally existing prey provide the food; in farming, it is the farmer.

Lowe (1988) provides statistics on the economics of salmon farming and ranching. In the latter, a return of 1% represents the break-even point while actually a return of 2% or more is usually observed. On the other hand, farming offers the product protection from threats of the open ocean, as farmed species are maintained from hatching to harvest. In 1985, herding activities accounted for over one third of the world salmon production. (Table 13-4).

Knowledge is slowly accumulating as to whether the farming and ranching of marine organisms are favorably or deleteriously affecting other members of ecosystems. In the former

Table 13-3: Estimated Aquaculture Production in 1985 in Metric Tons

Region	*Finfish*	*Crustacea*	*Molluscs*	*Seaweeds*	*Others*	*Total*
Africa	46.2	0.1	0.4			46.7
N. America	300.9	39.0	176.8	0.2		516.9
S. America	83.5	32.4	1.6	5.3		122.8
Asia and Oceania	4599.7	209.8	2115.4	3515.7	39.4	10480
Europe	370.9	0.3	591.5	4.5		967.2
USSR	296					296
Total						
1985	5697.2	281.6	2885.7	3527.7	39.4	12429.6
1980	3206.8	75.0	3299.7			
1975	2628.8	29.7	1961.2			
% Change 1975–1985	117	848	47			

Source: Rhodes 1988.

case problems arise from the entry of organic materials, fecal pellets, and unconsumed food, as well as of ammonia, which can fertilize the growth of planktonic organisms in undesirable ways, the so-called eutrophication process. Farms can overload the coastal system causing decreased water quality—even to the point where the culture activity is jeopardized.

In the case of ranching of larger numbers of fish, there is the haunting, but as yet unestablished problem of competition for food between herded organisms and wild species.

There are already conflicts between the establishment of maricultural activities and the loss of natural resources. For example, the depletion of mangrove forests, a valuable but declining marine ecosystem, is associated with shrimp farming in the south-east Pacific (Escobar, 1988). In Panama, 1% per year is the apparent loss rate. In Colombia, 5,000 hectares of mangroves are already dedicated to shrimp farming. And 60,000 of the 177,000 hectares of mangroves in Ecuador have already been turned over to salt water shrimp farming.

Table 13-4. The Sources of Market-Place Salmon

Source	*Quantity Tons*	*Percent of Total*
Wild Catch	561,000	63
Ranching	281,800	32
Farming	45,300	5
Totals	889,000	100

Source: Lowe, 1988.

On the other hand the intense raft culture of mussels in northwest Spain (about 0.1 million tons per year) has an overall positive affect on the associated food chains (Tenore *et al.*, 1985). The fecal wastes of the mussels provide sustenance to demersal fish and crabs, although it decreases the diversity of benthic organisms. Scallop recruitment may be negatively affected.

Overview

Coastal ocean space in the near future is subject to conflict in use, whereas the great expanse of open ocean space may be underutilized with respect to the waste disposal needs of a growing world population.

References

Brown, L.R. "The changing world food prospect: the nineties and beyond." *Worldwatch Paper* 85. 58 pp. (1988).

Capuzzo, J.M. and Lancaster, B.A. "Zooplankton population response to industrial wastes discharged at Deepwater Dumpsite-106." In "Wastes in the Ocean," Vol. 5. *Deep Sea Waste Disposal*. Edited by Kester *et al.* John Wiley & Sons, Inc. pp. 209–226 (1985).

Epstein, J. (1970). "Rate of decomposition of GB in seawater." *Science* 170: 1396–1398.

Escobar, J. (1988). "The South-East Pacific." *Siren*. No. 36. pp. 28–29.

French, H.F. (1988). "Combating Toxic Terrorism." *World Watch* 1: 6–7.

Hollister, C.D., Anderson, D.R. and Heath, G.R. (1981). "Subseabed disposal of nuclear wastes." *Science* 213: 1321–1326.

Kone, S. (1988). "Viewpoint." *The Siren*. No. 37, 2–3.

Linnenbom, V.J. (1971). "Final Report on First Post-Dump Survey of the Chase X Disposal Site." *Naval Research Laboratory Memorandum Report* 2273. Washington D.C. 40 pp.

Lowe, M.D. (1988). "Salmon Ranching and Farming Net Growing Harvest." *World-Watch* 1: 28–32.

NAS (1984). *Disposal of Industrial and Domestic Wastes. Land and Sea Alternatives*. National Academy Press. Washington D.C. 210 pp.

NAS (1985). *Dredging Coastal Ports*. National Academy Press. Washington D.C. 211 pp.

OTA (1987). *Wastes in Marine Environments*. Congress of the United States of America Office of Technology Assessment. 312 pp.

NOAA (1979). *Assimilative Capacity of US Coastal Waters for Pollutants*. Environmental Research Laboratories, Boulder, Colorado. 284 pp.

Park, K. (1989) In *Global Climate Change*. Paragon House Publishers, New York, NY.

Rhodes, R.J. (1988). "Status of world aquaculture: 1987." *Aquaculture Magazine Buyers Guide* 4 -18.

Tenore, K.R., J. Corral, N. Gonzalez, and E. Lopez-Jamar. "Effects of intense mussel culture on food chain patterns and production in coastal Galacia, NW Spain." In *Proceedings of the International Symposium on Utilization of Coastal Ecosystems: Planning Pollution and Productivity*. Edited by Ning Labbish Chao and W. Kirby Smith. Rio Grande, Brazil (1985).

FOURTEEN

MODIFYING The OCEAN

FOUR MEDITERRANEAN PROJECTS

Gerald Stanhill

Introduction

To seriously suggest modifying the oceans even today invites comparison with King Canute. To date the only global modification that man appears to have achieved is the inadvertent, shameful and near ubiquitous pollution caused by the estimated 6-million tons of solid and liquid wastes (Park 1989) now disposed of in the oceans. Fortunately, more serious widespread consequences of this pollution on the oceans' biological productivity and climate-modifying, physical properties have not been demonstrated.

The most plausible possibility that man is currently inadvertently modifying the oceans on a global scale lies in the suggestion that the increasing depth of the oceans (Barnett 1983) is due to a reduction in the volume of the southern cryosphere (Kukla and Bavin 1981) and that this has been brought about by the recent warming of the atmosphere (Watts 1983). This warming may be the result of the increase in the CO_2 concentration of the atmosphere caused by man's activities (Hansen *et al.* 1981).

However, most of the facts and all of the causal links in the above argument are in dispute, and even if substantiated many experts believe that the climatic effects of the CO_2 increase will be evident over the land surfaces long before any ocean modification has been detected (Klein 1982).

For the above reasons the subject chosen for this article is not ocean modification on a global scale, either intentional or inadvertent. It is rather the possibility of modification on a limited local scale illustrated by four plans to exploit the waters of the eastern Mediterranean—a relatively accessible and sheltered part of this inland sea.

All four projects link water and energy. Two seek to use the sea water to exploit gravitational differences with local land formations below sea level near the south and east coast in order to generate electricity. The very high insolation in this arid area permits a continuous inflow of water and hence production of electrical energy, even after the water levels have been equilibrated in the initial filling phase.

The two other projects discussed require inputs of energy to make the sea water usable and available for agriculture in the potentially productive desert areas to the south and east of the Mediterranean.

The Water Balance of the Mediterranean

Before describing the projects individually, some basic information on the sea's water balance is necessary. The distribution of precipitation and evaporation is shown in Figures 14-1 and 14-2. These illustrate the sharp gradients which exist in the area, even, to a lesser extent, over the sea itself. They also show the negative atmospheric balance of the sea as a whole. The fact that the water deficit is met by a net inflow from the Atlantic, rather than by fresh water from land runoff, explains the sea's high salinity (Gorgy and Salah 1974).

Independent estimates of the importance of the sea surface as a source of water vapor to the atmosphere are available from Peixoto and Oort's (1983) analysis of the atmosphere's water balance. Their results for the three winter months when the major precipitation occurs in the eastern basin are shown in Figure 14-3. This indicates that the western and southeastern

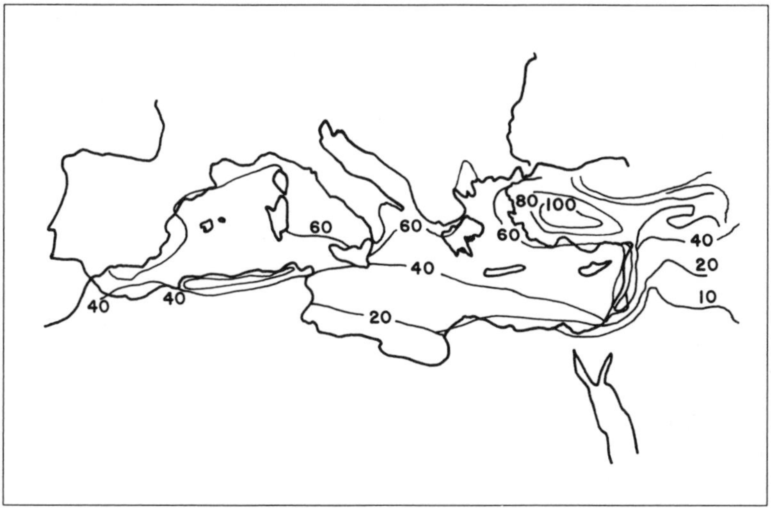

Figure 14-1: Annual total values of precipitation over the Mediterranean, CMS. Source: Baumgartner and Reichel 1975.

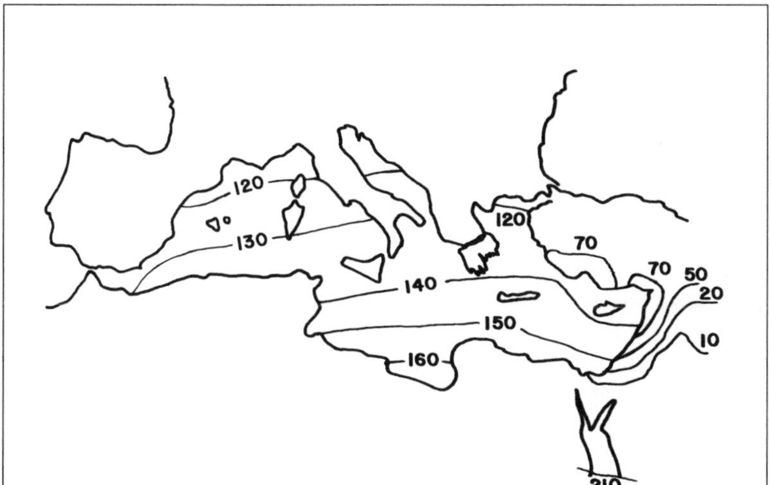

Figure 14-2: Annual total values of evaporation over the Mediterranean, CMS. Source: Baumgartner and Reichel 1975.

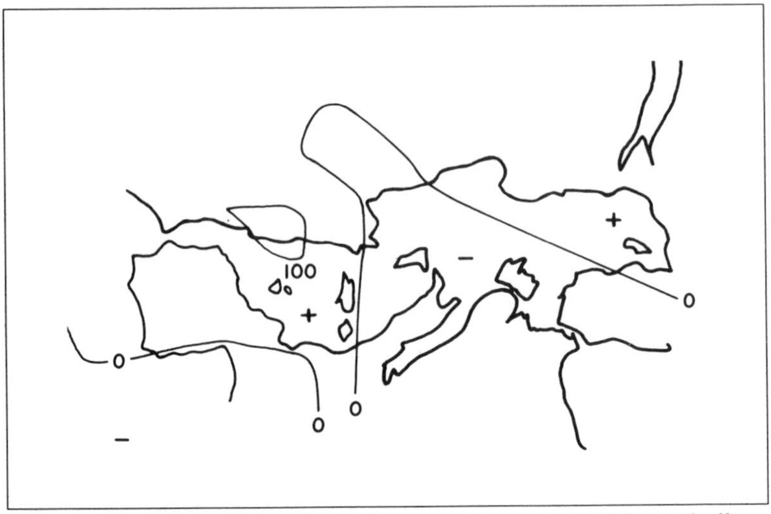

Figure 14-3: Winter time values of horizontal divergence of the vertically integrated total water vapor transport for months of December, January, February. Negative values indicate convergence with precipitation exceeding evaporation CMS. Source: Peixoto and Oort (1983).

Mediterranean are at this season areas of rather weak divergence supplying the water vapor transported eastward. By contrast, at this time the central Mediterranean is a region of weak convergence with the sea acting as a sink for atmospheric water vapor, with precipitation exceeding evaporation. For the year as a whole the boundary between divergence and convergence follows the northern border of the inland sea.

In order that the relevance of the projects to be described can be evaluated against the general oceanic environment as well as that for the Mediterranean, some additional comparative information is given in Table 14-1. The data presented there show the Mediterranean to be shallower, more arid and hence more saline and yet more biologically productive than the globally averaged oceans. However, the great variation in the earth's oceans disguised by such averaging makes it virtually certain that there are many other sea areas similar to the Mediterranean for which the projects to be discussed may also be relevant. In this context the enclosed seas, gulfs and bays of

Table 14-1: Physical and Biological Characteristics of the Mediterranean Compared with Globally Averaged Oceans

	Dimensions		*Water Balance*		*Fisheries Productivity**	
	Area	Depth	Precipitation mm y-1	Evaporation mm y-1	Salinity o/oo	Mean catch & landings 1978–1982 kg km-2 y-1
Mediterranean	2.512	1.365	395	1444	38	541
Globally averaged oceans	261.1	3.733	1066	1176	35	203

* Includes fishes, crustaceans and molluscs but not aquatic mammals or plants. Sources: Baumgartner and Reiches (1975) and FAO (1984).

the middle latitudes which border arid and semiarid lands are of particular interest. Many such areas of North and South America, Africa both north and south, Arabia and the Persian Gulf and Australia can be identified in Figure 14-4.

The Mediterranean-Dead Sea Project

The idea of generating power by mixing Mediterranean water with that of the Dead Sea—the terminal lake laying at the deepest point on the earth's surface more than a third of a kilometer below the level of the Mediterranean—is not a new one. The proposal to connect the two seas was made more than a century ago (Allen 1855) and has since then fired the imagination of many writers. However, it took the combination of the sharp increase in the price of oil and the decline in the level of the Dead Sea which occurred during the last decade to initiate detailed studies and planning of this project. The feasibility of the project was examined by two committees, and as a result of their recommendations, a company was established by the Israeli government and charged with the planning and construction of the project. The following brief account is based on the outline and appraisal published by the Mediterranean-Dead Sea Co. Ltd. (Arkin 1982) and a review article by the chairman and coordinator of the steering committee for the

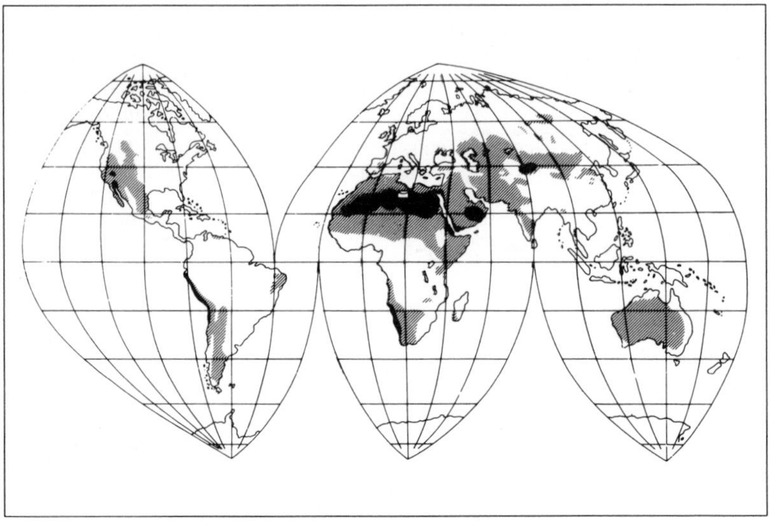

Figure 14-4: Desert and arid areas of the world. Source: Menenti (1984).
Deserts where there may be no rainfall during a year.
Arid zones where rainfall is less than potential evapotranspiration.

project published in 1983, (Neeman and Schul) with other individual sources as referenced.

The Dead Sea lies approximately 100 km to the east of the south-eastern shore of the Mediterranean. Its northern basin has an area of approximately 800 km^2 with a maximum depth of 325 m and contains 136 km^3 of salt-saturated water.

During the last decade its level—currently -406 m MSL—has dropped at an average rate of 0.4 m a year and is now more than 15 m below its record high level at the beginning of this century (Fig. 14-5).

An important factor to be considered in estimating the steady-state power producing capacity of the Mediterranean-Dead Sea project is the large fluctuation in the level of the Dead Sea that has occurred during historical times, reflecting the highly variable rainfall over its Jordan catchment basin (Klein 1961a, 1981b, 1982). To this natural variation must now be added the increasing exploitation of Jordan water during the last 50 years, first for power production when Lake Kinneret

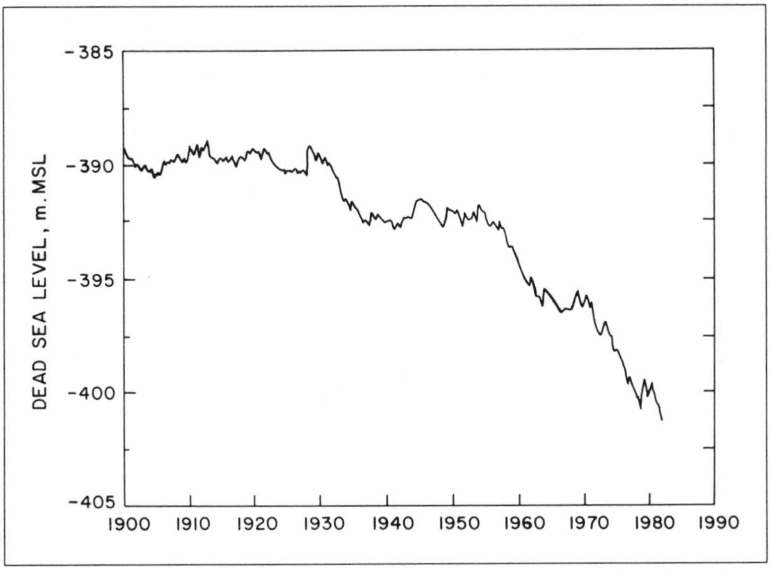

Figure 14-5: Changes in the Dead Sea level between 1900 and 1982. Source: Arkin (1982).

was dammed at its southern exit in 1932, and later when the Israeli and Jordanian water-carriers began to extract water for irrigation in 1964 and 1965, respectively.

The very shallow southern basin of the Dead Sea has an area of approximately 220 km2 which is now occupied by the evaporation pans of two potash plants. Following the drop in the Dead Sea level to -400 m MSL the continued existence of the southern water body is dependent on pumping from the deeper northern basin.

During the recent period the rate of evaporation from the deep northern basin of the Dead Sea has been estimated to be 1.38 m per year (Stanhill 1985). It is this rate, together with the maximum water level which will allow operation of the southern evaporation ponds for potash production, which determines the amount of Mediterranean water that can be mixed with the Dead Sea and hence the project's power-generating capacity.

Continuous deposition of salt in the potash evaporation ponds requires periodic elevation of the level of their surrounding dikes in any case, and it has been estimated that this would allow the Dead Sea level to be restored to a level approaching its maximum at the beginning of the century, i.e., -390 m MSL, within a period of approximately 20 years without interfering with potash production and after allowing for the large variation in natural water inflow to the Dead Sea.

The above statistics form the basis for the projected electrical power generation by the project. During the first 20 years—the filling phase—the hydroelectric plant with an installed capacity of 800 MW is estimated to be capable of producing 1.650 billion kWh a year, or 1.090 billion kWh after allowing for power needs for water pumping. This latter net value represents 5.1% of the projected national electricity generation at the beginning of this period from crude oil and coal plants. However, it represents 19% of the peak electricity demand, because operation of the hydropower station will be concentrated into periods of peak demand. The quantity of water moved per year during this period would be 1.58 x 109 m^3, i.e., 1.6 km^3 yr^{-1}.

During the subsequent steady state an average 0.96 km3 of Mediterranean water will be mixed annually to generate 1,080 billion kWh per year (770 million kWh net power production); at the beginning of this period this represents only 1.7% of the projected national thermal electricity generation but 9% of the estimated peak power demand.

A number of important scientific uncertainties are attached to the above estimates of the project's output, most of them concerning possible changes in the rate of evaporation resulting from mixing of the Mediterranean with Dead Sea waters. Reduction of the salinity, and hence increased vapor pressure of the water surface and, to a minor degree, increase in its surface area, will increase the volume of evaporation and hence generating capacity. However, an increased reflectivity of the water surface caused by significant gypsum precipitation and/or decreases in water surface temperatures and increases in air humidity caused by microclimate modification would have the opposite effect.

Although spectacular whitening of the Dead Sea surface has occurred more than 50 times in the past 2,000 years due to massive precipitation of salts (Bloch 1980), experiments on a pilot-plant scale and in the laboratory support the results of calculations that this is unlikely to result from mixing on the scale envisaged. The effects of reduced salinity and microclimate modification on evaporation are more certain but less clear. However by analogy with the nearby sweet water Lake Kinneret (Stanhill and Newmann 1978) evaporation from the Dead Sea is unlikely to increase by as much as 20% following implementation of the project.

The exact nature of the mixing of the waters is of considerable relevance, and this has been studied by a number of groups developing simulation techniques for predicting and optimizing the process (Vadasz, Weinter and Zvirin 1983).

Five optional routes for conveying water from the Mediterranean to the Dead Sea, and one from the Red Sea, were examined by the study group. The southernmost Mediterranean alignment shown in Figure 14-6 was chosen on economical and environmental grounds with special attention to the need to minimize the danger of ground water salinization.

The intake of the route selected lies near the southeast corner of the Mediterranean coast, north of the international border between Egypt and Israel, at 31°25'N. A covered rectangular canal 1.5 km long is to supply sea water to an underground pumping station with a power capacity of 65 MW which will elevate the water 100 m through a buried, concrete-embedded pressure tube 5.4 m in diameter and 7.6 km in length. The water will then be conveyed through the main, open canal of the system. This is to consist of an open concrete trapezoidal canal 30 m wide and 20 km long which will bring the water to the main tunnel, a concrete-lined pressure tunnel 5.5 m in diameter and 80 km long. The maximum depth of this tunnel below the surface is 550 m and three access shafts from the surface are planned at intermediate points. The tunnel's alignment is ESE to a point some 10 km south of Be'er Sheva from which it is to pass E to a point above the Dead Sea coast just south of the northern basin. Two reservoirs with capacities and elevations of 4.3 x 106 m3 at 81 m MSL and 7.4 x 106 m^3 at 53

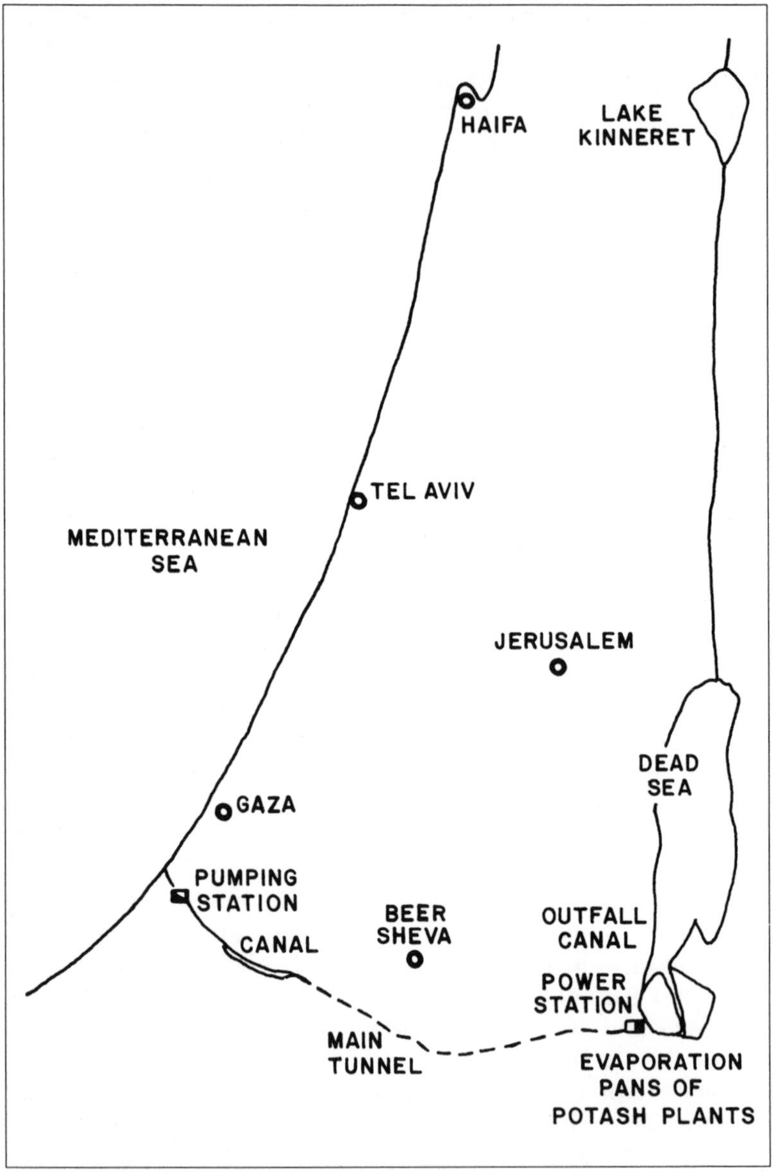

Figure 14-6. Currently proposed alignment and main features of the Mediterranean-Dead Sea Project. Source: Arkin (1982).

m MSL are to be connected with the tunnel on the eastern end above the coast and lead to the penstock, a vertical steel-lined shaft 420 m high. This will feed the underground power station—to consist of four turbines with a total installed capacity of 800 MW. Finally, the Mediterranean waters will reach the Dead Sea's northern basin via a 10 km long outfall canal.

The operation of the project currently envisaged is to restrict electricity generation at the power station to the 6–8 hours per working day when the demand on the national grid reaches its peak, thus giving 48 hours a week of operation at full capacity. By contrast, the coastal pumping station will operate only during off-peak hours, with two-thirds of its gross power requirements recouped at the power station. Thus, the project will operate as a pump storage scheme supplemented by the two regulatory reservoirs above the power station which will permit up to 35 hours of full discharge from the main tunnel to be stored during the weekend or other periods when full power generation is not required.

The cost of the project has been estimated at US $1 billion at 1981 prices.

The economic benefits are much more difficult to estimate than the costs as they incorporate the uncertainties in predicting changes in the future costs of fossil fuels (required to generate electricity in conventional power plants), rates of interest and discount rates for capitalization. Assuming 1%, 5% and 6% per year for the three rates, respectively, results in the project being financially profitable. This is increased to a minor extent if allowance is included for other quantifiable benefits such as the saving in investment that would otherwise be needed for alternative power stations, improvement in the operating efficiency of existing thermal power stations, and the reliability and frequency stability of the national electricity grid. Another benefit difficult to quantify is the diversification of national energy sources.

Many other ancillary projects have been suggested which could utilize the Mediterranean water before mixing with the Dead Sea, thus significantly increasing the project's profitability. These include the use of the water to cool inland power stations, for extracting oil from the shale deposits known to exist to the south of the proposed alignment, for desalinization based on waste heat from power stations, and for artificial inland water bodies to be used for tourism and mariculture.

Two further energy-generating projects utilizing the mixing of Mediterranean with Dead Sea water have been proposed in addition to the hydropower station. One seeks to exploit the rather minor differential heat of dilution which would be released when the salt-saturated Dead Sea water is diluted by the less saline Mediterranean water. A slightly greater energy generation would be forthcoming if the waters were first mixed with the even more concentrated end-brines from the potash separation process.

A more ambitious proposal is to use the lighter and cooler (because less saline) Mediterranean water to cover sections of the Dead Sea and hence convert them into floating solar ponds (Assaf 1976). Active research to solve the many technical problems involved in this project is underway. Although this proposal would add to the total energy-generating potential of the Dead Sea project, the negative evaporation-reducing effect of extracting stored solar heat on the capacity of the hydropower station must also be taken into account.

The Mediterranean-Qattara Depression Project

The Qattara Depression project is based, as was the previously described one, on the exploitation of the unlimited supply of water from the Mediterranean with the high potential evaporation loss from a below sea-level desert region to generate electrical power.

This idea is also not a new one and for more than a decade the Qattara Project Authority, established by the Egyptian government, has commissioned feasibility studies and surveys of the site. The results of these studies in the main take the form of unpublished reports. However, these are referred to and current plans are summarized in a publication by Bassler and Hamid presented at the 11th World Energy Conference held in 1980. The following account is based largely on this publication.

At its nearest point to the Mediterranean, the Qattara Depression lies less than 100 km south of the southeastern coast of the inland sea. Its area is very large, with 13.5 x 103 km^2 lying below the minimum projected steady-state working level of -50 m MSL. The benefits of this large evaporating surface are counterbalanced by the relatively shallow depth of the depression. At its deepest point this lies only 145 m below sea level; averaged over the area bounded by the -50 m MSL contour, the average depth is -74 m MSL.

The topography of the area between the edge of the depression and the Mediterranean constitutes the major technical and economical problem in the proposal. The land rises gradually southwards from the coast but drops very sharply near the depression. The elevation of the highland slopes parallel to the coast and rises from 150 m MSL in the east to 230 m MSL in the west. The depth at the floor of the depression also increases from east to west.

Almost as important for the economic evaluation of the project is the evaporation rate to be expected from an extensive sea water surface created in the depression. A number of estimates have been made using a variety of approaches ranging from evaporation pan and tank measurements to those based on the energy balance and bulk aerodynamic approaches. In all cases the measurements used were taken near to but not within the Qattara Depression. The results vary from 1.7 to 2.9 m per year with the most probable value between 1.75 m and 2.00 m per year. A comparison with estimates of the rates of evaporation from the southeastern Mediterranean and northern Red Sea (Fig. 14-2) supports the lower rather than the higher of these figures.

The design characteristics of the project are dictated by the rate of evaporation (which determines the steady state volume of water than can be added), the volume-surface relationship of the depression's topography (which determines the optimum operating depth of the water surface), and the electrical load characteristics of the Egyptian national electricity grid (which determines the seasonal and diurnal demand for power generation). However, another very important element is the capacity and alignment of the water-conveyance system.

The western LI alignment shown in Figure 14-7 is 74 km long. The current plan calls for two pressure tunnels each 68

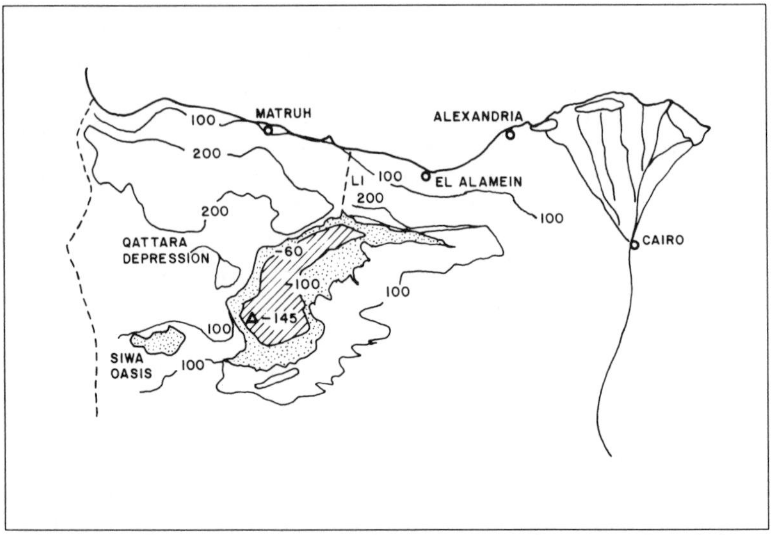

Figure 14-7: Currently proposed alignment and topography of the Qattara Depression Project. Source Bassler and Hamed (1980).
Area between 0 and -60 m MSL depression.
Area below -60 m MSL depression.
------ LI alignment.

km long with an internal diameter of 15 m lined with reinforced concrete. This will allow a flow of 800 m³/sec or 25.2 km3 per year. Such a system could fill the Qattara Depression with sea water to a depth of -60 m MSL within 23 years or, if the operating level is to be -50 m MSL, 28 years. These two depths are the critical ones for determining the optimum operating level. Between them the depression's volume increases by 63% but its surface area, and hence evaporation, by only 17%. Thus at deeper operating depths the reduction in evaporation compensates for the increased electricity generation per m3, whereas at shallower depths the increase in evaporating area does not compensate for loss of head.

The cost of this conveyance system was estimated to be US $66,000 per meter length of both tunnels, with an installed capacity of 320 MW and an annual electricity generation of 2,635 billion kW, the estimated investment cost per kW is US $17,174, including 15% for contingencies and 14% for indirect costs.

The total cost, including provision for pumped storage at an upper basin 200 m above sea level near the rim of the depression, is US $8.4 billion. At this cost the project is hardly economical and for this reason considerable attention has been given to other and cheaper modes of water conveyance.

One alternative examined was an open canal along the same alignment excavated by nuclear detonation. The canal proposed is 72.5 km long, 50 m deep and 300 m wide allowing a discharge of 1200 m^3/sec, or 50% more than the two-tunnel scheme. By contrast, the cost of such a canal was estimated to be only one-sixth of that for the tunnels and the cost per kW capacity one fifth, i.e., US $3,075 kW-1. The total cost of the entire nuclear-canal project, including pumped storage, was US $4.76 billion, or just over half that of the previous proposal.

Despite this, the technical and political uncertainties and difficulties associated with the use of nuclear explosives are apparently such that recent investigations have concentrated on alternative alignments using conventional construction methods. These examined a shorter eastern alignment which has the additional benefits of a lower overburden and less distance to the electricity demand center of Alexandria.

Such an alignment would consist of a combined tunnel and canal system. Three estimates made so far show a considerable reduction in construction costs, not only due to the shorter distance, but also to the lower cost per unit length of canal compared with tunnel construction.

Even with a cheaper eastern alignment the economic profitability of the Qattara scheme is uncertain. However, there are significant ancillary benefits which, although difficult to quantify, could substantially supplement the conservation of fossil fuels. These benefits include the provision of considerable employment during the construction phase, the avoidance of environmental pollution otherwise resulting from thermal electricity generation, and the increase in the area's tourist potential attributable to the presence of a large inland water body. In its early stages this lake could form the basis for fishery projects; later, with increasing salinity, opportunities for chemical industries would emerge.

Probably the most important fringe benefit of the Qattara Depression project would be an improvement in the profitability and efficiency of Egypt's national electrical power system. Currently two-thirds of the country's electricity is supplied by Nile hydropower plants. However, the availability of this power is severely limited by the needs of the irrigation system which determine and control the very seasonal release of water from the High and Aswan dams. The Qattara scheme would not be subject to this limitation and with the provision of pumped storage could be operated to improve substantially the functioning of the national power system.

Rainfall Enhancement by Vertical Mixing of the Eastern Mediterranean

The water balance studies of both the atmosphere and sea previously referred to and illustrated in Figures 14-1, 14-2, and 14-3 show that the eastern Mediterranean acts as a source of water to the atmosphere which, during the winter rainfall season, is transported eastward. The isotopic composition of rainfall collected in the semi-arid areas lying downwind provides evidence that this region of the sea is a significant source of the water charging the rain clouds and precipitated from them.

In 1982 G. Assaf (in Tzvetkov and Assaf 1982) suggested that the dependence of precipitation in a semi-arid region on the intensity of air-sea interaction occurring within a relatively limited time and spatial frame could be practically exploited in two ways. The first was to use measurements of sea heat storage at the beginning of the winter rainfall season to predict the amount of rain to be expected. In an area such as the Levant, where the annual rainfall has a coefficient of variation of 30% or more, and an annual total considerably less than the potential evapotranspiration demand, such a prediction would be of considerable economic importance. This is especially the case for agriculture as the yield of winter, rain-fed crops and the amount of water available for summer irrigation is dependent on, and limited by, rainfall.

The second mode of exploitation suggested was to increase rainfall by increasing heat storage in the eastern Mediterranean through mixing the cool and deep water with the warmer surface water prior to the rainfall season. The increased heat storage would enhance the energy subsequently available for latent heat transfer and consequently should lead to an increase in the amount of rainfall.

The following description of this project is based largely on the proceedings of a workshop held in 1982 (The Cherney Workshop on Weather Modification) at which research on a number of aspects of this work was described. A discussion of the physical basis of the project was subsequently presented (Assaf 1989) and in addition a number of more widely available publications reporting research on this topic have been referred to.

Correlation and Prediction

The natural, interannual variation in the heat storage in the eastern Mediterranean is considerable; before discussing its correlation with rainfall, the average magnitude and annual variation of this heat flux will be outlined.

Over the year a total of 4.2 GJ is gained and lost per m^2 of sea surface; at its coolest—in mid-March—the sea stores 0.7 GJ m-2 in its upper 200 m; at its hottest—in early September—the heat stored above 0°C is 2.8 GJ m-2. The annual cycle is shown as a rate in Figure 14-8 from which it can be seen that the maximum positive value of heat storage rate -28.5 MJ m-2 d-1, attained in June, equals the total radiant energy received in global radiation at that time of year, implying a very considerable additional advective and/or convective heat source.

The values shown in Figure 14-8 are averages based on measurements made in the area bounded by the 32° and 35° lines of latitude and longitude, respectively, and both the spatial and interannual variations are considerable. These variations are discussed by Hecht, Rosentroub and Bishop (1982) and the examples they present show a year-to-year variation at a given season reaching ±30 MJ m-2 heat storage. Expressed on a time basis, the season of maximum heat storage in late summer can vary interannually by ±one month.

Seasonal values of the changes in heat storage measured in the three degree area of the eastern Mediterranean between 34° and 35°E and 31° and 34°N during different years have

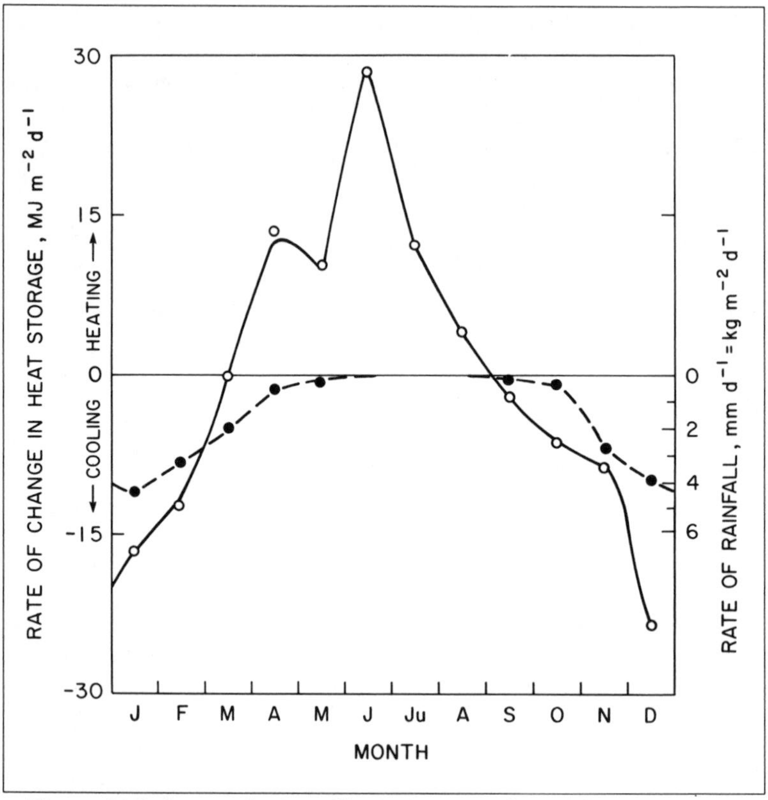

Figure 14-8: Seasonal rates of heat storage and rainfall, southeastern Mediterranean.
o—o heat storage change, MJ m-2 per day.
●—● rainfall rate, mm per day.
Note: the scales of energy and rainfall have been equated through the latent heat of vaporization of water at 20°C.
Sources: heat storage—Hecht, Rosentraub and Bishop (1982); rainfall rates represent averaged climatological standard normal for 1931–1960 period for Haifa, Tel Aviv and Jerusalem stations, coordinates as given in Table 14-2.

been presented by Tzvetkov and Assaf (1982). Their values, given in Table 14-2, were calculated from measurements listed in the US National Oceanographic Data Center Catalogue for 11 years between 1952 and 1969; they represent the difference

Table 14-2: Sea Heat Storage and Precipitation in the Southeastern Mediterranean

Winter season	*Initial sea temperature °C*	*Energy extracted[2] GJ m-2*	*Precipitation[3]*	
			Annual total kg m-2	*Subsequent seasonal total (mm)*
1952/53	20.3	2.30	558	471
1954/55	20.3	1.05	455	256
1955/56	20.3	1.46	697	242
1959/60	19.5	1.25	278	243
1960/61	20.8	1.80	504	400
1961/62	19.8	1.58	508	389
1964/65	20.1	2.09	718	524
1965/66	19.6	1.29	353	252
1966/67	20.5	2.76	82	615
1967/68	19.1	1.88	484	251
1968/69	20.4	2.09	706	525
Mean	20.1	1.78	540	378
Standard deviation	0.51	0.51	149	189
Coefficient of variation, %	2.5	28.7	27.6	50.0

1 In upper 138 m, when this sea layer is first completely mixed, i.e., November to December.
2 Difference between heat content of upper 138 m between completion of autumnal mixing and start of summer stratification, i.e., March to April.
3 Average of measurements at Haifa (34°46'E, 32°04'N, 20m MSL) and Jerusalem (35°13'E, 31°47'N, 810m MSL).
Source: Tzvetkov and Assaf (1982).

between heat stored in the upper 138 m layer of the sea from the first measurement date in winter when the profile is fully mixed (which ranges between November and December) to the first date in spring when summer stratification is seen (between March and April).

The seasonal energy loss from the cooling of the sea during this period averaged 1.78 GJ m-2, with individual yearly values ranging from a minimum of 1.25 to a maximum of 2.76 GJ m-2. The standard deviation for the 11 years was 0.51 GJ m-2, giving a coefficient of variation for heat loss of 29%. It is very significant that the same coefficient of variation is obtained from measurements of the seasonal rainfall during the same years taken at three sites representative of the downwind coastal area of Israel. This area is also approximately three square degrees. These data are also presented in Table 14-2.

Although the total rainfall, both at the Levant coast and inland, is well correlated with the total heat extracted during the winter, that of the later seasonal rain falling after the upper sea column is mixed in early winter and is even more highly correlated. The correlation with the average for the three coastal belt stations shown in Table 14-2 is 0.88; that for individual stations, as for inland ones at Amman and Damascus, is over 0.9.

However, the total seasonal heat loss is of no use as a predictor of rainfall; for this, some measure of the amount of heat stored at the beginning of the winter is needed. Analysis of the correlation between the sea temperature at this time (Table 14-2) and both total and subsequent seasonal rainfall shows correlation coefficients of 0.56. Thus, the interannual difference in the temperature of the sea column at the beginning of the winter, i.e., its heat storage, predicts only approximately 30% of the interannual variation in the subsequent rainfall.

For practical purposes the following rules have been suggested: If the sea temperature in the SSE Mediterranean is above 20.4°C at the beginning of the season, the annual rainfall in the coastal belt of Israel will be average or above; if it is below 19.8°C, rainfall will also be below average. There were no exceptions to these rules during the 11 seasons for which data were available.

The correlation between rates of heat release from the sea and rainfall on the coastal area downwind extends to the intra-annual distribution of these two quantities. Figure 14-8, based on long-term monthly averages, shows that for the greater part of the rainfall season, the energy released per unit area of cooling sea surface is more than sufficient to supply the latent heat for evaporation of the rain falling per unit land area.

A deeper understanding of the mechanisms involved would be gained if measurements of sea heat changes were available on a time basis corresponding to that typical of winter rainfall in this region, i.e., approximately 60 rain days per season clumped into spells typically three days in duration.

Causation and Control

Despite the inter- and intra-annual correlations, heat loss from the sea appears to be a necessary but not sufficient cause of rainfall in the Levant. For rain to occur, the typical cyclonic situation—with enhanced sea heat loss caused by the passing storm track—is essential. Without such situations originating outside the region, rainfall will be limited, however great the heat storage is at the beginning of the rainfall season.

In fact, a negative interaction between sea-heat loss and precipitation can occur. Thus, an above-average number of storm situations, and hence rainfall, at the beginning of the winter in October, has been shown to be associated with less than average rainfall in the remaining part of the season. The reason is that this preliminary mixing reduces the heat available to enhance evaporation during the subsequent midwinter cyclonic situations.

Despite these reservations, it seems likely that an increase in the amount of heat stored in the eastern Mediterranean would, on the average, lead to an increase in rainfall. This increase in heat storage could be achieved by mixing the cooler, deeper water with the heated surface layer during the summer season, thus increasing the depth of the heated layer.

How this mixing could be achieved, and what its costs and consequences could be, have been outlined by Assaf (1989). He projects a grid of floating vertical pipes, each 2 m in diameter and 80 m in depth, supported by a 4 m diameter buoy and distributed at a density of one per 10 km2.

To mix the sea during the summer heating season at the rate of 1 m3 s-1 would increase the depth of the heated upper layer from 50 to 55 m, i.e., by 10%, and would require an energy input of only 500 W to overcome the 2 kg m^{-3} density difference between the warm and cold waters.

The obvious local source of this energy is that of the waves which disperse on the Mediterranean coasts at a rate of 7 kW m-1. A number of ways in which this energy could be used to mix the water are discussed by Assaf (1984). Whatever the technology, the energy requirement is small—each of the mixing tubes would require 104 kW per year during a summer period of approximately 100 days—equivalent to 3.6 KJ per m^2 of mixed sea surface.

The results of a 10% increase in the depth of the upper mixed layer were calculated to increase the initial early winter water temperature by 0.5°C. The statistics of the relationship between this parameter and rainfall imply an increase in the rainfall over the coastal plain of Israel of 85 mm with an increase half this amount extending to the eastern plateau to the Jordan Rift valley at the longitude of Amman and Damascus (see Table 14-2 and Assaf (1984)). Assaf (1984) has calculated that a 10% sea increase in mixing during the summer over a 330 by 330 km area of the southeastern Mediterranean would increase the rainfall over a land area of 105 km^2 by 2 x 109 m^3, i.e. 2 km^3. Each mixing unit would thus generate 20,000 m^3 of additional rainfall.

The missing energy needed per unit of additional rainfall is very small and corresponds to 0.18 MJ m^{-3}.

Nuclear Desalination for Coastal Desert Agriculture

The fourth project to exploit Mediterranean waters, like the previous one, aims at using them as a source of water to improve the agricultural productivity of the semiarid land areas bordering the southern and eastern coasts. It differs from the precipitation-enhancement proposal in utilizing an established although very energy-intensive technology—desalination.

The use of nuclear energy to desalinate sea water for the irrigation of the potentially productive desert region of the northern Sinai coast formed the basis of the Eisenhower-Strauss plan. This was formally approved by the US Senate in 1967 as a contribution to achieving political stabilization in the region through economic development (Fried and Edlund 1971). Following this approval, technical and economic aspects of the proposal were intensively studied by a group at the Oak

Ridge National Laboratory and their report (Nuclear Energy Centers 1968) forms the basis of the following brief description.

The concept calls for an agro-industrial center powered by a dual purpose nuclear power plant at a suitable coastal site. Electricity generated by the reactor would be used for chemical and for metallurgical industries which would include production of the fertilizers needed for the agricultural enterprise. It would also be used to distribute the irrigation water. Steam from the power plant's turbine generators would provide the energy needed to desalinate water needed for irrigation. An artist's concept of this agro-industrial complex is shown in Figure 14-9 taken from the ORNL report (1968).

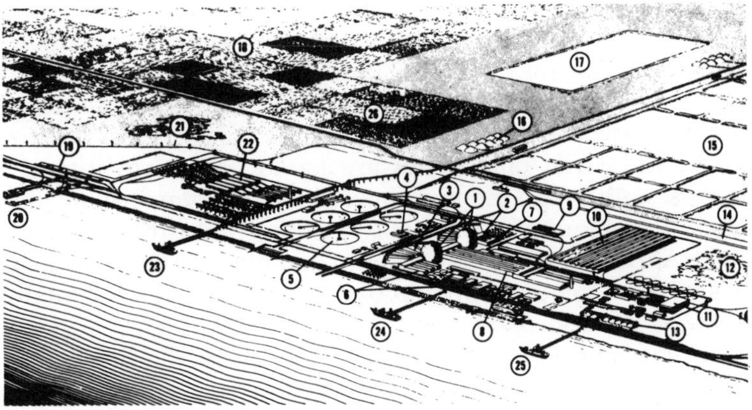

Figure 14-9: Artist's conception of agro-industrial complex on the shore of a coastal desert. Legend: 1. Nuclear reactors. 2. Steam turbines. 3. Seawater evaporators. 4. Central control facilities. 5. Seawater treatment plant. 6. Caustic chlorine production plant. 7. Electrolytic hydrogen plant. 8. Aluminum smelting plant. 9. Ammonia plant. 10. Aluminum fabrication. 11. Alumina plant. 12. Alumina plant waste. 13. Bauxite storage. 14. Railway yards. 15. Solar salt works. 16. Salt piles. 17. Bitterns ponds. 18. Irrigated farm. 19. Food warehouses. 20. Food export dock. 21. Phosphorus plant waste slag. 22. Electrical furnace phosphorus plant. 23. Phosphorus raw material import—salt export. 24. Cl_2, NaOH, NH_3 and Al export. 25. Bauxite import. 26. Main irrigation canal.
Source: ORNL Report (Nuclear Energy Centers 1968).

In selecting potential sites suitable for such a complex, a number of factors must be considered. For the agricultural enterprise to succeed, the chemical and physical properties of the soil are important. The plant nutrient concentration is less important than that of salt, as the former will in any case have to be supplemented with fertilizers, whereas to leach excessive salts with desalinated water is a very expensive process. The physical structure of the soil is important to allow efficient infiltration and drainage of the irrigation water; the latter can be improved by provision of an artificial drainage system, but this is extremely expensive. The climate should permit the rapid and year-round growth of a variety of crops—the year-long growing season is particularly important to allow continuous use of desalinated water without prohibitively expensive water storage facilities—and also permit the most efficient use of the capital-intensive system. Finally, the topography of the site should include a sufficient area of land whose slope, relief, and elevation are suitable for irrigation. "Sufficient" in this context refers to the water requirement corresponding to the desalination rate from the economically optimum size of a nuclear reactor.

The industrial enterprises are based on energy-intensive processes. Although the raw material for nitrogen fertilizer production is ubiquitous, those for two other industrial processes which appear suitable—aluminum and elemental phosphorus production—require supplies of bulky raw materials, bauxite, and rock phosphates.

To import these raw materials and export the finished industrial and agricultural products require transport facilities, in particular a suitable nearby port or potential harbor site.

At least two sites on the southeastern Mediterranean appear to satisfy most of the above requirements. One is the region inland from the northern coast of the Sinai Peninsula extending from El Arish (31°08'N, 33°48'E) to Gaza (31°30'N, 34°28'E). The second is the hinterland of the northern Egyptian coast west of Alexandria and centered on Burg el 'Arab (30°54'N, 29°32'E).

Two different levels of nuclear power and desalination technologies were examined in the ORNL study. These were a near-term option consisting of a light-water reactor linked to a multistage flash evaporation plant, and a far-term technology utilizing breeder reactors with a combination vertical tube and multistage evaporation plant for desalination. Three possible agricultural cropping plans were evaluated, all at the level of what is now currently the best commercial practice in desert-irrigated agriculture of the southwestern US. The crop rotations maximized either variety of crops or their production measured in monetary or calorific value. In all cases the industrial component of the complex was the same, using 1740 Mw (electric) power to produce the following daily amounts of primary products: 755 tons ammonia, 843 tons phosphorus, and 1,053 tons caustic chlorine.

Some of the salient features of the size and cost of the above combinations are listed in Table 14-3 although it should be pointed out that there have been important changes in the costs and performance of both nuclear power generation and desalination technologies in the two decades that have elapsed since the ORNL report was published.

By comparison, the changes in the agricultural sector are less significant. The three cropping systems examined permit different areas to be cropped for the same water use because of differences in the water requirements of the individual crops. In the southeast Mediterranean sites the areas of crop that could be grown with an annual production of 1.192 km^3 of desalinated water vary from 1,221 km^2 for the high-calorie system to 810 km^2 of summer crops and 1,134 km^2 of winter crops under the mixed cropping system and to 972 km^2 of summer and 1,296 km^2 of winter crops in the profit maximizing cropping plan. All three systems have winter wheat as their main crop from the point of view of both area and water requirements and should produce sufficient food to feed from 4.5 to 6.3 million people.

The gross-energy requirement for sea water desalination using the near-term technology, light water reactor and multistage evaporation plant was calculated to be 28.46 MJ m-3 —considerably less than most desalination plants actually operating, no doubt for reasons of scale economy. No less than 40% of the total energy requirement is represented by amortization of the energy embodied in the desalination plant.

Table 14-3: Some Characteristics of Agro-industrial Nuclear Centers

Technology level	*Near-term*		*Long-term*		
Power station size Mw (thermal)	11,100		11,900	11,900	11,900
Net electrical power Mw (electrical)	2,100		2,900	1,935	3124
Desalted water production Mm3yr-1	11,382		1,382	1,382	1,382
Farm size km2	1,296		1,296	1,296	1,296
Investment M US$					
Nuclear power plants	166		261	246	217
Turbine generator plants	120		118	83	20
Evaporator plant	403		279	279	279
Industrial complex	570	7301	570	570	0
Farm	306		306	306	306
Other items5	216	222	342	306	306
Total	1,781	1,947	1,876	1,790	1,035
Annual operating costs M US$					
Power and water plant	47	47	18	16	21
Industrial complex	133	152	133	133	133
Farm	56	56	56	56	62
Total	236	255	207	205	83
Annual sales M US$					
Industrial	347	407	347	347	0
Farm	194	104	194	194	194
Total	548	608	577	556	205
Income minus expenses	312	353	370	351	122
Internal rate of return, % y-1	14.6	16.1	16.5	16.4	10.1

1. Ammonia converted to fertilizer products.
2. ~1000 Mw electricity supplied to national grid.
3. Without electrical supply to grid.
4. Only agricultural production—no industry.
5. Includes grid tie, working capital, harbor, town and fuel inventory.

Source: ORNL Report (Nuclear Energy Centers 1968).

A comparison of the estimated performance of the projected desert agriculture with the actual current performance of Egyptian, Israeli, and Californian agricultures as taken from national statistics, is presented in Table 14-4. This shows that the coastal desert agriculture based on desalinated water is

Table 14-4: Comparative Statistics for Four Agricultural Systems in Mediterranean Climates

	Egypt 1972–1974	*California 1974*	*Israel 1969–1970*	*Nuclear desalinated coastal desert*
Cultivated area, km2	2,850	36,920	4,110	1,220
Irrigated, %	1000	83	42	100
INPUTS, per hectare per year				
Persons gainfully employed	1.85	0.08	0.20	0.06
Tractors	0.007	0.038	0.040	0.037
Livestock, animal units	1.99	1.35	0.84	3.73
Water applied m3	17,933	4,890	3,264	9,536
Fertilizers applied, kg[3]	146	156	458	560
Pesticides applied, kg	70	7	22	10
OUTPUTS, per hectare per year				
Persons fed[4]	11.3	6.8	7.8	19.2
Food of animal origin, %	8	38	33	10.0
EFFICIENCIES				
Labor: persons fed per persons employed	6	85	39	320
Labor: persons fed per persons employed	1.83	0.90	0.41	0.28
Water: water applied per person fed, m3	1,587	719	418	4

1. Calorie optimization cropping plan modified to increase animal production.
2. Based on following weighing factors: Camels 1.1, buffaloes, horses, mules 1.0, cattle, donkeys 0.8, sheep, goats and pigs 0.1, poultry 0.1.
3. Includes N (predominant), P205 and K20 only.
4. At one-million kcal per caput per annum, allowance included for seeds and non-edible grain fractions but not for storage and distribution losses.

Source: Stanhill (1979).

extremely efficient in terms of labor and water use, but this is at the expense of its energy efficiency. In this it poses a great contrast to the current Egyptian system which uses large inputs of renewable energy, i.e., human and animal labor and Nile water, with modest quantities of inputs based on non-renewable energy sources.

Discussion and Conclusions

All four projects discussed have in common an attempt to exploit the Mediterranean Sea for the benefit of the arid region bordering its southern and eastern shores. The volumes of water involved are enormous, between one and two cubic km a year in the case of the Dead Sea, rainfall enhancement, and nuclear-desalination projects, and more than 10 times this quantity—25 km^3 a year—for the Qattara Depression scheme. However, even this latter volume would represent less than a 1% increase in the natural rate of water loss and predominantly southeastward vapor transfer of Mediterranean water by natural evaporation.

The major contrast between the projects is that whereas the first two utilize water to generate energy, the other two require inputs of energy to desalinate sea water.

In the first case the power generation rates are very different because of the great contrast in the elevation differences. For the filling phase of the Dead Sea project the net power generation estimated is 2.48 MJ m^{-3} and in the steady-state phase 2.89 MJ m^{-3}. For the Qattara Depression project the energy produced per unit water volume was estimated at 0.37 MJ m^{-3}.

The two water-producing schemes also differ very much in their estimated energy requirements. Thus rainfall enhancement by summer sea mixing was calculated to require only 0.18 MJ m^{-3} which could be supplied by renewable wave energy, whereas nuclear desalination was estimated to sequester 28.5 MJ m^{-3} of non-renewable nuclear and fossil-fuel energy.

This contrast between the two types of projects persists even if the possibility of their interaction is considered. Such a possibility is suggested by the coincidence that the sites for the two energy-producing projects are close to those selected for the energy-requiring nuclear agro-industrial complexes. The energy produced by the Dead Sea and Qattara Depression projects could be used to desalinate a very small fraction of the water used for power generation to irrigate high-value winter export crops, in the natural "greenhouse" climate of both the Dead Sea and Siwa oasis regions.

The figures presented suggest that the rainfall enhancing, sea-mixing project is the energetically most attractive of the proposals. This is strongly reinforced by the fact that in this region the marginal water use efficiency of increased winter rainfall from crop production is as much as twice that of water used for summer-crop irrigation (Stanhill 1981).

Economically, the four projects also fall into two categories—food and energy production—and their feasibilities from this point of view will depend on future prices of, and markets for, these two commodities.

In the national contexts of the projects considered, food and energy, as well as the capital needed to implement the schemes, are all in short supply. Viewed from the wider regional point of view, however, the desalination projects might appear as the preferred choice, given the large fossil fuel, and hence capital resources of the Middle East as a whole and the water-limited food-production potential of the region.

It is hoped that this wider regional outlook of technological opportunities and economic needs may one day prevail and lead to a successful example of ocean modification to complement the cautionary tale of King Canute.

References

Allen W. 1855. "The Dead Sea: a new route to India." London: Longman, Brown, Green and Longman.

Arkin Y. 1982. "Mediterranean-Dead Sea Project. Outline and Appraisal." Jerusalem: Mediterranean-Dead Sea Company Limited, 45.

Assaf, G. 1976. "The Dead Sea: A scheme for a solar lake." *Solar Energy* 18: 293–299.

Assaf, G. 1989. "Enhancement of precipitation via sea mixing." In *Global Climate Change*. Edited by S. Fred Singer. New York: Paragon House Publishers. p. 285–296.

Barnett, T. 1983. "Recent changes in sea level and their possible causes." *Climatic Change* 5: 15–38.

Bassler, F. and M. Hamad 1980. "Mediterranean energy for Egypt from turbines in the Qattara depression." *Eleventh World Energy Conference,* Volume 1A: 30–36, 324.

Baumgartner, A. and E. Reichel 1975. *The World Water Balance*. Amsterdam: Elsevier, 175.

Bloch, M. 1980. "Dead Sea whiteness and its origin." *Israel Academy of Science and Humanities Proceedings* 19: 1–7.

FAO, 1984. *Yearbook of Fishery Statistics—Catches and Landings*, 1982, Volume 54. Rome.

Fried, J. and M. Edlund 1971. *Desalting Technology for Middle Eastern Agriculture*. New York: Praeger Publishers. 112.

Gat, J. and M. Rindsberg, 1982. "The isotopic signature of precipitation originating in the Mediterranean Sea area." In *The Charney Workshop on Weather Modification*. Caesarea October 27–29: 12. Yavne: Ormat Turbines Limited.

Gorgy, S. and M. Salah. 1974. "Mediterranean Sea." In *Encyclopedia Britannica* 15th edition 11: 854–858. Chicago: Encyclopedia Britannica.

Hansen J., D. Johnson, A. Lacis, S. Lebedeff, P. Lee, D. Rind and G. Russell 1981. "Climate impact of increasing atmospheric carbon dioxide." *Science* 213: 957–966.

Hecht, A., Z. Rosentroub and J. Bishop 1982. "Temporal and spatial variations of heat storage in the eastern Mediterranean Sea." *Proceedings of the Charney Workshop on Weather Modification*: 26.

Klein, C. 1961. "On the fluctuations of the level of the Dead Sea since the beginning of the 19th Century." Hydrological Paper number 7. Jerusalem: Hydrological Service: 83.

Klein, C. 1981. "The influence of rainfall over the catchment area on the fluctuations of the level of the Dead Sea since the 12th Century." Israel Met. Reas. Papers, number 3. Naftali Roseman Memorial Volume. Bet Dagan: Israel Meteorological Service: 29–58.

Klein, C. 1982. "Morphological evidence of lake level changes, western shore of the Dead Sea." *Israel Jour. Earth-Science* 31: 67–94.

Klein, W. H. 1982. "Detecting carbon dioxide effects on climate." With commentaries by R. Gilliland, J.K. Angell, P.M. Kelly, T.M.C. Wigley and P.O. Jones. In *Carbon Dioxide Reviews*: 1982. Edited by W.C. Clark, New York: Oxford University Press. pp. 213–241 and 242–252.

Kukla G. and J. Gavin. 1981. "Summer ice and carbon dioxide." *Science* 214: 497–503.

Menenti, M. 1984. "Physical aspects and determinations of evaporation in deserts, applying remote sensing techniques." Report 10: Institute Land Water Management Research. Wageningen: The Netherlands, 202 pp.

Ne'eman Y. and I. Schul. 1983. "Israel's Dead Sea Project." *Annual Review Energy* 8: 113–136.

Nuclear Energy Centers: Industrial and Agro-Industrial Complexes. 1968. ORNL-4290. Oak Ridge TN: 227.

Park, P. Kilho. 1989. "World Wide Pollution in the Oceans." In *Global Climate Change*. Edited by S. Fred Singer. New York: Paragon House Publishers. p. 207–244.

Peixoto, J. and A. Oort. 1983. "The atmospheric branch of the hydrological cycle and climate." In *Variations in the Global Water Budget*. Edited by A. Street Perrott *et al.* pp. 5–65.

Stanhill, G. 1979. "A comparative study of the Egyptian agro-ecosystem." *Agro-Ecosystems* 5: 213–230.

Stanhill, G. 1985. "An updated energy balance estimate of evaporation from the Dead Sea." *Israel Meteorlogical Research Papers* 4: 98–116.

Stanhill, G and J. Neumann. 1978. "Energy balance and evaporation in Lake Kinneret." Edited by C. Serruya. Amsterdam: *Monographiae Biologicae*, 173–181.

Tzvetkov E. and G. Assaf. 1982. "The Mediterranean heat storage and Israel precipitation." *Water Resources Research* 18: 1036–1040.

Vadasz P., D. Weinter and Y. Zvirin. 1983. "A halothermal simulation of the Dead Sea for application to solar energy projects." *Journal of Solar Energy Engineering* 105: 348–355.

Watts J. 1983. "Surface temperature anomalies for the northern hemisphere." In *Carbon Dioxide Review*: 1982. Edited by W. Clark. New York: Oxford University Press, 448–456.

PART FOUR:

OCEAN COMMERCE

FIFTEEN

CONSTRUCTION Of A SPACE In The SEABED

Yutaka Mochida

Introduction

To excavate under the seabed and construct a space for various purposes will become prevalent and more diversified.

Until recently, the seabed was used mainly as a source for minerals. In the future, however, it will be used for various purposes, e.g., storing of resources, seabed plants, seabed habitation, etc. Among them, one of the most important uses will be under sea tunnels for the purpose of transportation and communication across a strait.

Construction of Seikan Under Sea Tunnel which—has an entire length of 53.85 km—was completed and commercial operation began March 13, 1988. To date, the under sea tunnels completed and in use include Kanmon Under Sea Tunnel (3.6 km) and New Kanmon Under Sea Tunnel for the new JNR Super-express (Bullet) train which connects Honshu and Kyushu, two of the four main islands of Japan. Seikan Under Sea Tunnel is the one that connects Honshu with Hokkaido. In the future are planned the Kitan Strait Tunnel (about 30 km in length) that will connect Honshu with Shikoku, and the Houyo Strait Tunnel (about 40 km in length) that will

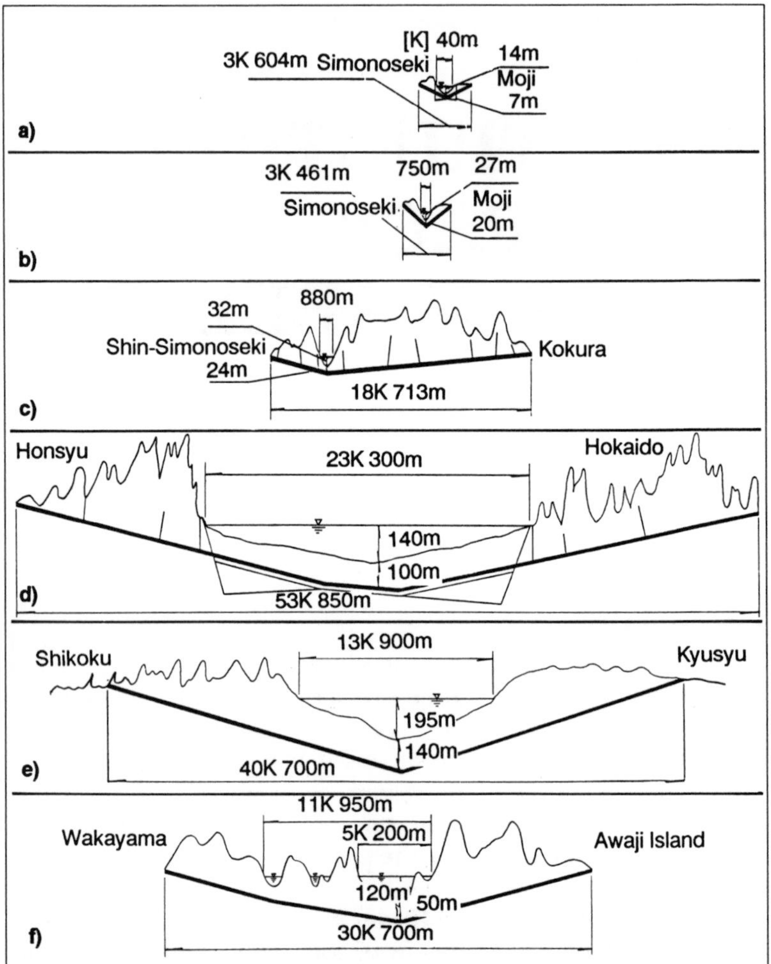

Figure 15-1A: Tunnels in Japan. a) Kanmon Tunnel—completed in 1944; b) Kanmon Road Tunnel—completed in 1958; c) Shin-Kanmon Tunnel—completed in 1974; d) Seikan Tunnel—completed in 1988; e) Houyu Tunnel (provisional); f) Kitan Tunnel (provisional).

connect Shikoku with Kyushu. In other parts of the world, either planned or under investigation, are the Channel Tunnel connecting the United Kingdom and the European continent

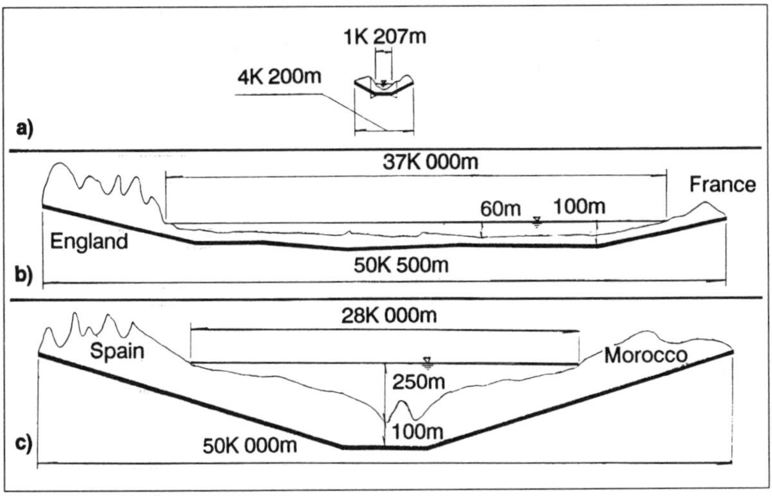

Figure 15-1B: Tunnels built in England. a) Marsey Railroad Tunnel—completed in 1886; b) Dover tunnel—in construction; c) Gibraltar Tunnel—under investigation.

begun in 1987, the Spain-Morocco Channel Tunnel (connecting the European continent with the African continent, about 50 km) and the Japan-Korea Tunnel (connecting Japan with Korea, about 250 km). (See Figure 15-1A, B and Figure 15-2.) I would like to view some of the problems which faced the sea tunnels based on the experience of construction of the Seikan Under Sea Tunnel.

Special Features of the Seabed Tunnel

In general, sea and tidal currents in the straits are known to be very strong, and changes in meteorological conditions can be very large, making the straits difficult for traffic. For these reasons, circulation or distribution of personnel and freight have been hindered in the straits and entirely different industrial structures and cultures had to be developed for a long time. Many attempts have been made to help solve these problems but problems in marine and meteorological conditions on the straits still remain unsolved, building a barrier against construction.

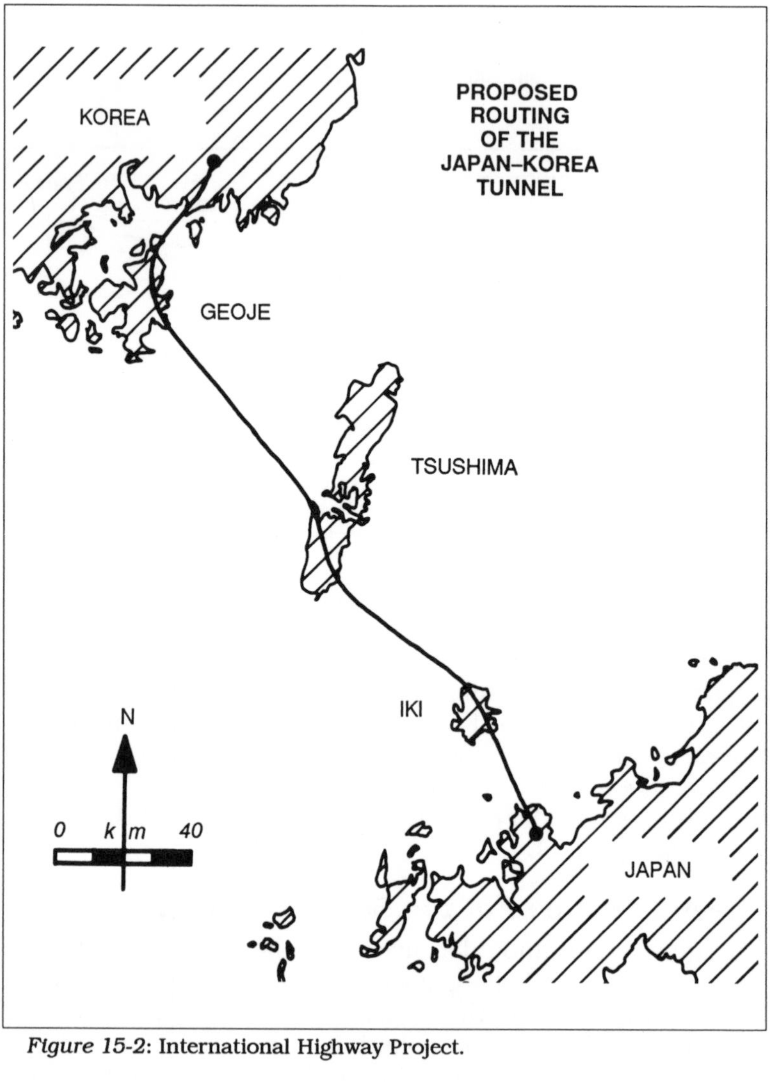

Figure 15-2: International Highway Project.

To connect a strait when the distance is small and shallow, a bridge may be considered. Taking into account the depth of water (140 m) and the velocity of sea current (as fast as 10 kt),

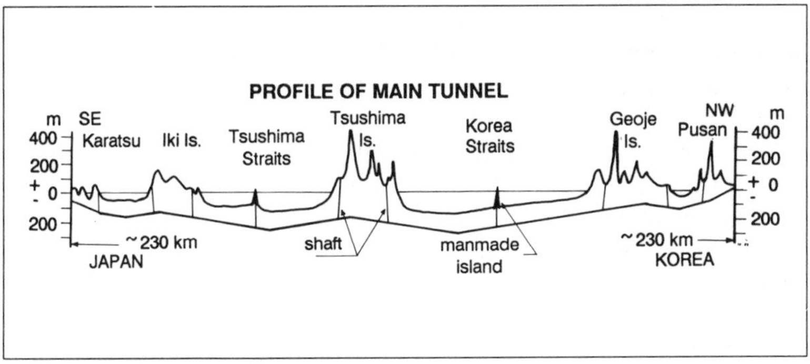

Figure 15-3: Profile of tunnel.

however, no such construction was considered feasible in the case of the Seikan Strait.

With the present level of technological capability there are still many difficult problems that have to be overcome in order to construct a space in the seabed. Two of the major problems are:

- Obtaining information on the geological conditions below the seabed.
- Dealing with, and designing for, seawater pressure and spring water.

Prior to construction, the most important matter is to obtain and sufficiently grasp the geological conditions below the seabed. Knowing geological conditions below the seabed has a far greater effect on the construction work than it would above ground. Therefore, prior to the commencement of construction work, it is necessary that detailed information on the natural conditions below the seabed—where the construction work will occur—be obtained and reasonable judgments based upon such information be made. However, there are many difficulties in collecting information on the natural conditions that exist below the seabed, i.e., seawater, constituting a thick barrier, in addition to the tremendous effects from sea current and meteorological conditions. Consequently, the investigation of the seabed will yield less accurate results than that which is performed above ground and will be time and money consuming.

What presents the most difficult problem is that there is a technical dichotomy—the difficulty of investigating the natural conditions below the seabed, yet the essentiality of this knowledge for construction work.

However, no matter how people are going to utilize space below the seabed in the future, more thorough understanding of the natural conditions is considered essential for the construction of these tunnels; such understanding is not only essential for the stability of construction, but also for their use and maintenance after completion.

Therefore, the technical understanding of natural conditions requires immediate attention. For this purpose, however, it is also necessary to upgrade science technologies in many fields at the same time. Also important is the training of personnel so that they can freely use such technologies and truly understand their nature. Ultimately, the training of capable personnel will, I think, become the key to the problem.

It is a matter of course that the space provided by excavation below the seabed will have to bear the water pressure corresponding to the depth of the water. The deeper the excavation, the more pressure, and this may present a serious problem for the stability of the excavated rockbed. Also, considerations against water pressure have to be given to the structures below the seabed. In the sea areas where construction has already been attempted, the deeper the water, the larger the water pressure problems were. On the other hand, where excavation is carried out in the seabed, without exception, spring water must be expected. Although how it should be dealt with—that is, whether it should be sealed to stop it from flowing, or removed—will be a problem. Also, there is a problem of the chemical resistance of structures due mostly to the chemical corrosion of seawater, which must be taken into consideration.

In addition to the points mentioned above, in providing a space in the seabed, other important environmental problems must be considered: Maintenance of living and working environments during the construction, drainage, and seawater pollution after completion, etc. Even though we note a gradual advance in these technologies in recent years, there is still much progress to be desired.

Inasmuch as we feel the need for advanced technologies in the environmental field, a major point must be the understanding of nature as well as the recognition of its present situation. The important and urgent nature of this point is truly international.

Specific Methods of Settling the Problems

How have these problems been settled in the construction of the Seikan Tunnel? (I dare not say they are solved well enough.) Basically, it was to remove the problematic conditions that the construction was carried out below the seabed. That is to say, to make the conditions for construction the same as construction carried out above ground, all special conditions inherent in the construction of a tunnel in the seabed had to be removed. By doing so, the same design and method of construction can be applied to construct a space below the seabed, and the results of technological development used therefore can also be applied to the construction of the tunnel below the seabed.

Specifically, the following were carried out: To obtain geological information below the seabed, a horizonal boring—seldom used above ground—was employed. Whichever method is used, it will always be difficult to understand the natural conditions of geology below the seabed. Normally, an exploratory boring (diameter $=\xi \sim 10$ cm) on each side of the tunnel to be drilled was carried out prior to excavation of the tunnel. The information that can be obtained from this boring on the natural conditions is as follows: types of rocks, faults, or bad conditions; a forecast of the quality and quantity of spring water; the generation of gas, etc.

By performing this pilot boring with certainty, far more accurate information of the natural conditions may be obtained than by normal exploratory investigations.

In the initial period of construction of the Seikan Tunnel, this pilot boring could only be executed from the boring station in the tunnel for a length of 200–300 m for various technical reasons, but in the latter part of the construction we were able to bore for a length of about 2,000 m, making it possible to foresee the natural conditions two years ahead of actual tunnel excavation. This was particularly helpful in estimating construction time. Thus we were able to prepare the construction schedule with an adequate time allowance. Thus a handicap imposed by the location of construction under the seabed was completely removed by the pilot boring executed prior to the tunnel excavation.

However, in order for the information obtained physically from this pilot boring to be useful, there needed to be trained personnel to judge the information along objective lines. The success of the construction work depended on how accurately these two items were taken care of. Consequently, as the most well-trained and knowledgeable personnel are those who could act as middlemen between nature and the tunnel, training these people was the most important job of all.

With these conditions satisfied, the conditions for the construction of the tunnel were then the same as for one built above ground. Solving the major problems of under sea tunnel construction together with further understanding of nature—which is more important on the seabed than above ground—did not enable us to conquer the nature of the seabed, but did allow us to use its special features to proceed with the construction work in harmony with it.

Dealing with water can be a problem of an extremely technical nature. Since the excavation of above-ground tunnels proceeds with an uphill grade towards the summit, any spring water can naturally be drained towards the tunnel mouth, presenting no problem (with the exception of shooting water at the upper part of the tunnel). But since excavation of an under sea tunnel proceeds with a downhill grade towards the center of the seabed, spring water will remain in the tunnel, requiring draining. If the amount increases too much, excavation has to be stopped. To allow excavation to proceed, there is no way but to stop the spring water. When the spring water is stopped, the water pressure will naturally be borne by rocks and structures around the tunnel. In the case of Seikan Tunnel, this water pressure was 240 t/m^2, which cannot normally be expected under usual tunnel excavation conditions. If the tunnel were to take this kind of water pressure completely by itself, as is the case of the subway or the underwater tunnel, the cost for construction would be tremendous and risks of wider excavation would be caused. In order to cope with the situation,

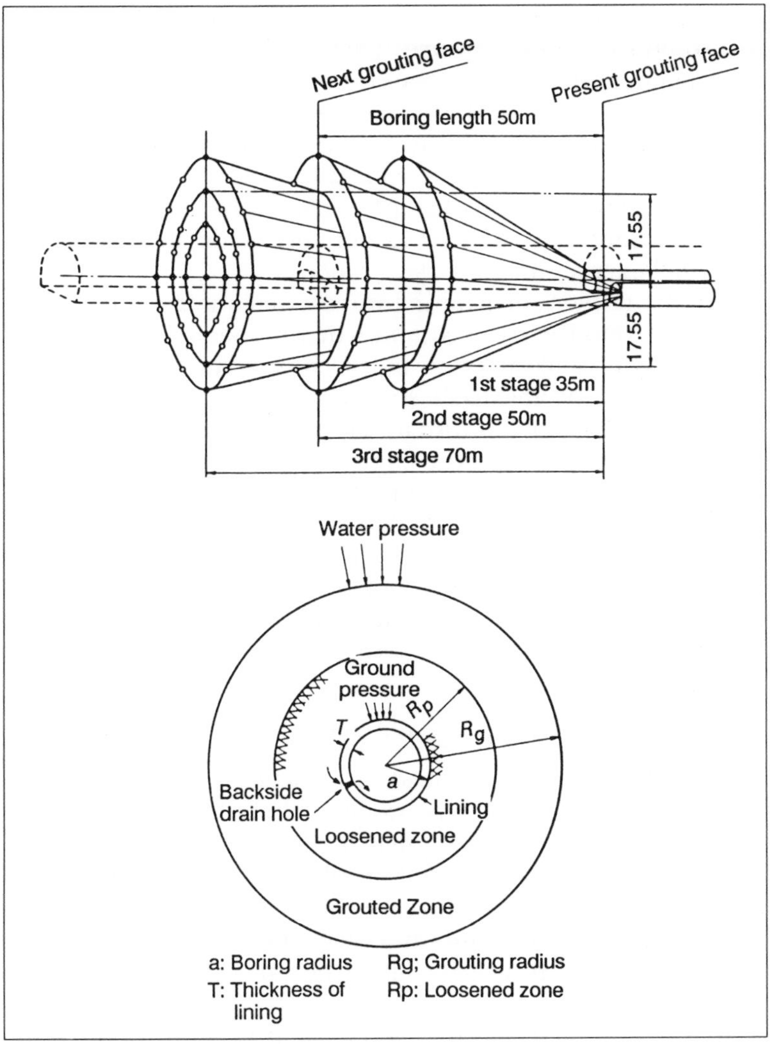

Figure 15-4: Conceptional illustration of grouting.

considerably vast areas of rockbed where the tunnel was to be dug had to be grouted prior to commencing the tunnel excavation. The area of grouting varied depending on the geology surrounding the tunnel so that the consolidated rockbed would withstand the water pressure. That is, the water pressure as a natural phenomenon was dealt with by consolidating the rockbed, a part of the seabed's nature. The material used for grouting was developed from materials with durability against seawater. By doing so, the rockbed itself was made impermeable—thereby able to withstand considerable water pressure. Thus, the conditions for excavation were made the same as that of tunnel excavation above sea level.

The actual work of grouting was carried out from numerous drill holes into the rockbed and when we had an aggregate of completely finished injected holes, consolidation was the definite result. To be able to do so, each and every one of the drill holes had to be grouted with a suitable method and results had to be thorough. Each of the engineers on site controlled these operations, and their judgment decided the success or failure of the construction work. As has been explained thus far, by making the seabed conditions almost equal to the conditions above ground by using pilot boring and grouting, the tunnel excavation work proceeded safely just as with tunnels above ground. And what makes it possible is the judgment of trained human beings.

Safety of Seabed Construction

Without limiting it to seabed construction, construction work as a whole must be executed safely without having an adverse effect on the surrounding environment. However, in seabed construction there are special problems in the working environment, due to the fact that we have to deal with an almost infinite volume of seawater and the work has to be carried out through a long passage from land (the part which has been dug initially).

In the construction of the under sea tunnel, one of the worst accidents possible is that a part of the tunnel collapses and becomes flooded. To prevent this disaster from occurring, the following preventive measures must be taken systemwide:

1. Provide emergency flood gates (all water pressure resistant type) at required locations, so that an excessive flood can be divided up into sections.

2. Provide an inclined shaft and a separate pilot tunnel where workers can take shelter.

3. Provide a drainage system with sufficient volume so that an abnormal flood can be dealt with.

4. Provide an emergency power-generating system that is capable of operating the drainage system, lifting system, etc.

5. Provide a communication system to and from the tunnel and provide a sufficient storage of emergency materials.

Worker safety in the tunnel was always considered most important. Therefore, a manual was prepared and workers were trained to understand the measures to take against abnormal floods; constant training was necessary so as to prevent panic conditions from occurring.

No matter how well we are prepared, disasters such as these could occur, because of human error. What is most important is how we were able to minimize the damage from such disasters.

Going back to technological development, there is still much to be desired in this respect, for there are many technological advancements still required for seabed construction. Also, again, the training of engineers in judgment and technical capabilities has to be carried out. These developments and training can only be promoted through trial and error. That is to say, if seabed construction is to be performed in a high-quality manner, some errors cannot be avoided. Therefore, by allowing a large margin for such errors in advance, a fatal blow may be prevented. Secondary and even tertiary protective measures against possible errors have to be taken in advance. Similarly, this could also be applied to measures against ventilation and fires. Since errors committed in the seabed could greatly affect other areas, sufficient measures must be taken to cope with human error. Teamwork and a sense of judgment have to be attained through constant training, etc.

Summary

The use of seabed space is expected to increase in the future, because of the relative constancy of water temperature, its aseismatic quality (similar to that of the tunnel) and the effective utilization of land space, etc. On the seabed, unless the work proceeds with better planning than that which goes on above ground, the damage sustained from an error could be much greater. And due to the fact that there are large factors which depend upon the judgment of human beings, we could say that the work done in the seabed is extremely prone to human error.

It has been 40 years since the Seikan Tunnel investigation initially started and 20 years since the work was undertaken. At last it is completed. Thanks to the effort of overcoming the handicaps of being in the seabed and of understanding its extremely difficult nature, we were able to come this far. We were not able to conquer the nature of the seabed, but we were able to excavate the tunnel, learning how to work in harmony with its nature. By fully demonstrating our capability to know the characteristics of nature, we were able to proceed with the work.

We had to face the need for the development of numerous peripheral technologies in order to make use of the power of nature through this project, but we are thankful for the fact that the worldwide advancement of technology brought fruitful results for us.

SIXTEEN

HIGHWAYS UNDER The OCEAN

A COMMENTARY

Avraham Melamed

The project of construction of transportation tunnels under the ocean bottom is very inspiring, as it may provide new options to strengthen economic, social, and cultural ties between islands or countries separated by stretches of water.

The significance of such projects cannot be over-emphasized when one tries to imagine how different a course history might have taken, for example, if a land bridge had existed from Italy through Sicily to Tunisia. Certainly North Africa would not have developed so differently from southern Europe. And would Great Britain have become the same maritime world power if it had been part of the European continent?

Nevertheless, there are many factors working against carrying out sea-tunnel projects. In some cases, such as the English Channel Tunnel, security and political considerations work against the project. In most other situations, plans for construction of sea tunnels are rejected on purely economic grounds. Beyond a certain distance, or a certain depth of the sea, the alternative ferry system is simply cheaper than the sea tunnel.

Technological changes may cause some shifting of the break-even point, but the basic consideration of the economic alternatives would always put a limit to the length or depth of tunnel projects.

In some particular situations, some unique factors may work in favor of sea-tunnel projects. I would assume that, in Japan, the ties between the various parts of the nation living on separate islands, combined with opening better prospects for development of some lesser developed regions, played an important role in deciding to construct the sea tunnels.

With its high level of technology and great economic resources, Japan may undertake an important role in leading the way in this field for the rest of the world.

The risk undertaken in deciding to go ahead with a long sea-tunnel at a great depth under the bottom of the sea is far greater than in ordinary projects of a similar financial scope. This is so mainly because exploratory drilling work is required to know the geotechnical conditions ahead of decision-making. But complete exploration is often too costly to carry out. Hence one has to decide to undertake the project without reliable estimates of the funds required for its execution. Only later, in the course of actual construction, is the geotechnical information gradually obtained from horizontal boreholes drilled ahead of the progressing tunnels.

In view of these difficulties, the outstanding pioneering role of Japan in sea tunneling should be emphasized. May we wish Japan success in this enterprise that others may follow elsewhere.

SEVENTEEN

The EARLIEST VOYAGERS

Willard Bascom

Intercontinental voyaging has been going on for a very long time. The earliest European explorers—Leif Ericson, Columbus, de Gama, Cabral, Magellan, Cook—were by no means the first to reach the Americas, round Africa, or visit mid-Pacific islands. Without detracting from their valuable contributions, one can observe that the descendants of earlier explorers were already living on the remote lands they visited.

The questions of who first reached the Americas by sea, when they arrived, and what culture they brought, have long been the subject of controversy. The debate has been primarily between those who believe the cultures of ancient America were independently developed and those who think a significant diffusion of ideas resulted from trans-oceanic contacts. The independent inventionists admit the possibility that "with miraculous good fortune" contacts were possible, but they doubt that any substantial amount of culture was transferred in this way. The diffusionists believe there were repeated contacts and cite cultural similarities to support that view.

Most arguments have been about whether cultural traits or objects that are similar on both sides of the Atlantic or Pacific were brought to the Americas or invented here. These include such things as similarities in pottery, tools, burial practices, architecture, luxury goods (jade and turquoise), worship of animals and design motifs. There is also controversy over the origins of cultivated plants (peanuts, gourds, cotton), chickens, and carved or molded representations of elephants.

This author is familiar with the cultural evidence reviewed by such authors as Riley (1971) and Jett (1978). However, this paper will minimize it in favor of other kinds of evidence whose collective importance has been largely overlooked.

These are:

1. The accounts of many accidental voyages across the Pacific and the logical reasons why desperate people would have been driven to cast their lots on the sea, however great the risk.

2. The fact that a number of remote islands including Hawaii, Easter, and New Zealand had long been inhabited when they were first reached by Europeans.

3. The knowledge that many small boats, sometimes poorly built, sailed and provisioned, have crossed the oceans in the last two centuries.

4. The variability of ocean winds and currents over the last few thousand years that would make ocean crossings in primitive craft impossible in some years but virtually unavoidable in others.

5. The existence of clay and stone portraits of foreigners mixed with those of Amerinds in many pre-Columbian collections.

Before discussing those points I shall review what is known about early sea travel and trade so that some of the indirect evidence to be discussed can be related to probable voyages.

Evidence of Early Sea Travel

It seems unlikely that our remote ancestors ever intentionally crossed the open sea for unknown destinations. More likely the first voyages were toward lands that were visible across the water. The earliest evidence we have, confirmed by radiocarbon dating, is that the human race, whose development began in Africa or Asia, reached Australia 40,000 years ago (Johnstone 1980). At that time, during the Wisconsin glacial period, the sea level was some 50 meters below its present stand (Fairbridge 1965). Although a land bridge connected Australia with New Guinea, those sea travellers would have had to negotiate at least

180 km between Java and Timor or 95 km between Celebes and the Moluccas by island-hopping (Johnstone 1980). None of the sea distances were great and the next island may always have been in sight, but inter-continental voyaging had begun.

Some of the best evidence we have about early voyages comes from the Mediterranean. About 6,500 B.C., obsidian was brought on several occasions from the Aegean island of Melos to the Franchthi Cave on the Peloponnesian peninsula of Greece, a sea distance of 120 km. Similar finds on Crete and Cyprus dated at about 6,200 B.C. (Johnstone 1980) show that sea trade had begun between peoples who lived beyond each other's horizons. Seafarers where becoming bolder. Sicily, visible across the water from the Italian mainland, and Malta, visible from Sicily, are known to have been inhabited by 5,000 B.C. The Canary Islands and Ceylon were reached by Neolithic peoples at least by 3,000 B.C. Populations spread by sea as new lands were opened by the new sea transport systems.

Until about the fourth millennium B.C. there is little direct evidence about the nature of the boats that were used, but there is a wide spectrum of suggestions. Single logs, possibly shaped and probably paddled; several logs tied together to form a raft; hide- or bark-covered frames; bladder floats connected in various ways; bundles of reed or papyrus; and dugout canoes were possible means of Neolithic navigation.

Although in recent years it has been demonstrated that very small boats of nearly any design can cross the ocean, none of the styles mentioned seems likely to have borne settlers to the Canary Islands, for example; there must have been something larger. About that time Middle East civilization had developed to the point where ship forms were recorded. Outlines of ships with sails and paddles or oars were scratched on rock, painted on vases, and sculpted in cylinder seals; models of ships survive from that period made of wood, clay, and silver. Some of these had paddles and one had a step for a mast, but the renderings are too crude to show details of construction. Many of the early ships represented look like they were made for inland waters, but we do not know.

Then in 1954, to everyone's surprise, a real ship from this period, complete in every detail, was found in a boat-tomb alongside the Cheops pyramid, apparently buried with the Pharaoh in 2,590 B.C. It was dissembled, but every piece, including lashings, oars, and ceremonial carvings, was present. It took eight years of substantial effort by a team of Egyptians to reassemble it into the form shown in Figure 17-1, after which it was placed in a museum alongside the pyramid that has never been opened to the public (Jenkins 1980). Once the Cheops ship was exhumed from its nearly airtight-watertight tomb and put together, historians learned how much was known about shipbuilding 4,500 years ago and how greatly the seagoing capabilities of that time had been underestimated.

Figure 17-1: Painting of Cheops ship as it looked on the Nile in about 2,600 B.C. This ship is still in existence in a museum at the great pyramid (Bascom).

The Cheops ship was not intended for long-distance voyaging, and we do not know that the Egyptians ever had such desires. Rather, it seems to have been much like the standard Nile barges of the time but embellished by an ornamental bow and sternpost and a royal chamber.

The hull is 43.4 m long and 5.9 m wide and has two longitudinal stiffeners, each 23 m long and 45 cm deep, made from Lebanese cedar. The Cheops ship looks seaworthy, and its length is as great as two of Columbus' ships placed end-to-end. It was intended to be ceremonially rowed (while being towed), but if that basic hull had been ballasted and equipped with sails like those shown on artwork of the period, a knowledgeable sailor could have crossed any ocean.

The discovery of this complete vessel, 2,000 years older than most of the ancient ship fragments dug from the bottom of the Mediterranean by archaeologists, immediately dispelled the thought that Egyptians were restricted to reed boats. If technology is available, people tend to use it, and plainly such a ship was the product of many hundreds of years of development. It gives tangible meaning to the first formally recorded sea trade in which an earlier Pharaoh, Snefru, brought "forty ships with cedar logs" from Lebanon in about 2,650 B.C. (Casson 1959). This was plainly not a first voyage; it hints at an extensive sea trade in the eastern Mediterranean that began in the sixth millennium. Direct evidence is slim; but it must have included Egypt, for archaeologists digging in Crete have found stone bowls from the Nile valley and some Egyptian tombs have contained early Minoan material.

A more convincing argument derives from the wind structure in the Mediterranean which decreed the trade routes used in the Greek-Roman periods (Bascom 1976). The winds of summer, when sea trade was conducted, made it easy to sail down to the coast of North Africa. To return, it was common practice to sail eastward along Libya and Egypt, then north along the coast of present day Israel, Lebanon and Syria, and westward along the coast of Turkey. Such routes, probably discovered and followed by coasting vessels long before Cheops, led inevitably to international trade. Compared to going overland through mountain regions and hostile locals, the sea was a more convenient route, even considering the limitations of primitive ships.

We have no evidence of what the ships were like that formed the transition between small craft for quiet waters and seagoing vessels, but we have ideas about how that came about. Figure

17-2 shows the most likely manner in which the single log developed into a ship. The dugout log at the top took on a shape that was easier to propel and was lightened by the removal of excess wood. Then the narrow log was widened using heated stones, water, and props to hold the gunwales apart.

Figure 17-2: The development of the ship. Dugout log (top) is widened by seaming with hot rocks and held open with props (center), then side boards are sewn on (left) and finally ribs, mast, and deck are added.

When this was done there was often insufficient freeboard to operate in waves or with much load. Therefore, boards were sewn with fibers along the upper rim (gunwale) to increase the freeboard as shown in the lower left. Eventually it was discovered that a substantial number of boards could be sewn one above the other to form a hull. If need be, braces and stiffeners were added for strength and to insure the boat kept its shape. Finally a sail was added. Such boats are still built in Bangladesh. Thus the original log became a keel to which planks could be attached by sewing (or mortising), and the structure stiffened with ribs. The Cheops ship shows these three features, and uncounted versions of each must have been tried. It is not unlikely that ships of similar capability were developed about the same time in southern and eastern Asia.

Several hundred years before the Cheops ship was purposely entombed near Cairo, some pottery was accidentally buried on the opposite side of the earth at Valdiva, Ecuador, the westernmost point of South America. A formal archaeological excavation on the coastal plain there sponsored by the Smithsonian Institution and the Ecuadorian government found some Jomon-Japanese-like potsherds at a depth of 10 m. The find was carbon-dated at 3,000 B.C. Some of the pieces are now on display at the Smithsonian in Washington D.C., along with photos of ancient Jomon pottery and a chart showing the hypothesized route of the voyagers across the North Pacific. According to Meggers and Evans (1966), this archaeological investigation "brought to light facts that can lead to only one conclusion: a boatload of inadvertent voyagers from Japan strayed ashore in the New World some 4,500 years before Cortez reached Mexico." Evidence of later voyages about 100 B.C., in the form of well-made models of Oriental houses (Figure 17-3) and figures, is in an adjacent display.

Accidental and Forced Voyages

The arrival of Jomon Japanese in Ecuador some 4,200 years ago raises the question of motives. Why would they, or any ancient who knew nothing of the ocean beyond the horizon, suddenly embark on a voyage? We cannot answer for any specific person, but here are some plausible suggestions.

An important clue comes from a paper given by Charles W. Brooks before the California Academy of Sciences in March 1975. In "Japanese Vessels Wrecked in the North Pacific Ocean" he recorded the accidental drifts of 60 junks; for 37 of these he personally interviewed those who were saved or witnesses to the find. Brooks states the problem. "Once forced from the coast of Japan by the stress of weather, the rudders are soon washed away; then these vessels fall off into the trough of the sea and roll their masts out." Then they drift at the whim of winds and currents. Twenty-five of these junks came ashore in

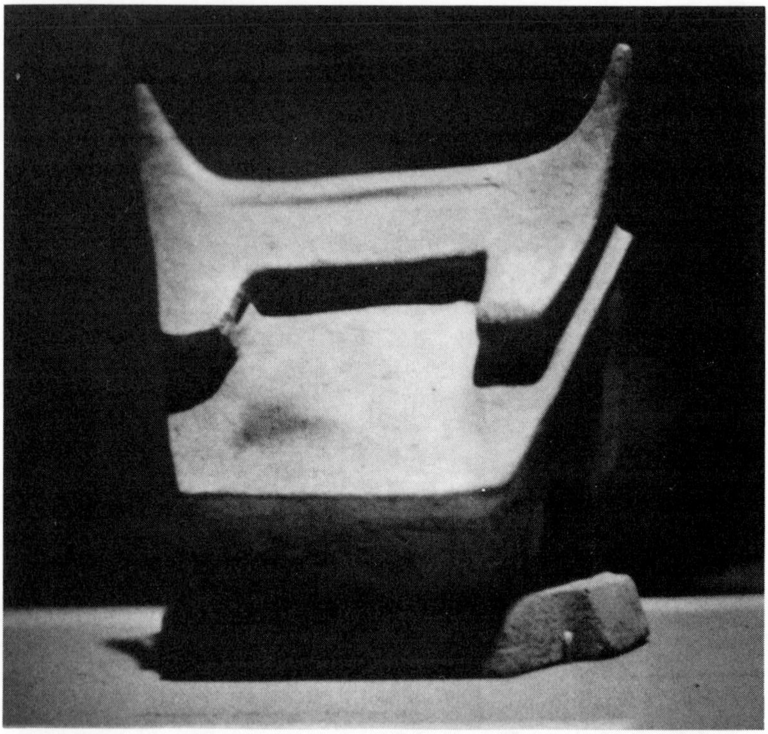

Figure 17-3: Pottery house model (12 cm high) recovered at La Tolita, Ecuador. Style is similar to Han Chinese or proto-historic Japanese (Smithsonian).

the following places: Aleutian Islands; near Sitka, Alaska; Queen Charlotte Island, Washington; Oregon; California; Mexico; within 18° of the equator; and Hawaii. In 33 of the 60 drifters 222 persons survived; the average time of crossing for 15 of the junks was seven months.

Brooks' example number eleven is illuminating. In March 1815 the brig *Forrester*, cruising off Santa Barbara, California, sighted a junk drifting without masts or rudder. Although it was blowing a gale, Captain Adams boarded the junk and found the captain, carpenter, and one seaman surviving; 14 bodies were in the hold. He took the three aboard, and with careful nursing they were well enough in a few days to tell how they had been dismasted 17 months previously on a voyage from Osaka to Yedo (Tokyo).

In collaboration with Professor George Davidson of the US Coast Survey, Brooks collected information on 36 other wrecks going back to 1613. He comments, "The number of junks, of which no record exists, which have thus suffered during the past 19 centuries must be very large, probably many thousand vessels." The finds at Valdiva are understandable in the light of this evidence of drift voyaging.

The accidental discovery of Brazil in 1500 by Pedro Alvares Cabral, only 44 days after he left Portugal, is an indication of the ease of crossing the Atlantic in some years. His intention was to round Africa, but he had been warned to sail well to the west to avoid the doldrums; equatorial winds and currents carried his ships to the strange coast (Worcester 1969) where he encountered cannibal women whom he called Amazons.

There are some data about forced voyages. Casson (1959) quotes Herodotus on two of these: first, the circumnavigation of Africa by Phoenicians under orders from Pharaoh Necho in about 600 B.C. They duly reported a strange circumstance: the sun was on their right side as they sailed west, a preposterous idea for Mediterranean sailors. Second, the intended voyage of the Persian Satapses around Africa in the opposite direction about 480 B.C. It seems Satapses had violated one of the ladies of King Xerxes' court and was sentenced to be impaled. His mother interceded, suggesting the voyage as an alternative, and so the young man started out. He sailed past Gibraltar, down the coast of Morocco, and eventually turned back when he reached the doldrums. Upon returning to Persia he was impaled for not having completed the trip. One suspects that he would have continued if he had known the outcome.

Some voyagers probably did foresee the result if they did not take to the sea. One can imagine several sets of likely circumstances. For example, a king is defeated in battle. With a few loyal retainers he escapes to the waterfront, seizes the best of the boats available, and sails away.

Or, there is famine in the land. A few hardy people could reach the coast with no more than the vague feeling that there are other lands beyond the sea where things are better. Perhaps the sailors were fishermen who had heard stories of distant lands; perhaps the motivation was pestilence. During the time when the Mediterranean was a "Roman lake" there was no local escape for revolting Jews or gladiators or pirates or escaped slaves. If they could reach the Gates of Hercules and keep going they had a slim chance—not much, but the alternative was crucifixion. Many voyagers of ancient times must have been persons with nothing to lose and, doubtless, many of them were lost.

Inhabited Islands

The best evidence for long-distance ocean voyaging by primitive peoples is well known to everyone. Very remote Pacific Islands, including Hawaii, Easter, and New Zealand, had been inhabited for hundreds of years when first discovered by Europeans. Studies by Buck (1938), Suggs (1959), and others indicated that the Polynesians had island-hopped eastward from the Indo-Chinese mainland beginning before 1700 B.C. and had reached the Marquesas in about 120 B.C. Presumably this long history of eastward explorations continued, since the voyagers did not know that north and east of the Marquesas is the largest area of open ocean on earth. Even so, they found Easter and the Hawaiian group, which are but tiny dots in the blue expanse. Can anyone doubt that other sailors exploring eastward from the same bases also came upon the mainland of North and South America, which formed a barrier thousands of miles long directly in their path? As Suggs (1959) notes, their "obsidian spear heads, unmistakable in form and material, were recovered from a prehistoric Indian tomb on the Chilean coast."

These island sailors voyaged in dugout canoes that were made with great care, according to traditional procedures that combined mysticism and craftsmanship. Most had a single outrigger and could sail with either end forward but some were double hulled. In early times these apparently were made of huge logs but the natives of remote islands still make canoes of small logs with raised (sewn) gunwales that are capable of going hundreds of miles across open water. Their migrations were generally eastward, against the prevailing trade winds. Since these craft do not sail particularly well into the wind, the question often arises as to how they managed to voyage eastward so successfully.

The answer is that the winds do not always blow from the east. Almost every year there is a month or so when the winds are contrary. At that time one can imagine that young men, enticed by the evidence of drifting objects and overflying birds, would find it hard to resist sailing east to see what was there, knowing that in a few weeks the wind would shift and bring them safely home again. In such a manner they racheted eastward for a thousand years until the jumping-off point at the Marquesas Islands was reached.

Ocean Crossings in Very Small Boats

The question of whether very early voyagers had vessels that were capable of ocean crossings has already been answered in one way by the discussion of Mediterranean and Polynesian craft. A different kind of answer comes from a study of the small boats that have crossed the oceans in the last hundred years or so.

In the last 20 years many small boats have made intercontinental solo voyages trying to set records, and it is common knowledge that well-planned crossings in a modern sailboat are not unusual. Hugo Vilhen's Atlantic crossing in the six-foot-long *April Fool* (Vilhen 1971) and Gerry Spiess' Atlantic and Pacific crossings in the 10-foot *Yankee Girl* (Spiess 1981) are examples.

If we go a little further back in time, their predecessors traveled in boats much more like those that could have been used by ancient voyagers. For example, the 20-foot open dory used by Alfred Johnson in 1876 to cross the Atlantic in 46 days (Merrien 1954) is not unlike an Egyptian boat in the Mellon Museum in Pittsburgh that was used 3,700 years earlier.

Johnson was the first to cross the Atlantic alone (as far as we know); he did so to celebrate the centennial of the US. Afterwards, not thinking his voyage was exceptional, he returned to solo halibut fishing on the Grand Banks. Two of the hundreds who followed him are remarkable because of the limitations they put on provisions carried and the boats used. Alain Bombard crossed the Atlantic from Casablanca to the Barbados in

65 days in a rubber dinghy. What made the trip so remarkable was that he sailed without any stores of food or water to prove his theory that man could live off the sea for a long time by fishing and catching rain water (Barker 1973). He was soon followed by Hannes Lindeman who first crossed from West Africa to Haiti in a dugout canoe. Still not satisfied, Lindeman repeated the trip, this time going from West Africa to New York in a rubberized fabric fold-boat. Dr. Alan Petersen, a young M.D. with no sailing experience, was caught in Shanghai by the 1939 Japanese bombing attack and stayed to help the wounded. By the time he was ready to leave, no regular transport was available, so he bought a river junk and sailed across the Pacific to San Francisco (Petersen 1952). Dozens of other examples are given by Borden (1967) and Kehoe (1971).

Thus it is apparent that nearly any kind of boat, however small, can make it across and that its occupants can survive with minimal provisions if they are lucky enough to have favorable winds and currents.

Climatic Influences

Another factor, important in early voyaging, needs to be considered. Good statistics on ocean weather for the last few thousand years are not available, but the evidence of tree rings and ice cores is that temperatures and rainfall can vary substantially from year to year.

The Kuro Siwa, or Japanese current on which the junks drifted across the North Pacific, does not always move at the same speed along the same path. Sometimes it throws off great eddies or gyres to the north or south that would cause a drifting object to circle back to the west. A few years ago three buoys instrumented for satellite tracking were released off Japan in what was believed to be the main stream of the current. One buoy went northwest to Kamchatka, one went south to the Philippines and one went due east where it circled some deep sea-mounts. None followed the expected great circle route towards Vancouver Island. In other years the current doubtless flows fast and direct to the American coast. Wind patterns also change from year to year, sometimes helping, at other times hindering, small-craft passage.

Columbus crossed the Atlantic at the beginning of the "little ice age," generally an unfavorable period for sailing which lasted from 1430 to 1850 (NAS 1975). He was successful because he stayed below latitude 30° (Morrison 1942). Major unexpected changes in winds and currents related to the 1981–1983 El Niño in the Pacific remind us of the difficulty of predicting or hindcasting such events in the remote past. Figure 17-4 shows the times of temperature changes, as recorded in tree rings, for the last 3,500 years, correlated with glacier fluctuations (La Marche 1975). There is no simple way to relate these data to ocean winds and currents; they are presented to show the substantial climatic changes in the period being discussed.

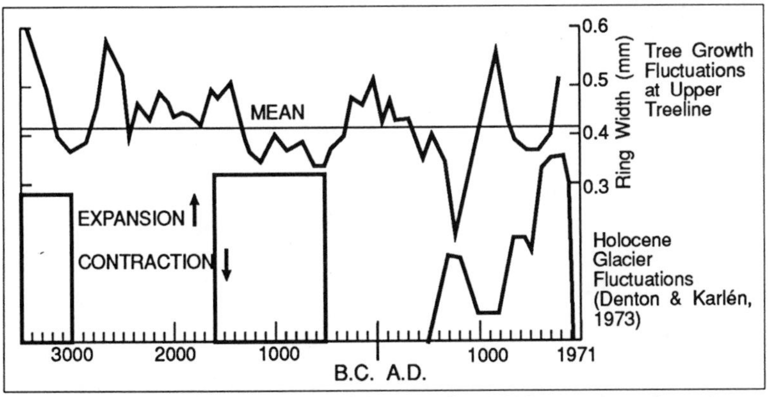

***Figure 17-4*: Climatic records of the past few 1000 years based on ring widths of bristlecone pine. Advance and retreat of Alaskan glaciers below (La Marche 1975).**

The point is that over the last few thousand years there must have been numerous times when ocean weather conditions were such that any accidental or purposeful voyage, in almost any kind of a boat, would have been successful.

Portraits in Clay

The final kind of data relating to early voyaging to the Americas are the most controversial because they are so close to being the hard, clinching evidence long sought to settle the question of diffusion versus independent invention. It is the finding in meso-America of many portrait heads of persons who represent all the races of man and clearly are not pre-Columbian Amerinds. In "Unexpected Faces in Ancient America," Dr. Alexander von Wuthenau (1975) presents dozens of photos of these small heads in clay or stone of people who clearly came from Africa, Asia, the Middle East and Europe. I have examined and photographed some of those in his personal collection (Figure 17-5). They are well-modeled portrait heads, most of which are 6–8 cm high. These heads are fashioned in different styles, made from different kinds of clay, and were found in different parts of Mexico and Central America. We do not know when they were made, nor are there any confirming data. They were "found," not carefully dug by archaeologists, so they are out of context and undatable. This makes them unacceptable as evidence to many anthropologists.

One can understand the need to be cautious about such matters, because there is the possibility that such pieces could be of post-Columbian manufacture. However, I am inclined to think that the large number of such heads, made with greater skill than is generally found among present-day modelers, found over the last hundred years at many remote locations, means that a great many of them are ancient. Moreover, many of these heads are of specific individuals with details of facial characteristics such as scars. Many very good replicas of ancient clay pieces, including heads, have been offered to me by the vendors who hang around historic sites in Mexico, but I have never been shown a head representing a foreigner. Apparently there is no market for such anomalous pieces, whether old or recent.

An interested person soon develops the habit of looking for foreign faces in museum displays. I will give two examples. In the Rufino Tamayo Mexican Pre-Hispanic Art Museum in Oaxaca, a group of eleven 13-cm-high terracotta female figurines from Panuco, Tamaulipas, are described as being of the Huastec culture (1250 B.C. to 200 A.D.). One of these figurines has black features and hair; the rest seem to be native peoples.

In the Diego Riviera Museum in Mexico City, the room nearest the entrance displays an unmistakably black acrobat (22 cm)

Figure 17-5: Some of Alexander von Wuthenau's "Unexpected Faces in Ancient America." All are believed to be pre-Columbian, possibly as early as 1,000 B.C. Location of find is given. The reader is invited to decide for himself the origin of the people represented. a) Vera Cruz, Mexico, b) La Venta, Mexico, c) Tlapacoya, Mexico, d) Tlatilco, Mexico, e) La Hueteca, Mexico, f) Iximche, Guatemala.

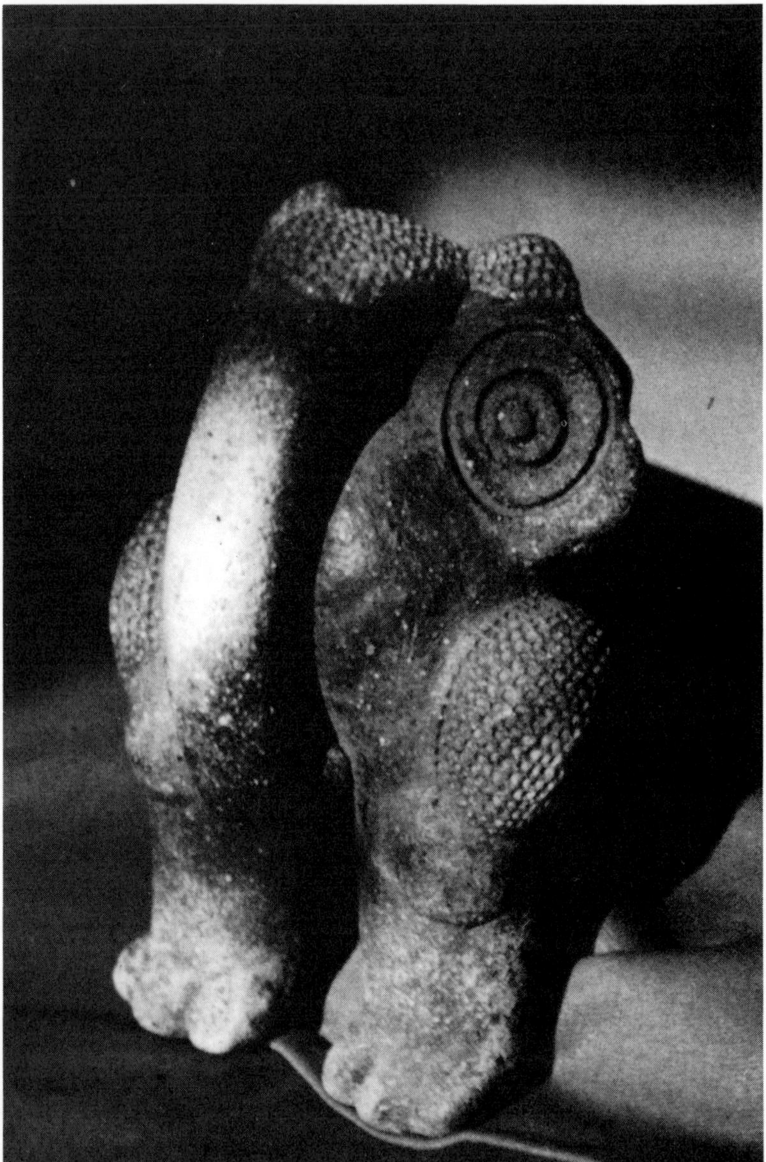

Figure 17-6: Elephant-like clay object found near San Jose, Costa Rica (10cm) (Owned by Thelma Dunlop).

with head down and back so steeply arched his feet are above his head. An adjacent case exhibits the face of an Oriental (12 cm). Both are dated 1100–600 B.C. There are over 100 other heads on display in this museum, but only these two are recognizably foreign. (Other foreign-looking heads are said to be present in the reserve collection.) Sometimes animal figures are found that look as though the sculptor was working from memory or descriptions rather than a live model (Figure 17-6).

These clay portraits need to be explained. The most logical view is that they are as authentic as the non-foreign heads in the same museum, and that they accurately represent the persons (or descendants of persons) who came by sea. Now that it can be shown that ocean crossings have been possible for a long time, that explanation becomes increasingly credible.

Conclusion

Evidence has been presented about the kind and availability of boats in ancient times and the reasonable chance that people aboard could survive long enough to cross an ocean—if they were lucky enough to make the attempt at a favorable time. Actual sea crossings thousands of years ago have been documented, and it is very likely that the original sailors (or their descendants) left their faces to prove they made it.

These people were the original ocean explorers. Although we cannot name them or say exactly when or how they crossed, we owe them a nod of respect. They were the earliest voyagers.

References

Barker, R. 1973. *Against the Sea*. New York: St. Martins' Press.

Bascom, W. 1976. *Deep Water, Ancient Ship*. New York: Doubleday.

Borden, C. 1967. *Sea Quest*. Philadelphia: Macrae Smith Company.

Brooks, C. 1975. "Report of Japanese Vessels Wrecked in the North Pacific Ocean." San Francisco: California Academy of Sciences.

Buck, P. 1938. *Vikings of the Pacific*. Chicago: University of Chicago Press.

Casson, L. 1959. *The Ancient Mariners*. New York: Minerva Press.

Fairbridge, R. 1965. "The Changing Level of the Sea." *Scientific American.*

Jenkins, N. 1980. *The Boat Beneath the Pyramid.* New York: Holt, Rinehart and Winston.

Jett, S. 1978. *Pre-Columbian Transoceanic Contacts, Ancient Native Americans.* San Francisco: W.H. Freeman.

Johnstone, P. 1980. *Sea-Craft of Prehistory.* London: Routledge and Kegan Paul Limited.

La Marche, Denton and Karlen in *Understanding Climatic Change.* Washington, D.C.: National Academy of Sciences Printing Office.

Kehoe, A. "Small boats on the North Atlantic." In Riley, C., C. Kelley, C. Pennington, and R. Rands, eds. 1971. *Man Across the Sea.* Austin: University of Texas Press.

Meggers, B. 1971. *Contacts from Asia Quest for America.* New York: Praeger.

Meggers, B. and C. Evans, 1966. "Transpacific Contact in 3000 B.C." *Scientific American,* Volume 214m Number 1.

Merrien, J. 1954. *Lonely Voyagers.* New York: G.P. Putnam's Sons.

Morrison, S.E. 1942. *Admiral of the Ocean Sea.* Boston: Little, Brown and Company.

Petersen, A.E. 1952. *Hummel, Hummel.* New York: Vantage Press.

Spiess, G. 1981. *Alone Against the Atlantic.* St. Paul: Fair Winds Publishing Company.

Suggs, R. 1959. *The Island Civilizations of Polynesia.* New York: New American Library, Incorporated.

von Wuthenau, A. 1975. *Unexpected Faces in Ancient America.* New York: Crown Publishing Company.

Vilhen, H. 1971. *April Fool.* Chicago: Follett Publishing Company.

Worcester, D. 1960. *Brazil.* New York: Charles Scribner's Sons.

EIGHTEEN

The EARLIEST VOYAGERS

A COMMENTARY

Mangalam Srinivasan

This commentary will complement the fascinating presentation of Willard Bascom on "The Earliest Voyagers." Although Bascom includes statements reflecting his recognition of early voyagers outside the realm of the Occident, references to voyagers from South and Southeast Asia have been somewhat inadequate. This, I realize, may have to do with the fact that, as H.G. Wells once suggested, world history as written by European historians stands apart from and unconnected to the history of the non-Occidental world in general and South Asia in particular. This commentary will try to provide selective evidence of early Indian seafaring and maritime activities in search of new shores and opportunities.

Scarce, but nevertheless important, evidence of river barges which approach the dimensions of small ships has been recovered in the Mohanjadaro-Harappa excavations, indicating trade between Indus Valley people and those who lived outside the Indian continent. This is further confirmed by the fact that "Indus seals and other objects have been found in Sumer at levels dating between about 2300 and 2000 B.C. Evidence of Sumerian exports to India is very scant and uncertain.... The finding of Indus seals suggests that merchants from India actually resided in Mesopotamia; their chief merchandise was probably cotton" (Basham 1954).

By the time of the Buddha, the long and rugged coastal waters of India had already been circumnavigated several times, with a few ships even advancing beyond the monsoon seas onto the open ocean. Before the beginning of the Christian era there were Indian settlements in Burma, Malaya, and parts of Indonesia.

Linguistic evidence abounds testifying to the great maritime activities of the Tamil kingdoms and those of others in ancient India. According to one scholarly account,

> Even a few Hebrew words are believed by some to be of Indian origin, notably koph, "a monkey" (Sanskrit-kapi) and tukki, "a peacock" (Tamil-togai). Though the details of the book of Kings may not be historically accurate, the statement that the navy of Tarshish brought to King Solomon gold and silver, ivory, apes and peacocks shows that the Hebrews received commodities from India at an early period. It has been suggested that the land of Ophir, from which King Hiram of Tyre brought gold, precious stones and "almug" trees to Solomon was Supara, the ancient port near Bombay. This suggestion is strengthened by the fact that in the Septuagint, the Greek version of the Old Testament, the word occurs as Swfara; these almug trees may have been sandal, one of the Sanskrit words for which is valguka from which the Hebrew word may be derived (Basham 1954).

Sugar, rice, iron (a much-valued commodity—Indian iron was said to have been of very high strength and purity), live animals, birds, and exotic herbs and roots were much in demand in several parts of the ancient world, especially in Rome. Emperor Claudius was said to have "even succeeded in obtaining from India a specimen of the fabulous phoenix, probably a golden pheasant, one of the loveliest birds of India" (Basham 1954).

Indian merchant ships, mostly from Tamil kingdoms in southern India, traded with the West as well as the East, especially China. Popular articles such as gem stones, silk, perfumes, cotton, spices and luxury commodities drained the Roman coffers of gold—by one account some 600,000 lbs. annually—and this wealth made its way into the coffers of kingdoms in southern India, prompting Pliny to state, "so dearly do we pay for our luxury and our women."

There is contemporary evidence, both literary and archeological, to suggest that Indian mathematicians, philosophers, magicians, conjurers, and even astrologers went in these ships to be of assistance to the Roman emperors for the experience as well as for the gold. This adverse balance of trade (India imported precious little from Rome except gold!) has been cited as one reason for the financial difficulties of the Roman Empire from the reign of Nero onwards.

The early Tamil literature is full of references to the 'Yavanas' —a term usually used to denote Greeks but often taken to mean any foreigner, especially from Europe. The Tamils traded with the Greeks, Egyptians, Romans, and others, which is amply illustrated by the *Periplus of the Erytherean Sea, The Periplus, Ptolemy's Geography*, as well as by early Tamil poems.

One author describes the early voyages around the first and second centuries A.D. of the Tamil kings in these words:

> The second century A.D. Tamil poem "Pattinapaalai" mentions how goods brought to the ancient Chola port of Puhar piled up as if without limit and we read of tortoise shells, aromatic woods and manufactured goods brought from Southeast Asia. Most of this trade seems to have been in the hands of South Indian merchants but it is quite probable that some Southeast Asian merchants too came to India. Another early Tamil poem, 'Mathuraikäanci' describes merchant colonies speaking different languages at the Chola capital. The ancient Indian port of Kviripattinam is described in the Cilapatikaaram: "The sun shone over the open terraces, over the warehouses near the harbour and over the turrets... In different places, the onlookers' attention was caught by the sight of the abodes of the Yavanas, whose prosperity never wanted. At the harbour were to be seen sailors from many lands, but to all appearances, they lived in one community..." (Ramaswamy 1982).

During the great social and cultural revival and renaissance under the Tamil Chola Kings Rajaraja I and Rajendra I, shipping and seafaring flourished. They developed a "positive maritime policy" and were said to have had a "regular navy"—perhaps the only significant navy in the annals of India prior to that of the British in India. Rajaraja I Chola conquered Ceylon with his navy; and his son Rajendra I sent out a great naval expedition, which occupied parts of Burma, Malaya, and Sumatra, as well as suppressed the piratical activities of the Indonesian kings which had been interfering with the trade between India and China. Rajendra's naval expedition is considered "unique in the annals of India."

The Southeast Asian Scene

It is very clear that shipping and early voyaging between India and Southeast Asia, on the one hand, and China on the other, were extensive. Considerable evidence exists that Indian ships and sailors routinely traveled to Southeast Asia and China, but few pieces of evidence are available that ships and sailors from these countries arrived and docked in Tamil ports. Some evidence to the effect that Malay ships and Burmese boats rode the high seas to trade with India appears in Malay literature and history.

Roman and other European demand for Indian spices sent Indian ships eastward in search of more spices, especially in the Indonesian Islands with their plentiful supplies of cinnamon, cardamon, and camphor. In the course of search for more spices for reexport to the West, the Indian merchants discovered that these islands, especially Java and Sumatra, were rich in gold as well. The Vayupurana, an ancient Sanskrit text, describes Sumatra as a land rich "in mines of gold and gems and in ocean mines," perhaps a reference to alluvial gold. *Jataka Tales* gives the following description of an Indian ship that went to Sumatra in search of thin gold: "800 cubits in length, 20 fathoms in depth having three masts of sapphire, a cordage of gold, silver sails and oars and rudders of gold" riding the waves to these islands appropriately named "the Golden Land." That these Southeast Asian ports were important is borne out by the fact that the disturbances along the silk route between China and the West, due to raids by the Central Asian hordes, had deflected the trade routes toward the sea—from China to the ports of the Coromandel Coast of the Tamils, from whence these goods found their way to the Mediterranean and Rome.

With the decline of the Greco-Roman empires, Indian trade turned more toward China and China increased her demand for Indian goods such as silk, jewelry, spices, oilseeds, perfumes, cotton and other luxury commodities. Unlike the West from where India imported precious little, some Chinese goods desired by the Indians, notably pottery and silk, were imported into India.

Wilfred Schoff notes, in his introduction to the *Periplus of the Erythraean Sea*, (1960) that the "growth of civilization in India created an active merchant marine, trading to the Euphrates and Africa, and eastward we know not whither."

The ports on the west and east coasts of peninsular India bristled with seafaring activities. Important and desired commodities found their way from every part of India to these ports to be shipped to the Mediterranean and the Persian Gulf from the West and to China from Kaviripoompattinam in Tamilnadu. Shipping between India and China was entirely controlled by the Tamils. Shipping between the Western ports and the West was controlled by early Tamil kings, and later by the various kings of Malabar and the Arabs, until the Portuguese through bitter battles with both, gained control of all trade routes to and from India and the West. Some historians, both Indian and Occidental, have ventured to suggest that the great discovery voyages by Columbus, Vasco da Gama, Magellan and the subsequent empire-building enterprises of the European West can be ascribed to the desire of Europe to get its hands on the "spices" and "gems" of India! Numerous topical references are found in history, literature, and contemporary folklore to the ancient kingdoms. Suggestions are made even in popular Dutch expressions such as "as expensive as pepper." It was reported that a pound of ginger cost an Englishman as much as "a full-grown sheep." The spices found their way not only to the West but to China as well, making ginger a basic ingredient to Chinese cooking, along with sesame and other tropical Indian products. It is believed that Alaric and the Goths "demanded pepper as ransom when he besieged Rome in 408 A.D." And much later the English landlords collected parts of their rents from tenants in pepper. (Basham 1954).

The Art of Shipbuilding

European writers of recent times often ignore the contemporary evidence presented in Indian history and literature as well as in their own on the state of the art of Indian shipbuilding. When they do mention the seafaring activities they often dismiss the reference with a notation that shipping in India did not equal that of the Vikings, the Spanish, the Portuguese or of the English. This notion is due to the fact that the periods for comparison are inequitably chosen. For example, the much-reduced seafaring, according to one historian, corresponds to the time of the Muslim invasion of India. Religious sanctions came to be imposed on Hindus who ventured to cross the seas. As the historian put it, "the Muslim invasions encouraged Xenophobia and the people who had planted their colonies from Socotra to Borneo became, with religious sanction, a nation of landlubbers" (Morarjee 1960). It is true that after the Middle Ages the Chinese and the Arabs outstripped the Indians in the art of shipbuilding as India came under foreign domination internally.

However, the earlier achievements in shipbuilding are comparable to the efforts of the West. Several references are available as to the art of shipbuilding in ancient India. Atharva veda Samhita describes Indian ships riding "well the waves, broad in beams and spacious, comfortable, resplendent, with strong rudders and faultless in build." Pliny has recorded that the Indian ships were built with prows at each end. Arrian describes dockyards, galleys of 30 oars, and transport vessels. According to Marco Polo, Indian ships were double planked, built of fir timber, caulked with oakum and with iron nails used in construction. A 15th century Italian traveller, Nicolo Conti, recorded that "the natives of India build ships larger than ours, capable of containing 2,000 butts and with five sails and so many masts. The lower part is constructed with triple planks in order to withstand the force of tempests to which they are much exposed" (Basham 1954).

In addition to shipbuilding, Indians, especially the Tamil kings, did much to encourage sea trade. The Chola kings built lighthouses and wharfs "where the beautiful great ships of Yavavavas discharged their merchandise to be examined by customs officials, stamped with the king's seal, and stored in warehouses. Kavirippattinam, now a decaying fishing village silted up by river mud, had an artificial harbor, built, according to a late Sinhalese source, by soldiers captured by the great King Karikalan in a raid on Ceylon." Early Greek, Roman, and Tamil references indicate the existence of many flourishing ports, the chief among them being Musiri (known to the Greeks as Musiris), Korkai, and Kaviripattinam, all in the Tamil kingdoms, Bhrgukacha, Supära near modern Bombay on the West Coast and Patala on the Indus delta. Basham writes:

> ...coastal shipping plied to the south and to Ceylon, and westwards to the Persian Gulf and the Red Sea until, in the 1st century A.D., seamen took to using the monsoon winds to sail straight across the Indian Ocean to the ports of South India. In the East the Ganges Basin was served by the river port of Campä, from which ships sailed down the Ganges and coasted to the south and Ceylon. By Mauryan times (300 B.C.), with the eastward expansion of Aryan culture, Tämraliptï became the main seaport of the Ganges Basin...

From Tämraliptï ships sailed not only to Ceylon, but, from before the beginning of the Christian era, to Southeast Asia and Indonesia.

References

Basham, A.L. 1954. *The Wonder That Was India*. New York: Grove Press, Inc.

Morarjee, S. 1960. "Shipping in Ancient India." *The Times of London Annual*, p. 60.

Ramaswamy, S. 1982. "Full Ship A-Sail, Plying the Eastern Route." *The India Magazine*, pp. 4–11.

NINETEEN

OCEAN CITIES

THE CASE OF VENICE AND ITS SAFEGUARDING

Roberto Frassetto

Ocean cities, born in different historical times in strategic locations for conquest or defense, power, and trade, since the beginning of this century, with industrial development, face ever increasing problems in the need of expansion or in the search for survival.

The natural and anthropogenic changes in the physical environment, the rapid technical evolution in trade, ocean and air transports, commerce and management, the changes in the cost and productivity of labor, the relation of harbor activity to the surrounding inland capacity of commercial absorption, are the complex causes of the perplexities in the ocean cities' existence.

Each of such cities as Tokyo, Hong Kong, Bangkok, Amsterdam, Wilmington, New Orleans, and Athens, to name just a few, is exposed to one or more of these problems; but all of these problems are incredibly gathered in Venice, a unique model of complex questions of survival, not only as an ocean city but as a historical center of unreproducible cultural value. Can this gem of an ocean city, the Queen of the Sea of the fifteenth century, powerful and rich, embellished with all possible treasures of art in an island surrounded and crossed by water, with an enchanting natural environment, today in distress and decaying, be revitalized and saved? Must an old ocean city die to leave new younger cities to be created or can it be rejuvenated for modern society's needs? Can it be saved from aging, decay, and abandon?

Poets, scientists, architects and engineers, politicians, economists, and administrators all see it in a different way. The poets abandon themselves to a passive romantic resignation to fate. Scientists and engineers are active in finding the truth to understand the pathology of its decadence and decay and to find a therapy: they believe that the long-term survival of the Queen of the Sea is achievable. Politicians require too much time to understand and use the scientific and technical information in a social-transition period where offers, demands, political ambition, education, and the capacity of management are in question. As a consequence, action and intervention are slow.

Is the solution to the problems of Venice to let her sink? This is the way a foreign romanticist like James Morris sees it: "She has died several deaths already."

As a Great Power, she died prematurely in 1498, when Vasco da Gama found a sea route to the Orient. As a political entity, she died posthumously in 1797, when Napoleon's cockaded soldiers disembarked in the Piazza San Marco. As an island phenomenon she died in 1846, when the railway causeway was built across the lagoon. As a working city she is dying all the time, as her commercial and industrial energies are drained away to the mainland and she is left to the degradation of mass tourism.

Letting her sink would redeem this long and squalid decline. Imagine her there at the end, La Serenissima, Bride of the Adriatic, enfolded at last by the waters she espoused, her gilded domes and columns dimly shining in the green and, perhaps at very low tides, the angel on the summit of the Campanile to be seen raising his golden forefinger (for he stands in an exhortatory pose) above the sandbanks. This would be the true Venetian end: an end in the grand manner, such as Tintoretto would portray in vast brown canvases on rotting chapel walls, and Byron celebrate in romantic elegy:

"O Venice! Venice! when thy marble walls
Are level with the waters, there shall be
A cry of nations o'er thy sunken halls,
A loud lament along thy sweeping sea!"

It is a counsel of perfection, and it will not happen. For one thing it would take too long—one cannot hang around for the apocalypse—and for another the world would not allow it. Far from letting Venice sink, the world community is beginning to see the survival of that astonishing city as an allegorical necessity of our time.

Scientists were called to study and describe the environmental and geophysical mechanisms in which originate the threats to the safeguarding of the city and to indicate the possible remedies, after the major flood of the century. In November 1966 seawater and floating pollution, including heavy oil, reached a level of over 1.50 meters in some parts of the historical center of Venice which suffered damage for a long time thereafter.

How and why is Venice sinking? Why are floods more frequent and more severe? Why are stones and bricks eroding and losing their consistency? How are erosion and accretion going to change the lagoon and how would the closure of gates at the lagoon entrances, needed to prevent the largest floods, penalize its port and its commercial activity? And how can a commercial ocean city, more than 1,000 years old, face the evolution of modern society and the shift from ship-borne to air-borne transportation? There are many answers to be carefully formulated, keeping in mind that the cultural value of a historical ocean city can and must be saved for posterity.

The History of Venice

It is known that the Venitii occupied the center islands of the present lagoon of Venice in 500 A.D., taking refuge from the Teutonic invaders. Artifacts of the Bronze Age have, however, been found in some excavations in the center of Venice, but it is difficult to place them in history.

As an ocean city, however, Venice was already the trade and communication bridge between Europe, the Mediterranean and the Orient in A.D. 1100. Her fleet brought thousands of soldiers of different countries to Palestine in several crusades. In 1200, Dante visited the Arsenal and was stunned by its magnificence and the intense industrial activity, which he described in the *Inferno* (Canto XXI, 7–15).

In the following centuries the Doges sent the Venetian ships and army to conquer not only the far lands of the eastern Mediterranean but also the nearby Adriatic coastal land.

From 1260 to 1295 Marco Polo's Oriental expeditions took place, on a quest for trading profits, establishing communication between the Pope and Christianity, Venice and its commerce, and the Mongol Empire.

In 1423 Doge Tommaso Moceningo described the naval power of Venice: A total of 36,000 men was employed in military and commercial ships out of 150,000 inhabitants. Forty-five galleys with 11,000 sailors, 360 round-bottomed vessels of considerable dimension with 8,000 men and 3,000 smaller ships with 17,000 men made up this powerful fleet (Figure 19-1).

The Venetians were not particularly fond of large-scale, long-term enterprises involving many people from different families. They preferred undertakings of a fixed duration with an average life-span of three to five years. It was the fast changes in trade and marine transport that induced the Venetians to favor short-term, joint enterprises.

Very interesting and efficient were the coordination methods called the "*Colleganza*" and the "*Moana*." The members of the richest noble families, engaged in politics and military expeditions, would organize their commercial investments through a form of partnership association called a "*colleganza*" or alliance with travelling merchants who were entitled to a quarter share of the profits. This was a type of administration for overseas investments in which a commissioned agent, the "*colleganza*" worked, not for a share of the profits, but for a percentage of the business he handled. He was the operator that today would be called "*commissario.*"

At other times the joint owners of the galleys of a convoy would set up a common fund, thus giving life to the type of association known as "*Maona*" in order to purchase the goods that would make for a worthwhile cargo.

Figure 19-1: Venice in 1500. In its glorious days obscuring the old power of Byzantium, Venice became in 1500 the queen of the sea, the most powerful harbor and shipbuilding city of the world. On Ascension Day, with the greatest ceremony of each year, the Doge married the sea throwing a precious ring in the Adriatic, just off the Venetian coast, from the luxurious ship *Bucintoro*, seen on the right of this picture. In the middle of the fifteenth century the Arsenal of Venice covered 25,500 square meters, employed from 2,000 to 3,000 people and was the largest industrial complex of the world. With its organizational characteristics it was the forerunner of modern industry, having created the assembly-line and vertical integration.

After 1500 the powerful nobles, enriched through generations by commerce and military expeditions, became interested in land properties, agriculture, art, and culture, beginning their period of decadence.

Splendid villas and estates were built along the Venetian rivers which are now the pride of the region. With changing times and conditions, a new class of merchants grew up, opening updated trades with renewed vigor. As a class they were never to attain political power, but they often collected great fortunes. They also promoted the realization of basic modifications of the lagoon of Venice.

Nature, with its continuous, relentless activity, was changing the unstable system of the lagoon which was gradually silting up as a result of alluvial deposits from the rivers that flowed into it. The brackish water was also becoming unbearable with insects, and men stepped in to reverse the natural process by digging canals and dredging the lagoon where ships and the city activity needed revitalization and deeper lagoon waters.

"*Acqua di mare fa buon porto*" the Venetians were saying, meaning that salted seawaters were making a good harbor. This is not true in many harbors of the world built in deep estuaries of large rivers, but it was true for the lagoon harbors.

In a few centuries, the Venetians diverted the two small rivers, the Brenta and the Sile, to flow around the lagoon directly into the sea, letting the ocean tides flush the lagoon with salubrious salt water and recycle the urban organic wastes flowing ever since, and amazingly so even today, into the lagoon (Figure 19-2).

This work continued into the 18th century until nature's trend reversed again. This time the sea was overtaking with its action of erosion and accretion, with sediment transports.

Dikes and walls were constructed by a typical organization of Venice: "the Magistrato alle Acque," a very severe agency which had the charge to study and change the lagoon to adapt it to the changing needs of the city's activity, but also had the power to condemn any citizen who would not respect the lagoon waters and keep it clean. Hands were cut off of the thieves, the tongues of liars, and the heads of lagoon offenders. This dreadful terror was however much more effective than the relentlessness and carelessness of present times when the citizens accuse an intangible, everchanging government of the decay of the city and do not assume their own responsibility and action.

With a new leisure decadence in the last two centuries, Venice became an easy prey for Napoleon's armies and for the Austrians.

The nearby harbor of Trieste was taking over the commercial trade and since the early 1700s became the major port of the Austrian Empire.

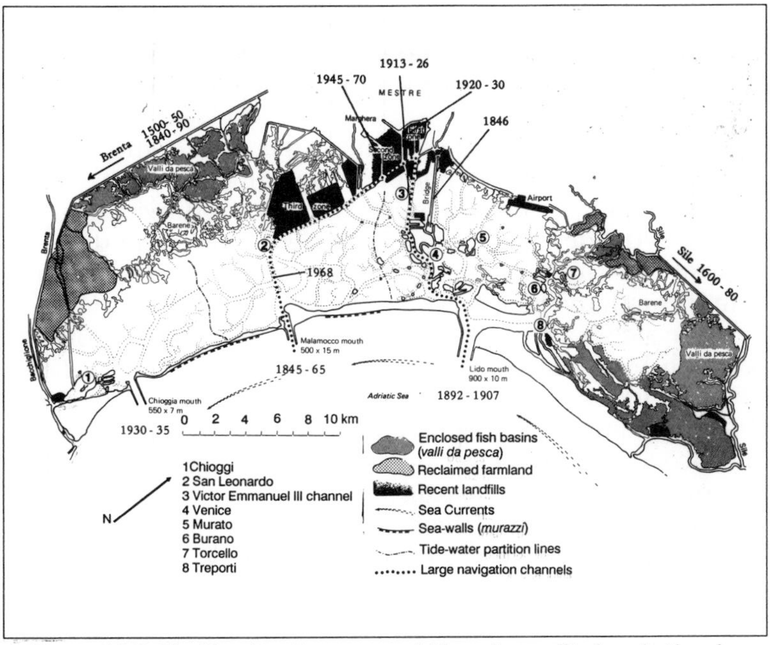

Figure 19-2: The Venetian Lagoon would have been silted-up in time by the solid transport of rivers flowing into it. Beginning in 1500 up through 1970 the Venetians diverted rivers, dug channels, made jetties at the three mouths connecting the lagoon to the sea, created fish ponds and land reclamation for industries, trying to preserve some natural beauty while also creating the needed ways for ship traffic, a large harbor and a good shipyard for commerce and industry.

During the occupation of Venice by the Austrians, no major success was reached to give new life to Venice as an ocean city, even though some lagoon maintenance and a new Malamocco entrance to the lagoon was made.

In 1829 Venice became a free port for about half a century, but this solution did not help to give new life to Venice's commercial activity.

In 1846 the railroad linked the island of Venice to the mainland, about three miles away.

In 1880 Italy took over Venice and during a flourishing Italian economy, the main harbor, which was for many centuries on the island of San Giorgio in front of San Marco

Square, the residence of the ship agents, was transferred to near the railroad station, in hopes of a new trend in commerce; but from 1888 to 1896 a new crisis in the economic management of Venice took place.

At the beginning of this century, the Italian government decided to renew the harbor of Venice. In 1913 a new canal, the Vittorio Emanuele, was opened to allow a direct line from the sea to the developing industrial city of Marghera through the historical city, a shorter and more economic access for ships than through the long Malamocco canals.

In the 1920's a new industrial harbor was created in connection with 58 new firms, among which were several mineral and chemical industries. As a consequence, in the decade 1928–1938 the number of laborers grew four times, causing in turn the uncontrolled development of Mestre-Marghera, the inland part of the Venice municipality.

It is at this time that the big trauma of Venice took place. Because labor costs were lower than those in other ocean cities, the industrial harbor of Venice, despite its 15 km distance from the sea and its meandering narrow access channels, where tugs and pilots needed particular experience and attention to navigate, was favored by all shipping companies as the nearest point of access to central Europe and as the needed base for the booming local industrial area.

This development was seen as of economic benefit to Venice and as a step for acquiring new power and wealth, pretending to make of Venice again the major northeast port of the Mediterranean Sea for European markets and the most direct and convenient line to the Far East (through the Suez Canal) and to the Middle East. As a final thoughtless decision a refinery was created in front of Venice for local and export use.

During the following 20 years the ship cargo traffic increased from about 2 million tons in 1950 to about 15 tons in 1970. The number of industrial establishments increased from 130 to 240 and the number of employees from 22,000 to 37,000 within a few years (Figure 19-3).

New land was reclaimed from the lagoon to give space to further planned industries and harbor facilities (Figure 19-4). In the decade 1958–1968 land reclamation increased from 6

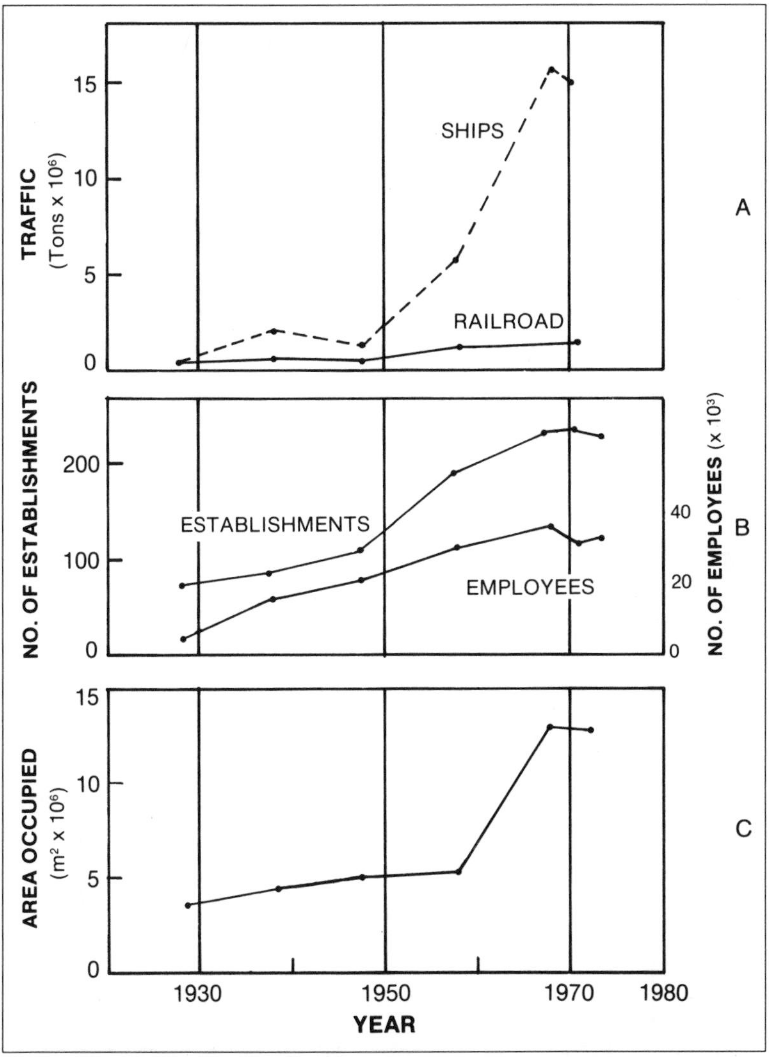

Figure 19-3: A disorderly and unplanned development of human activity in the Venetian municipality gave birth to an episodic increase (1930–1970 but specifically 1950–1970) in ship traffic (A), the number of establishments and employees (B), and land reclamation for industries (C). The population, looking for new jobs, migrated from the historical center to the inland part of the municipality (D, next page). At the occurrence of the big flood in 1966 the trends changed and the industrial crisis started.

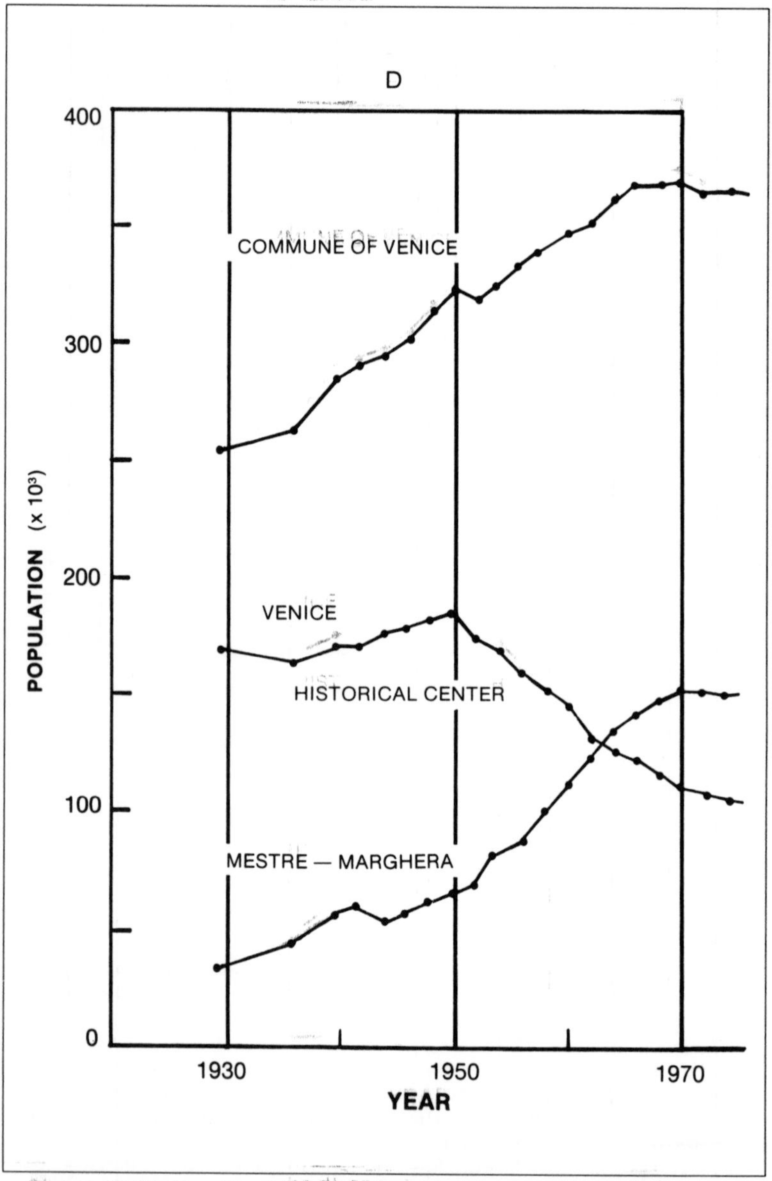

Figure 19-3D: Results of the disorderly and unplanned development of human activity in the Venetian municipality. (Continued from the preceding page.)

Figure 19-4: Venice today. A view of the inland oil refineries and chemical industries developed from 1930 to 1970 just over a mile across the lagoon, from the historical center of Venice.

million to about 13-million square meters, reducing the natural extension of the Venetian lagoon to 70% of the one of 1900. This process would have continued for speculations if a general alarm was not sounded. It was after the big flood of November 1966 (Figures 19-5, 19-6, 19-7) that the entire population of Venice and of the world woke up to realize the serious damage that the industrial boom had done to the delicate structures of the city of Venice. A new crisis in the social and economical life of Venice took place.

The cost of labor, very convenient in the 1930's, had become prohibitive in the 1960's through the reclamations of self created and overdemanding trade unions. The ship traffic and commercial trade for central Europe was diverted to Rotterdam and to other large, more economic harbors providing updated facilities and inland river ship trade.

Because of the floods the ground floors of the greatest number of houses in Venice became unhealthy due to humidity and salt absorption. The active population preferred to migrate and live on the mainland at lower costs and eventually commute to

Figure 19-5: Venice in 1700 and today. A painting by Canaletto shows the life in San Marco Square in 1700. The lower photograph shows a flood today. Floods increased in levels and frequency with land subsidence. Modern technology can find a remedy to this threat after sound scientific research of natural and human-induced geophysical phenomena.

Figure 19-6: "*Acqua alta*" of small amplitude are experienced frequently. Nevertheless each one means several hours of inconvenience for people in the area of St. Mark's and the Doges' Palace. [Photo: Unesco/A.F.I.]

Figure 19-7: During the disastrous storm surge of November 4, 1966, waves assaulted the sea-walls protecting the barrier islands of the lagoon. [Photo: Ermanno Reberschak.]

the historical center for daily work.

The harbor, now crowded with too many and unsatisfied workers, government supported, gradually became a heavy burden on the state finances and on the taxpayer. This problem has not been overcome yet.

Stone and brick structures in the beautiful historical city of Venice, exposed to physical and chemical processes of the natural environment, aged at an unpredicted rate and the results impressed the national and international cultural world (Figure 19-8). The long-term dilemma "the safeguarding of Venice" or the "unconditioned industrial development of an ocean city," gave birth to extensive discussions and polemics, some of which must still find a solution. But no effective decision making, in terms of costs, benefits, and priorities to solve this problem could be adopted by engineers, economists, and politicians without the information from careful scientific and technical research.

The Geophysical Problem

The physical safeguarding of Venice is threatened by natural and man-induced land subsidence, wind-induced storm surges, seismic movements and earthquakes, water and air pollution, coastal and lagoon erosion, and land reclamation, all of which pose increasing consequences of distress to the population and to its activity and severe damage to monuments, dwellings, harbor structures, and waterways.

This delicate geophysical problem is a unique challenge for scientists. In order to establish a scale of priority, it was decided to approach the problem with sequential research programs to save Venice for 10, 100, or 1,000 years.

In the decade of research from 1968–1978, the basic information to save Venice from major calamities for a few decades has been achieved. Engineers and administrators were provided with an accurate description of causes and effects and suggestions for useful intervention.

One of the first products of scientific research was a mathematical model for the forecasting of ocean storm surges causing floods (to Venetians the "*acqua alta*"). This model is now used by a city service to warn the population and the harbor organizations in time to save their properties and adjust their activity in accordance with the expected level and duration of the "*acqua alta*." For this application the warning is made by deep horns, with reiterated blows, six hours in advance while a telephone-answering system gives the details on levels, time,

Figure 19-8: With the increase of floods and air pollution the aging and decay processes of bricks and stones, of which the city is built, has reached alarming conditions for the survival of monuments and dwellings. An *ad hoc* practical therapy for water proofing and consolidating antique structures is needed to withstand the hostile environment and time—a role of science and technology still to be properly filled.

and duration. The six-to-nine hours forecast has an accuracy of a few centimeters in water level and few minutes in time of peak tide. This forecast, however, will not be sufficient for ship routing, to avoid the stand-by time to ships which could reach, in the future, the entrances of the Venetian lagoon when they are closed, during the few hours of the peak of storm surges. A prediction of 12 hours or more, which is desirable for ship routing, may be achieved at the conclusion of ongoing international meteorological studies on a regional and semi-planetary scale. This is part of the present research program for long range weather forecasting (up to six days).

The reason for the militations of the present predictive model is that the Adriatic Sea has approximately a six-hour response time to atmospheric forcing. For a longer period forecast, it is necessary to predict the nature and strength of the meteorological perturbation, when it is still over the Atlantic, much before it delivers its energy over the Adriatic Sea, while in transit from west to east.

The "*acqua alta*" is the result of a combination of astronomical tides, storm surges and seiches (the natural oscillation of basins such as the Adriatic Sea), each of which has its period or phase. When they are in phase, at spring tide and during severe storms, the sea level can reach more than two meters above mean sea level. When they are out of phase, even during strong storms, the resulting effect may be negligible.

The "*acqua alta*" has been reported in history since the first men found refuge in the Venetian lagoon islands, before medieval times; but the frequency of floods has increased in time, following the variations of natural-land subsidence due to tectonic and isostatic processes.

With the present urban plaimetry at a level from about 40 to 200 centimeters above mean sea level, Venice suffers the consequences also of eustatic variations. The global sea level, after the last glacial period, kept increasing over 30 meters in 6,000 to 7,000 years and kept at an even level, with fluctuations of a few meters for a few thousand years, reduced to a few centimeters in the last two thousand years, according to different sources (see Figures 19-9A, B, C). There are opinions that a return to a glacial period in the next several thousand years

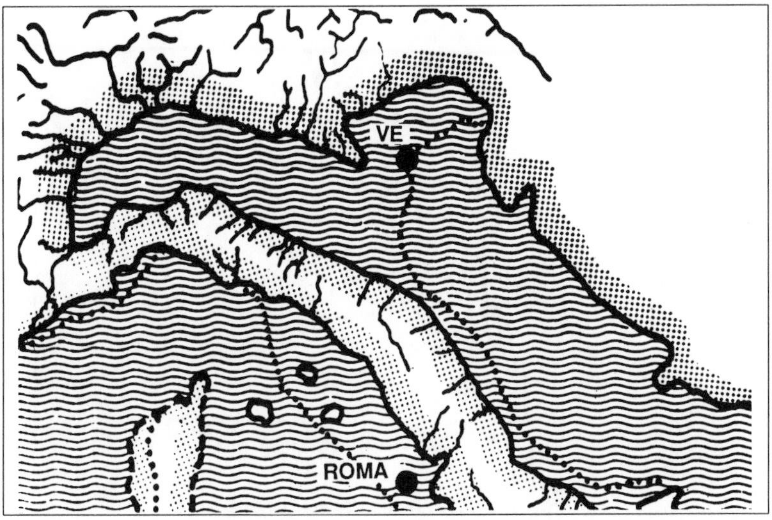

Figure 19-9A: The variation of sea level in geological times. Isostatic and eustatic theories. Pliocene—more than 2 million years ago.

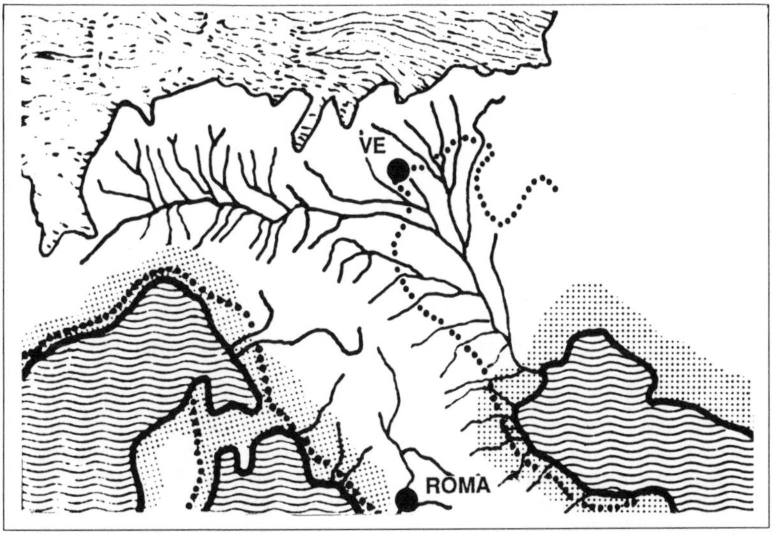

Figure 19-9B: The variation of sea level in geological times. Isostatic and eustatic theories. Pleistocene—during the last Würm glaciation about 20,000 years ago the coastline probably reached the mid-Adriatic Sea.

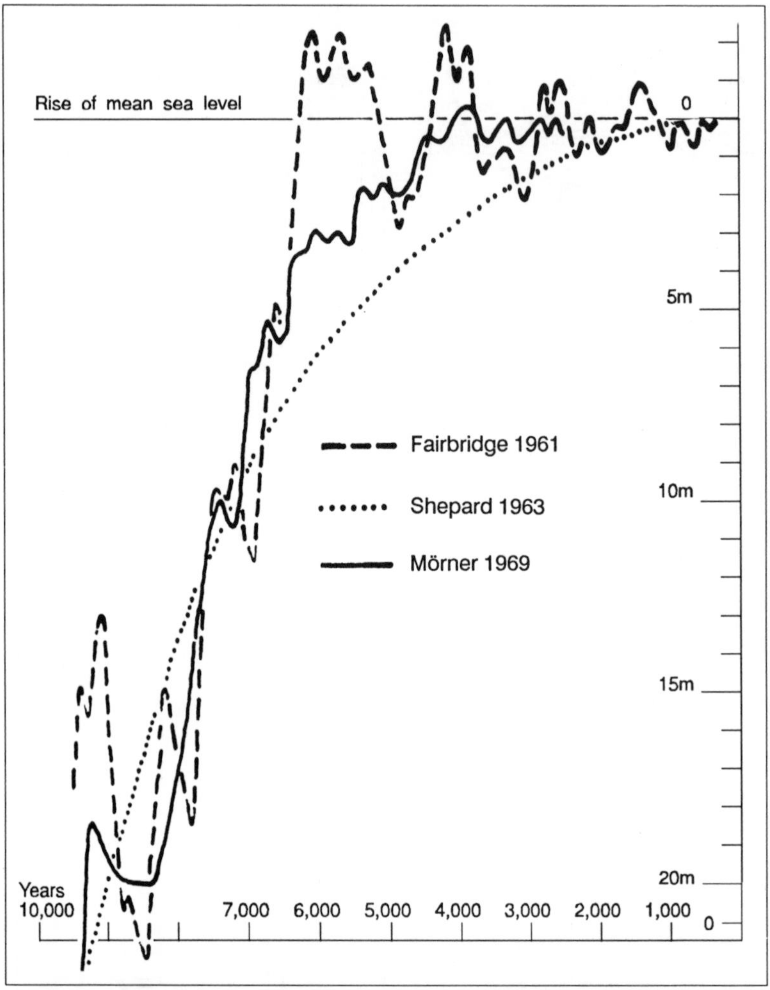

Figure 19-9C: The variation of sea level in geological times. Isostatic and eustatic theories. Holocene—the rise of mean sea level in the last 10,000 years, according to three theories. Since 2,000 years ago the variation appears to be on the order of 1 mm/year, while 5,000 years ago it was on the order of 1 cm/year. Secular variations are also expected as a modulation of the general tendency. According to various theories, in the next 2,000 years one should expect a new glacial period and a decrease in m.s.l. if anthropogenic factors do not change significantly the natural climate, as is the case of CO_2 increase in the global atmosphere.

should be due, but the present increase in carbon dioxide and dust in the atmosphere traps heat in the lower atmosphere and the Antarctic, as well as other world glaciers, continues to melt. The planetary mean sea level is therefore now still rising at an estimated rate of about 10 centimeters per century. Land subsidence and sea level rising are cumulative in Venice and account for about 20 centimeters per century.

Since 1930, with the development of industry and modern domestic needs, the requirements for water, pumped from artesian wells, increased. Progressively deeper aquifers had therefore to be exploited, particularly between 1950 and 1970 (Figure 19-10A), when the rate of industrial activity on the borderland of the Venetian lagoon, and the local population had a boom. A boom that was badly planned and that demonstrated its incompatibility with the environment and the character of Venice.

The processes of soil compaction and soil subsidence, both natural and man-induced, increased the frequency of floods. These processes have been described by scientists who gave clear evidence of the effect of water pumping from the artesian wells exploiting aquifers at different depths and different distances from the historical center (Figures 19-10B, C, D).

As a consequence the municipality requested the closure of all artesian wells located within five miles of the historical center and along the border of the Venetian lagoon. The five aquifers existing to depths of 300 meters were therefore newly fed by percolating rain waters, collected in the entire basin of the Venetian region from the mountains to the sea, and a small rebound was experienced. The man-induced subsidence which had been 5 mm/y (10 cm in 20 years) is now under control, leaving the natural subsidence rate of about 20 cm per century relative to sea level unsolved.

The second major endeavor for the safeguarding of Venice is its protection from severe floods.

Brackish water from the lagoon invades the lowest depressions of the Square in front of the Church of San Marco (Figure 19-6) when the ocean tide reaches 63 cm above the commonly used level of reference, which was the mean sea level (m.s.l.) measured in 1897. Those 63 cm correspond to 40 cm above the

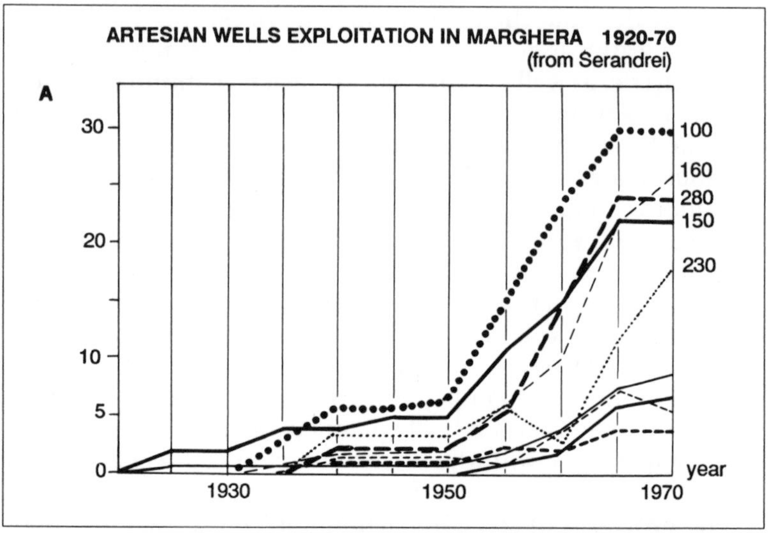

Figure 19-10A, B, C: Water Exploitation, Subsidence and Flood Frequency, 1950–1970 Increase. As a consequence of uncontrolled industrial development, the need for clean fresh water for industries increased and artesian wells with powerful pumps exploited aquifers at different depths (A, above), causing the abatement of the static levels (piezometric levels) in different areas (land, historical center, industrial area) (B, below) and the sinking of the soil relative to the Mean Sea Level (m.s.l.) (C, facing page, top).

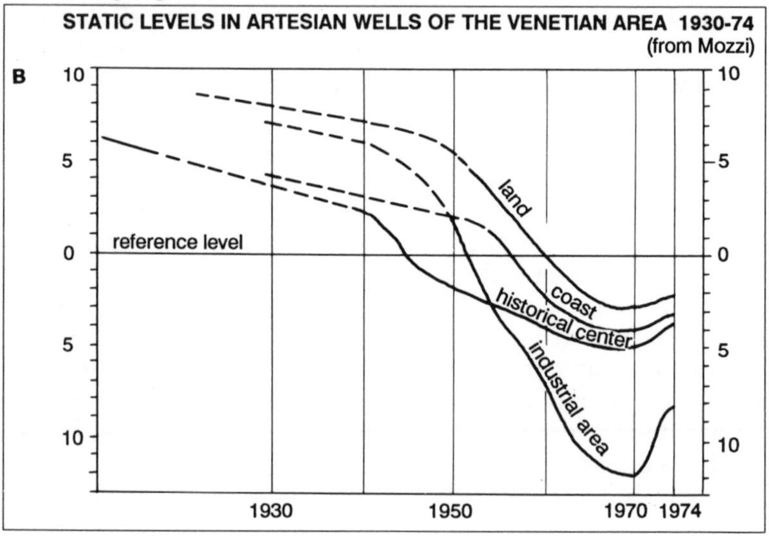

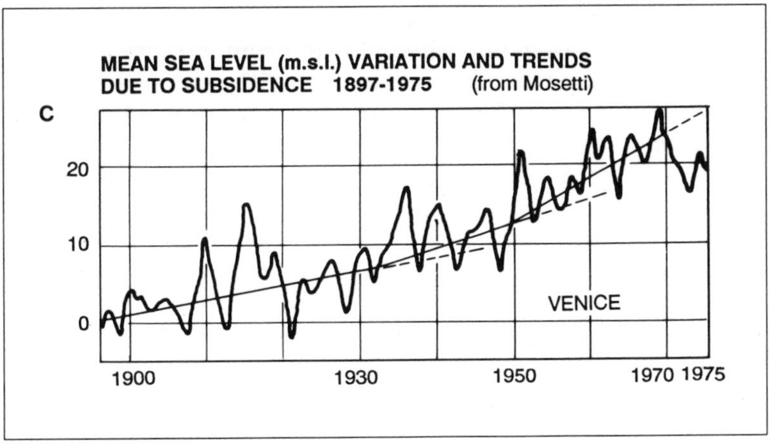

Figure 19-10C

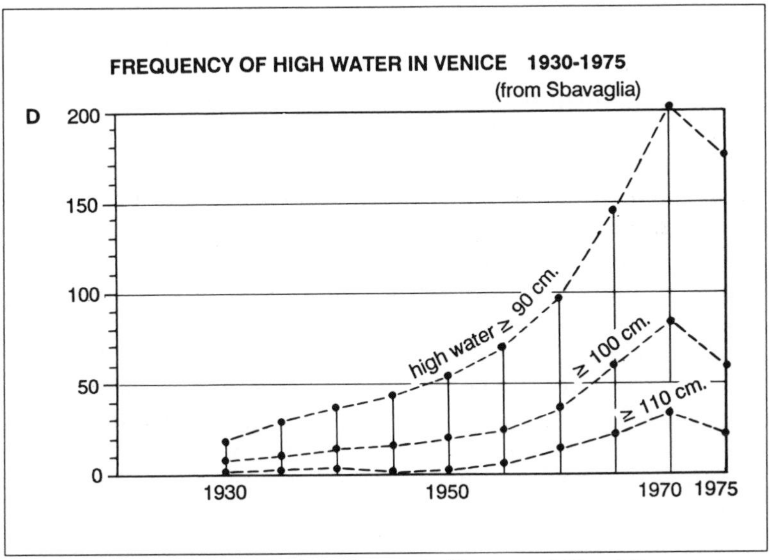

Figure 19-10D: Water Exploitation, Subsidence and Flood Frequency, 1950–1970 Increase. The frequency of floods reaching 80 to 110 cm above the level of reference increased. The relation between human activity (Figure 19-3) and the geophysical threats due to men are evident particularly between 1950–1970. After that date, with an industrial crisis and the world alarm for the safeguard of Venice, the trends have changed.

m.s.l. of today. From neap tide to spring tide, from when the sun and moon are in opposite phase to when they are in phase, the astronomical tide range varies from 50 to about 100 centimeters. This means that the water exceeds the m.s.l. by 25 to 50 centimeters.

The astronomical tides therefore are not yet a severe threat to the city even though at their maximum height they form a few pools in San Marco Square, unfortunately the lowest area of the city, and as Napoleon said the most beautiful square in the world.

It is when the southern wind blows, particularly in the case of cyclonic perturbations, that the seawater, forced up to the Venetian coast, enters the lagoon joining the tide, to flood the city. The "*acqua alta*" is called "*eccezionale*" when it exceeds about 100 centimeters above the level of reference. When these conditions occur, about five percent of the city is flooded. A project for the construction of gates at the three entrances of the lagoon, through which the seawater flushes in and out with the tide, has been approved.

The construction of the gates can be completed in five years, pending the grant of funds from the government. Its present cost would be on the order of one billion dollars, to be divided, in principle, into five yearly installments. This project satisfies three main enforced conditions: 1) avoiding further penalties to the port activity; 2) preventing major floods in the city; and 3) preventing the increase of the pollution of the lagoon waters.

1) The project contemplates gates which can be closed at will, as in Figures 19-11A, B.

The statistics of the last 20 years of sea-level variation show that high water 100 cm or more over the level of reference occurs (on an average) seven times a year and high water above 120 cm twice a year. The frequency increases rapidly with lower levels.

By selecting 100 cm as the safety level which must not be exceeded in the lagoon, the penalties to ship traffic would amount on the average to a total of 34 hours per year, with a minimum of zero hours in one year like 1974.

One must consider that about 8,000 ships a year of an average of 10-to-20 thousand tons, could get through the three gates of the lagoon if the planned growth and renovation of the lagoon harbors (Venice, Marghera, Chioggia) will be realized by the year 2000. This means about one ship per hour. Ships however do enter the lagoon mostly during daylight and find their berth during working hours. This reduces the maximum penalty to ship traffic from about 6 to 12 A.M. during the winter. In summer, in fact there are no significant nor frequent

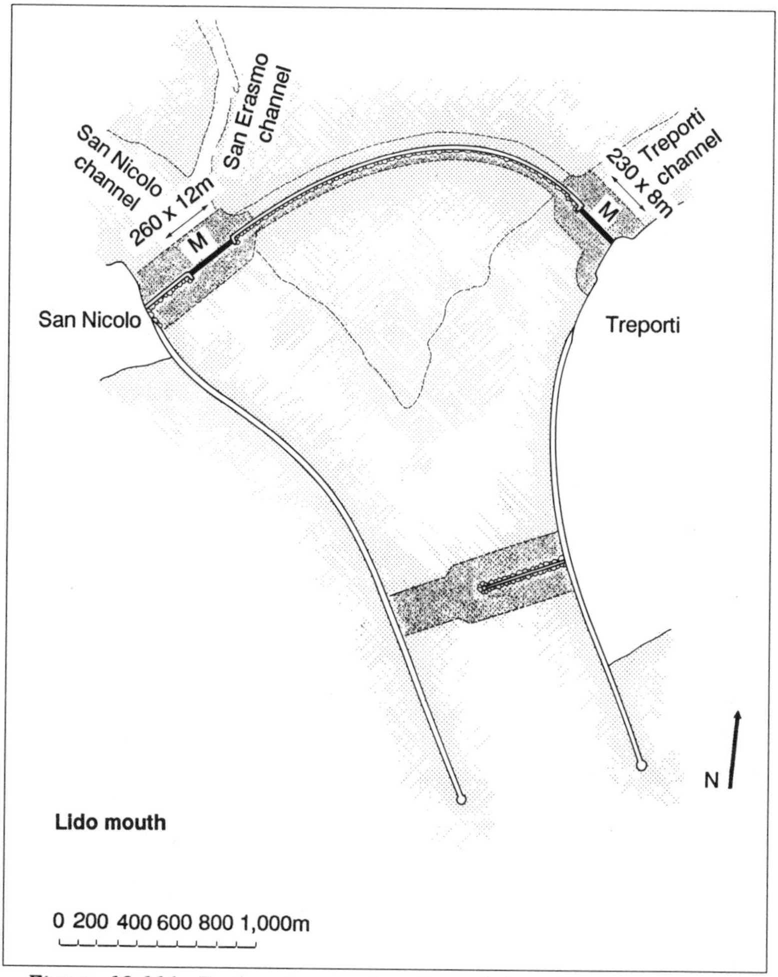

Figure 19-11A: Engineering works planned for the closure of the mouths. M indicates the location of mobile floodgates.

storm surges and, as a consequence, no closure of gates.

2) The project prevents the "*acqua alta eccezionale*" in the Historical Center.

For the maneuvering of the gates, an operation center is foreseen which controls the forecasts of storm surges, the changes in the quality and levels of the lagoon waters, the ship traffic, and the harbor activity.

When the seawater level is expected to raise more than 1 m above the level of reference, flood-gates are lifted from the bottom to close the three lagoon entrances at the exact time when the level of safety is reached on the sea side (Figure 19-11B).

The city of Venice is thus protected from exceptionally high waters. To protect the 5% of the city flooded with water levels below one meter, other interventions in the historical center are proposed, because the closure of the lagoon gates would penalize ship traffic too often.

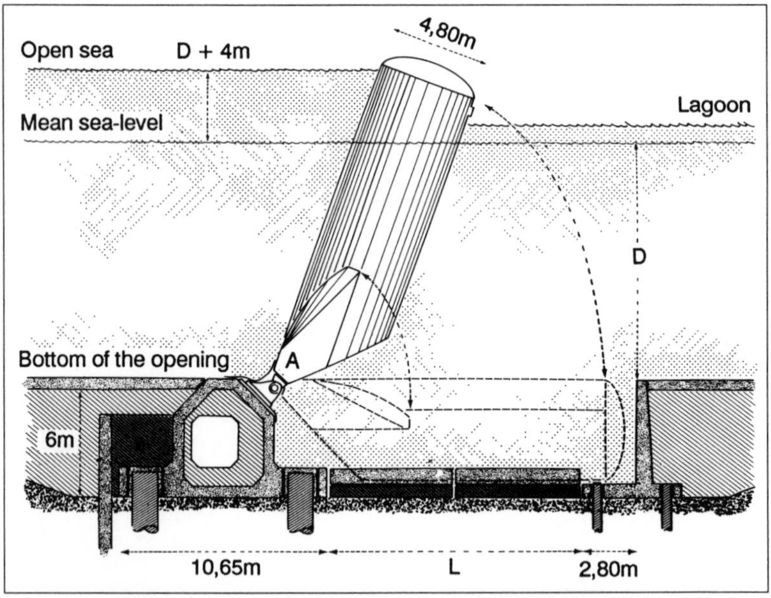

Figure 19-11B: Cross-section of planned mobile floodgates.
A = Rotation axis
B = Depth of the opening
C = Width of the gate

Among these interventions there is one which contemplates isolating the depressed zone from the lagoon water with artistically designed borders. Another intervention contemplates the application of the "mud jacking" technique which consists in carefully spaced injection of neutral consolidating material at depths from 5 to 20 meters, lifting the depressed area a few centimeters.

3) The project improves flushing of the lagoon.

The "*Progettone*," so called because it is a big project, similar in grandeur to the 15th-century projects which diverted the rivers from the lagoon to flow directly into the sea, considers, in fact, a fixed restriction of the width of the lagoon entrances where the water is shallow, and mobile flood gates on the deeper navigable channels as seen in Figures 19-11A, B.

Because of the restriction, the exchange of water from the sea to the lagoon is permanently reduced by an estimated 5%, which the project's engineers considered acceptable because other actions are planned to reduce the inflow of polluted waters with interventions at the source (i.e. agriculture, industry, urban waste disposals).

In the summer, however, when the tidal excursion is reduced and high temperatures trigger the mechanism of eutrophication (abnormal growth of algae and the death of fishes from anoxia) the gates can be operated out of phase, inducing a forced flushing, during night time when ship traffic is minimized or non-existent. This flushing could be obtained by letting the tide in through one gate and out through another, generating a one way artificial circulation. This would considerably improve the present flushing mechanism based on the to-and-fro tidal flow and a mixing process rather than a circulation process, which occurs only when strong winds blow from the northeast.

Concluding Remarks

Ocean cities, in populated countries of the world, have occupied most of the strategic natural sites of the coasts, where commercial ports could offer efficient services and good protection to ships from ocean storms. It would be impossible to find an available natural coastal defense to create a new harbor in these countries today unless it were artificially made at great expense and risk.

Most ocean cities are by now centuries old and have their historical value and must survive age.

Fishing villages along the coast, in minor bays, full of color and pleasant environments, are becoming attractive as residences for people in search of a corner of peace, natural beauty, or old time rustic flavor, while fisheries are becoming industrialized, a business for large enterprises.

Historical centers in ocean cities are being rebuilt or restored for a new life, as a cultural testimony to the past, for use as residences, for business, and administrations, and properly modified for modern living and comfort. As a consequence, a great variety of problems arise everywhere in the art of restoring, consolidating and waterproofing the antique decaying structures and materials, in preserving attractive or precious decorations or architectural works of art from an insidious ocean environment.

Venice is demonstrating how complex this task is, in modern times when everybody is in a hurry to accomplish things in the shortest possible time even for the shortest possible duration at the minimum cost and effort. In times of an economy of waste, durability and restoration have been confined only to the most precious properties of the world. But times are changing and the taste and respect for attractive minor products of the past is getting hold of more and more people and particularly of many far-seeing city administrators, for the benefit of future communities.

The technique of destroying to rebuild is no longer acceptable on a large scale. The respect for the past history of the natural environment, for values other than practical money-making is taking over in the new urbanistic activities along with the rejuvenation of old cities.

Napoleon rebuilt Paris for the enjoyment of many centuries of posterity. Jaques Chaban Delmas, a determined mayor, in 1947 rebuilt and rejuvenated, with the cooperation of the entire population, the city of Bordeaux. Venice, despite the intrigues of politics and financial difficulties, will be preserved; Athens needs a lot of studies and plans.

The role of science, of interdisciplinary scientific and technical research as the basis for providing sound information concerning interventions and the decision making of political and responsible administrative authorities, is facing new challenges. Ocean cities need to be restored and protected from natural and anthropogenic environmental threats: a task for the joint, intelligent cooperation of physicists, architects, engineers, urbanists, chemists, artisans and responsible business men. They need to be safeguarded from short and long-term natural calamities such as earthquakes, *tsunamis*, storm surges, floods, erosion and accretion, and subsidence. These threats must be demonstrated, understood, and simulated in models, and predicted for decision-making authorities.

Credible and documented scientific information must reach interdisciplinary completeness, an opportunity for scientists to overcome disciplinary boundaries. This information must be transferred to the decision-making agencies, an opportunity for scientists to become more involved in the practical application of their findings and in helping correct political planning.

TWENTY

OCEAN CITIES

A COMMENTARY

Uri Marinov

The History of Venice

Venice as an ocean city was established more than 1,000 years ago. A review of the city's history reveals its rapid development as a military and industrial complex until the middle of the 16th century when it became "the largest industrial complex of the world and the forerunner of modern industry, having created the assembly line." In the 16th century the citizens of the city, affluent from commercial, industrial, and military activities, "became interested in land properties, agriculture, art, culture; beginning their period of decadence." Accelerated economic development throughout the centuries was linked with deleterious effects on the environment, including the blockage of the lagoons and the creation of unsanitary conditions.

In an effort to alleviate the deterioration of the environment, seawater was brought in to flush the lagoons and remove the domestic and industrial waste. This worked, more or less, for 200 years until the seawater's effects on the city became noticeable. At that time, awareness of the importance of maintaining the water quality of the lagoons resulted in the establishment of an institute, probably one of the first environmental institutions in the world, to protect water quality and to enforce very stringent laws. The importance given to the protection of water quality is evident in the type of punishment meted out: thieves had their hands cut off, liars their tongues, and the "the heads of the lagoon offenders were cut." There are some environmental administrators around the world today who might wish for such a severe system of penalties.

Further deterioration of Venice's environment came about in the 19th and 20th centuries, through uncontrolled and very rapid economic development, which was stopped abruptly only by the terrible effects of the floods of November 1966. These floods served as a symbol and warning to the people of Venice and the world. They revealed the fragility of Venice's urban development, the sensitivity of its environment, and the deterioration of the very fabric of its life as a result of inadequate evaluation and assessment of its environment in the decision-making processes.

Rapid industrial development unaccompanied by environmental considerations, coupled with manmade mistakes and incomplete solutions, led to pollution, deterioration of air and water quality, houses unfit for human habitation, and finally an exodus of residents from the historic city center. In addition to the manmade forces, the natural forces of tides, earthquakes, and floods led to an increase of up to 20 cm in the water level per century, bringing about a threat that Venice would sink and disappear. Is the "Queen of the Sea," the "Bride of the Adriatic" and the square that was considered by Napoleon as the "most beautiful in the world" under threat of death—in addition to the many times it has already died, according to James Morris? Is it justifiable to be as pessimistic as the author who ends his paper by saying that Venice's problems "gave birth to extensive discussions and polemics some of which ended in productive plans but few in effective, clever interventions?"

What Happened in Venice

What lessons can be learned from analyzing the history of those 1,000 years? In hindsight, utilizing our new knowledge of the inter-relationship of population, technology, urbanization and energy, it is clear that in Venice man was oblivious to his environment, setting himself above the rules and processes of nature and the environment, and thus jeopardizing life itself.

The city grew very rapidly, ignoring the physical basis of its foundation, and started to sink. The accumulation of waste caused unsanitary conditions and as a solution seawater was brought in to flush the lagoons. The sea then levied a heavy toll by causing erosion and floods which interrupt the life of the residents, and at times cover up to 5% of the historic city center. The solution to this is a proposed plan to build floodgates at the three entrances to the lagoon, at the price of $1 billion, which would control the seawater flushes.

Environmentalists are usually quite concerned over such large-scale projects which drastically change the existing natural environment. Will the Venetians repeat the mistakes of the past? Do they understand all the environmental consequences of such a project? Have they evaluated the plan, not only from an economic and technological point of view, but also from its effects on the natural environment?

The most important lesson we should learn from the history of Venice is that, if we want to continue to live on the planet earth, we need to mobilize all our resources in trying to predict and forecast the consequences of our activities. The role of science is not only to treat the negative effects of an action, but also to try to predict and to prevent it. Environmental effects caused by man should be prevented and should only be treated as a last resort. Natural disasters should be forecast as much as possible, with all precautions taken to reduce or eliminate their effects.

What Should Be Done

During the last several decades people sensitive to environmental degradation, observing Venice, London, Lake Tahoe, and Los Angeles, among others, came to the erroneous conclusion that the only solution to smog, eutrophication, noise, and other environmental problems is to stop economic growth. This conclusion—born of panic—resulted in a worldwide setback to the environmental movement, especially in the developing world. The answer to pollution is not zero growth, but controlled growth, accompanied by environmental management. The world as a whole, as well as each country, district, and large city, must incorporate environmental management into its political, economic, and social structures.

Such a system of environmental management should fulfill several functions:

1. Identification of the major problems which affect the geographical area of responsibility, and setting up an order of priorities for action.

2. Environmental policy must be founded upon specific principles, foremost among which should be cooperation and integration between environmental protection and development planning. Other components of the policy should include concentration on prevention rather than treatment, the establishment of realistic standards, encouragement of public participation, and implementation of inter- and multi-disciplinary approaches to every action and decision.

3. Monitoring and assessment is an essential component of environmental programs. Rational management of the environment should be based on reliable data—essential for enforcement, alert and warning systems—and setting up of standards for the purpose of intermittent control of industrial plants.

4. The cornerstone of environmental management is the introduction of environmental considerations into the decision-making processes for all major projects, in the same way as economic, technical and social aspects are considered. In many instances, environmental planning is implemented with the aid of formal Environmental Impact Statements which help to formalize the processes.

5. Comprehensive modern legislation consisting of laws, regulations, and bylaws is an important aid in the implementation of environmental goals.

6. Without enforcement, environmental legislation is meaningless, and it should usually be carried out by highly motivated, professionally trained inspectors rather than by the police.

7. Environmental education and information is a necessary supporting measure in any environmental management program. Its functions are many and multi-faceted, and include the increasing environmental awareness of the public and decision-makers; training of professional manpower; and incorporating

environmental dimensions into the formal education framework.

8. The role of research has been exaggerated at times. In many cases elaborate and expensive research programs have been carried out in areas unrelated to real environmental issues with no interrelationships with the decision-makers. Mission-oriented programs of research are sometimes necessary to comprehensive environmental management programs, but their linkage to decision-makers is essential and should be guarded.

9. International cooperation is vital in solving common environmental problems which transcend geographical or political borders.

Summary

It is safe to say that had Venice implemented a comprehensive environmental management program 1,000 years ago, or even 100 years ago, many of its current problems could have been prevented. For obvious reasons, decapitation cannot be used today as an effective measure for environmental control, but better, and more justified, means to achieve environmental goals do exist.

What we need is the collective will of the people to achieve sustainable development, and through it a better future. Some of us look at the world as a Petri dish, a dish which has a limited amount of food and moisture, where very rapid growth of bacteria is followed by depletion of nutrients and rapid death. Others, and let's hope the majority of people, look at the world as a "Space Ship" where all the resources are recycled, and a team of astronauts cooperate to achieve optimum conditions for continuing long flights. Whether the world will be a Petri dish or a "Space Ship" depends only on us, and Venice could be one of the first places where this will be demonstrated.

EPILOGUE

The UNITY Of The OCEAN

Athelstan Spilhaus

> And God said, "Let the waters under the heaven be gathered together unto one place, and let the dry land appear"; and it was so.

The ocean is one. It was so and it is so to this day. The land that appeared was once one, Pangaea, but it separated into islands we call continents, isolated from each other by the vast expanse of the ocean.

Land people, isolated from one another, find strains on their unity as people. Sea people are different. The ocean breeds a unity in people from all lands who go to sea. The ocean selects a certain type of person from all of the races of humanity that come upon it. This type of person stays with the ocean. The rest are cast back ashore to join the quarrels among land people. There is a unity of sea people. Sea people are simply those with understanding, passion, and commitment to the sea.

All people, land or sea, work to live in harmony with nature. We can mold nature to supply our needs but not bend her too much or she springs back. Yet, at sea, because of its vastness, majesty, and forces which we understand less than those encountered on land, sea people find their unity and communication because they must work together and assist each other in times of peril.

The original lingua franca was a polyglot of Mediterranean languages, literally the Frankish language, developed by seafarers who not only needed to communicate with each other for mutual assistance at sea but also to communicate with the people in their ports of call in the Mediterranean.

When commerce spread worldwide, kinds of English, such as Pidgin English in the western Pacific and Orient, were developed not by scholars but by practical seafarers as port languages. Thus, from the sea came the use of a unified language called English, the present lingua franca of the global navigators. The language resulting from the unity of the seas has now spread to land and air.

Crews of early ships were polyglot. Vessels at sea were the original melting pot. The United States has prided itself as a melting pot, but with greatly increased international communication across the seas and through the air what country now has not the opportunity to become a melting pot? If it avails itself of this opportunity, the melting pot creates an alloy of quality often stronger than any one of its original components. This opportunity wells from the unity of the ocean.

The sea is three times bigger than the aggregate of the islands we call continents. In the sea there is opportunity for creative work of people to unite. What ocean scientist does not appreciate Hokusai's wave? What artist of the sea does not appreciate the beautiful mathematics of the waves on the ocean surface and within the sea? What musician that appreciates DeBussy's "La Mer" or other great music from any country inspired by the majestic noises of the sea, would not enjoy the "song of the whale" brought to human ears by modern science? Who among those who relish the works of Conrad, Masefield, and Melville can fail to see that these literary masterpieces use as the seabed of their authenticity and beauty the ordinary everyday experiences of seamen? So, the unity of the ocean creates a unity of creative work.

When we discuss the science underlying human work at sea, we find that we must consider earth's history, the beginnings of life, involving chemistry, the physics of atmospheric and ocean forces and movement and their interaction. And to understand the world ocean, we now go from space to the deepest abysses of the sea. Thus the unity of the ocean contributes to the unity of science if we are to understand it.

Intellectual humanity strives to overcome its ignorance. In Chapter 38 of Job, the Lord questions, "Who is this that darkeneth counsel by words without knowledge?" Yet, how often do our leaders darken counsel without the sea, without knowledge? In the same chapter, Job was chided, "Where wert thou when I laid the foundations of the Earth? Declare if thou hast understanding." We are still trying to discover the origins of the earth and the laying of its foundation. "Who hath laid the measures thereof... who hath stretched the line upon it?" Measuring the great earth was started by Eratosthenes by measuring the distance between two places in Egypt when the sun was overhead and reflected from the water in a deep well, and at the other place, simultaneously casting a shadow which could be measured. Now we are still "stretching the line" around and upon the earth with our newest satellite geodesy. "Or who shut up the sea with doors?" The whole of Holland is protected now from the sea by manmade doors with locks.

"The waters are hid as with a stone and the face of the deep is frozen." We are still trying to "see" through the waters below the face of the deep with sonar and other modern means.

"Hast thou entered into the springs of the sea or hast thou walked in the search of the depth?" Our aquanauts enter the springs of the sea and, two at least, have walked in the search of the depth.

I have, using mathematical projections, and, of course, the geodetic measurements of shorelines that separate ocean from land, drawn a map, the first picture of the whole ocean emphasizing its unity (Figure 21-1; refer also to frontispiece). The land islands that we call continents fringe the edges. It shows the ocean as the heart of our world.

Is it art? Is it science? Or is it both, unified, to give us understanding and joy?

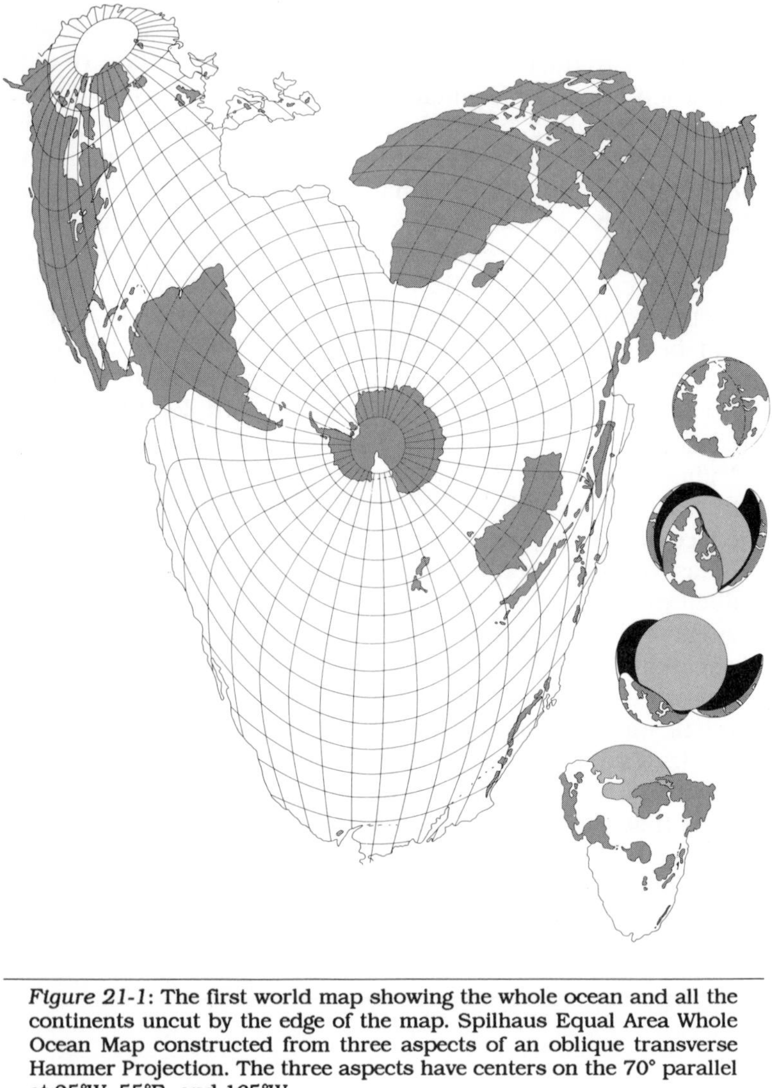

Figure 21-1: The first world map showing the whole ocean and all the continents uncut by the edge of the map. Spilhaus Equal Area Whole Ocean Map constructed from three aspects of an oblique transverse Hammer Projection. The three aspects have centers on the 70° parallel at 25°W, 55°E, and 165°W.

CONTRIBUTORS

Robert Abel: President of the New Jersey Marine Science Consortium, Fort Hancock, New Jersey.

Roger G. Barry: Professor at the Cooperative Institute for Research and at the Department of Geography, University of Colorado, Boulder, Colorado.

Willard Bascom: Director of the Southern California Coastal Research Project, Long Beach, California.

Hugh W. Ellsaesser: Physicist at the Lawrence Livermore National Laboratory, Livermore, California.

Roberto Frassetto: Director of Research at the Laboratory for the Study of Sea Dynamics, National Research Council, Venice, Italy.

Joel Gat: Professor of Geochemistry at Weizmann Institute, Rehovoth, Israel.

Edward D. Goldberg: Professor of Chemistry, Scripps Institution of Oceanography, La Jolla, California.

Eric B. Kraus: Professor Emeritus and Senior Research Associate of CIRES, University of Colorado, Boulder, Colorado.

Gunnar Kullenberg: Professor at the Institute of Physical Oceanography, University of Copenhagen, Copenhagen, Denmark.

Helmut Landsberg: Professor Emeritus at the Institute for Physical Science and Technology, University of Maryland, College Park, Maryland. (deceased)

Abraham Lerman: Professor at the Department of Geological Sciences, Northwestern University, Evanston, Illinois.

Uri Marinov: Director of the Environmental Protection Service, Jerusalem, Israel.

Avraham Melamed: Senior partner of Tushia Consulting Engineers, Ltd., Tel Aviv, Israel.

Yutaka Mochida: Former Director of Undersea Tunnel Division, Japan Railway Construction Public Corporation, Yokohama, Japan.

Hans Oeschger: Professor of the Physics Institute, University of Bern, Bern, Switzerland.

S. Ishtiaque Rasool: Distinguished visiting scientist at the Jet Propulsion Laboratory, California Institute of Technology, Pasadena, California.

S. Fred Singer: Professor of Environmental Sciences, University of Virginia, Charlottesville, Virginia.

Athelstan Spilhaus: President of Pan Geo, Middleburg, Virginia.

Gerald Stanhill: The Volcani Center, Institute of Soils and Water, Ministry of Agriculture, Bet-Dagen, Israel.

Don Walsh: Former Professor of Ocean Engineering at the Institute for Marine and Coastal Studies, University of Southern California, Los Angeles, California.

LIST OF FIGURES

LIST OF TABLES

Index

T

U

V

W

Z

DATE DUE			
OCT 10 2014			